Logical Options

Logical Options:
An Introduction to Classical and Alternative Logics

John L. Bell, David DeVidi, and Graham Solomon

broadview press

National Library of Canada Cataloguing in Publication Data

Bell, J.L. (John Lane)
     Logical options: an introduction to classical and alternative logics

ISBN 1-55111-297-3

1. Logic. I . DeVidi, David, 1962–   . II. Solomon, Graham, 1957–   . III. Title.

BC71.B44 2001   160   C2001-930186-3

Broadview Press Ltd. is an independent, international publishing house, incorporated in 1985.

North America:
P.O. Box 1243, Peterborough, Ontario, Canada K9J 7H5
3576 California Road, Orchard Park, NY 14127
Tel: (705) 743-8990; Fax: (705) 743-8353
E-mail: customerservice@broadviewpress.com

United Kingdom:
Turpin Distribution Services Ltd.,
Blackhorse Rd, Letchworth, Hertfordshire SG6 1HN
Tel: (1462) 672555; Fax: (1462) 480947
E-mail: turpin@rsc.org

Australia:
St. Clair Press, P.O. Box 287, Rozelle, NSW 2039
Tel: (02) 818-1942; Fax: (02) 418-1923

www.broadviewpress.com

Broadview Press gratefully acknowledges the financial support of the Book Publishing Industry Development Program, Ministry of Canadian Heritage, Government of Canada.

PRINTED IN CANADA

Contents

Preface

First courses in formal logic taught in philosophy departments normally cover classical propositional and predicate logic, use a natural deduction derivation procedure, and at least sketch proofs of basic properties such as soundness, completeness, and (failure of) decidability. More advanced courses might focus on classical modal logic, or on the incompleteness theorems of formalized arithmetic, on recursion and computability, on model theory, or perhaps introduce alternatives to classical logic such as intuitionistic logic, relevance logic, and linear logic, alternative logics which are nowadays widely discussed by philosophers, computer scientists, and mathematicians. There are a lot of choices for second and third courses in logic.

This book introduces some of the main extensions of and alternatives to classical logic: many sorted logic, second-order logic, modal logic, intuitionistic logic, three-valued logic, fuzzy logic, and free logic. It is designed to be useful for philosophy students and professional philosophers who have learned some classical first-order logic and would like to learn more about other logics discussed in the contemporary philosophical literature. It will be useful also for students in other disciplines in which alternative logics are studied and applied.

The book uses the tree derivation procedure, an elegant method refined by Smullyan and Jeffrey, among others, from Beth's semantic tableaux method and Gentzen's sequent calculus. The tree method has some advantages over natural deduction for nonclassical logics, the chief advantage being that it is more closely tied to the semantics than is natural deduction. The principal disadvantage of trees—in the eyes of those instructors, often philosophers, who prefer natural deduction—is that, in general, proofs using the tree method, while requiring considerably less ingenuity to construct than those using natural deduction, do not, unlike the latter, reflect the way actual reasoning proceeds. It is not our contention, however, that students need not be taught natural deduction. On the contrary, we hope that they will have learned that method in a first course in logic, and in any case we provide a sketch of the method at the end of our first chapter.

We suspect this book will prove most useful for a second course in logic, but it is self-contained enough to be used in a first course where the instructor does not intend to spend much time on such matters as translation between ordinary and formal languages. For readers who have a first course in logic but are unfamiliar with trees, Chapters 1 and 2 give a self-contained introduction to a tree method for classical predicate logic with identity. Chapter 2 also contains an introduction to the small amount of very elementary set theory that is necessary for the rest of the book. Experience tells us that a good many students have no acquaintance with this set theory, so that many simple examples and straightforward metatheoretical arguments elude them. Readers who are already familiar with trees from books by Smullyan, Jeffrey, Hodges, and others, and with elementary set theory, might just quickly review Chapters 1 and 2 before moving on to the rest of the book.

We don't expect instructors to cover all the material in this book in a one-term course. It is certainly possible to make a swift review of classical predicate logic and then cover the material on set theory, postulate systems, second-order logic, propositional modal logic and propositional intuitionistic logic—possibly replacing a detailed treatment of metatheory by a liberal discussion of philosophical issues such as the difference between first-order and second-order logic, the nature of necessity and possible worlds, and the virtues of abandoning bivalence. Or, after reviewing classical logic, one might cover in depth modal logic, intuitionistic logic and free logic. Or one could introduce students to a wide variety of systems and approaches to them by starting with the discussion of various proof methods in chapter 1, then surveying various modal logics, three valued and intuitionistic logic, and the approaches and systems discussed in Chapter 6.

If you enjoy working through this book, we expect you will also enjoy the following books which introduce or take further many of the topics we discuss:

George Boolos, *The Logic of Provability*, (Cambridge: Cambridge University Press, 1993)

David Bostock, *Intermediate Logic*, (Oxford: Clarendon Press, 1997)

Marcello D'Agostino, Dov M. Gabbay, Reiner Hähnle and Joachim Posegga, *Handbook of Tableau Methods*, (Dordrecht: Kluwer Academic Publishers, 1999)

Melvin C. Fitting, *Intuitionistic Logic, Model Theory and Forcing*, (Amsterdam: North-Holland Publishing Company, 1969)

Melvin C. Fitting, *Proof Methods for Modal and Intuitionistic Logic*, (Dordrecht: D. Reidel Publishing Company, 1983)

Robert Goldblatt, *Logics of Time and Computation*, Second Edition, (Stanford: CSLI Publications, 1992)

Wilfrid Hodges, *Logic*, (Harmondsworth: Penguin, 1977)

Richard Jeffrey, *Formal Logic: Its Scope and Limits*, Third Edition, (New York: McGraw-Hill, 1991)

Maria Manzano, *Extensions of First Order Logic*, (Cambridge: Cambridge University Press, 1996)

Anil Nerode and Richard Shore, *Logic for Applications*, Second Edition, (New York: Springer-Verlag, 1997)

Sally Popkorn, *First Steps in Modal Logic*, (Cambridge: Cambridge University Press, 1994)

Stephen Read, *Thinking About Logic*, (Oxford: Oxford University Press, 1995)

Greg Restall, *An Introduction to Substructural Logics*, (London: Routledge, 2000)

Raymond Smullyan, *First Order Logic*, (New York: Springer-Verlag, 1968)

A. M. Ungar, *Normalization, Cut-Elimination and the Theory of Proofs*, (Stanford: CSLI Publications, 1992)

We'd like to acknowledge all the logicians who have contributed to the development of the various logics we describe. We also thank our students for comments and suggestions. David DeVidi thanks the Social Sciences and Humanities Research Council of Canada for financial support during his work on this book.

Very few textbooks are free of errors. Please let us know about typos, exercises that are insufficiently clear, or other mistakes!

John L. Bell
Department of Philosophy
University of Western Ontario
jbell@julian.uwo.ca

David DeVidi
Department of Philosophy
University of Waterloo
ddevidi@watarts.uwaterloo.ca

Graham Solomon
Department of Philosophy
Wilfrid Laurier University
gsolomon@wlu.ca

Chapter 1

Classical Propositional Logic

1.1 Introductory Remarks

1.1.1 Some Basic Concepts

While philosophers claim logic as one of the traditional sub-disciplines of their field (along with metaphysics, epistemology, and ethics), nowadays logic is also studied by mathematicians, computer scientists, cognitive scientists and linguists, among others. But to understand the basics of modern logic, it is still worthwhile to begin by considering the subject's roots as the study of good reasoning. Among other things, this allows us to introduce some of the basic concepts which will play a central role in our discussions throughout this book.

When you attempt to persuade someone rationally that she ought to believe something, the appropriate method to adopt is to offer reasons. For this procedure to have any chance of success, two things are required: first, the reasons you offer must be less contentious at least among the parties to the discussion than the claim you are trying to establish; secondly, the reasons on offer need to be related to that claim in the right sort of way—as we often say, the claim in question should *follow from* the reasons you offer.

To discuss this process systematically, it is convenient to isolate some of the key ideas in the form of definitions.

DEFINITION 1.1 A *statement* is a sentence which makes an assertion, which is to say that it is a sentence which could be true or could be false.

DEFINITION 1.2 An *argument* is a collection of statements divided into *premises* and *conclusions*.

A few remarks are in order about these definitions. First, while there is obviously an important relationship between assertions and sentences which, grammatically speaking, are declarative in form, it is important to

1

notice that people in fact use sentences of various grammatical forms (and even non-sentences in some cases) to make assertions. For instance, you might tell a long-winded friend that you are hungry and think it is time to eat by interrupting him and saying "Are you hungry?" We will be assuming that in such cases there is always a declarative sentence available which, taken at face value, has the same content as the assertion made in such cases by other means. The examples we will use of arguments in English will therefore include only premises and conclusions which are declarative in form.

There are a couple of different things to notice about our definition of 'argument.' First, our definition allows for arguments with more than one conclusion, though we will confine attention almost entirely to cases where arguments have a single conclusion. In some specialized contexts, the extra flexibility is useful. Secondly, the *premises* are obviously playing the role played by the reasons in the preceding informal description. But notice that our definition doesn't require that anybody ever takes the premises to be grounds for believing the conclusion. It doesn't require that the argument was ever used, uttered, or thought by anybody, nor that there be any relationship between the premises and the conclusion—beyond their being part of the same collection of statements in which one is designated the conclusion, of course. Indeed, *any* collection of statements, with one designated the conclusion, counts as an argument. There are various advantages to using such a broad definition of 'argument.' The most important is that it disentangles the questions "Is this an argument?" and "Is this argument any good?" because there is no minimum standard of plausibility a group of statements must meet to count as a real argument. Let's turn to that second question now.

As we have said above, being a rationally persuasive argument rests on two conditions: the premises must be rationally acceptable, and the conclusion must follow from the premises. Logic alone is little help when it comes to deciding whether the first condition is met. Rather, logic is concerned with investigating this relation of "following from."

"Following from" is not a perfectly precise notion. In many contexts, for instance, we are willing to say that someone has presented a good argument (so that the conclusion follows from the premises) if the truth of the premises is enough to make the conclusion *likely*. Consider, for instance, the following argument:

1. Bob and Debbie handed in identical 4000 word term papers.

2. The academic regulations stipulate that students must work independently on term papers.

---

3. Bob and Debbie violated the academic regulations.

(Here we use a horizontal line to indicate that the statement beneath the line is the conclusion.) While it is extremely unlikely that these premises could both be true and the conclusion false, it is not *impossible* that two people write the same essay coincidentally. Nevertheless, the evidence in this sort of case would certainly be regarded as strong enough to warrant an academic penalty.

However, there is another, stricter reading of the phrase "follows from," where what is required is not merely that the premises would, if true, make the conclusion likely, but that the premises would, if true, *guarantee* the truth of the conclusion. Consider the following argument, for example:

1. Either this man's dead, or my watch has stopped.

2. This man isn't dead.

---

3. My watch has stopped.

Here there is *no* possibility that the premises be true and the conclusion fail to be true. It is this, stricter sense of "follows from" that, for most logicians, is the subject of investigation.

DEFINITION 1.3 An argument is *valid* if its conclusion is true in any case in which all of its premises are true.

DEFINITION 1.4 A *counterexample* to an argument is a case in which all its premises are true but its conclusion is false.

Thus an argument is valid provided it has no counterexamples, and invalid if it has counterexamples. As an example of an invalid inference, consider the following:

1. Either this man's dead, or my watch has stopped.

2. This man is dead.

---

3. My watch has stopped.

This inference is invalid, because the situation in which this man is dead and my watch hasn't stopped constitutes a counterexample.

Another notion which is a central concern of logicians is *consistency*.

DEFINITION 1.5 A set of statements is *(logically) consistent* if there is some case in which all the statements in the set are true. It is *(logically) inconsistent* if there is no such case.

Notice that it is possible for a set of statements to be consistent even if all members of the set are in fact false. For instance, the set {This man is dead, My watch has stopped} is consistent, because it *could be* the case that both statements are true. That in fact this man is alive and my watch hasn't stopped is immaterial.

1.1.2 Formal Logics

Logic, one could say without too much violence to the traditional meaning of the word, *is the science of valid inference.* But logicians, by and large, are more concerned with some sorts of valid argument than others. Consider again the valid argument above. Notice that it doesn't matter what statement one puts in place of the simple sentences "This man is dead" or "My watch has stopped." Provided one leaves the occurrences of 'or' and 'not' in place, the argument remains valid. The validity of this argument depends, in a sense which is difficult to specify, on the *form* of the argument, and not on its content. Most logicians would say that not all valid arguments are like this. For instance, if one argues that "Bob is my brother, so Bob is male," one has given a valid argument (the premise could not be true and the conclusion false), but this depends on the *meaning* of the words 'brother' and 'male,' and so on content and not merely on form. The sort of logic that is most likely to be studied is often called *formal logic* to indicate that it is the first sort of validity that is under investigation, and not the second.

By now perhaps it looks rather as though logicians have narrowed their subject too much. Logic is the science of good argument, but only one component of being a good argument is investigated, namely the relationship between premises and conclusions. But not all cases in which the premises support the conclusion are of interest, only those where the truth of the premises would guarantee the truth of the conclusion. And not even all of these arguments are of interest. Rather, the cases of interest are those in which this guarantee is due (somehow) to the form of the argument. One might wonder how much can be left to say, after all this narrowing of focus.

Quite a lot, as it happens. One will sometimes meet people, even professional academics, who somewhere have acquired the idea that formal logic is just classical first-order predicate logic (i.e., what they learned as undergraduates), and that since during the past 100 years this system has become fairly well-understood, there's not much left for logicians to do. In writing this book one of our hopes is that our readers won't be tempted to believe such a claim. We hope this in part because we will investigate various *different systems of formal logic.* This multiplicity arises for at least a couple of reasons.

Formal logics are, among other things, methods for considering the class of valid arguments *systematically.* One thing a good systematic theory does is to organize the relevant phenomena in such a way that one can describe them and reason about them efficiently—a good theory should be simple and elegant. But a good theory will also cover a large portion of the phenomena. Predictably, there is a trade-off between these virtues. That is, in general, one can generate a theory which covers a larger portion of the valid arguments only by accepting a system which is more complex and difficult to work with, and one increases simplicity, normally, only at the cost of comprehensiveness of the system. So, one reason for the variety of formal logics is that these different logics represent different trade-offs between simplicity and comprehensiveness.

In the early sections of this book, we will look at the best known example of this. First we will look at classical propositional logic, perhaps the simplest logic that captures an interesting fragment of the class of valid arguments. This is an extremely simple system that is fun to work with and which is surprisingly useful. But it is just too weak a system for many purposes, which is why a first course in logic typically also introduces students to the second system we will look at, classical predicate logic. This system captures many valid arguments which escape propositional logic, but it is somewhat more complicated. Several of the other systems we will consider in this book are designed to capture valid arguments left out of account by classical propositional and predicate logic.

But there is another reason for the variety of different systems of formal logic, one which is more philosophical. Some philosophers and mathematicians contend that classical logic counts as valid some arguments which are actually not valid, or at least which are not valid without some further presuppositions. Thus, some argue that so-called *intuitionistic logic*—which will be discussed later on—is an advance over classical logic in the sense that it counts as valid just those arguments which are *genuinely* valid. Its use will not put one at risk of "false positives," i.e., at risk of declaring an invalid argument valid. The difference between classical and non-classical logic plays an important role in many current debates in philosophy, as we will discuss further in Chapter 5, so some acquaintance with these systems seems required of anyone hoping to understand these debates.

EXERCISES 1.1.1
For each of the following claims, determine whether it is true or false, and briefly explain your answer.

1. If an argument is valid it remains valid when you add a new statement to the set of premises, regardless of what that new statement is.

* 2. No valid argument may have a contradiction as its conclusion.

3. An invalid argument can be turned into a valid argument by replacing the conclusion with its denial.

1.2 Propositional Logic

1.2.1 Preliminaries

There are two preliminary points needed to understand classical propositional logic.

First, recall that we are assuming that all the statements in an argument are *assertions*, and so are capable of being true or of being false. We now strengthen this assumption, adopting the *principle of bivalence*.

DEFINITION 1.6 (PRINCIPLE OF BIVALENCE) Every sentence gets exactly one of the two truth values *True* or *False*. (We denote these truth values $\top$ and $\bot$ respectively.)

Secondly, the class of valid arguments with which we will be concerned are those which owe their validity to the occurrence in them of complex statements which are constructed out of simpler ones according to *truth-functional rules*.

DEFINITION 1.7 (TRUTH FUNCTIONALITY) The truth value of any complex statement built up according to the syntactical rules of the system is unambiguously determined by the truth values of its constitutive parts.

Clearly, given the principle of truth-functionality, to investigate the validity of inferences we need to begin by considering how their constituent statements are formed, and how these are then to be assigned truth values. As the basic ingredients from which we shall fashion all such statements we shall assume that we have available a stock of *elementary statements*. It might be helpful to think of these as simple declarative sentences like "It is raining," "The cranes are flying," etc., though we don't assume this as part of the official characterization of elementary statements. What we do assume is that these statements can be assigned truth values arbitrarily and entirely independently of one another. (So, if "Bob is smart" is one elementary statement, "Bob is stupid" can't be another one, because the truth values of these statements are not independent of one another: that is, if it is true that Bob is smart, then it is false that he's stupid, and if he's stupid then it's false that he's smart, though of course "stupid" doesn't mean "not smart" since it's quite possible to not be smart without being stupid either. And "$2 + 2 = 4$" is not a candidate for being an elementary statement, either, since it can't be assigned the value $\bot$.) From elementary statements we obtain compound statements by applying the syntactical operations of our system. We will use only four, which can usefully be thought of as akin to the English language operations "and," "or," "if ... then," and "not." In this way we obtain, e.g., statements such as "It is raining and the cranes are flying," "If it is raining, the cranes are not flying," etc.

We will use *formal languages* to facilitate our discussions of the properties of the various systems of logic in this book. We now introduce a language, which we will call $\mathcal{L}$, which is suitable for discussions of propositional logics. We do so in two stages: first, we introduce the vocabulary for the language. Later we will specify which arrangements of the vocabulary are *grammatically correct* or *well-formed*.

DEFINITION 1.8 (BASIC VOCABULARY FOR $\mathcal{L}$) The items in the vocabulary for $\mathcal{L}$ fall into two mutually exclusive collections.

1. We assume that there is an infinite stock of *elementary statements*. We shall use italic capital letters from the beginning of the alphabet,

usually A, B, and C, possibly with subscripts, to denote elementary statements. Elementary statements will also be called *statement letters*.

2. Our language includes the symbols $\wedge$, $\vee$, $\rightarrow$, and $\neg$, which are called *logical operators*.

The logical operator $\wedge$ is usually read "and," $A \wedge B$ is called the *conjunction* of A and B, and A and B are called the *conjuncts* of $A \wedge B$. The operator $\vee$ is usually read "or," and $A \vee B$ is called the *disjunction* of A and B, and A and B are called the *disjuncts* of $A \vee B$. One often reads $A \rightarrow B$ as "if A, then B," and $\rightarrow$ is called the *implication sign*, or, sometimes, just the *arrow*. $A \rightarrow B$ is called an *implication* or *conditional* statement. A is the *antecedent* of $A \rightarrow B$, and B its *consequent*. The operator $\neg$ is usually simply read "not," and $\neg A$ is called the *negation* or the *denial* of A.

Two things should be kept in mind about these suggested readings of the operators. Not all uses of "and" in English are cases where it is used as a truth functional operation to conjoin two sentences. ("He was black and blue after the game" doesn't mean "He was black after the game, and he was blue after the game," for instance.) Similar points apply to the other operators, of course. More importantly, in ordinary language there are many expressions which have different meanings (in the sense that they can be used to communicate different things to a listener or reader), but which perform the same truth-functional operation. For example, in some contexts one might decide to say "He's small, but he's slow" instead of "He's small, and he's slow," to register one's surprise that such a small person could be slow. But as far as what one can validly infer about the truth of the statements "He's small" and "He's slow," these differences do not matter at all. Since it is valid inference we are concerned to study here, we can ignore these subtle differences of meaning for our purposes. Indeed, attending to them would be like asking after the colour of cannon balls when your job is to calculate trajectories. So, while we read $\wedge$ as "and," we could as well have chosen to read it as "but," or as "although," or as "in spite of," or as any of several other expressions which perform the same truth-functional role. Similarly, we might have read $\vee$ as "unless" instead of "or," and we could have read $A \rightarrow B$ as "A implies B" or "A only if B." With a bit of ingenuity, many other readings could be suggested for these connectives.

Using these symbols, statements are obtained by starting with the statement letters—which of course count as the simplest kind of statement—and applying the logical operators $\wedge$, $\vee$, $\rightarrow$, and $\neg$, to these, using parentheses and brackets as necessary to eliminate ambiguity, to obtain $A \wedge B$, $(A \wedge B) \vee C$, $(A \rightarrow B) \vee C$, $\neg[(A \rightarrow B) \vee C]$, etc. Formally:

DEFINITION 1.9 (DEFINITION OF STATEMENT OF $\mathcal{L}$) First, some notation: We will use italic capital letters from the second half of the alphabet, usually P, Q, and R, sometimes with subscripts, to denote arbitrary statements.

1. Any statement letter is a statement.

2. If P and Q are statements, so too are $(P \land Q)$, $(P \lor Q)$, $(P \rightarrow Q)$, $\neg P$.

3. Nothing else is a statement.

We shall feel free to replace parentheses by square brackets, and to omit parentheses in statements when we feel that their omission aids readability. If the reader is in doubt about how to read a particular statement, parentheses (or brackets) can always be replaced according to the following rules. (1) If a statement does not begin with a $\neg$, the outermost parentheses may be omitted. So we write, e.g., $A \land B$ for $(A \land B)$. (2) If the left member of a pair of parentheses is preceded by a $\neg$, that pair of parentheses will never be omitted, so in restoring parentheses you will never add a pair of parentheses whose left member immediately follows a $\neg$. So, don't be confused by $\neg A \lor B$. It is $(\neg A \lor B)$, and *this is not the same as* $\neg(A \lor B)$. (3) When there are two or more occurrences of the operators $\rightarrow$, $\lor$, and $\land$ enclosed in a single pair of parentheses, these are ranked in that order, and if there are two occurrences of the same symbol, the one further left has a higher rank. Add a new pair of parentheses that encloses the symbol occurrence with the lowest rank. Repeat as necessary. Consider, for example, $A \rightarrow B \lor C \rightarrow D$; after applying (1), we have the whole statement inside a single set of parentheses. The lowest ranked operator is the $\lor$, so we get $(A \rightarrow (B \lor C) \rightarrow D)$. The leftmost $\rightarrow$ has higher rank than the other, so we should add parentheses which enclose the statements immediately on either side of the rightmost $\rightarrow$. So we get $(A \rightarrow ((B \lor C) \rightarrow D))$.

EXERCISES 1.2.1
Suppose that P, Q and R are statements of $\mathcal{L}$.

1. Which of the following are statements of $\mathcal{L}$? For those which are not, explain why they are not.

 (a) $((\neg\neg P \rightarrow P) \rightarrow (P \rightarrow P))$.

 (b) $(P \land \neg P)\neg Q$.

 * (c) $((((P \lor Q) \lor R) \land P)$.

2. Restore all the parentheses to the following statements according to the above rules.

 * (a) $\neg P \land \neg Q \rightarrow \neg\neg P$

 (b) $\neg P \lor \neg Q \lor \neg R \land \neg P$

 * (c) $P \rightarrow Q \lor R \land R \rightarrow P$

 (d) $(P \rightarrow Q \rightarrow Q \rightarrow R) \rightarrow (P \rightarrow R)$

1.2.2 Truth Values, Valuations, and Validity

DEFINITION 1.10 The rules for computing the truth values of compound statements are as follows.

1. $P \wedge Q$ is true if P and Q are both true, and false if at least one of P and Q is false.

2. $P \vee Q$ is true if at least one of P and Q is true, and false if both P and Q are false.

3. $\neg P$ is true if P is false, and false if P is true.

4. $P \rightarrow Q$ is false when P is true and Q is false, but true in all other cases.

REMARK 1.1 (REMARK ON THE TRUTH VALUE OF $P \rightarrow Q$) The idea here is that we want a statement of the form $P \rightarrow Q$ to be false exactly when the truth values of P and Q constitute a counterexample to the validity of the inference from P to Q, that is, when P is true and Q is false.

These rules may be summed up in the form of *truth tables*. In such tables we use $\top$ for "True" and $\bot$ for "False."

P	Q	$P \wedge Q$	$P \vee Q$	$\neg P$	$P \rightarrow Q$
$\top$	$\top$	$\top$	$\top$	$\bot$	$\top$
$\top$	$\bot$	$\bot$	$\top$	$\bot$	$\bot$
$\bot$	$\top$	$\bot$	$\top$	$\top$	$\top$
$\bot$	$\bot$	$\bot$	$\bot$	$\top$	$\top$

By comparing this table and definition 1.9, you should be able to convince yourself of the following fact: if you know the truth values of all the statement letters which make up a compound statement, you can calculate the truth value of the whole statement. (Example: If A and B are true and C is false, then we can calculate the truth value of $(A \wedge C) \rightarrow (C \vee B)$. First, since C is false, $A \wedge C$ is false. But this statement is the antecedent of a statement of the form $P \rightarrow Q$ (i.e., it is P, while $C \vee B$ is Q.) If P is false, then $P \rightarrow Q$ is true, so the entire sentence is true.) Similarly, if you know the truth values of all the statement letters occurring anywhere in a collection of statements, you can calculate the truth value of every member. We will sometimes use as a convenient shorthand the notation $[\![P]\!]$ to denote the truth value of a statement P.

Recall definition 1.3, where we said that an argument is valid if its conclusion is true in any case in which all of its premises are true. In the context of classical propositional logic, what we mean by *cases* are the (truth) *valuations*.

DEFINITION 1.11 A *valuation* is an assignment of a truth value (and only one!) to each statement letter of $\mathcal{L}$. If V is a valuation and P is a statement of $\mathcal{L}$, we will sometimes write $[\![P]\!]^V$ for the truth value of P under V.

DEFINITION 1.12 An argument is *truth-functionally valid* if its conclusion is true under every valuation on which all its premises are true. A *truth-functional counterexample* for an argument is a valuation under which the conclusion is false and all its premises are true.

According to our definition the valuations assign truth values to all the infinitely many statement letters of $\mathcal{L}$. But it is not hard to see that the truth value of any particular statement P will depend only on the truth values of those statement letters that occur in P. So, returning to the sentence $(A \land C) \rightarrow (C \lor B)$, we can consider all the relevant cases by constructing the table:

A	B	C	$(A \land C)$	$\rightarrow$	$(C \lor B)$
T	T	T	T	T	T
T	T	⊥	⊥	T	T
T	⊥	T	T	T	T
T	⊥	⊥	⊥	T	⊥
⊥	T	T	⊥	T	T
⊥	T	⊥	⊥	T	T
⊥	⊥	T	⊥	T	T
⊥	⊥	⊥	⊥	T	⊥

We can see from this table that the sentence will be true under *every* valuation. The reason we can see this is not that the table lists all the valuations for $\mathcal{L}$—it doesn't list *any* valuation in its entirety. But every valuation will agree with one of the rows in this table in what it assigns to A, B and C, and these are the relevant bits of any valuation if our purpose is to calculate the truth value of this sentence, so this is all the information we need. In this table there are $2^3 = 8$ rows, because there are 3 statement letters in the sentence. If we had n statement letters $A_1, \ldots, A_n$, we would need 2^n rows in our table to ensure we had all the relevant information about all valuations.

Now we will look at a few examples which illustrate how we can use these facts to test arguments for truth-functional validity.

1. It is raining and the cranes are flying.

---

2. It is raining.

This has the form

$$A \land B$$
$$\therefore \quad A$$

The inference is valid since, according to the truth table for $\land$, whenever the premise $A \land B$ is true, so is the conclusion A. Thus, there can be no truth-functional counterexample to this argument.

1. It is raining or the cranes are flying.

2. It isn't raining.

---

3. The cranes are flying.

This has the form

$$A \lor B$$
$$\neg A$$
$$\therefore \quad B$$

We want an answer to the question "Are there any truth-functional counterexamples to this argument?" Since in a counterexample the conclusion, in this case B, must be *false*, we only need to consider such cases. Accordingly, by examining the table:

A	B	$\neg A$	$A \lor B$	B
$\top$	$\bot$	$\bot$	$\top$	$\bot$
$\bot$	$\bot$	$\top$	$\bot$	$\bot$

we can see that in no case in which the conclusion is false are *both* premises true, and so we see that there are no truth-functional counterexamples. Accordingly, the argument is truth-functionally *valid*.

Next, consider the argument:

1. If it is raining, then the cranes are flying.

2. It is raining.

---

3. The cranes are flying.

This has the form

$$A \rightarrow B$$
$$A$$
$$\therefore \quad B$$

Examine the truth table for possible counterexamples (conclusion false):

A	B	A	$A \rightarrow B$	B
$\top$	$\bot$	$\top$	$\bot$	$\bot$
$\bot$	$\bot$	$\bot$	$\top$	$\bot$

Neither of these cases constitutes a counterexample, so the inference is *valid*.

Next, the argument:

1. If it is raining, the cranes are flying.

2. The cranes are flying.

---

3. It is raining.

This one has the form

$$A \rightarrow B$$
$$B$$
$$\therefore \quad A$$

The following line in the truth table is a counterexample (in fact the only one):

A	B	B	$A \rightarrow B$	A
$\perp$	T	T	T	$\perp$

The inference is, accordingly, (truth-functionally) *invalid*.

1. If it is raining, the cranes are flying.

2. If the cranes are flying, the bears are restless.

---

3. If it is raining, the bears are restless.

This has the form

$$A \rightarrow B$$
$$B \rightarrow C$$
$$\therefore \quad A \rightarrow C$$

Now the only possible counterexamples arise when the conclusion $A \rightarrow C$ is false. This can happen just when A is true and C is false. Therefore we need merely examine the two lines in the truth table in which this occurs. These are the following:

A	B	C	$A \rightarrow B$	$B \rightarrow C$	$A \rightarrow C$
T	T	$\perp$	T	$\perp$	$\perp$
T	$\perp$	$\perp$	$\perp$	T	$\perp$

Since in neither of these lines are both premises $A \rightarrow B$ and $B \rightarrow C$ true, neither constitutes a counterexample, so there are none, and the inference is, accordingly, *valid*.

EXERCISES 1.2.2
Using methods similar to those used in the text, determine whether each of the following inferences is valid (i.e., identify the truth-functional form of the inference, then display the relevant part of the truth-table for the inference, and explain why it shows validity or invalidity).

1. (a) If heartaches are commercials, we are all on TV.
    (b) We are not all on TV.
    _____
    (c) Heartaches are not commercials.

2.* (a) If heartaches are commercials, then we are all on TV.
    _____
    (b) If we are not all on TV, then heartaches are not commercials.

3.* (a) If heartaches are commercials, we are all on TV.
    (b) Heartaches are commercials or the cranes are flying.
    (c) We are not all on TV.
    _____
    (d) The cranes are flying.

4. (a) If heartaches are commercials, we are all on TV.
    (b) Heartaches are commercials or the cranes are flying.
    (c) We are not all on TV.
    _____
    (d) The cranes are not flying.

1.2.3 Implication, Tautology, and Other Important Concepts

We shall use the notation

$$P_1, \ldots, P_n \vDash_{\mathrm{PC}} Q$$

to indicate that the inference from the statements $P_1, \ldots, P_n$ to the statement Q is truth-functionally valid. Thus the validity of the first three inferences above may be symbolized:

$$A \wedge B \vDash_{\mathrm{PC}} A, \quad A \vee B, \neg A \vDash_{\mathrm{PC}} B, \quad A, A \rightarrow B \vDash_{\mathrm{PC}} B.$$

The subscript "PC" in this notation stands for Propositional and Classical. We will often write $P \vDash Q$ in place of $P \vDash_{\mathrm{PC}} Q$, when the context makes clear that it is classical propositional logic we are discussing.

DEFINITION 1.13 When $P_1, \ldots, P_n \vDash Q$, we say that $P_1, \ldots, P_n$ (truth-functionally) *imply* Q, or that Q (truth-functionally) *follows from* $P_1, \ldots, P_n$.

Sometimes conclusions are obtainable without using premises. For example, consider the premiseless "argument":

1. If it is raining, then it is raining.

This "inference" is valid because in its truth table

$$\begin{array}{c|c} A & A \to A \\ \hline \top & \top \\ \bot & \top \end{array}$$

the conclusion $A \to A$ is always true: there are no counterexamples.

DEFINITION 1.14 A statement which is true in all possible cases is called (truth-functionally) *valid* or a (truth-functional) *tautology.*

An argument with a tautology as its conclusion is *always* valid, regardless of what its premises are. We shall use the symbol $\top$ to stand for a fixed tautologous statement, which for definiteness we shall take to be the statement $A \to A$ (although any tautology will do). The symbol $\top$ is, then, doing double duty: it indicates both a truth value and a particular statement. Notice that we then have

$$P \models \top$$

for any statement P.

DEFINITION 1.15 A set S of statements is said to be (truth-functionally) *satisfiable* or *consistent* if there is at least one case in which all the members of S are true, and (truth-functionally) *unsatisfiable* or *inconsistent* if not.

This concept is related to that of validity in the following way.

PROPOSITION 1.1 *If $P_1, \ldots, P_n \models Q$, then the set $\{P_1, \ldots, P_n, \neg Q\}$ is unsatisfiable, and conversely.*

For to say that $\{P_1, \ldots, P_n, \neg Q\}$ is unsatisfiable is just to assert that $P_1, \ldots, P_n$, and $\neg Q$ are never simultaneously true, which, given the principle of bivalence, amounts to asserting that $\neg Q$ is false, i.e. Q is true, whenever all of $P_1, \ldots, P_n$ are.

In particular, it follows that if $\{P_1, \ldots, P_n\}$ is unsatisfiable, $P_1, \ldots, P_n \models Q$, for *any* statement Q. That is, *inconsistent premises yield any conclusion whatsoever.*

DEFINITION 1.16 A single unsatisfiable statement (e.g., $A \wedge \neg A$) is called a (truth-functional) *contradiction.* A statement which is neither a (truth-functional) tautology nor a (truth-functional) contradiction is said to be (truth-functionally) *contingent.*

Thus a contradiction is a statement which is *always false.* We shall use the symbol $\bot$ to stand for a fixed contradiction, which for definiteness we take to be the statement $A \wedge \neg A$ (although, as in the case of $\top$, it matters not which particular contradiction we choose). Notice that we now have

$$\bot \models P$$

for any statement P. A contingent statement is one which is true in at least one case, *and* false in at least one case. Any statement is either tautologous, contradictory, or contingent: we shall presently develop an efficient technique for deciding which.

1.2.4 Equivalence and Expressive Completeness

Two statements are called (logically) *equivalent* if they take the same truth values in all possible cases. Accordingly, we make the following definition.

DEFINITION 1.17 Two statements of $\mathcal{L}$ are *truth-functionally equivalent* if they have the same truth value under all truth valuations.

For example, consider the truth tables for the statements $A \rightarrow B$ and $\neg B \rightarrow \neg A$:

A	B	$A \rightarrow B$	$\neg B \rightarrow \neg A$
$\top$	$\top$	$\top$	$\top$
$\top$	$\bot$	$\bot$	$\bot$
$\bot$	$\top$	$\top$	$\top$
$\bot$	$\bot$	$\top$	$\top$

Since $A \rightarrow B$ and $\neg B \rightarrow \neg A$ have the same truth value on every line of the table, they are equivalent.

We write $P \equiv Q$ to indicate that the statements P and Q are equivalent. We may think of $\equiv$ as a kind of equality between statements, since if $P \equiv Q$, then for every valuation V, $[\![P]\!]^V = [\![Q]\!]^V$. We leave it to the reader as an exercise to show that, for any statements P and Q, the following assertions amount to the same thing:

$$P \equiv Q \qquad [P \vDash Q \text{ and } Q \vDash P].$$

In connection with $\equiv$, we can define a new logical operator "$\longleftrightarrow$" called *bi-implication* (or *equivalence*) as follows:

P	Q	$P \longleftrightarrow Q$
$\top$	$\top$	$\top$
$\top$	$\bot$	$\bot$
$\bot$	$\top$	$\bot$
$\bot$	$\bot$	$\top$

Thus $P \longleftrightarrow Q$ has value $\top$ exactly when P and Q have the same truth value. It follows from this that $P \equiv Q$ holds when and only when the statement $P \longleftrightarrow Q$ is valid. The statements P and Q are called the *components* of $P \longleftrightarrow Q$.

It is easy to check the following equivalences:

$$P \equiv \neg\neg P \tag{1.1}$$
$$P \lor Q \equiv \neg(\neg P \land \neg Q) \tag{1.2}$$
$$P \land Q \equiv \neg(\neg P \lor \neg Q) \tag{1.3}$$
$$P \rightarrow Q \equiv \neg P \lor Q \tag{1.4}$$
$$P \longleftrightarrow Q \equiv (P \rightarrow Q) \land (Q \rightarrow P) \tag{1.5}$$

EXERCISES 1.2.3

*   1. Prove that $A \equiv B$ if and only if $A \vDash B$ and $B \vDash A$.

2. Use truth tables to establish that each of the claims 1.1–1.5 is true.

3. Show the equivalence of $A \lor B$ to each of the following:

    (a) $(A \rightarrow B) \rightarrow B$

*   (b) $(A \rightarrow B) \longleftrightarrow B$

    (c) $(A \longleftrightarrow B) \rightarrow A$

4. Show the equivalence of $A \land B$ to each of the following:

    (a) $(A \rightarrow B) \longleftrightarrow A$

    (b) $(A \longleftrightarrow B) \longleftrightarrow [(A \longleftrightarrow B) \rightarrow A]$

5. Consider two new binary connectives, $\not\rightarrow$ and $\not\leftrightarrow$, which we interpret as follows: $P \not\rightarrow Q$ has the value $\top$ if P is false and Q is true, and is false otherwise; $P \not\leftrightarrow Q$ is true if P and Q have different truth values, and false if they have the same truth value. Show that $A \land B \equiv (A \not\rightarrow B) \not\rightarrow B$, and that $A \lor B \equiv [(A \not\rightarrow B) \not\rightarrow B] \not\leftrightarrow (A \not\leftrightarrow B)$.

It is not hard to show in a rigorous way that $\rightarrow$ and $\longleftrightarrow$ are in a natural sense *expressible* in terms of $\{\land, \lor, \neg\}$, and hence in terms of $\{\land, \neg\}$ and $\{\lor, \neg\}$ (see the exercises below). That is, our language $\mathcal{L}$ includes one unary (i.e., one-place) logical operator (viz., $\neg$) and three binary operators ($\land, \lor, \rightarrow$), as primitive symbols, and we've since added a defined symbol ($\longleftrightarrow$) which is another binary operator. We've interpreted these as five distinct *truth functions* of the appropriate sort: an *n-ary truth function* is an assignment of a unique truth value to every possible sequence of n truth values, so the truth tables for the connectives obviously give unary or binary truth functions. If we are using a truth function to interpret a connective, we often extend this usage and refer to the connective as an *n-ary truth function on statements*. But now we see that any truth-functional statement which can be expressed using the resources of $\mathcal{L}$ and its interpretations could have been expressed, though perhaps in a more complicated way, using a language which includes only $\land$ and $\neg$ (or $\lor$ and $\neg$).

The question now arises as to whether *every* possible truth function on statements is so expressible. Notice that there is nothing that restricts us to unary or binary truth functions. What we are asking is whether all truth functions which take any number of statements as input can be expressed using only $\wedge$, $\vee$, and $\neg$. The answer, as we shall see, is *yes*.

DEFINITION 1.18 (DISJUNCTIVE NORMAL FORM) Let us suppose we are given a truth function H of n statements. Let $A_1, \ldots, A_n$ be distinct statement letters. For each valuation, a corresponding (truth) value of $H(A_1, \ldots, A_n)$ is obtained. We display this situation in the form of a truth table:

A_1	A_2	$\ldots$	A_n	$H(A_1, \ldots, A_n)$
$\top$	$\top$	$\ldots$	$\top$	$*$
$\top$	$\top$	$\ldots$	$\bot$	$*$
$\vdots$				$\vdots$
$\bot$	$\bot$	$\ldots$	$\bot$	$*$

First, consider the case where at least one of the entries in the H column is $\top$. For each row in which $H(A_1, \ldots, A_n)$ has value $\top$, we do the following. First, for each A_i, we define A_i^* to be A_i if the given valuation assigns $\top$ to A_i, and to be $\neg A_i$ if not. Next we form the conjunction $A_1^* \wedge \cdots \wedge A_n^*$. Notice that this conjunction is true precisely under the given valuation and no other. (More precisely, it is true under all and only the infinitely many valuations which assign the values to $A_1, \ldots, A_n$ which are specified in the row in question.) Now we form the disjunction of all these conjunctions arising from the $\top$ cases of the given truth table. The resulting statement is called the *disjunctive normal form* (d.n.f.) of the given truth function. Clearly, its truth table is identical to that of the given truth function.

It remains to consider the case in which the given truth function always takes the value $\bot$. Here we may take the disjunctive normal form to be, e.g., $A_1 \wedge \neg A_1$, since that sentence, too, uniformly takes the value $\bot$ for all valuations.

Since d.n.f.s contain only the logical operators $\wedge, \vee,$ and $\neg$, it follows that every possible truth function can be expressed in terms of $\wedge, \vee,$ and $\neg$ (see exercises for the details), and so every statement is equivalent to one whose only logical operators are these. We sum this up by saying that the set $\{\wedge, \vee, \neg\}$ is *expressively complete*. Moreover, since $\wedge$ is expressible in terms of $\vee$ and $\neg$ (cf. formula 1.2), and $\vee$ in terms of $\wedge$ and $\neg$ (cf. formula 1.3), we may infer that each of the sets $\{\wedge, \neg\}$ and $\{\vee, \neg\}$ is expressively complete.

Before proceeding further, let us consider a d.n.f. in a concrete case. Consider a three-place truth-function given by the truth table

A	B	C	$H(A, B, C)$
$\top$	$\top$	$\top$	$\top$
$\top$	$\top$	$\bot$	$\bot$
$\top$	$\bot$	$\top$	$\top$
$\top$	$\bot$	$\bot$	$\top$

and the information that in all the remaining cases $H(A,B,C)$ is false. In the first row, $H(A,B,C)$ is true. Since A is true in that row, A^* is just A, and similarly for B^* and C^*. The second row we can ignore, since $H(A,B,C)$ is false. In the third row, B^* is $\neg B$, since B is false in that row. And so on. Eventually, we calculate that the d.n.f. of $H(A,B,C)$ is

$$(A \wedge B \wedge C) \vee (A \wedge \neg B \wedge C) \vee (A \wedge \neg B \wedge \neg C).$$

As we have seen, for the purposes of truth functional logic we could have gotten by with only two primitive logical operations. This raises the question of whether we might have made do with only one. We shall see that, if we consider only operations which take two or fewer statement letters, there are exactly two of these.

DEFINITION 1.19 We define the logical operators $|$ —*nand*— and $\downarrow$ —*nor*— by means of the following truth tables.

P	Q	$P \mid Q$	$P \downarrow Q$
T	T	$\bot$	$\bot$
T	$\bot$	T	$\bot$
$\bot$	T	T	$\bot$
$\bot$	$\bot$	T	T

The symbols $|$ and $\downarrow$, so defined, are also known as the *Sheffer stroke* and the *Peirce arrow* respectively.

Clearly,

$$P \mid Q \equiv \neg(P \wedge Q) \qquad \text{and } P \downarrow Q \equiv \neg P \wedge \neg Q.$$

First, we show that $|$ and $\downarrow$ are each expressively complete. To do this it suffices to show that $\neg$ and $\vee$ are both expressible in terms of $|$, and $\neg$ and $\wedge$ in terms of $\downarrow$.

Evidently $P \mid P \equiv \neg(P \wedge P) \equiv \neg P$, so $\neg$ is expressible in terms of $|$. Now

$$P \mid Q \equiv \neg(P \wedge Q) \equiv \neg P \vee \neg Q,$$

so

$$\neg P \mid \neg Q \equiv \neg\neg P \vee \neg\neg Q \equiv P \vee Q.$$

Hence, recalling that $\neg P \equiv P \mid P$, we see that

$$P \vee Q \equiv (P|P)|(Q|Q),$$

and so $\vee$ is expressible in terms of $|$.

Similarly, $\neg P \equiv P \downarrow P$ and $P \wedge Q \equiv (P \downarrow P) \downarrow (Q \downarrow Q)$. Therefore $|$ and $\downarrow$ are each expressively complete.

We next show that $|$ and $\downarrow$ are the *only* expressively complete logical operations on two or fewer statement letters.

First, notice that there are four unary truth functions: the familiar ¬, the function ⊤(P), which assigns ⊤ whatever P's value, the analogously defined ⊥(P), and *id*(P), which leaves the truth value of P unchanged. We observe that *id*(P) can't express ¬, neither ⊤(P) nor ¬ can express ⊥(P), and ⊥(P) can't express ⊤. So none of these is expressively complete.

Now suppose that H(P, Q) is expressively complete. If H(⊤, ⊤) were ⊤, then any statement built up using only H would take the value ⊤ when all its statement letters take the value ⊤. So ¬A would not be expressible in terms of H. Therefore H(⊤, ⊤) = ⊥. Similarly, H(⊥, ⊥) = ⊤. So we obtain the partial truth table

P	Q	H(P, Q)
⊤	⊤	⊥
⊤	⊥	
⊥	⊤	
⊥	⊥	⊤

If the second and third entries in the last column are ⊤, ⊤ or ⊥, ⊥ then H is | or ↓. If they are ⊥, ⊤, then H(P, Q) ≡ ¬P; and if they are ⊤, ⊥, then H(P, Q) ≡ ¬Q. So in both of these cases H would be expressible in terms of ¬. But as we have already seen, ¬ is not expressively complete by itself. So H is | or ↓, as claimed.

EXERCISES 1.2.4

* 1. Show that any statement in which → occurs one or more times is equivalent to a statement in which the only connectives which occur are ∧, ∨ and ¬. [Hint: This is obvious if the statement is simply P → Q and → occurs in neither P nor Q, simply because (1.4) is true. But → need not be the main operator, and it need not occur only once. What is needed is a general method which, when applied to an arbitrary statement of £, will eliminate all occurrences of → and result in a statement equivalent to the one with which we began. It may prove useful to employ the *ranking* of occurrences of → defined on page 8.]

2. Show that any statement in which ⟷ occurs is equivalent to one in which the only connectives are ∧, ∨ and ¬.

3. Show that any statement in which only the connectives ∧, ∨ and ¬ occur is equivalent to one in which only ∧ and ¬ occur.

4. Show that any statement in which only the connectives ∧, ∨ and ¬ occur is equivalent to one in which only ∨ and ¬ occur.

5. In the text the notion of a disjunctive normal form *for an n-place truth function* is discussed. This is easily generalized in a way which legitimates talking about the disjunctive normal form *of a statement*. One way of obtaining a d.n.f. of a statement is to draw a truth table for the statement, then employ the method described above for obtaining the d.n.f. from a truth table. Use this method to obtain a d.n.f. for each of the following statements.

(a) $A \wedge B \rightarrow C \vee D$.

(b) $((A \rightarrow B) \rightarrow (A \rightarrow C)) \rightarrow (D \rightarrow C)$

* (c) $(A \longleftrightarrow B) \rightarrow (C \longleftrightarrow A)$

(d) $\neg A \vee \neg B \rightarrow A \wedge \neg A$.

1.2.5 Arithmetical Representation of Statements and Logical Operations

Statements and logical operations can be nicely expressed within *binary arithmetic*: the arithmetic of 0 and 1.

First, we describe the rules of binary arithmetic. We suppose given the two numbers 0,1 and two operations $+$ and $\cdot$ on them subject to the following rules:

$$0 + 0 = 1 + 1 = 0 \qquad 0 \cdot 0 = 0 \cdot 1 = 1 \cdot 0 = 0$$
$$0 + 1 = 1 + 0 = 1 \qquad\qquad 1 \cdot 1 = 1$$

We shall think of statements as determining *binary functions* (that is, functions taking just the values 0 and 1) as follows. Statement letters A,B,C, ... will be regarded as variables taking values 0,1: we think of 1 as representing the truth value $\top$ and 0 as representing the truth value $\bot$. Then the operation $\wedge$ corresponds to $\cdot$ and the operation $\neg$ to the operation $1 + \ldots$ of adding 1.

Given this, how do we interpret $\vee$ and $\rightarrow$? We argue as follows.

$$\begin{aligned}
[\![A \vee B]\!] &= [\![\neg(\neg A \wedge \neg B)]\!] \\
&= 1 + (1 + [\![A]\!]) \cdot (1 + [\![B]\!]) \\
&= 1 + 1 + [\![A]\!] + [\![B]\!] + [\![A]\!] \cdot [\![B]\!] \\
&= 0 + [\![A]\!] + [\![B]\!] + [\![A]\!] \cdot [\![B]\!] \\
&= [\![A]\!] + [\![B]\!] + [\![A]\!] \cdot [\![B]\!]
\end{aligned}$$

And

$$\begin{aligned}
[\![A \rightarrow B]\!] &\equiv [\![\neg A \vee B]\!] \\
&= 1 + [\![A]\!] + [\![B]\!] + (1 + [\![A]\!]) \cdot [\![B]\!] \\
&= 1 + [\![A]\!] + [\![B]\!] + [\![B]\!] + [\![A]\!] \cdot [\![B]\!] \\
&= 1 + [\![A]\!] + [\![A]\!] \cdot [\![B]\!].
\end{aligned}$$

In this way any statement P gives rise to a binary function called its *binary representation*, which we shall denote by the corresponding lower-case italic letter, p. In that case, *tautologies* are those statements whose binary representations take only value 1, and *contradictions* those statements whose binary representations take only value 0.

When, for example, is $P \rightarrow Q$ a tautology? Exactly when the corresponding binary representation $1 + p + p \cdot q$ is constantly 1. But this is the case precisely when $0 = p + p \cdot q = p \cdot (1 + q)$, that is, when at least one of p and $1 + q$ is 0. In other words, if $p = 1$, then $1 + q = 0$, i.e. $q = 1$. But this means that the value of p never exceeds the value of q: we shall write this as $p \leqslant q$. Writing $\Longleftrightarrow$ to indicate equivalence of assertions, this means that:

$$P \vDash Q \iff P \rightarrow Q \text{ is a tautology} \iff p \leqslant q.$$

That is, *in the binary representation,* $\vDash$ *corresponds to* $\leqslant$. By the same token,

$$P \equiv Q \iff p = q.$$

That is, *in the binary representation,* $\equiv$ *corresponds to* $=$.

The binary representation sheds light on expressive completeness. For example, the expressive completeness of $\{\wedge, \neg\}$ translates into the assertion that any binary function can be expressed in terms of the operations $\cdot$ and $1 + \ldots$, while that of $|$ into the assertion that any binary function can be expressed in terms of the single binary function $1 + x \cdot y$.

In light of this close connection between bivalent truth-functions and binary arithmetic, we will *henceforth often use 0 and 1 to refer to $\perp$ and $\top$, respectively.*

EXERCISES 1.2.5
Let $\max(x, y)$ be an operation which chooses the *larger* of two numbers x and y (and which chooses x if they are equal), and let $\min(x, y)$ be the analogous operation which chooses the minimum. Define $0 - 0 = 1 - 1 = 0 - 1 = 0$ and $1 - 0 = 1$. Show, using these definitions, that:

1. $[\![A \wedge B]\!] = \min([\![A]\!], [\![B]\!])$.

2. $[\![A \vee B]\!] = \max([\![A]\!], [\![B]\!])$.

*   3. $[\![A \rightarrow B]\!] = 1$ if $[\![A]\!] \leqslant [\![B]\!]$, and $1 - ([\![A]\!] - [\![B]\!])$ otherwise.

4. $[\![\neg A]\!] = 1 - [\![A]\!]$.

1.3   Trees for Classical Propositional Logic

Since an argument is valid if and only if it has no counterexamples, to test an argument for validity it suffices to conduct an exhaustive search for counterexamples. If none are found, then the inference is valid.

In the case of truth-functional validity (and, as we will see later in the book, also in the case of many other sorts of validity) *trees* are an efficient and elegant device for unearthing counterexamples.

Consider, for example, the (valid) argument

$$A \lor B$$
$$\neg A$$
$$\therefore \quad B$$

To obtain its tree form, we start by listing its premises and the *negation* of its conclusion:

$$A \lor B$$
$$\neg A$$
$$\neg B$$

These statements will be true in exactly the cases in which there are counterexamples to the original inference. Now we continue, generating a tree-like structure:

Here the statements A, B, $\neg A$, $\neg B$, and $A \lor B$ *occupy* positions, or as we shall call them, *nodes*[1] in the tree. The statement occupying the top node is a disjunction and requires analysis: $A \lor B$ is true in all those cases in which A is true and all those cases in which B is true, and in no other cases. We indicate this by writing A and B at the ends of a fork at the foot of the tree. At the same time we tick the statement $A \lor B$ to indicate that all its true cases have been taken into account. *Ticking a statement is, accordingly, equivalent to erasing it.*[2] Finally we write $\times$ at the foot of each path through the tree in which a statement occupies one node and its negation another. Such paths are called *closed*. In this particular tree *all* paths are closed; under these conditions the tree itself is said to be *closed*. And, as we shall see, the inference is then valid.

Why is this? Because the procedure was designed so that when we ticked a statement, we displayed all the possible ways in which that statement can be true. The various paths then represent all the ways in which the initial statements (i.e., the statements with which we began the tree) could possibly be true; that is, each path represents a potential counterexample to the original inference. In the case of a closed path, the "possibility" it represents does not really exist. Accordingly, if all paths are closed, then it is impossible for all the initial statements of the tree to be (simultaneously)

---

[1] We shall often identify a node in a tree with the statement occupying it.

[2] In accordance with the remark in the footnote above, we shall frequently use the locution "to tick a given node" as a synonym for "ticking the statement occupying the given node."

true. In other words, there are no counterexamples to the original inference and so it is valid.

In contrast, observe what happens when we test an invalid inference, e.g.,

$$A \lor B$$
$$A$$
$$\therefore \quad B$$

In this case the tree looks like this:

The left-hand path is not closed. Moreover, the only unticked statements which occur on that path are either statement letters or the negations of statement letters, or, as we shall say, they are all *literals*. What this means, for present purposes, is that they need no further analysis because the branch in question supplies us with the counterexample we were seeking. When the only unticked statements on an unclosed path in a tree are literals, we say that path is a *completed* (or *finished*) *open path*. You will recall that a counterexample in classical propositional logic is a valuation under which all the premises are true but the conclusion is false. To describe the counterexamples represented by a completed open path, note which literals occupy nodes in the path—in this case they are A and $\neg B$. The corresponding counterexamples are those in which unnegated statement letters are assigned the value 1 and negated statement letters get the value 0—so in this case, counterexamples are those valuations under which A is true and B is false. This is easily checked by considering the corresponding row of a truth table for this argument:

A	B	A ∨ B	A	B
1	0	1	1	0

We next describe the various *tree rules*.

1.3.1   Tree Rules for Classical Propositional Logic

In the procedure just sketched, there are two reasons we can have for ceasing to work on a given path: the path closes, or the path becomes a completed open path. It would be very convenient to have a procedure which ensures that we always arrive at one or another of these outcomes for every path on a tree. Clearly, to get such a procedure we would need rules for "analyzing" all statements which are non-literals.

Given what has already been said, it should be clear what the rule must be for handling disjunctive statements.

RULE 1.1 (DISJUNCTION) Tick a disjunction occupying a node and write the disjuncts at the end of a fork drawn at the foot of each open path containing the ticked node.

$$P \vee Q \; ✔$$
$$P \qquad Q$$

On the other hand, a disjunction is *false* when and only when both disjuncts are false. Thus we have the rule:

RULE 1.2 (NEGATED DISJUNCTION) Tick a negated disjunction occupying a node and write the negations of the disjuncts in a column at the foot of each open path containing the ticked node.

$$\neg(P \vee Q) \; ✔$$
$$\neg P$$
$$\neg Q$$

Since a conjunction is true exactly when both conjuncts are true, we need the rule:

RULE 1.3 (CONJUNCTION) Tick a conjunction occupying a node and write the conjuncts in a column at the foot of each open path containing the ticked node.

$$P \wedge Q \; ✔$$
$$P$$
$$Q$$

On the other hand, a conjunction is false exactly when either conjunct is false. So we have the rule:

RULE 1.4 (NEGATED CONJUNCTION) Tick a negated conjunction occupying a node and write the negations of the conjuncts at the end of a fork drawn at the foot of each open path containing the ticked node.

$$\neg(P \wedge Q) \; ✔$$
$$\neg P \qquad \neg Q$$

Since $P \rightarrow Q \equiv \neg P \vee Q$, we can introduce the rule:

RULE 1.5 (IMPLICATION) Tick an implication occupying a node and write the negation of the antecedent and the consequent at the ends of a fork drawn at the foot of each open path containing the ticked node.

$$P \rightarrow Q \quad \checkmark$$
$$\diagup \qquad \diagdown$$
$$\neg P \qquad \qquad Q$$

Since an implication is false exactly when the antecedent is true and the consequent false, we have:

RULE 1.6 (NEGATED IMPLICATION) Tick a negated implication occupying a node and write the antecedent and the negation of the consequent in a column at the foot of each open path containing the ticked node.

$$\neg(P \rightarrow Q) \quad \checkmark$$
$$P$$
$$\neg Q$$

Since a bi-implication is true exactly when both components are true, or both are false, we need the rather complicated-looking rule:

RULE 1.7 (BI-IMPLICATION) Tick a bi-implication occupying a node and draw a fork at the foot of each open path containing the ticked node. At the ends of each of these write in columns the components, and, respectively, the negations of the components, of the ticked node.

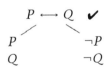

$$P \longleftrightarrow Q \quad \checkmark$$
$$\diagup \qquad \diagdown$$
$$P \qquad \qquad \neg P$$
$$Q \qquad \qquad \neg Q$$

A bi-implication is false exactly when one component is true and the other false, hence:

RULE 1.8 (NEGATED BI-IMPLICATION) Tick a negated bi-implication occupying a node, and draw a fork at the foot of each open path containing the ticked node. At the ends of these write in columns the first component and the negation of the second, and, respectively, the negation of the first and the second.

$$\neg(P \longleftrightarrow Q) \quad \checkmark$$
$$\diagup \qquad \diagdown$$
$$P \qquad \qquad \neg P$$
$$\neg Q \qquad \qquad Q$$

Finally, since $\neg\neg P \equiv P$, we can adopt a rule which tells us, essentially, to erase double-negations.

RULE 1.9 (DOUBLE NEGATION) Tick a negated negation occupying a node and write the doubly-negated statement at the foot of each open path containing the ticked node.

$$\neg\neg P \;\checkmark$$
$$P$$

It is natural to think of the rules listed above as coming in pairs. For each binary connective, there are two rules, one for when statements of that form are affirmed, and one for when they are negated. This nice symmetry is broken by the fact that we have only one rule for the negation operators. We can regain it by regarding the rule which allows us to close a branch containing both P and $\neg P$, somewhat artificially, as the "affirmative" negation rule. We can then summarize these rules as follows:

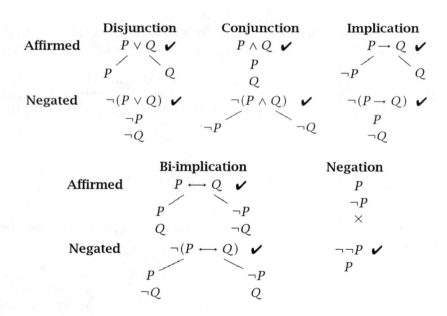

1.3.2   Trees as a Test for Validity

To test an argument for validity, begin with a tree consisting of a single path containing its premises and the negation of its conclusion. If there are non-literals on an open branch of the tree, choose one and apply the rule which allows you to tick that statement—for any non-literal, there will be exactly one such rule. Do this repeatedly until you are finished, i.e., until the only unticked nodes in any remaining open paths are literals. (A tree obtained in this way is called a [finished] *tree associated with* the given argument.) If any tree associated with an argument is closed, i.e. if all its paths are closed, the original inference is valid.

A few remarks about this process are in order. When carrying it out, you should be sure before any particular application of any rule that you have marked all the closed paths with an ×. Obviously, as a practical matter, this will save some effort. In any case, it is strictly speaking *incorrect* to add things to the bottom of a closed path, since all the rules state that certain statements are to be added only to open paths on which the node occurs. Secondly, observe that there can be more than one tree associated with a given argument, depending on the order in which the rules are applied. In this connection, notice that we say that the argument is valid if there is *some* tree associated with it which is closed. In the case of classical propositional logic, it turns out that if some tree for an argument closes, then all trees for that argument close, so in a sense it doesn't really matter in what order you decide to apply the rules. (It can make a significant difference to how complicated the resulting tree is, so some foresight in choosing, for instance, to apply rules which don't require branching before applying those which do will certainly be rewarded by requiring less work. But the final answer will be the same regardless.) As we shall see in later chapters, in other systems things are sometimes not quite so simple.

We now give some examples of the use of this test. First, consider the argument $(A \wedge B) \vee C$, $\neg A$, therefore C. A tree for this argument is:

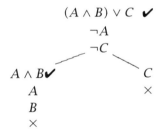

The tree is closed, so the argument is *valid*.

What about the argument $A \vee B$, $C \vee A$, $\neg A$, therefore $C \wedge B$?

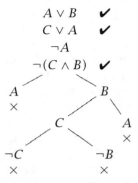

Once again, the tree closed, so the argument is valid. Next, let's consider the argument $A \rightarrow B$, $B \rightarrow C$, therefore $A \rightarrow C$.

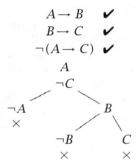

Again, the argument is valid. Notice that in this case we saved some work by first applying the negated implication rule to the third node of the tree. It is a useful exercise to draw the tree which results by first applying the implication rule to the first and second lines to see that one can generate unnecessary work for oneself by not paying attention to such things.

1.3.3 Further Applications of the Tree Method.

Counterexamples from the associated tree.

Any open path remaining in a finished tree associated with an argument determines a counterexample to it (and so establishes its invalidity). And conversely, any counterexample is determined by an open path in any such tree.

For example, the argument $A \vee B$, $C \vee D$, therefore C, is invalid.

Consider the following finished tree associated with this argument:

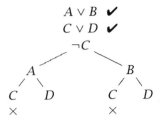

Each open path in this tree determines a counterexample to the given inference. For example, the left hand open path, nodes of which are occupied by
A, $\neg C$, D, but by neither B nor $\neg B$, determine as counterexamples all cases
in which $[\![A]\!] = 1$, $[\![C]\!] = 0$, $[\![D]\!] = 1$ regardless of the truth value of B.
That is, we obtain two classes of counterexamples: those in which $[\![A]\!] = 1$,
$[\![B]\!] = 1$, $[\![C]\!] = 0$, $[\![D]\!] = 1$, and those in which $[\![A]\!] = 1$, $[\![B]\!] = 0$, $[\![C]\!] = 0$,
$[\![D]\!] = 1$. Similarly, the right hand open path determines as counterexam-
ples all cases in which $[\![B]\!]$, $[\![C]\!]$, $[\![D]\!]$ are 1, 0, 1 respectively, regardless of
the truth value of $[\![A]\!]$. In total we get the three distinct counterexamples—
the two listed above, and those valuations in which $[\![A]\!] = 0$, $[\![B]\!] = 1$,
$[\![C]\!] = 0$, and $[\![D]\!] = 1$. These are all the counterexamples to the given
inference.

In this connection we observe that the open paths in the *other* finished
tree associated with the above invalid argument, viz.,

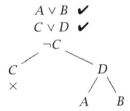

of course determine exactly the same counterexamples as were obtained
before.

Tree test for Satisfiability

Recall that a set of statements is satisfiable or consistent if there is at least
one case in which all the members of the set are true. We can use trees to
test sets of statements for truth-functional satisfiability. Given a (finite) set
S of statements, start a tree with the members of S in a column. Then S is
satisfiable precisely when there is an open path through the finished tree.
Each open path determines a truth valuation that makes all the members of
S true.

We illustrate this by the following example. Consider the set of statements $\{A \lor B, \neg(A \land B)\}$. One relevant finished tree is

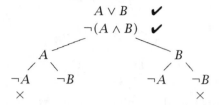

There are two open paths in which the literals A, $\neg B$; $\neg A$, B respectively,
occupy nodes. Thus the valuations making the given set of statements true
are where $[\![A]\!] = 1$ and $[\![B]\!] = 0$ or where $[\![A]\!] = 0$ and $[\![B]\!] = 1$.

Tree test for tautologousness

To determine whether a given statement is a tautology, start a tree with
its *negation*. Then the given statement is *a tautology* precisely when the
resulting finished tree is *closed*.

For example, consider the statement $(A \land B) \lor (\neg A \lor \neg B)$. To test for
logical validity, we construct the following tree:

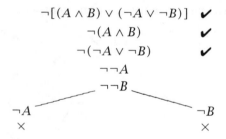

Since this (finished) tree is closed, the statement in question is a truth-
functional tautology.

Tree test for contradictions

To test whether a given statement is a contradiction, start a tree with the
(unnegated) statement. Then the statement is a *contradiction* precisely when
the resulting finished tree is *closed*.

For example, to test whether the statement $A \land (A \rightarrow B) \land (A \rightarrow \neg B)$ is a contradiction, construct the following tree:

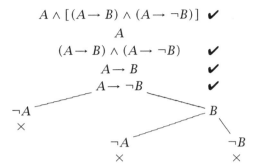

Since this (finished) tree is closed, the given statement is a contradiction.

EXERCISES 1.3.1

1. Use trees to determine which of the following arguments are truth-functionally valid. For those which are not, use the tree to determine all the valuations which are counterexamples.

    (a) $A \wedge (B \rightarrow C) \therefore (A \wedge C) \vee (A \wedge \neg B)$

* (b) $\neg A \vee B, B \rightarrow C, C \vee D \therefore A \vee D$

    (c) $A \rightarrow \neg A, \neg A \rightarrow C \therefore C \wedge \neg C$

2. For each of the following sets of statements, use trees to determine whether or not it is truth-functionally consistent. For those which are consistent, use the tree to determine under which valuations they are all true.

    (a) $\{A \rightarrow (D \longleftrightarrow C), C \wedge D, \neg C, A\}$

* (b) $\{\neg\neg\neg A \rightarrow \neg\neg B, \neg B \rightarrow \neg A, \neg(A \rightarrow B)\}$

    (c) $\{C \wedge \neg A, C \longleftrightarrow (C \rightarrow A), (C \vee A) \rightarrow \neg(C \wedge A)\}$

3. For each of the following statements, use trees to determine whether it is a truth-functional tautology, a truth-functional contradiction, or truth-functionally contingent.

    (a) $(A \rightarrow B) \vee (B \rightarrow A)$

* (b) $\neg(A \longleftrightarrow B) \rightarrow (\neg A \longleftrightarrow \neg B)$

    (c) $[A \rightarrow (B \rightarrow C)] \rightarrow [(A \rightarrow B) \rightarrow C]$

    (d) $(A \rightarrow \neg A) \wedge (\neg A \rightarrow C) \rightarrow C$

4. (a) Explain the relationship between the use of the tree method as a test for consistency and its use as a test for contradictoriness.

* (b) Explain the relationship between the use of the tree method as a test for validity and as a test for consistency.

5. Let τ be a finished tree with one initial statement P. Show how to use τ to obtain a disjunctive normal form for P.

1.4 Metatheorems

We turn now to the task of supplying some arguments designed to justify the claims we have made concerning the use of trees in establishing validity and satisfiability. Before getting started, we need some terminology.

DEFINITION 1.20 If we apply a tree rule of the form

P is called the *premise* and $\{Q, R\}$ the *list of conclusions* of the application. Similarly, when applying a tree rule of the form

P is called the *premise* and $\{Q, R\}$ and $\{Q', R'\}$ the *lists of conclusions*.

DEFINITION 1.21 (CORRECTNESS AND COMPLETENESS OF A RULE) We call a tree rule r *correct* if whenever the premise of r is true under a given valuation, then all the statements in *at least one* of r's lists of conclusions are also true under the valuation. And let us call r *complete* if the converse holds, that is, the premise of r is true under a given valuation whenever all the statements in at least one of r's lists of conclusions is true under the valuation.

Clearly, *all the tree rules we have introduced are correct and complete in the above senses.*

Next, we observe that the process of constructing a finished tree *always terminates.* For the tree starts with a finite number of statements, each of which has finite length.[3] The tree grows by a process of choosing an unticked statement occupying a node of an open path, ticking it and adding at the foot of each open path running through that node some finite number of statements. Since we begin with a tree with a single path, and each application of a rule adds only a finite number to the total number of open paths in the tree (it can at most double it, in fact, since at most two branches come out of the bottom of each open path), at every stage there are only finitely many open paths on the tree. Hence at every stage only finitely many statements are added to the tree. Moreover, each of these additions is *shorter* than the ticked one. Eventually the point must be reached at

---

[3]We define the *length* of a statement to be the total number of symbols in it.

which all unticked statements occupying nodes of open paths have lengths 1 or 2, (i.e., are literals) and the process ends.

Given a set S of statements, let us say that a tree starts with S if the statements of S occupy the top nodes of the tree, that is, those preceding any node which arises as the result of applying a tree rule. Now we can establish

THEOREM 1.2 (CORRECTNESS OF THE TREE METHOD)
If a finite set S of statements is satisfiable, there will be an open path through any tree that starts with S.

To prove this, observe first that, if all the statements occupying nodes in a path ψ of a tree are true under a given valuation, then ψ is open. For if both a statement and its negation occupied nodes in ψ, then, since one of them has to be false under the given valuation, we would violate the hypothesis on ψ.

Now suppose that under some valuation V all the members of S are true. Consider the following property of a tree τ.

(∗) τ starts with S and contains a path ψ such that all statements occupying nodes of ψ are true under V.

By the observation above, any tree satisfying (∗) contains an open path.

We claim that, if τ has property (∗), so does any tree τ^* obtained from τ by applying a tree rule. For suppose that (a) all the statements occupying nodes in a certain path ψ through τ are true under V and (b) we extend τ to τ^* by applying a tree rule to one of its statements. Clearly we may assume that this statement is in ψ, for if not, then ψ is unaffected and is a path of τ^*. Accordingly in the transition from τ to τ^* the path ψ is extended to a new path, or extended and split into two new paths, by applying some tree rule. Since any tree rule is correct, all the statements occupying nodes in the new path, or all those occupying nodes in at least one of the new paths, are true under V. But this shows that τ^* has property (∗), as claimed.

It follows that *any* tree starting with S has property (∗), and hence contains an open path. Hence any complete tree will include a complete open path and, as we have seen, the process of tree construction for finite sets of sentences always terminates with a complete tree.

As an immediate consequence of this, we obtain the

THEOREM 1.3 (ARGUMENT CORRECTNESS OF THE TREE METHOD)
If a tree associated with an argument is closed, the argument is valid.

Now we prove the converse of the above correctness result, that is, the

THEOREM 1.4 (ADEQUACY OF THE TREE METHOD)
If there is an open path through a finished tree starting with a given set S of statements, then S is satisfiable.

To prove this, let τ be a finished tree starting with S containing an open path ψ. Let V be the valuation under which those statement letters occupying nodes of ψ are assigned 1, and all others 0. We claim that all statements occupying nodes of ψ are true under V.

First, notice that all statements of lengths 1 or 2 occupying nodes of ψ are true under V. For those of length 1 are statement letters and are accordingly true under V by definition. And any one of length 2 is a negation $\neg A$ of a statement letter A; since ψ is open, A cannot occupy a node of P, and so is false under V. Thus $\neg A$ is true under V.

Now suppose that, if possible, some statement occupying a node of ψ is false under V. Let P be such a statement of *shortest* length. Then by the above the length of P must be at least 3, so a tree rule, r say, may be applied to P. Since τ is finished, some list L of conclusions obtained by applying r to P is already part of ψ. But each statement in L is shorter than P, and so must be true under V. Since r is complete, it follows that the premise P of the specified application of r is also true under V. Therefore the falsity of P is refuted, and the claim above follows.

The truth of the claim immediately yields the adequacy result.

As an immediate consequence, we obtain the converse of argument correctness, that is,

THEOREM 1.5 (ARGUMENT ADEQUACY OF THE TREE METHOD)
If an argument is valid, then any finished tree associated with it is closed.

EXERCISES 1.4.1
*   1. Explain clearly why Theorem 1.2 follows from Theorem 1.1.

2. Explain clearly why theorem 1.4 follows from 1.3.

1.5   Other Proof Methods

The tree method we employed in the preceding section has many advantages when investigating properties such as consistency, validity, and so on: it is very easy to use, and since the tree rules reflect very directly the intended meanings of the logical connectives many of the proofs of metalogical results are fairly direct and easy to understand. We will therefore use this method more than any other in this book.

But the tree method is by no means the only proof method, and some others have their own advantages in other situations. We will turn next to the task of briefly describing some other methods, and indicating their relationship to the tree method.

1.5.1 Classical Propositional Calculus

In this section we describe a formal system—the *propositional calculus*—for *proving* propositional statements and as a result obtain a purely syntactical characterization of valid propositional inferences and tautologies. To set up the system we choose certain tautologies as *axioms* and lay down a certain *rule of inference* which will enable us to construct deductions.[4]

The propositional calculus (PC) has as axioms all statements of any of the forms (1)-(10) below.

1. $P \rightarrow (Q \rightarrow P)$

2. $[P \rightarrow (Q \rightarrow R)] \rightarrow [(P \rightarrow Q) \rightarrow (P \rightarrow R)]$

3. $(P \wedge Q) \rightarrow P$

4. $(P \wedge Q) \rightarrow Q$

5. $P \rightarrow (Q \rightarrow (P \wedge Q))$

6. $P \rightarrow (P \vee Q)$

7. $Q \rightarrow (P \vee Q)$

8. $(P \rightarrow R) \rightarrow [(Q \rightarrow R) \rightarrow ((P \vee Q) \rightarrow R)]$

9. $(P \rightarrow Q) \rightarrow [(P \rightarrow \neg Q) \rightarrow \neg P]$

10. $\neg\neg P \rightarrow P$.

The sole rule of inference for PC is widely known by the Latin name *modus ponens* ("proposing mode"):

$$\frac{P, \quad P \rightarrow Q}{Q} \tag{MP}$$

In words, from P and $P \rightarrow Q$, infer Q.

DEFINITION 1.22 Let S be a set of statements. A *deduction* from S is a finite sequence $P_1, \ldots, P_n$ of statements such that, for any $i = 1, \ldots, n$, P_i is either (a) an axiom, (b) a member of S, or (c) inferrable using MP from earlier members of the sequence, i.e., there are numbers $j, k < i$ such that P_k is $P_j \rightarrow P_i$.

A deduction from the empty set of statements is called simply a *proof*. A deduction (or proof) with last statement P is called a *deduction* (or *proof*) *of P*. We write $S \vdash_{PC} P$ to indicate that P is *deducible* from S, i.e. that there is a deduction of P from S. If S is empty, so that P is *provable*, i.e. there is a proof of P, we write just $\vdash_{PC} P$, and call P a *theorem* of PC.

---

[4]In what follows we shall omit the logical operator $\longleftrightarrow$ in forming statements, and the rules governing $\longleftrightarrow$ in constructing trees. The reader will recall that $\longleftrightarrow$ was, after all, introduced by its being defined by $p \longleftrightarrow q \equiv (p \rightarrow q) \wedge (q \rightarrow p)$.

EXAMPLE 1.1
The following is a proof of the statement $P \rightarrow P$.

1.	$(P \rightarrow [(P \rightarrow P) \rightarrow P]) \rightarrow ([P \rightarrow (P \rightarrow P)] \rightarrow (P \rightarrow P))$	by Ax.2
2.	$P \rightarrow [(P \rightarrow P) \rightarrow P]$	by Ax.1
3.	$[P \rightarrow (P \rightarrow P)] \rightarrow (P \rightarrow P)$	by MP on 1, 2
4.	$P \rightarrow (P \rightarrow P)$	by Ax.1
5.	$P \rightarrow P$	by MP on 3,4

We now establish the important

THEOREM 1.6 (DEDUCTION THEOREM)
For any set S of statements and any statements P,Q:

$$S, P \vdash_{PC} Q \quad \text{if and only if} \quad S \vdash_{PC} P \rightarrow Q.$$

Proof: First, suppose that $S \vdash_{PC} P \rightarrow Q$. Then there is a deduction $P_1, \ldots, P_n$ with $P_n = P \rightarrow Q$ of $P \rightarrow Q$ from S. Clearly, if we add the sequence P, Q to the end of this sequence, the result is a deduction of Q from S, P. Therefore $S, P \vdash_{PC} Q$.

Conversely, suppose that $S, P \vdash_{PC} Q$. Then there is a deduction $R_1, \ldots, R_n$ of Q from S, P (so that Q is R_n). We claim that $S \vdash_{PC} P \rightarrow R_i$ for any $i = 1, \ldots, n$.

Now, if the claim were false, then there is a least number k such that it is *not* the case that $S \vdash_{PC} P \rightarrow R_k$. There are then four possibilities: (1) R_k is an axiom; (2) R_k is in S; (3) R_k is P; (4) R_k is deducible using MP from some R_i and R_j with $i, j < k$, where R_j is $R_i \rightarrow R_k$. We show that in each of these four cases $S \vdash_{PC} P \rightarrow R_k$. This will contradict the assertion that the claim is false for R_k, and it must accordingly be true.

Case (1). R_k is an axiom. In this case the sequence of statements R_k, $R_k \rightarrow (P \rightarrow R_k)$, $P \rightarrow R_k$ is a proof of $P \rightarrow R_k$, so that $S \vdash_{PC} P \rightarrow R_k$.

Case (2). R_k is in S. In this case the same sequence of statements as in case (1) is a deduction of $P \rightarrow R_k$ from S.

Case (3). R_k is P. Here we have $\vdash_{PC} P \rightarrow R_k$ by Example 1.1, so a fortiori $S \vdash_{PC} P \rightarrow R_k$.

Case (4). For some $i, j < k$, R_j is $R_i \rightarrow R_k$. Since k was assumed to be the *least* number for which it is not the case that $S \vdash_{PC} P \rightarrow R_k$, and $i, j < k$, we must have $S \vdash_{PC} P \rightarrow R_i$ and $S \vdash_{PC} P \rightarrow R_j$, i.e., $S \vdash_{PC} P \rightarrow (R_i \rightarrow R_k)$. But

$$[P \rightarrow (R_i \rightarrow R_k)] \rightarrow [(P \rightarrow R_i) \rightarrow (P \rightarrow R_k)]$$

is an instance of axiom 2. Hence, applying MP,

$$S \vdash_{PC} (P \rightarrow R_i) \rightarrow (P \rightarrow R_k)$$

and applying it once more,

$$S \vdash_{PC} P \rightarrow R_k.$$

We have obtained a contradiction in each case, so the claim is true. In particular, taking $i = n$, we get $S \vdash_{PC} P \rightarrow R_n$, i.e. $S \vdash_{PC} P \rightarrow Q$. This completes the proof.

Our next result is the

THEOREM 1.7 (SOUNDNESS THEOREM FOR THE PROPOSITIONAL CALCULUS)
Any theorem of PC is a tautology. [5]

Proof: Note first that, if a valuation satisfies both P and $P \rightarrow Q$, then it satisfies Q. Thus if both P and $P \rightarrow Q$ are tautologies, so is Q. In other words, MP leads from tautologies to tautologies.

It is also not hard to show that any axiom of PC is a tautology. One easy way to do so is to apply the tree method to test the axiom forms (1)–(10) for tautologousness. We leave this as an exercise for the reader.

Hence any deduction in PC consists entirely of tautologies, and the result follows.

THEOREM 1.8 (COROLLARY)
PC is consistent in the sense that for no statement P do we have both $\vdash_{PC} P$ and $\vdash_{PC} \neg P$.

We are next going to establish a strengthened version of the Soundness Theorem. This is much easier to prove if we modify slightly the procedure for constructing trees.

DEFINITION 1.23 An *extended tree* is a tree obtained by allowing, in addition to all the usual rules for constructing trees, application of:

RULE 1.10 (EXCLUDED MIDDLE FOR TREES (EM)) At any time in the construction of a tree, one may extend any open path by writing any sentence and its negation at the ends of a fork drawn at its end.

---

[5] Notice that we use the terms "correctness" and "adequacy" for systems of tree rules, whereas we use "soundness" and "completeness" for similar properties of the propositional calculus and some other systems. Terminology for these properties varies across the literature: some authors use "soundness" and "completeness" for systems of tree rules, and reserve the name "adequacy" for the combination of these properties, while others use "correctness" and "adequacy" as we do and reserve the name "completeness" for their combination, and so on. Our usage reflects an old idea that trees (which some authors call "truth trees"), and their cousins, semantic tableaux, are somehow too closely related to the intended interpretations of the formulas to be properly classified as "syntactical" methods of proof. We don't agree with this, but we follow these authors by using different terminology for trees and for other sorts of proof procedure. Having all four terms available is useful to us in later chapters when we distinguish between, for instance, rule-soundness and rule-correctness for related but distinct properties.

Clearly, the EM rule is correct in the sense of definition 1.21. (The rule has no premises, but under *any* valuation either P or $\neg P$ will be true.) It follows, just as for ordinary trees, that the use of extended trees is argument correct. That is, if an extended tree associated with an argument is closed, then that argument is valid.

Now we prove the

THEOREM 1.9
Let S be a (finite) set of statements and P a statement. If $S \vdash_{PC} P$, then there is a closed extended tree starting with $S, \neg P$.

Proof: Suppose that $S \vdash_{PC} P$. Then there is a deduction $P_1, \ldots, P_n$ of P from S. We claim that for any $i = 1, \ldots, n$ there is a closed extended tree starting with $S, \neg P_i$.

Suppose on the contrary that the claim is false. Then there is a least number k such that there is no closed extended tree starting with $S, \neg P_k$. There are then two possibilities, each of which we show leads to a contradiction. Case 1: $k = 1$. In this case P_k is either an axiom or a member of S. If it is an axiom, then it is a tautology, so there is a closed tree τ starting with $\neg P_1$. If we append S to the top of τ, we obtain a closed tree starting with $S, \neg P_1$. If, on the other hand, P_1 is in S, then the tree consisting of just $S, \neg P_1$ is already closed.
Case 2: $k > 1$. By hypothesis there is, for each $i < k$, a closed extended tree starting with $S, \neg P_i$. We show that from this we may conclude that there is a closed extended tree starting with $S, \neg P_k$.

Now P_k is either an axiom, a member of S, or inferrable using MP from previous P_i. In each of the first two cases we obtain a closed extended tree just as we did in the case $k = 1$. In the last case there exist numbers $i, j < k$ such that P_j is $P_i \to P_k$. As we have just observed, there are closed extended trees τ_1, τ_2 starting with $S, \neg P_i$ and $S, \neg P_j$, i.e. $S, \neg(P_i \to P_j)$, respectively. Start a new extended tree as follows (notice the use of EM):

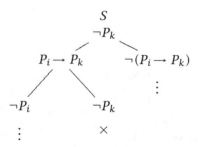

If to the left-hand branch of this tree we append τ_1 pruned of its top nodes (i.e., of the lines S, P_i) and to the right-hand branch τ_2 pruned of its top nodes, we obtain a closed extended tree starting with $S, \neg P_k$.

Thus in all cases we contradict the assumption that the claim is false. Accordingly it is true; in particular, taking $k = n$, we obtain a closed extended tree starting with $S, \neg P$. This proves the theorem.

As a consequence of this and the argument correctness of extended trees, we obtain the

THEOREM 1.10 (STRENGTHENED SOUNDNESS THEOREM FOR PC)
If $S \vdash_{PC} P$, then $S \models P$.

Our final task will be to prove the converse of this.

Let us call a set S of statements *formally inconsistent* if $S \vdash_{PC} P$ and $S \vdash_{PC} \neg P$ for some statement P. We now establish the following facts:

PROPOSITION 1.11 *(A) S is formally inconsistent if and only if $S \vdash_{PC} Q$ for all statements Q. (B) $S \vdash_{PC} P$ if and only if $S, \neg P$ is formally inconsistent.*

Proof of (A): Clearly, if $S \vdash_{PC} Q$ for all statements Q, then S is formally inconsistent. To establish the converse, we begin by showing that $\vdash_{PC} \neg P \to (P \to Q)$. First, note that the following sequence is a deduction of Q from $\neg P, P$:

1.	$\neg P$	
2.	P	
3.	$P \to (\neg Q \to P)$	Ax.1
4.	$\neg P \to (\neg Q \to \neg P)$	Ax.1
5.	$\neg Q \to P$	by MP on 1,3
6.	$\neg Q \to \neg P$	by MP on 2,4
7.	$(\neg Q \to P) \to [(\neg Q \to \neg P) \to \neg \neg Q)]$	Ax.9
8.	$(\neg Q \to \neg P) \to \neg \neg Q$	by MP on 5, 7
9.	$\neg \neg Q$	by MP on 6,8
10.	$\neg \neg Q \to Q$	Ax.10
11.	Q	by MP on 9,10

So $\neg P, P \vdash_{PC} Q$. Two applications of the deduction theorem now give $\vdash_{PC} \neg P \to (P \to Q)$ as claimed.

Now if S is formally inconsistent, we have $S \vdash_{PC} P$ and $S \vdash_{PC} \neg P$. Since $\neg P \to (P \to Q)$, two applications of MP yield $S \vdash_{PC} Q$. This proves (A).

Proof of (B): If $S \vdash_{PC} P$, then $S, \neg P \vdash_{PC} P$ and $S, \neg P \vdash_{PC} \neg P$ so $S, \neg P$ is formally inconsistent.

Conversely, suppose that $S, \neg P$ is formally inconsistent. Then by (A), $S, \neg P \vdash_{PC} \neg \neg P$. So by the deduction theorem $S \vdash_{PC} \neg P \to \neg \neg P$. Now we have

$$P \to P, P \to \neg P \vdash_{PC} \neg P$$

as the following deduction shows:

1. $P \rightarrow \neg P$
2. $(P \rightarrow P) \rightarrow [(P \rightarrow \neg P) \rightarrow \neg P]$ Ax.9
3. $P \rightarrow P$
4. $(P \rightarrow \neg P) \rightarrow \neg P$ by MP on 2,3
5. $\neg P$.   by MP on 1,4

Since $\vdash_{PC} P \rightarrow P$, it follows that $P \rightarrow \neg P \vdash_{PC} \neg P$. So, substituting $\neg P$ for P, we get $\neg P \rightarrow \neg\neg P \vdash_{PC} \neg\neg P$. But $\neg\neg P \rightarrow P$ is an axiom, so an application of MP yields $\neg P \rightarrow \neg\neg P \vdash_{PC} P$. But we have already observed that $S \vdash_{PC} \neg P \rightarrow \neg\neg P$, so another application of MP yields $S \vdash_{PC} P$ as required. This proves (B).

Let us call the collection which includes exactly those statements which occupy nodes of a tree before any tree rule is applied the *initial set of statements* of that tree. We now sketch a proof of the

THEOREM 1.12
The initial set of statements of any closed tree is formally inconsistent.

Proof (sketch): Let us define the *depth* of a tree to be the length of its longest path, where we count the length of paths as follows: the length of the initial set of statements is 1, and each additional node on the path increases the length of the path by 1. Suppose that the assertion of the theorem is false. Then there is a closed tree with a *formally consistent* (i.e., not formally inconsistent) set of initial statements. Among these choose one, τ say, of least depth, d say. Then τ is a closed tree whose set S of initial statements is formally consistent. We shall derive a contradiction from this.

There are two cases to consider.
Case 1: $d = 1$. In this case τ is identical with S. Since τ is closed there must be some statement P for which both P and $\neg P$ are in S. Clearly S is then formally inconsistent.
Case 2: $d > 1$. In this case, by assumption, the set of initial statements of any closed tree of depth less than d is formally inconsistent. Now examine the statements at level 2 of τ. We claim that however these statements were obtained, we can always conclude that S is formally inconsistent.

For example, suppose that the statements at level 2 of τ arise by applying the $\vee$-rule to a statement in S of the form $P \vee Q$. Then τ starts thus:

If in τ we fuse S with P and expunge Q as well as all nodes following it, we get a closed tree (recall that τ was assumed closed) of depth less than d with

S, P as its set of initial statements. But then S, P is formally inconsistent. Similarly, S, Q is formally inconsistent. Since $P \vee Q$ is in S, it follows that S is formally inconsistent. (For if R is any statement, we have $S, P \vdash_{PC} R$ and $S, Q \vdash_{PC} R$ so that $S \vdash_{PC} P \rightarrow R$ and $S \vdash_{PC} Q \rightarrow R$. Two applications of MP and Axiom 8 now yield $S \vdash_{PC} P \vee Q \rightarrow R$; but since $P \vee Q$ is in S, MP yields $S \vdash_{PC} R$. Since this holds for any statement R, S is formally inconsistent.)

Similar arguments work for the other rules; in all cases we conclude that S is formally inconsistent.

We have shown that assuming the theorem false leads to a contradiction. So the theorem is proved.

EXERCISES 1.5.1
Supply the details for the rules left out of the above proof. (Hint: For the $\rightarrow$ rule, it may help to begin by showing that $P \rightarrow Q \vdash_{PC} \neg Q \rightarrow \neg P$.)

As a consequence of this, we finally obtain the

THEOREM 1.13 (COMPLETENESS THEOREM FOR PC)
For any set S of statements, and any statement P, if $S \vDash P$, then $S \vdash_{PC} P$.

Proof: If $S \vDash P$, then by inference adequacy any finished tree τ associated with the inference of P from S is closed. It follows from the previous theorem that the set $S, \neg P$ of initial statements of τ is formally inconsistent. Hence, by fact (B), $S \vdash_{PC} P$.

EXERCISES 1.5.2
* 1. Show that every axiom of PC is a tautology.

2. Explain clearly why Theorem 1.7 follows from Theorem 1.6.

1.5.2 Natural Deduction

The classical propositional calculus has nice features that are very useful for metatheoretic investigations. Proofs *within* the calculus, on the other hand, can be cumbersome, and the adoption of this system involves the acceptance of *axioms*, a step which might be thought to raise thorny philosophical issues. The tree method, as we've seen, is an efficient search procedure for counterexamples, one which eliminates the need for axioms. And since the tree rules closely reflect the intended semantics for our language, the metatheoretical results can be proved in a straightforward and illuminating way. But neither of these proof methods can plausibly be said to reflect faithfully a significant fragment of the various strategies that are commonly used in deductive reasoning. We turn now to consider a *natural deduction* system for classical propositional logic. As the name suggests, one of the virtues claimed for such systems is that the proofs one can construct in them more closely reflect our actual deductive practice (at least when we reason well). The system we consider also eliminates the need for axioms.

Finally, some advocates of natural deduction approaches to logic contend that they provide an *analysis* of the *meaning* of the logical connectives. On the other hand, metatheoretic results are somewhat more awkward to prove for this system than for the others.[6]

Natural deduction systems are typically constructed by specifying, for each logical operator, two sorts of rules. First, we have *introduction rules.* Roughly speaking, these encode answers to the question, "What must we know before we can infer a statement which has the operator in question as its main logical operator?" The other sort of rules are called *elimination rules*, and these (roughly speaking) encode answers to the question "What can we infer if we know a statement with the operator in question as its main operator?" For example, a bit of reflection should be enough to make clear that the most sensible response to a challenge to prove the statement $P \wedge Q$ is to set about trying to prove P and to prove Q. Conversely, the obvious answer to the question of what can be inferred from $P \wedge Q$ is that you can infer P and you can infer Q. There are thus two $\wedge$-Elimination rules.

RULE 1.11 ($\wedge$-INTRODUCTION ($\wedge$I)) If you have proved P and you have proved Q, then you can infer $P \wedge Q$.

$$\frac{P \qquad Q}{P \wedge Q}$$

RULE 1.12 ($\wedge$-ELIMINATION ($\wedge$E)) If you have proved $P \wedge Q$, then you can infer P; if you have proved $P \wedge Q$, you can infer Q.

$$\frac{P \wedge Q}{P} \qquad\qquad \frac{P \wedge Q}{Q}$$

The elimination rule for $\rightarrow$ should present no difficulties, since it is a version of modus ponens, the lone rule we used in the propositional calculus.

RULE 1.13 ($\rightarrow$-ELIMINATION ($\rightarrow$E)) If you have proved both $P \rightarrow Q$ and P, you can infer Q.

$$\frac{P \rightarrow Q \qquad P}{Q}$$

To understand what is formalized by the introduction rule for $\rightarrow$, as well as several of the other rules we are about to encounter, one needs to reflect on what is involved when in the course of constructing an argument one says, "Well, suppose ... ." For example, if one argues as follows: "Suppose there is no God. Then the burning bush didn't talk to Moses (or at least, if it did, it wasn't God's voice speaking through the tree). So it would follow that the Bible contains falsehoods. Hence, if there's no God the Bible contains falsehoods." Notice the following things about this argument: First, the original premise is not *asserted*, but is merely *supposed*. Even if one

---

[6]Natural deduction systems were independently devised by Gerhard Gentzen and Stanislaw Jaśkowski in the late 1920s.

believes that God exists, it is no use objecting to this argument that the first premise is false, since it is at no point claimed to be true. Secondly, in the statements between the supposition and the conclusion, the argument proceeds as though the supposition were established. So these claims, too, are not asserted by the arguer—rather, they are only asserted to be the case *under the supposition* that there is no God. Finally, the conclusion is conditional in form and so is the sort of statement we have been symbolizing using →. But this statement *is* asserted by the arguer, and not merely under the supposition. This can be done because the assumption has been, in effect, built into the conclusion by its being placed in the antecedent.

In our presentation of the rules, we indicate that a statement *P* is a supposition rather than an assertion by writing [*P*].

RULE 1.14 (→-INTRODUCTION (→I)) If, under the supposition that *P*, you can prove *Q*, then you can infer *P* → *Q*.

$$[P]$$

$$\vdots$$

$$Q$$

$$\overline{}$$

$$P \to Q$$

The elimination rule for ∨ makes a double use of this sort of reasoning under a supposition. This rule is sometimes called a *constructive dilemma*, and it is a pattern of argument one frequently encounters in ordinary life. For instance, a philosophy student might run up against the following argument. "Look, you're never going to get rich. Either you're going to be a philosopher, or you'll quit and do something else. Suppose you do continue and become a philosopher. Since philosophers make about as much money as poets, you won't get rich. So suppose you quit. Then you'll be doing something you're not interested in, so even if it's something other people get rich doing, it won't make you rich." Once again, we are not concerned with whether this is a sound argument or not, merely in the (valid) pattern of inference involved. The arguer begins by asserting a disjunction, then constructs *two* subarguments. In effect, two (→I) arguments are constructed, one beginning with each of the two disjuncts of the first premise, and both of which reach the same conclusion (viz., you won't get rich). On the basis of all this, the final conclusion (which was stated in the first sentence of the passage) is inferred.

RULE 1.15 (∨-ELIMINATION (∨E)) If you have proved *P* ∨ *Q*, and can prove *R* under the supposition that *P*, and can prove *R* under the supposition that

Q, then you can infer R.

$$\frac{P \vee Q \quad \overset{[P]}{\overset{\vdots}{R}} \quad \overset{[Q]}{\overset{\vdots}{R}}}{R}$$

The rule of $\vee$-Introduction is straightforward, provided one remembers that $\vee$ does not indicate that there needs to be any particular relationship between the two disjuncts. If one proves either disjunct, then one has proved the disjunction, however silly it might seem to connect the two statements in question.

RULE 1.16 ($\vee$-INTRODUCTION ($\vee$I)) If you have proved P, then you can infer $P \vee Q$; if you have proved Q, then you can infer $P \vee Q$.

$$\frac{P}{P \vee Q} \qquad \frac{Q}{P \vee Q}$$

We turn next to the rules for negation. It is commonly asserted that in the context of a debate the side arguing the affirmative bears the burden of proof because, typically, it is extremely difficult to prove a negative statement. One way that this is done when it can be done is to say something like, "Well, suppose that were true, ... ," then to show that something *already known to be false* follows. That is, one shows that the claim in question *could not possibly be true*. This $\neg$-Introduction rule, which formalizes this sort of reasoning, is often called *reductio ad absurdum*.

RULE 1.17 ($\neg$ INTRODUCTION ($\neg$I)) If under the supposition that P one can prove, for some statement Q, both Q and $\neg Q$, then one can infer $\neg P$.

$$\frac{\overset{[P]}{\overset{\vdots}{Q}} \quad \overset{[P]}{\overset{\vdots}{\neg Q}}}{\neg P}$$

It is with the elimination rule for negation that we appeal to the principle of bivalence. If $\neg\neg P$ is true, then $\neg P$ must be false (that's what negation means, after all). But then what about P? We know that it cannot be false, for then $\neg P$ would be true as well as false. But by bivalence, P must be either true or false, so since it is not false we can conclude that it is true. So, since we are for the present assuming the principle of bivalence, we may adopt the following rule.

RULE 1.18 ($\neg$ ELIMINATION ($\neg$E)) If you have proved $\neg\neg P$, then you can infer P.

$$\frac{\neg\neg P}{P}$$

There are various ways of organizing proofs using these rules. One relatively economical and perspicuous way is to write proofs with numbered lines and annotations indicating the rule used at each step. We also need some way of keeping track of which suppositions we are reasoning under at any point in our proofs. In short proofs, this is relatively easy to do informally, and we will count on the reader to be able to do this in our short examples below. In lengthier proofs, it is useful to annotate each line with the line numbers of all the suppositions under which the statement occurs. For the remainder of this discussion of natural deduction we write $S \vdash P$ to indicate that there is a *proof* in our natural deduction system of the statement P whose *initial assumptions* are all members of the set of statements S. If S is empty, we write $\vdash P$. A *proof* is a sequence of statements which begins with some set of *initial assumptions* which are taken as proved. Each subsequent statement in the sequence is either a supposition or it follows from other members of the sequence by application of one of the rules to earlier members of the sequence. P is proved from the initial assumptions if and only if it occurs in the sequence under no suppositions.

When presenting natural deduction proofs as linear sequences in this way, one needs to have available an additional, seemingly unbelievably trivial rule. We might call it the rule of *repetition*: A sentence which occurs earlier in a proof can be repeated at any later stage, provided its earlier occurrence did not depend on any supposition which is not being made at the later place. The use of this rule often passes unremarked: for instance, in the first proof below, we use the fact that line 3 contradicts line 1 to justify line 4. Strictly speaking, we ought to *repeat* line 1 under the supposition made at 2. Since this move is rather obviously available, we leave it out.

That we don't show this rule the respect of giving it the same sort of introduction as the others doesn't merely reflect the fact that we often use it without mention. Rather, we leave it out because there are other methods of presenting natural deduction proofs (which give them a more tree-like appearance, in fact) which render the addition of this rule unnecessary. However, this doesn't mean that the repetition rule is as uninteresting as it might seem: a crucial difference between natural deduction systems for some *relevance logics* and for classical logic is that unrestricted use of repetition is ruled out in the relevance logics.[7]

---

[7]Loosely and roughly, relevance logics are attempts to devise formal logics in which the relation of *implication* is closer to what we mean when we say that one statement *follows from* another. In the systems we shall consider in this book, *everything* is implied by a contradiction, but it is rather unnatural to say that "Snow is white" *follows from* "Bob is over 6 feet tall and Bob is not over 6 feet tall" (at least, it seems unnatural until you've taken a few courses in formal logic!). The guiding idea is that something can follow from something else only if the two claims are relevant to one another. We shall not be able to pursue relevance

EXAMPLE 1.2

1. Prove $\neg(P \vee Q) \vdash (\neg P \wedge \neg Q)$. We note that what requires proving is a conjunction. The most direct way to achieve this is to derive both of the conjuncts, joining them together in the end with $\neg I$. Each of the conjuncts is a negation, so a likely strategy for proving each of these is to use $\neg I$. From this point, it is not difficult to fill in the remaining details.

1.	$\neg(P \vee Q)$	Premise
2.	P	Suppose for $\neg I$
3.	$P \vee Q$	From 2, by $\vee I$
4.	$\neg P$	By $\neg I$ from 2, since 3 contradicts 1.
5.	Q	Suppose for $\neg I$
6.	$P \vee Q$	From 5 by $\vee I$
7.	$\neg Q$	By $\neg I$ from 5, since 6 contradicts 1
8.	$\neg P \wedge \neg Q$	From 4, 7 by $\wedge I$

2. Show $\vdash P \vee \neg P$. We are asked here to prove a disjunction. However, a little reflection will make clear that the strategy of trying to prove one or other disjunct and then applying $\vee I$ isn't going to work, since each of these statements could well be logically indeterminate, and something is seriously wrong with our rules if they render indeterminate statements provable. The proof below shows an *indirect* way of proving statements which can be used in classical logic: start with the negation of the statement to be proved, use $\neg I$, then follow that with $\neg E$.

1.	$\neg(P \vee \neg P)$	Suppose for $\neg I$
2.	P	Suppose for $\neg I$
3.	$P \vee \neg P$	From 2, by $\vee I$
4.	$\neg P$	By $\neg I$, since 3 contradicts 1.
5.	$\neg P$	Suppose for $\neg I$
6.	$P \vee \neg P$	From 4 by $\vee I$
7.	$\neg \neg P$	By $\neg I$, since 6 contradicts 1
8.	$\neg \neg (P \vee \neg P)$	By $\neg I$ from 1, since 7 contradicts 4.
9.	$(P \vee \neg P)$	From 9 by $\neg E$

It is instructive to consider a curious relationship between the tree rules and the natural deduction rules. One can regard the tree rules for $\wedge$, $\vee$, and $\rightarrow$ as essentially the natural deduction intro rules for those connectives,

---

logic in this book. A good place to begin the investigation of relevance logic is *Entailment: The Logic of Relevance and Necessity*, by A.R. Ross and Nuel Belnap, Princeton University Press, 1975.

written upside down. Upside down, ∧I can be read as "from $P \wedge Q$, infer *both P and Q*." There are two ∨I rules, so taking them upside down one would expect to get two parts. So, upside down, ∨I can be read as "from $P \vee Q$, infer *either P or Q*." To see why this applies also to →I is slightly more complicated. The tree rule says "from $P \to Q$ infer *either ¬P or Q*." To get this from the natural deduction rule, we appeal to bivalence: either ¬P is true or P is true, and, according to the intro rule, if you had P you'd have Q. So if you have $P \to Q$, then either you'd have ¬P or you'd have Q.

The tree rule for double negation is just the natural deduction rule ¬E. But notice that the tree derivation method as a whole involves the procedure illustrated in our previous example. We begin by applying something akin to ¬I, i.e., to the reductio method: to prove by tree rules that Q follows from X, we take the set X, ¬Q and apply the rules until we arrive at a closed tree. This shows the *inconsistency* of the set X, ¬Q. From this we can conclude that X implies ¬¬Q. However, in our practice we reject ¬Q and accept Q, which shows that we are relying on the principle of bivalence to underwrite our use of trees.

EXERCISES 1.5.3

1. It is relatively straightforward to prove that anything provable in the propositional calculus is also provable in classical natural deduction.

    (a) Show that any axiom of the propositional calculus is provable in the natural deduction system.

  * (b) Use this result to show that anything provable in the propositional calculus is provable in the natural deduction system.

2. We can show that ∧I is a *derived rule of inference* for the propositional calculus by reasoning as follows. Suppose we are given P and Q. Since $P \to Q \to (P \wedge Q)$ is an instance of axiom 5, two applications of modus ponens yield $P \wedge Q$. So, $P, Q \vdash P \wedge Q$.

    (a) Show that all the other rules of the natural deduction system are derived rules of inference for the classical propositional calculus. (Hint: you may want to make liberal use of the deduction theorem.)

    (b) Derive that any statement provable in the natural deduction system is provable in the propositional calculus.

1.5.3 Sequent Calculus

It will be useful to begin with some notation and terminology. We will, for the duration of this section, use the letters W, X, Y, and Z to denote *sequences* (or *ordered lists*) of statements. Sequences differ from sets of statements in two respects: the order in which the statements occur in a sequence matters, while in a set it is irrelevant; and the same statement can occur twice in a sequence, while in a set it cannot. A *sequent* is an array of the form $X \vdash Y$. Informally, $X \vdash Y$ can be read as saying that if *all* the formulas in X are true in a valuation V then *at least one of* the formulas in Y is true in V. The X component of $X \vdash Y$ is called the *antecedent* or *left component*; Y is called the *succedent* or *right component*. Finally, in our statements of the various rules it is important to remember that any of the sequences W, X, Y, and Z can be empty.

The *sequent calculus* is a system of rules for operating on sequents. There are two kinds of rules. *Structural rules* tell us how to add formulas to a sequence, delete redundancies from a sequence, and how to change the order of formulas within a sequence. Operational rules tell us how to introduce the connectives $\wedge$, $\vee$, $\rightarrow$, and $\neg$ on the left and right of $\vdash$. There is also one axiom scheme, the Identity Axiom $P \vdash P$. Derivations in the sequent calculus always start with an instance of this axiom.

DEFINITION 1.24 (RULES FOR THE SEQUENT CALCULUS)
1. Identity Axiom Scheme: For any formula P, $P \vdash P$ is an axiom.

2. Structural Rules:

Thinning (or Weakening):

$$\text{Left-thin} \quad \frac{X \vdash Y}{P, X \vdash Y} \qquad \text{Right-thin} \quad \frac{X \vdash Y}{X \vdash Y, P}$$

Contraction:

$$\text{Left-con} \quad \frac{P, P, X \vdash Y}{P, X \vdash Y} \qquad \text{Right-con} \quad \frac{X \vdash Y, P, P}{X \vdash Y, P}$$

Interchange (or Permutation):

$$\text{Left-int} \quad \frac{W, P, Q, X \vdash Y}{W, Q, P, X \vdash Y} \qquad \text{Right-int} \quad \frac{X \vdash Y, P, Q, Z}{X \vdash Y, Q, P, Z}$$

Cut:

$$\frac{X \vdash Y, P \qquad P, W \vdash Z}{X, W \vdash Y, Z}$$

Before we give the operational rules, some explanation of the structural rules is in order. *Thinning* formalizes the property of valid arguments that the addition of an arbitrary formula to the list of premises or to the list of conclusions makes no difference to the validity of the argument. That is, if Y validly follows from X, then you can infer that Y validly follows from X and P, and, similarly, if Y validly follows from X then you can infer that Y or Q validly follows from X. *Contraction* formalizes the property that a formula may be used more than once in a proof, and hence that more than one occurrence of a given formula on the left, or on the right, is redundant. *Interchange* formalizes the property that the order of formulas in the premise list, or in the conclusion list, is unimportant. The *Cut* rule formalizes the transitivity of deductions. Simplifying slightly, it says that if P validly follows from X, and Z validly follows from P then you can "cut" P out and infer that Z validly follows from X.

3. Operational Rules.

Left-∧:
$$\frac{P,X \vdash Y}{P \wedge Q, X \vdash Y} \qquad \frac{Q,X \vdash Y}{P \wedge Q, X \vdash Y}$$

Right-∧:
$$\frac{X \vdash Y,P \qquad X \vdash Y,Q}{X \vdash Y, P \wedge Q}$$

Left-∨:
$$\frac{P,X \vdash Y \qquad Q,X \vdash Y}{P \vee Q, X \vdash Y}$$

Right-∨:
$$\frac{X \vdash Y,P}{X \vdash Y, P \vee Q} \qquad \frac{X \vdash Y,Q}{X \vdash Y, P \vee Q}$$

Left—→:
$$\frac{X \vdash Y,P \qquad Q,W \vdash Z}{P \rightarrow Q, X, W \vdash Y, Z}$$

Right—→:
$$\frac{P,X \vdash Y,Q}{X \vdash Y, P \rightarrow Q}$$

Left-¬:
$$\frac{X \vdash Y,P}{\neg P, X \vdash Y}$$

Right-¬:
$$\frac{P,X \vdash Y}{X \vdash Y, \neg P}$$

As in natural deduction, there are several styles of setting up proofs using the sequent calculus rules. We'll use an annotated linear style in order to make the proofs easier to follow. So we define a *proof in the sequent calculus* to be a series of sequents which begins with one or more axioms and which is such that every non-axiom in the series arises from earlier sequents by application of one of the rules. The final sequent in the series is *proved*.

EXAMPLE 1.3
1. Prove $\vdash \neg\neg A \rightarrow A$. We might begin our attempt to generate a proof by reasoning as follows. We must begin with an identity axiom, and $A \vdash A$ is a likely candidate. Furthermore, if we want to conclude with an application of Right→ (as seems a likely strategy, given what we

are trying to prove), we know we will need to have $\neg\neg A$ on the left. So we will need to introduce negations. The negation rules tell us that negation symbols can be added by moving formulas from one side of $\vdash$ to the other.

1.	$A \vdash A$	Axiom
2.	$\vdash A, \neg A$	From 1, by Right $\neg$
3.	$\neg\neg A \vdash A$	From 2, by Left $\neg$
4.	$\vdash \neg\neg A \rightarrow A$	From 3, by Right $\rightarrow$

2. Prove $\vdash A \rightarrow (B \rightarrow A)$.

1.	$A \vdash A$	Axiom
2.	$B, A \vdash A$	From 1, by Left-thin
3.	$A \vdash B \rightarrow A$	From 2, by Right $\rightarrow$
4.	$\vdash A \rightarrow (B \rightarrow A)$	From 3, by Right $\rightarrow$

3. Prove $\vdash A \vee \neg A$.

1.	$A \vdash A$	Axiom
2.	$\vdash A, \neg A$	From 1, by Right $\neg$
3.	$\vdash A, A \vee \neg A$	From 2, by Right $\vee$
4.	$\vdash A \vee \neg A, A$	From 3, by Right-int
5.	$\vdash A \vee \neg A, A \vee \neg A$	From 4, by Right $\vee$
6.	$\vdash A \vee \neg A$	From 5, by Right-con

Notice that in the proofs of $\vdash \neg\neg A \rightarrow A$ and $\vdash A \vee \neg A$, but not of $\vdash A \rightarrow (B \rightarrow A)$, we have steps with two formulas on the right side of $\vdash$. Steps with two or more formulas on the right are called "multiple conclusion" steps. It turns out that classical logic sequent calculus *requires* multiple conclusion steps (or some comparable procedure). You won't find proofs that do not use multiple conclusion steps for $\vdash \neg\neg A \rightarrow A$ and $\vdash A \vee A$, or for $\vdash (\neg A \rightarrow \neg B) \rightarrow (B \rightarrow A)$, though you can prove $\vdash (A \rightarrow B) \rightarrow (\neg B \rightarrow \neg A)$ without any multiple conclusion steps.

EXERCISES 1.5.4
Find sequent calculus proofs for:

* 1. $\vdash (\neg A \rightarrow \neg B) \rightarrow (B \rightarrow A)$

* 2. $\vdash (A \rightarrow B) \rightarrow (\neg B \rightarrow \neg A)$

REMARK 1.2 Considering again the third example above, it will become clear that it can be quite tedious to write out the structural rules all the time. When working in sequent calculus for classical logic most logicians simply treat the sequences W, X, etc., as *sets* instead of *ordered lists*, which has the effect of "building in" structural rules. But it is the structural rules that in a significant way are definitive of classical logic when it is formulated as a sequent calculus.

Logical systems which have exactly the same operational rules as classical logic but give up one or more of the structural rules are called *substructural logics*. For example, intuitionistic logic, which we consider in more detail in Chapter 5, can be regarded as a substructural logic which does not allow multiple conclusions and so restricts Right-thin to the form

$$\frac{X \vdash}{X \vdash P}.$$

Some other substructural logics drop or restrict both the Right and Left Thinning rules. Doing so yields sequent calculus versions of *relevance logics*. *Linear logics* drop or restrict the Contraction rules as well as the Thinning rules. There are intriguing philosophical motives behind the investigation of these logics, which we can only briefly mention here. Thinning allows us to introduce "irrelevant" formulas in the course of a proof. Relevance logicians argue that only "relevant" formulas should be used when proving a conclusion from a set of premises. Of course, it is difficult to precisely define *relevance*, but in terms of the sequent calculus approach to logic the status of the thinning rule is central. Such logicians typically reject the theorems $P \rightarrow (Q \rightarrow P)$ and $P \rightarrow (\neg P \rightarrow Q)$, which require thinning in their proofs. The Contraction rule embodies the idea that it doesn't matter how many times you use a particular formula in a proof. But if formulas are thought of as *resources*—like dollar bills or nickels and dimes—or are used to model such resources, then it is important to keep track of the number of times a given formula is used. You can't spend the same dollar bill more than once in the course of a purchase. It is not obvious that formulas, in so far as they are statements that have truth values, should be regarded as resources like dollar bills. Perhaps it is necessary that contraction holds for truth-preserving inference. On the other hand it is not obvious we should agree that to be a *logic* a system must model truth-preserving inference between statements.[8]

Though the Cut rule is in practice very useful, it is in principle dispensable in classical propositional logic. That is, any proof which employs Cut can be transformed (*normalized*) into a proof of the same sequent in which Cut is not employed. Moreover, normalized proofs have the nice property that only *subformulas of the premises and conclusions* occur in the proof, i.e., in a normalized proof of $X \vdash Y$ only subformulas of X and Y occur.[9]

---

[8]We are just at the edge of deep philosophical issues about the nature of proof and logic. For a useful account which provides many more of the details of substructural logics, see Kosta Dosen and Peter Schroeder-Heister, *Substructural Logics* (Oxford: Clarendon, 1993).

[9]The definition of *subformula* is as follows: Each sentence letter is the only subformula of itself. The subformulas of $\neg P$ are $\neg P$ together with all the subformulas of P. The sub-

An examination of the statement of the Cut rule makes clear that it allows us to make use of a formula P in the course of a derivation which need not be a subformula of any formula in W, X, Y, or Z. On the other hand, normalized proofs are typically longer, and are sometimes very much longer, than proofs which make use of Cut.

REMARK 1.3 The tree method, as originally formulated, uses only rules which decompose formulas into subformulas. But it is certainly possible to add a version of the cut rule to the tree method. Indeed, this is precisely what we did when we added the rule of *excluded middle for trees* to simplify our proof of the equivalence of the tree method and the propositional calculus.

EXERCISES 1.5.5

1. Show that $P_1, P_2, \ldots, P_m \vdash Q_1, Q_2, \ldots, Q_n$ is a provable sequent whenever $P_1, P_2, \ldots, Pm, \neg Q_1, \neg Q_2, \ldots, \neg Q_{n-1} \vdash Q_n$ is a provable sequent. (Hint: First, observe that application of Right Negation to $X, -Q \vdash Q$ produces $X \vdash Q, \neg\neg Q$. Secondly, prove that $X \vdash Y, \neg\neg Q$ implies $X \vdash Y, Q$.)

2. We have not proved it, but the sequent calculus is sound and complete for truth-functional semantics. That is, $X \vdash Y$ is a provable sequent if and only if $X \vDash P_1 \vee \cdots \vee P_n$, where $P_1, \ldots, P_n$ are the statements in the sequence Y, and conversely. Using these assumptions:

   (a) Show that if Q validly follows from P_1, P_2, P_3 by the classical tree rules, then $P_1, P_2, P_3 \vdash Q$ is a provable sequent.

   (b) Show that if $P_1, P_2, P_3 \vdash Q_1, Q_2$ is a provable sequent, then there is no open tree for the set $\{ P_1, P_2, P_3, \neg Q_1, \neg Q_2 \}$.

REMARK 1.4 The proofs requested in the second of these exercises make use of metatheoretical results relating different proof procedures to a common formal semantics. It is worth considering how to prove such facts in more strictly proof-theoretic fashion. As a first step, notice that it is possible to convert the Left Operational Rules of sequent calculus into tree rules for $P \wedge Q$, $P \vee Q$, and $P \rightarrow Q$, and the Right Operational Rules of sequent calculus into tree rules for $\neg(P \wedge Q)$, $\neg(P \vee Q)$, $\neg(P \rightarrow Q)$, and $\neg\neg P$. Consider the operational rules "upside down," and convert any formula P on the right side of the $\vdash$ symbol in an operational rule into $\neg P$ for a tree rule. For example, written upside down Left$\rightarrow$ is

$$\frac{P \rightarrow Q, X, W \vdash Y, Z}{X \vdash Y, P \qquad Q, W \vdash Z}$$

formulas of $P \wedge Q$, $(P \vee Q, P \rightarrow Q)$, are that statement together with all the subformulas of P and all subformulas of Q. The subformulas of a sequence S of statements are just the subformulas of the statements which occur in S.

which, (ignoring the X,Y,W,Z components) gives us the tree rule

This makes obvious that there is some important relationship between sequent proofs and trees, but it is only the first step in a proof that every
sequent proof can be converted to a tree proof (or conversely). What about
that clause about ignoring X, Y, Z, W? There are axioms involved in sequent
proofs, but not on trees. What effect does that have? It is worth reflecting
on what complications are involved in attempting such a proof.

It is also worth considering possible conversion procedures from sequent calculus rules to natural deduction rules, and vice versa. The reader
is invited to consider the straightforward relationship between the sequent
calculus Right Operational Rules and natural deduction Introduction Rules,
and also to consider how the relationship between Left Operational Rules
and Elimination Rules is more complicated.

Proofs of such facts which directly compare the systems of rules are typically much more involved than the sorts of proofs which detour through a
semantics. On the other hand, those proofs can also yield a deeper understanding of the relationships between proof systems.[10]

---

[10]For a good study of relations between natural deduction and sequent calculus, see An-
thony M. Ungar, *Normalization, Cut-Elimination and the Theory of Proofs*, CSLI Lecture Notes
No. 28 (Stanford: CSLI, 1991). And see David Bostock, *Intermediate Logic* (Oxford: Clarendon, 1997) for a wide-ranging introductory comparison of various proof methods for classical
logic.

Chapter 2

Classical Predicate Logic

2.1   Introductory Remarks

The concept of truth-functional validity employed in Chapter 1 is restricted in that it does not cover a large class of arguments which are clearly logically correct. Consider, for example, the following argument:

1. All Cretans love all animals.

2. All horses are animals.

3. Epimenides is a Cretan.
   _____

4. Someone loves all horses.

   This argument is patently not truth-functionally valid: probably the best we can do to symbolize it in the language of propositional logic is C, H, E, therefore S. Still, given the usual reading of the terms "all" and "some," it is logically correct. Moreover, its correctness derives from the grammatical structure of the statements constituting it, which is to say that it is *formally valid*, in the sense mentioned in the introductory remarks to Chapter 1. However, it involves grammatical structure which is beyond the power of the language of propositional logic to represent, most notably because it involves in an essential way predicates—"(is a) horse," "(is an) animal," "(is a) Cretan"—and relations—"loves."

   In order to symbolize this argument and others like it we need to enlarge our logical vocabulary. Thus, as in algebra, it is natural to begin by introducing variables $x, y, z, \ldots$ to refer to arbitrary individuals, and then to write, for example, "Ax" for "x is an animal," "Cx" for "x is a Cretan," "Hx" for "x is a horse," and "Lxy" for "x loves y." In the example we do not merely refer to arbitrary individuals, though. We also refer to a specific individual, Epimenides, and we do so by using his *name*. If we want to represent this argument in a way suitable to capture what it is about its form which makes it logically correct, it will be useful to have the same ability in our formal languages, so we write, for example, e for "Epimenides." The symbols A, C and H are *predicate symbols*, L is a *relation symbol*, and e a *name*. Finally, notice that the statements which make up the example argument make assertions about, for instance, how many Cretans love all horses (all of them), how many people love all horses (someone does, i.e., at least one person does), and so on. The logical correctness of this argument depends crucially on the arrangement of this sort of claim in the premises and the conclusion. We therefore introduce two symbols, $\forall$ and $\exists$, called the *universal* and *existential quantifier*, respectively: the expression "$\forall x$" will symbolize the phrase "for all (or any) x," and "$\exists x$" the phrases "for some x," or, equivalently, "there exists an x."

To put our argument in symbolic form, we first write it in the following way:

1′. For any individual x, if x is a Cretan, then for any individual y, if y is an animal, then x loves y.

2′. For any individual x, if x is a horse, then x is an animal.

3′. Epimenides is a Cretan.

4′. For some individual x, for all individuals y, if y is a horse, then x loves y.

Now 1′—4′ can be symbolized directly in terms of our enlarged logical vocabulary thus:

1″. $\forall x[Cx \rightarrow \forall y(Ay \rightarrow Lxy)]$

2″. $\forall x(Hx \rightarrow Ax)$

3″. Ce

4″. $\exists x \forall y(Hy \rightarrow Lxy)$

The logical system associated with the enlarged vocabulary of variables, predicate and relation symbols, names, and quantifiers is called *predicate* or *quantificational* logic. Statements formulated within this vocabulary will be called *predicate* or *quantificational statements*.

2.2 Tree Rules for Classical Predicate Logic

2.2.1 Rules for Quantifiers

In order to be able to employ the tree method to test arguments within predicate logic (such as the one above) for validity, we need to formulate new tree rules governing the quantifiers. In the case of $\forall$, we shall be guided by the usual meaning of generality, namely, that whenever we assert that *all* individuals under consideration have a certain property, then, given any individual, *that* individual has, or, as we shall sometimes say, *instantiates* the property. We call this the principle of *universal instantiation*. The corresponding tree rule may be formulated thus:

RULE 2.1 (UNIVERSAL INSTANTIATION) When a statement of the form $\forall v \varphi(v)$ occupies a node of an open path of a tree,

1. if a name n appears in the path, write $\varphi(n)$ at its foot unless $\varphi(n)$ already occupies a node of the path (in which case writing it once more in the path would be redundant);

2. if no name appears in the path, choose some name n and write $\varphi(n)$ at its foot.

Do not tick the line $\forall v \varphi(v)$.

Let us observe this rule in action. Consider the argument:

1. Juliet loves all who love Romeo.

2. Romeo loves himself.

---

3. Juliet loves herself.

The argument may be symbolized as follows, using r as a name for Romeo, j for Juliet, and writing Lxy for "x loves y":

$$\forall x(Lxr \rightarrow Ljx)$$
$$Lrr$$
$$\therefore \ Ljj$$

Just as we did when constructing trees for arguments in classical propositional logic, we start off with the premises of the argument followed by the negation of its conclusion, and then continue so as to obtain a closed tree in the following way:

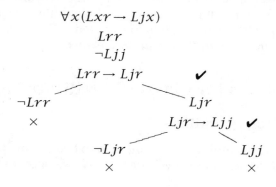

In this example we used the UI rule twice, to obtain the fourth and sixth lines. That is, $\forall x(Lxr \rightarrow Ljx)$ is $\forall x\varphi(x)$, while $Lrr \rightarrow Ljr$ is $\varphi(r)$ and $Ljr \rightarrow Ljj$ is $\varphi(j)$. Notice that both applications were made to the same node (the top one), and in both the variable v was x, and $\varphi(v)$—that is, $\varphi(x)$—the expression $Lxr \rightarrow Ljx$. The two applications differed, however, in respect of the name substituted for x: in the first case it was r and in the second j. In the first case we obtained $\varphi(r)$ by substituting r for x in $\varphi(x)$, and in the second $\varphi(j)$ by substituting j for x in $\varphi(x)$.

From the fact that we had to apply UI *twice* to the same statement, it should now be apparent why we do not tick a statement to which UI has been applied. Indeed, in this example we had to continue to apply it with every name actually appearing in the path in question before the path (and the tree) finally closed.

Let us now consider an example of an application of UI in which no names are initially given. Here the tree method will be used to test satisfiability rather than validity. Consider the statements:

1. All unicorns are fleet.

2. No unicorns are fleet.

Using the obvious notation, these apparently conflicting hypotheses concerning unicorns are expressible as the statements occupying the first two nodes of the following tree, which tests their joint satisfiability:

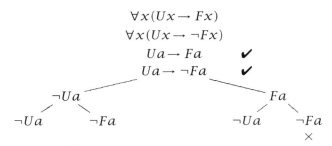

The third node here results by applying UI to the first node, at the same time introducing the new name a. Once this name has been introduced into the path, it must be used in the application yielding the fourth line from the second, because clause (1) of the UI rule now applies.

Note that the tree is finished since no further applications of UI can be made. We do not introduce any further new names, because neither clause of the rule applies: a occurs on the path, so (2) doesn't apply, and applying (1) by substituting a for x in either of the first two lines would simply introduce onto each path a sentence which already occurs on the path.

The tree has three finished open paths. Each of these open paths may be regarded as representing a possible *domain* or *universe of discourse* in which all the statements occupying lines in it are true. In general, the objects comprising the domain associated with an open path correspond to the

names appearing in that path. In our example, there is only one such name—
a—present, so that each domain of discourse has exactly one element, which
we take to be named by a. Since the statement $\neg Ua$ occurs in each path,
the statement "a is not a unicorn" holds in each domain of discourse. In
the second open path the statement $\neg Fa$ appears, so the statement "a is
not fleet" holds in the associated domain of discourse. The third open path
contains the statement Fa, so "a is fleet" holds in the associated domain of
discourse. On the other hand, the first path contains neither Fa nor $\neg Fa$, so
in the corresponding domain of discourse a can be fleet or not indifferently.
In fact, since the object named by a is the *sole* individual in each domain of
discourse, we see that in each of these contexts the statement $\neg Ua$ has the
stronger meaning that *nothing* is a unicorn. Thus each domain of discourse
represents a "world" in which no unicorns exist, so that any assertions about
all unicorns, including our two conditions above, automatically come out
true, and are therefore jointly satisfiable there.

We turn now to the existential quantifier $\exists$. First, we note that, assuming
the principle of bivalence, there is a simple connection between $\exists$ and $\forall$.
To see what it is, imagine that we have a domain of discourse consisting of
three people, named by, say, a, b, and c. Consider the two statements

1. Someone (in our domain of discourse) is Canadian. $\exists x Cx$

2. Everyone (in our domain of discourse) is Canadian. $\forall x Cx$

It is clear that in our domain of discourse the statement $\exists x Cx$ is equivalent
to the disjunction
$$Ca \lor Cb \lor Cc,$$
and the statement $\forall x Cx$ to the conjunction
$$Ca \land Cb \land Cc.$$
Therefore the negated statement $\neg \exists x Cx$ is equivalent to
$$\neg(Ca \lor Cb \lor Cc),$$
which by De Morgan's laws (i.e., the law that $\neg(P \land Q) \equiv \neg P \lor \neg Q$ and
$\neg(P \lor Q) \equiv \neg P \land \neg Q$) is equivalent to
$$\neg Ca \land \neg Cb \land \neg Cc.$$
But this last statement asserts that each, and so every, individual in our
domain of discourse satisfies $\neg Cx$; in other words, it is equivalent to the
statement $\forall x \neg Cx$.

It is evident that the correctness of this line of reasoning is independent
both of the nature of the predicate Cx and of the number of individuals in
the domain of discourse. Thus we may draw the general conclusion that,
for any formula $\varphi(v)$, writing $\equiv$ for equivalence as usual,
$$\neg \exists v \varphi(v) \equiv \forall v \neg \varphi(v).$$

An analogous argument shows that also

$$\neg \forall v \varphi(v) \equiv \exists v \neg \varphi(v).$$

Thus, in our example above, negating the statement "Someone is Canadian" is equivalent to asserting "Everyone is non-Canadian" and negating the statement "Everyone is Canadian" to asserting "Someone is non-Canadian." [1]
    All this justifies the following

RULE 2.2 (NEGATED QUANTIFICATION) If a statement of the form $\neg \forall v \varphi(v)$ (or $\neg \exists v \varphi(v)$) occupies a node of an open path, tick it and write at the feet of all open paths containing that node the same statement with $\exists v \neg$ in place of $\neg \forall v$ (or with $\forall v \neg$ in place of $\neg \exists v$).

$$\neg \forall v \varphi(v) \ \checkmark \qquad \neg \exists v \varphi(v) \ \checkmark$$
$$\exists v \neg \varphi(v) \qquad\quad \forall v \neg \varphi(v)$$

We now require a rule for the existential quantifier. This is:

RULE 2.3 (EXISTENTIAL INSTANTIATION (EI)) Given an unticked statement of the form $\exists v \varphi(v)$ occupying a node of an open path, check to see whether the path contains a node occupied by a statement of the form $\varphi(n)$. If not, choose a name n *that has not been used anywhere in the path* and write the statement $\varphi(n)$ at its foot. When this has been done for every open path in which the statement $\exists v \varphi(v)$ occupies a node, tick the node occupied by the given statement.

$$\exists v \varphi(v) \qquad \checkmark$$
$$\varphi(n) \quad (n \text{ new})$$

It is important to observe in applying this rule that the name n introduced *must not be already present in the path*. This is imperative because we want n to name an individual *about which we assume nothing except that it satisfies $\varphi(v)$*; individuals that have already been named may have properties that conflict with this supposition. For example, consider the following (true) premises:

1. Someone is Canadian, i.e., $\exists x C x$.

2. Don DeLillo is not Canadian, i.e., $\neg C d$.

---

[1] The reader may be wondering why we inserted the qualification that this convenient relationship between the universal and existential quantifiers holds "assuming the principle of bivalence." More precisely, it depends on De Morgan's laws. These hold in classical logic, and in Chapter 1 we used the principle of bivalence to justify the rules of classical logic which make it easy to show that De Morgan's laws are valid. As we shall see in our discussion of intuitionistic logic in Chapter 5, De Morgan's laws are not all valid in some contexts where bivalence in not assumed, and this relationship between the two quantifiers consequently fails in those contexts as well.

Were we allowed to use the old name d instead of being forced to introduce a new one, we would be able to generate a closed tree from these premises:

$$\exists x Cx \;\checkmark$$
$$\neg Cd$$
$$Cd$$
$$\times$$

where we have (incorrectly!) applied EI to the first node to obtain the third. This would mean that the premises are not jointly satisfiable, in other words, that from the assertion "Someone is Canadian," we would be able to infer "DeLillo is Canadian." Using the same line of reasoning, we would in fact be able to make this inference about *anyone*. Incorrectly applied, EI can lead to absurdities such as these.

Correctly applied, on the other hand, EI leads in our example to

$$\exists x Cx \;\checkmark$$
$$\neg Cd$$
$$Ca$$

where a is a new name, denoting, as it were, an "archetypal Canadian," whose identity is not further specified.

Armed with these new rules for quantifiers, let us return to the argument with which this chapter began, and see if there is a tree associated with it which closes. Here is one:

This tree does close.

2.2.2 Identity

We frequently need to assert that two names refer to the same, or different, things, as, for instance, in the (correct) argument

1. Yesterday I was home.

2. Monday I was out.

---

3. Yesterday was not Monday.

Writing a for "yesterday," b for "Monday," and Hx for "I was home on day x," we still lack a way of symbolizing statement 3. We rectify this by introducing the symbol =, called the *identity* or *equality symbol*, which we agree is to be written in between variables or names, as in $x = y$, $n = x$, or $m = n$. As a convenience, we also introduce the diversity or inequality symbol $\neq$, so that the statements $x \neq y$, $n \neq x$, $m \neq n$ serve as abbreviations for $\neg(x = y)$, $\neg(n = x)$, and $\neg(m = n)$, respectively.[2]
   Now our argument may be symbolized

$$Ha$$
$$\neg Hb$$
$$\therefore \ a \neq b.$$

   If we negate the conclusion of this argument so as to investigate its validity in the usual way, we start off with

$$Ha$$
$$\neg Hb$$
$$\neg(a \neq b) \ \checkmark$$
$$a = b$$

with the fourth line justified by the negated negation rule. Now if a and b are truly identical, then any property possessed by a should be shared by b (and vice versa), so from the first and fourth of these statements it should be permissible to infer

$$Hb$$
$$\times$$

As a result the tree will close.
   This idea leads us to introduce the following

---

[2] The inequality symbol thus has a status similar to that of $\longleftrightarrow$. It is not officially part of the language, but is convenient enough to have available that for most purposes we simply ignore its secondary status.

RULE 2.4 (RULE FOR IDENTITY) If an open path contains a node occupied by a statement of the form $m = n$ and also a node occupied by a statement P in which one of the names m or n appears one or more times, write at the foot of the path a statement Q obtained by replacing one or more of the occurrences of that name in P by the other name (so, e.g., if P is Hm, Q would be Hn, and if P is $\forall x Axmn$, Q might be $\forall x Axmm$ or $\forall x Axnn$), provided that Q does not already occupy a node of that path:

$$m = n$$
$$P$$
$$Q$$

It is also a characteristic feature of identity that every individual is self-identical. We formulate this idea as a tree rule by closing any path which terminates with a statement of the form $n \neq n$. Thus we introduce the

RULE 2.5 (RULE FOR NON-IDENTITY (OR DIVERSITY)) Close any path that contains a node occupied by a statement of the form $n \neq n$:

$$n \neq n$$
$$\times$$

These rules enable us to establish the four basic laws of identity, viz., substitutivity, reflexivity, symmetry, and transitivity.

Substitutivity.

$$\varphi(a)$$
$$a = b$$
$$\therefore \quad \varphi(b)$$

The validity of this inference is confirmed by the fact that the following tree closes:

$$\varphi(a)$$
$$a = b$$
$$\neg\varphi(b)$$
$$\varphi(b)$$
$$\times$$

where we have used the rule for identity to obtain the fourth line from the first two.

Reflexivity. We may always validly infer, for any a, that $a = a$.

The validity of this inference follows immediately from the rule for non-identity.

Symmetry.

$$a = b$$
$$\therefore \quad b = a$$

The correctness of this inference follows from the closed tree

$$a = b$$
$$b \neq a$$
$$b \neq b$$
$$\times$$

in which the third statement is obtained from the first two by the rule for identity, and closure from the rule for nonidentity.

Transitivity.

$$a = b$$
$$b = c$$
$$\therefore \quad a = c$$

The correctness of this inference results from the fact that the following tree is closed:

$$a = b$$
$$b = c$$
$$a \neq c$$
$$a \neq b$$
$$\times$$

where the last statement arises from the second and third by the rule for identity.

2.2.3 Functions

Relationships such as motherhood or fatherhood have the property that each individual determines a specific, indeed unique, individual (the individual's mother or father, respectively) with respect to which it stands in that relationship. The introduction of devices called *function symbols* into our logical vocabulary will enable us to give symbolic expression to this fact.

Thus consider, for example, the relation M of motherhood on the domain of discourse consisting of all persons. We introduce the function symbol m to stand for "mother of," so that $m(x)$ is to be read "mother of (person) x." Then there are two equivalent ways of expressing the statement "y is the mother of x," viz.,

$$Mxy \text{ and } y = m(x).$$

Thus, for example, if a names Liza Minnelli, then $m(a)$ names Judy Garland.

Names and variables are noun-like terms, and function symbols may be applied to terms of this sort to yield new terms. Thus we may write, for example,

$$m(m(x)) = \text{mother of mother of } x = \text{maternal grandmother of } x.$$

Similarly, if in addition we introduce the function symbol f for "father of," then

$$m(f(x)) = \text{mother of father of } x = \text{paternal grandmother of } x$$

etc.

In general, we may introduce a function symbol in connection with a relation R precisely when R has the two following properties:

Existence For any x, there exist y such that Rxy.

Uniqueness For any x, y, z, if Rxy and Rxz, then $y = z$.

When these conditions are satisfied, then for any x there is a *unique* y such that Rxy, and so we can introduce a function symbol f with the meaning that, for any x, $f(x)$ denotes this uniquely determined y. Thus, for any x and y, the following conditions are equivalent:

$$y = f(x) \text{ and } Rxy.$$

Function symbols may also be employed in trees, where such terms as $f(a)$, $f(m(a))$, etc., are counted as names. However, *in doing this we must at the same time insist that when the EI or UI rule requires us to introduce a new name, it must be a simple one, i.e. a new letter not already used.* To illustrate, we establish the validity of the inference

$$\forall x(f(a) = x)$$
$$\therefore \quad \forall x(f(x) = a).$$

(An example of this form of argument in English is: "Everybody's Adam's father, therefore Adam's everybody's father.") The tree for this argument is

$$\forall x(f(a) = x)$$
$$\neg\forall x(f(x) = a) \quad ✔$$
$$\exists x(f(x) \neq a) \quad ✔$$
$$f(b) \neq a$$
$$f(a) = f(b)$$
$$f(a) = a$$
$$f(b) = a$$
$$\times$$

The tree is closed and the inference valid. Notice that in the fourth line EI was applied to the third line, introducing a new letter b.

EXERCISES 2.2.1

1. Prove that the following inferences are valid by constructing suitable trees.

* (a) $\forall x(Px \vee Qx), \exists x Px \to \forall x(Sx \vee Tx), \neg \forall x Sx, \neg \forall x Qx \therefore \exists x Tx.$

(b) $\forall x Px, \forall x Qx \therefore \forall x(Px \wedge Qx).$

(c) $\forall x Px \to \forall x Qx \therefore \exists x \forall y(Px \to Qy).$

2. Let P be a statement and Qx a one-place predicate. Establish the validity of the following statements.

(a) $\forall x(P \wedge Qx) \longleftrightarrow (P \wedge \forall x Qx).$

(b) $\forall x(P \vee Qx) \longleftrightarrow P \vee \forall x Qx.$

* (c) $\exists x(P \wedge Qx) \longleftrightarrow (P \wedge \exists x Qx).$

(d) $\exists x(P \vee Qx) \longleftrightarrow (P \vee \exists x Qx).$

(e) $\forall x(P \to Qx) \longleftrightarrow (P \to \forall x Qx).$

* (f) $\forall x(Qx \to P) \longleftrightarrow (\exists x Qx \to P).$

(g) $\exists x(P \to Qx) \longleftrightarrow (P \to \exists x Qx).$

(h) $\exists x(Qx \to P) \longleftrightarrow (\forall x Qx \to P).$

3. Determine, using trees, which of the following statements are valid. For each statement which is not valid, use the tree to obtain a case in which it is false.

(a) $\exists x(Px \to \forall y Py).$

* (b) $\exists x(\exists y Py \to Px).$

(c) $\forall x \forall y \forall z[(Rxy \wedge Ryz) \to Rxz].$

* (d) $(\exists x Px \wedge \exists x Qx) \to \exists x(Px \wedge Qx).$

(e) $\forall x(Px \vee Qx) \to (\forall x Px \vee \forall x Qx).$

4. Use trees to show that each of the following inferences is valid.

(a) $a = b, \neg Fab \therefore \neg \forall x Fxx$

* (b) $\forall x[Fx \to \exists y(Gyx \wedge x \neq y)], \exists x Fx \therefore \exists x \exists y(x \neq y)$

(c) $\forall x \forall y[f(x) = f(y) \to x = y] \therefore a \neq b \to f(a) \neq f(b).$

2.3   Predicate Languages and Their Interpretations

The reader has probably observed that we have been calling an argument formulated in predicate logic *valid*, or *correct*, if the tree beginning with the argument's premises and negated conclusion closes. But a look back at definition 1.3 will confirm that we are making some important presumptions in doing this. An argument is valid if and only if its conclusion is true in any case in which all of its premises are true. We have not so far showed for arguments of predicate logic that having an associated tree which closes guarantees that this will be the case. Indeed, we have not yet even specified what the relevant sort of "case" is for arguments in predicate logic—as we will soon see, these are called *interpretations* of the language in which the argument is formalized. Much of the rest of this chapter will be devoted— in several stages—to carrying out the task of legitimating the way we have been speaking so far. The stages will be seen to be of independent interest.

2.3.1   The Languages

We have so far been very informal in our discussions of quantified state- ments and have thus been relying on the good sense of the reader. However, if our proofs in the remainder of this chapter are to be rigorous, we need a precise statement of just what counts as a language, and a clear explanation of related syntactic notions.

  A first point to notice is that while in the case of propositional logic we were able to confine attention to a single language, in predicate logic it is much better to allow for many different languages. As in the propositional case, we begin by describing the vocabulary of these languages. All the predicate logic languages share a common *logical vocabulary*.

DEFINITION 2.1 The vocabulary of every predicate language includes:

  1. A (countably) infinite set of *individual variables,* $v_1, v_2, v_3, \ldots$.

  2. The *binary propositional connectives,* $\land$, $\lor$, $\rightarrow$, and the *unary proposi- tional connective,* $\neg$.

  3. The *quantifiers,* ($\forall$) and ($\exists$).

  4. The *punctuation marks,* (and).

Some languages include a further logical symbol, and some do not:

  5 The *identity symbol,* =.

These are the only logical symbols of languages for predicate logic.

Unlike other logical symbols, the identity sign is a 2-place *predicate symbol.* If the vocabulary of a language $\mathcal{L}$ includes the identity symbol, we say that $\mathcal{L}$ is a language *with identity.* Otherwise we say it is a language *without identity.*

  Other than whether it is with or without identity, what distinguishes one language of predicate logic from all others is its *non-logical vocabulary.*

DEFINITION 2.2 The non-logical vocabulary of a language $\mathcal{L}$ for predicate logic consists of

1. A set of *non-logical predicate symbols*, P_1, P_2, P_3, ... If $\mathcal{L}$ is without identity, this set includes at least one member, while if $\mathcal{L}$ is a language with identity, then this set may be empty. On the other hand, in either case it might be *infinite*.

2. A (possibly empty, finite but non-empty, or infinite) set of *names*.

3. A (possibly empty, finite but non-empty, or infinite) set of *function symbols*.

While the set of predicate symbols can be infinite, in practice we shall consider languages where this set is rather small. Each predicate symbol and each function symbol is assigned a number $\geqslant 1$ called its *arity*. If the arity of a predicate P (or function symbol f) is n, we often say that P (or f) is an *n-place predicate symbol* (*n-place function symbol*). If P is an n-place predicate symbol for $n \geqslant 2$, we often say that P is an n-place *relation symbol*.

We will now specify some *notational conventions*, some of which we have been using already without commenting on them. First, we will use $\mathcal{L}$ as a variable in our metalanguage (i.e., English) to designate languages for predicate logic, and will rely on context to fix its reference in particular cases. When more than one language is being considered at a time, we will use subscripts to distinguish them. We will use small italic letters from the end of the alphabet, usually x, y, and z, to designate individual variables, and will employ subscripts with these from time to time as well. We will use other small italic letters, especially f, g and h, to designate function symbols. Small italic letters other than x, y and z, especially a, b, c, m and n will also be used to designate names. While there is overlap in these uses of small letters, there will be enough information available from the context and from the way the letter is used to make clear whether it is being used to designate a name or a function symbol. We will use capital italic letters, especially P, Q and R, possibly with subscripts, to designate predicate symbols. We often write, e.g., $Pxyz$, and understand by this that P is a 3-place relation symbol. In the special case of a 2-place relation symbol, we often write, e.g., xPy instead of Pxy, and we always do so when P is the identity symbol (which is to say, we write the more readable $x = y$ in place of $= xy$).

Just as in our discussion of the language of propositional logic, once we have a vocabulary available for our language, we need to specify which arrangements of the elements of the vocabulary are grammatical, hence potentially meaningful, and which are not. In the propositional case, since the smallest grammatical unit was a statement, all the grammatical expressions of the language were statements. The basic form of statements in predicate logic is to attribute some property to some object or to say that some objects stand in some relation to one another, with the result that the *grammatical expressions* of languages for predicate logic come in two groups. The first, the *terms* of the language, have the grammatical role of referring to objects.

The second, the *formulas*, attribute properties to objects or say they stand in certain relations. We will use t and s, often with subscripts, to designate terms, and will use lower case Greek letters, especially φ, ψ, α, β to designate formulas.

DEFINITION 2.3 The class of *terms* of $\mathcal{L}$ is defined recursively as follows.

1. The individual variables and names of $\mathcal{L}$ are *terms of $\mathcal{L}$*.

2. If f is an n–place function symbol of $\mathcal{L}$ and $t_1, \ldots, t_n$ is a sequence of (not necessarily distinct) terms of $\mathcal{L}$, then $f(t_1, \ldots, t_n)$ is a *term of $\mathcal{L}$*.

3. Nothing else is a *term of $\mathcal{L}$*.

DEFINITION 2.4 The class of *formulas* of $\mathcal{L}$ is defined recursively as follows.

1. If P is an n–place predicate symbol of $\mathcal{L}$, and $t_1, \ldots, t_n$ is a sequence of (not necessarily distinct) terms of $\mathcal{L}$, then $Pt_1 \ldots t_n$ is a *formula of $\mathcal{L}$*.

2. If φ and ψ are formulas of $\mathcal{L}$, then $(\varphi \wedge \psi)$, $(\varphi \vee \psi)$, $(\varphi \to \psi)$ and $\neg\psi$ are all *formulas of $\mathcal{L}$*.

3. If φ is a formula of $\mathcal{L}$ and x is an individual variable which occurs in φ, and neither $(\forall x)$ nor $(\exists x)$ occurs in φ, then $(\forall x)\varphi$ and $(\exists x)\varphi$ are both *formulas of $\mathcal{L}$*.

4. Nothing else is a formula of $\mathcal{L}$.

If a formula of $\mathcal{L}$ has the form described in clause (1) of this definition, we say it is an *atomic formula*. If it has the form described in clause (3), we say it is a *quantified formula*. If it has the form described in clause (2), we say it is a *truth-functional formula*. Note that a truth-functional formula might well have occurrences of quantifiers in it (for instance, $(\forall x)Px \vee \neg Pa$ is a truth-functional formula).

We remark that clause (3) of this definition is more complicated than the similar clause used by some authors. We introduce two restrictions, both in aid of readability of formulas. First, we require that x occur in φ before we can append an x-quantifier to it. This counts as ungrammatical so-called "vacuous quantifications," e.g. expressions such as $(\forall x)(\forall y)Py$. We also require that neither $(\exists x)$ nor $(\forall x)$ occur in φ if either of them is to be appended to φ. This restriction helps make it clear at a glance which quantifier a given occurrence of a variable x is bound by, in the sense defined below, by decreeing ungrammatical expressions such as $(\exists x)[(\exists x)Px \to Px]$. Other authors will allow such formulas, relying on their definitions to ensure that it is unambiguous that the third occurrence of x is bound by the second occurrence of $(\exists x)$, while the fourth x is governed by the first $(\exists x)$. According to the present definition, this expression is not a formula, because in forming it the leftmost $(\exists x)$ would need to be added to the formula $[(\exists x)Px \to Px]$. This is ruled out because there is already an occurrence of $(\exists x)$ in that formula. Note, however, that this doesn't mean that we might not have two occurrences of, say, $(\exists x)$ in a single formula. For instance, $(\exists x)Px \wedge (\exists x)Qx$ is a formula, because each of $(\exists x)Px$ and $(\exists x)Qx$ is a formula, so we can form it using clause (2) of the definition.

We will continue our practice of substituting brackets for parentheses in aid of readability, and of deleting parentheses when we feel this is in aid of readability. Sometimes we might even add parentheses which, strictly speaking, are superfluous, for the same reason. For instance, we sometimes include parentheses around identity formulas, because $(\forall x)(x = y)$ is easier to read than $(\forall x)x = y$. This is the cost of writing $x = y$ for $= xy$. On the other hand, we normally abbreviate $\neg(t_1 = t_2)$ to $t_1 \neq t_2$. Finally, we note that we will extend our conventions for the replacement of parentheses from the propositional case (see the comments following definition 1.9) to the present case. Furthermore, we extend the convention governing parentheses preceded by $\neg$ to cover parentheses preceded by $(\forall x)$ and $(\exists x)$ as well: if the left member of a pair of parentheses is preceded by a quantifier, we do not delete that pair. So $(\forall x)Px \to Ra$ is $[(\forall x)Px \to Ra]$, and *not* $(\forall x)(Px \to Ra)$. Finally, when there is no danger of ambiguity we omit the parentheses around $(\forall x)$ and $(\exists x)$.

There is an important distinction between such expressions as " ... is a fishmonger" and "Sarah is a fishmonger." Each is a perfectly grammatical expression of English, but only the second is a complete sentence which can be used straightforwardly to make a statement. The complete grammatical (declarative) sentences of natural languages are an important subclass of the grammatical expressions of the language, because they *make an assertion*, which is to say that they say something which might be either true or false. Native speakers of such languages are typically very good at distinguishing complete grammatical sentences from other expressions of the language. We want to be able to draw a similar distinction in languages for predicate logic, and for similar reasons. It is useful to make the following preliminary distinction.

DEFINITION 2.5 If φ is a formula and x is a variable, then every occurrence of x in φ is either *free* or *bound*, and it is not both.

1. If φ is atomic, then all occurrences of x in φ are *free occurrences*.

2. If φ has the form $\alpha \wedge \beta$, $\alpha \vee \beta$, $\alpha \to \beta$ or $\neg\alpha$, then an occurrence of x is free in φ if and only if that occurrence is free in whichever of α or β it is.

3. All occurrences of x are *bound* in $(\exists x)\varphi$ and $(\forall x)\varphi$.

If an occurrence of x in φ is free, then that occurrence of x is *bound by* the occurrence of $(\exists x)$ or $(\forall x)$ in $(\exists x)\varphi$ or $(\forall x)\varphi$.

DEFINITION 2.6 (STATEMENT OF L) The *set of free variables of* φ, which we denote by FV(φ), is the set of all variables which have at least one free occurrence in φ. A formula φ is a *statement of* L if and only if FV(φ) is empty, i.e., there are no free occurrences of variables in φ. We often refer to statements of L as *sentences*.

Just as in the propositional case, we will use the italic capital letters P, Q, and R to designate statements of L.

REMARK 2.1 If we assume that the language L contains at least one name, then the class of statements of L can also be picked out by the following definition:

1. An n-place predicate symbol of L followed by a sequence of n (not necessarily distinct) names of L is a statement. (In particular, bearing in mind our convention about how to write identity formulas, if a and b are names, $a = b$ is a statement.)

2. If P and Q are statements of L, then $P \wedge Q, P \vee Q, P \rightarrow Q$ and $\neg P$ are all statements of L.

3. If P is a statement of L, and P^* is the formula which results by replacing one or more occurrences of a particular name by a variable x *which does not occur in P*, then both $(\exists x)P^*$ and $(\forall x)P^*$ are statements of L.

4. Nothing else is a statement of L.

We extend the use of the term "atomic formula" and say that sentences formed under clause 1 are *atomic statements*. If L contains no names, it will obviously contain no atomic statements. The reader might find it instructive to see how the restrictions in clause (3) of this definition correspond to those of clause (3) in definition 2.4.

EXERCISES 2.3.1
Let L be a language with identity whose non-logical vocabulary consists of a two place predicate R, a one place predicate P, and the names a and b.

1. Which of the following expressions are *statements of* L? For those which are not, explain why they are not.

     (a) $(\forall x)(\exists y)Rxy \rightarrow x = y$

     (b) $(\forall x)(Rxa \rightarrow Rbx)$

  * (c) $(\forall x)[Rxa \wedge (\forall y)(x = y \rightarrow (\exists x)Ryx)]$

     (d) $(\forall x)Rxa \wedge (\exists x)Rbx$

  * (e) $(\forall a)Pa$

2. For each of the following expressions, identify its set of free variables.

(a) $\forall x (Px \rightarrow Rxa)$

* (b) $\forall x Px \rightarrow \exists y Rxy$

(c) $\forall x (Px \rightarrow \forall y Rxy \rightarrow Py)$

2.3.2 Interpretations: Preliminary Remarks

The central idea we need is that of an *interpretation* of the vocabulary of a language $\mathcal{L}$ for predicate logic, a concept which generalizes that of a valuation of statement letters (cf. definition 1.11). The reader will recall that in the propositional case valuations assigned appropriate "meanings" (i.e., truth-values) to the non-logical vocabulary. This done, definition 1.2.2, which gives the "natural" reading to the logical vocabulary of the language, enables us to assign meanings to all the grammatical expressions of the language. In the case of languages for predicate logic, we can have many more sorts of non-logical vocabulary, so there is more work for an interpretation to do. In particular, an interpretation $\mathcal{M}$ of our logical vocabulary now consists of:

1. A nonempty set M, called the *universe* of $\mathcal{M}$;

2. An assignment, to each name, if there are any, of a definite element of M (which we shall call the *interpretation under $\mathcal{M}$* of that name);

3. An assignment, to each n–place function symbol, of an n–place function from M into M (which we shall call the *interpretation under $\mathcal{M}$* of that function symbol);

4. An assignment, to each n–place predicate symbol, of a definite n–place relation among the elements of M, where we understand a "1–place relation" to be a *property*. (We shall call this the *interpretation under $\mathcal{M}$* of that relation).

Once an interpretation of our non-logical vocabulary has been fixed, it becomes possible to assign a definite truth value to each statement based on that vocabulary by giving the identity symbol, the logical operators, and the quantifiers their natural meanings. This is best illustrated by an example.

Suppose our vocabulary contains one binary predicate symbol L and one name a. Consider the interpretation $\mathcal{M}$ whose universe is the set of positive integers $\{1, 2, 3, \dots\}$, a is interpreted as the number 1, and L is interpreted as the "less than" relation $<$. Let us determine the truth values of the statements

(1) $\exists x Lax$ (2) $\forall x Lax$ (3) $\forall x \exists y Lxy$

under $\mathcal{M}$. To do this we use $\mathcal{M}$ to "translate" these statements into assertions possessing truth values as follows. The "translation" of (1) is:

1. There is a number x such that $1 < x$,

which is obviously true. The interpretation of (2) is

   2 For all numbers x, $1 < x$,

which is clearly false since it is not the case that $1 < 1$. Finally, the interpretation of (3) is

   3 For any number x, there is some number y such that $x < y$,

which is obviously true.

     This example should be sufficient to introduce the way in which any interpretation for $\mathcal{L}$ can be made to yield a definite truth value—truth or falsity—for each statement of $\mathcal{L}$: we call this the *truth value of P under* $\mathcal{L}$. Equipped with this notion, we can define an *argument* in $\mathcal{L}$ to be (*classically*) *quantificationally valid* if, for any interpretation $\mathcal{M}$, whenever all the premises of the argument are true under $\mathcal{M}$, so is its conclusion. A statement P of $\mathcal{L}$ is (classically quantificationally) *valid* if it is true under any interpretation. And a set of statements S is satisfiable if there is an interpretation under which all the statements in S are true.

     Of course, we have yet to show that, for instance, an argument is valid in this sense if a tree associated with the argument closes. To do so requires a more rigorous presentation of interpretations. For this, it is useful to have some acquaintance with some of the basic concepts of *set theory*, which will also prove useful for the further development of logic later in the book.

2.4   Set Theory

2.4.1   Sets

We are all familiar with the idea of a *set*, also called a *class* or *collection*.[3] As examples, we may consider the set of all coins in one's pocket, the set of all human beings, the set of all planets in the solar system, etc. These are all *concrete* sets in the sense that the objects constituting them—their *elements* or *members*—are material things. In mathematics and logic we wish also to consider *abstract* sets whose members are not material things, but abstract entities such as numbers, lines, ideas, names, etc. We shall use the term *set* to cover concrete and abstract sets, as well as sets which contain a mixture of material and abstract elements. However, while a set might collect together things which are abstract or concrete, it must collect *individual things*. This distinguishes a set from, for instance, a container

---

[3] In a more rigorous presentation of set theory, the words 'set' and 'class' are usually used to mark an important distinction—every set is a class, but not conversely. The distinction is fundamentally important to discussions of the foundations of mathematics, but we ignore it here since our goal is only to introduce those set theoretical concepts we will be employing in our logical investigations below. We likewise must ignore many other important set theoretical concepts and facts, some of which would be very important if we intended to pursue other areas of formal logic, for instance model theory.

of water. A bucket might include a gallon of water, but it does not contain individual waters. In a room which includes several containers of water, we can sensibly talk about the *set of containers of water in the room*, but *not* of the *set of all the water in the room*.

If S is a set, and a is an element of S, we say that *a belongs to* or *is a member of* S, and write

$$a \in S.$$

If b does not belong to S, we write $b \notin S$.

In a given context, there will be a set to which all the objects we wish to consider (i.e., all the things we are talking about in the context) belong: this set is called the *universal set* or *universe of discourse* for that context and will be denoted by UD. It is important to remember that the universal set will not always be the same but will vary with the context: it can, in fact, be any set whatsoever. For example, if we are discussing the properties of the natural number system, UD will be the set of all natural numbers. If we are discussing people, we shall want UD to be the set of all human beings.

Once a universal set has been specified, we can consider *properties* and *relations* defined on it. Suppose, for instance, that the universal set UD is the set of all people. Then examples of properties defined on UD are denoted by the expressions

$$x \text{ is female} \qquad x \text{ is male} \qquad x \text{ is Canadian}$$

and examples of relations on UD are denoted by the expressions

$$x \text{ is taller than } y \qquad x \text{ is married to } y.$$

Here x and y are being used as variables which are understood to *range* over UD. This means that, when the variables in each expression are replaced by names of elements of UD (in the case at hand, names of human beings), a statement having a definite truth value is obtained. (If the resulting statement is true, the elements are said to *satisfy* the expression in question, and the elements named are said to *possess* the property or to *stand in* the relation in question.) For example, if in the expression "x is female" we replace x by "Arnold Schwarzenegger" we obtain the false statement

$$\text{Arnold Schwarzenegger is female,}$$

while if in the expression "x is taller than y" we make the same substitution for x and replace y by "Danny DeVito" we obtain the true statement

$$\text{Arnold Schwarzenegger is taller than Danny DeVito.}$$

The most direct way of specifying a set is to list its elements explicitly. Thus, for example,

$$\{2, 3, \text{Romeo}, \text{Juliet}\}$$

denotes the set whose elements are the numbers 2 and 3 and the persons
Romeo and Juliet. And

$$\{\text{Juliet}\}$$

denotes the set whose sole member is Juliet. This notation is, however, of
no use when the number of members of the set we are trying to specify is
infinite, or finite but excessively large. To specify such sets we must instead
state the characteristic property that an object must have to be a member
of the set. A special notation involving (one-place) *predicates* is used for
this purpose. For example,

$$\{\, x \mid x \text{ is Canadian} \,\}$$

denotes the set of all people who are Canadian, with the understanding that
the variable x ranges over the universal set of all people. Similarly,

$$\{\, x \mid \exists y (x = y^2) \,\}$$

denotes the set of all natural numbers which are perfect squares, provided
that it is understood that the variables x and y range over the universal
set of all natural numbers. In general, if $\varphi(x)$ is a predicate (with one free
variable) defined on a universal set UD, we write

$$\{\, x \mid \varphi(x) \,\}$$

to denote the set of all elements of UD satisfying the predicate $\varphi(x)$. This
set is called the set *determined* by φ.

It is also convenient to have a notation for the empty set, that is, the set
which has no members. We use the symbol $\varnothing$ to denote this set. Thus, for
example, if x ranges over the the natural numbers, $\{\, x \mid x^2 = 2 \,\}$ is identical
with $\varnothing$. This is the case because there is no natural number whose square
is 2.

Two sets A and B are said to be *equal*, and (as usual) we write $A = B$, if
they have the same members, that is, if

$$\forall x (x \in A \iff x \in B).$$

If the sets A and B are determined by predicates φ and ψ defined over a
common universal set UD, that is, if A is $\{\, x \mid \varphi(x) \,\}$ and B is $\{\, x \mid \psi(x) \,\}$,
then

$$A = B \iff \forall x [\varphi(x) \iff \psi(x)].$$

That is, two sets are equal exactly when their determining predicates are
equivalent. This observation is constantly employed in establishing the
equality of sets.

If A and B are sets, we say that A is a *subset* of B, or that A is *included*
or *contained* in B and write

$$A \subseteq B$$

if every member of A is a member of B, that is, if

$$\forall x (x \in A \Rightarrow x \in B).$$

In the opposite event we write $A \nsubseteq B$. For example,

$$A = \{1, 2, 3\} \subseteq \{0, 1, 2, 3\} = B.$$

Notice that this is not the same as $A \in B$, since the elements of B are 0, 1, 2 and 3 and A is not one of these. Notice also that, for any set S, $S \subseteq S$.
   Clearly

$$A = B \iff (A \subseteq B \text{ and } B \subseteq A).$$

If A and B are determined by predicates $\varphi(x)$ and $\psi(x)$ defined on a universal set UD, then

$$A \subseteq B \iff \forall x [\varphi(x) \Rightarrow \psi(x)].$$

   Each predicate φ defined on a universal set UD determines a subset of UD, namely $\{x \mid \varphi x\}$. And conversely, each subset A of UD determines a predicate defined on UD, namely the predicate $x \in A$. In view of this, we can say that predicates defined on a universal set and subsets of that set amount to the same thing.
   If A is a set, considered as a subset of a universal set UD, its *complement* CA is defined by

$$CA = \{x \mid x \notin A\}.$$

It is important to notice that CA depends on the universal set UD. For example, if A is the set of positive natural numbers, and if UD is the set of all natural numbers, then CA is $\{0\}$, while if UD is the set of all integers, then CA is the set $\{\ldots, -2, -1, 0\}$.
   If A and B are sets, their *union* $A \cup B$ and *intersection* $A \cap B$ are defined by

$$A \cup B = \{x \mid x \in A \text{ or } x \in B\}$$

and

$$A \cap B = \{x \mid x \in A \text{ and } x \in B\}$$

respectively.
   For example,

$$\{1, 2, 3\} \cap \{2, 3, 4\} = \{2, 3\},$$
$$\{1, 2, 3\} \cup \{2, 3, 4\} = \{1, 2, 3, 4\},$$
$$\{1, 2, 3\} \cap \{0, 4\} = \varnothing$$
$$\{x \mid x \leqslant 0\} \cap \{x \mid x \geqslant 0\} = \{0\},$$

assuming in the last case that UD is a set of numbers *which includes 0.*

EXERCISES 2.4.1

* 1. Explain why $\varnothing$ is a subset of any set.

2. Prove that, for any subsets A, B, C of a universal set UD:

   (a) $C C A = A$

   (b) $A \subseteq A$

* (c) $A \cup C A = \text{UD}$

   (d) $A \cap C A = \varnothing$

   (e) $A \cap (B \cup C) = (A \cap B) \cup (A \cap C)$

* (f) $A \cup (B \cap C) = (A \cup B) \cap (A \cup C)$

   (g) $A \cap (B \cap C) = (A \cap B) \cap C$

   (h) $A \cup (B \cup C) = (A \cup B) \cup C$

* (i) $C(A \cap B) = C A \cup C B$

   (j) $C(A \cup B) = C A \cap C B$

* 3. For subsets A and B of a universal set UD, prove that the following are equivalent:

   (a) $A \subseteq B$

   (b) $C B \subseteq C A$

   (c) $A \cup B = B$

   (d) $A \cap B = A$

   (e) $A \cap C B = \varnothing$

   (f) $C A \cup B = \text{UD}$

4. Let $A \setminus B$—the *relative complement* of B in A—denote the set $\{ x \mid x \in A \wedge x \notin B \}$.

   (a) Prove that $A \setminus B = A \setminus (A \cap B)$ and $A = (A \cap B) \cup (A \setminus B)$.

* (b) Are the following always true? $(A \setminus B) \cup B = A$, $(A \setminus B) \setminus B = A$. Explain.

2.4.2   Relations

Given any two individuals a and b, we assume that we can form another individual $\langle a, b \rangle$ called the *ordered pair* with first component a and second component b. If a and b are distinct, the ordered pair $\langle a, b \rangle$ is different from the ordered pair $\langle b, a \rangle$: it follows that $\langle a, b \rangle$ cannot be the same as the set $\{a, b\}$, since always $\{a, b\} = \{b, a\}$. Generally speaking, ordered pairs $\langle a, b \rangle$ and $\langle c, d \rangle$ are said to be *equal* precisely when their first and second components are pairwise identical, that is, if $a = c$ and $b = d$. Thus

$$\langle a, b \rangle = \langle c, d \rangle \iff a = c \text{ and } b = d. \tag{$*$}$$

The concept of ordered pair can be introduced in a variety of ways, for instance by defining

$$\langle a, b \rangle = \{\{a\}, \{a, b\}\}.$$

We shall not, however, be concerned with the exact definition of $\langle a, b \rangle$: we will only need to know that it satisfies condition $(*)$ above.

We shall also assume that we can form ordered triples $\langle a, b, c \rangle$, quadruples $\langle a, b, c, d \rangle$—in general, for any $n \geqslant 2$, ordered n-tuples $\langle a_1, \dots, a_n \rangle$. Again, all we need to know about these is that

$$\langle a_1, \dots, a_n \rangle = \langle b_1, \dots, b_n \rangle \iff a_1 = b_1 \text{ and } \dots \text{ and } a_n = b_n.$$

Given two sets A and B, the set of all ordered pairs $\langle a, b \rangle$ with $a \in A$ and $b \in B$ is called the *Cartesian product* of A and B: it is denoted by $A \times B$. Cartesian products arise frequently in mathematics (and implicitly in logic). For a familiar example, consider the usual plane from (Euclidean) geometry, which extends indefinitely in all directions. Once one chooses two perpendicular lines in the plane and a unit of distance, one can assign to each point on the plane its *Cartesian coordinates*, which will be a pair of real numbers. Furthermore, each ordered pair of real numbers will correspond to a point on the plane. In effect, this procedure involves identifying the geometric plane with $\mathbb{R} \times \mathbb{R}$, the Cartesian product of two copies of the real line. (This fact is really the starting point of René Descartes' analytical approach to geometry, which translates some difficult problems in geometry into easier problems in algebra—hence the term "Cartesian.")

Similarly, given n sets $A_1, \dots, A_n$, the set containing all ordered n-tuples $\langle a_1, \dots, a_n \rangle$ with $a_1 \in A_1, \dots, a_n \in A_n$ is called the *Cartesian product* of $A_1, \dots, A_n$ and denoted by $A_1 \times \cdots \times A_n$. If all the As are identical with a fixed set A, then $A_1 \times \cdots \times A_n$ is written A^n and called the nth *(Cartesian) power of A*.

EXERCISES 2.4.2

1. Prove that $A \times (B \cup C) = (A \times B) \cup (A \times C)$, $A \times (B \cap C) = (A \times B) \cap (A \times C)$, and $A \times (B \setminus C) = (A \times B) \setminus (A \times C)$.

* 2. Prove that if $C \neq \varnothing$, then $A \subseteq B \iff A \times C \subseteq B \times C$.

We often have occasion to consider *binary relations*. A binary relation may be regarded as a *property of ordered pairs*, that is, as a (one-place) *predicate defined on a Cartesian product of two sets*. Since, as we have observed, a predicate defined on a set amounts to the same thing as a subset of that set, it follows that *a binary relation is essentially just a subset of a Cartesian product of two sets*. This is best illustrated by an example.

Consider the binary relation of *marriage between women and men*. Writing W for the set of women, and M for the set of men, the marriage relation may be identified with the set R of ordered pairs $\langle a, b \rangle$ in which a is a woman, b is a man, and a is married to b. Thus R is a subset of $W \times M$: we naturally say that R is a *relation between W and M*. In general, a subset of the Cartesian product $A \times B$ of two sets A and B is called a (binary) *relation between A and B*. If H denotes the set of all human beings, then the relation R is clearly also a subset of $H \times H$: it is accordingly natural to say that R is a *relation on H*. Generally, a subset of a Cartesian product $A \times A$ is called a (binary) *relation on A*.

Similarly, a subset of $A_1 \times \cdots \times A_n$ is called a *relation among $A_1, \ldots, A_n$* and a subset of a Cartesian power A^n an *n-ary relation on A*.

If R is an n-ary relation, it is customary to write $Ra_1 \ldots a_n$ for $\langle a_1, \ldots, a_n \rangle \in R$. More particularly, if R is a binary relation, it is common practice to write aRb for Rab: the former is read "a bears the relation R to b."

EXERCISES 2.4.3

1. Let A, B and C be sets, let R be a relation between A and B, and let S be a relation between B and C. We define the *composite relation $S \circ R$* between A and C to be the set of all pairs $\langle a, c \rangle$ with $a \in A$ and $c \in C$ such that, for some $b \in B$, we have aRb and bSc. Let R and S be the parenthood and sisterhood relations on the set of human beings. What are $S \circ R$, $R \circ S$, $R \circ R$, and $S \circ S$?

2. If R is a relation between sets A and B, the inverse relation R^{-1} between B and A is defined to be the set of all pairs $\langle b, a \rangle$ such that aRb.

   (a) What is R^{-1} when R is (i) the marriage relation, (ii) the parenthood relation, (iii) the brotherhood relation, on the set of human beings?

   * (b) Let R be a relation between A and B, and S a relation between B and C. Prove that $(S \circ R)^{-1} = R^{-1} \circ S^{-1}$, and that $(R^{-1})^{-1} = R$.

2.4.3   Equivalence Relations

The idea of equivalence is of universal importance: in fact all abstractions met with in everyday life involve this idea. For instance, a hitchhiker seeking a ride in a passing vehicle will ignore all the properties of such a vehicle except its mobility: as far as he or she is concerned, all moving vehicles are equivalent, regardless of type.

This idea of equivalence is given precise expression in set theory through the concept of *equivalence relation*. An equivalence relation on a set A is a relation R on A satisfying the following conditions for all $a, b, c \in A$:

1. Reflexivity: aRa,

2. Symmetry: $aRb \iff bRa$,

3. Transitivity: $(aRb \text{ and } bRc) \implies aRc$.

As examples of equivalence relations we have:

· The identity relation on any set A consisting of all ordered pairs of the form $\langle a, a \rangle$ with $a \in A$.

· The relation R on the set of all human beings defined by aRb if and only if a and b have the same parents.

· The relation R on the set of natural numbers defined by mRn if and only if m and n have the same remainder when divided by 2.

· The relation of logical equivalence on the set of all statements.

If R is an equivalence relation on a set A, and $a \in A$, the *equivalence class of R containing a*, written $[a]_R$, is the set comprising all members of A which bear the relation R to a, that is,

$$[a]_R = \{ x \mid xRa \}.$$

For example, the equivalence classes of the first three relations above are, respectively: all sets of the form $\{a\}$ for $a \in A$; all families of siblings; the set of even numbers and the set of odd numbers.

EXERCISES 2.4.4
* 1. Prove that any two equivalence classes are either disjoint or identical.

2.4.4 Orderings

The idea of an *ordering relation*, or *ordering*, is another important concept in everyday life. Whenever we make a comparison, for example, when we say that something is bigger, or heavier, or more interesting than something else, we are implicitly employing the idea of ranking or ordering with respect to the property in question.

In set theory this idea is captured by making the following definition. An *ordering* on a set A is a relation—often written $\lhd$—on A which satisfies the following conditions for all $a, b, c \in A$:

1. Reflexivity: $a \lhd a$

2. Transitivity: $(a \lhd b$ and $b \lhd c) \Rightarrow a \lhd c$

3. Anti-symmetry: $(a \lhd b$ and $b \lhd a) \Rightarrow a = b$.

Notice that the difference between the definition of an ordering relation and the definition of an equivalence relation is that the condition of symmetry is replaced by the condition of anti-symmetry.

The obvious examples of ordered sets are sets of numbers (the reals, the rationals, the natural numbers) ordered as usual. However, these examples have another feature not shared by all orderings. If $\lhd$ in addition satisfies the condition of

4. Totality: for all $a, b \in A$, $a \lhd b$ or $b \lhd a$

then ◁ is called a *total ordering* on A. Obviously, all total orderings are orderings. But it is an important fact that many orderings are not total. An ordering which is not total will be referred to as a *partial ordering*. If ◁ is an ordering (partial or total) on A, we will say that A is *partially* or *totally ordered by* ◁. If neither $a ◁ b$ nor $b ◁ a$, we say that a and b are *non-comparable* elements of A (with respect to ◁).

EXAMPLE 2.1

· The set of natural numbers is totally ordered by the relation ⩽ of increasing magnitude. It is partially, but not totally, ordered by the relation | of divisibility: $m \mid n$ if and only if m is a divisor of n.

· The power set $\mathcal{P}A$ of a set A is the set whose elements are all the subsets of A. (For example, if $A = \{1, 2\}$, then $\mathcal{P}A = \{\varnothing, \{1\}, \{2\}, \{1, 2\}\}$.) The inclusion relation ⊆ is a partial ordering on $\mathcal{P}A$. If A has more than one element, it is *not* a total ordering.

EXERCISES 2.4.5

*   1. Prove the claims made in the previous example.

2. If ◁ is a (partial, total) ordering on a set A, prove that its inverse $◁^{-1}$ is also a (partial, total) ordering on A.

3. A relation on a set A which is both reflexive and transitive is called a *preordering* on A. For example, the relation *at least as tall as* is a preordering on the set of human beings.

   (a) Prove that the relation P *logically implies* Q is a preordering on the set of all statements.

* (b) If R is a preordering on A, prove that the relation S defined by aSb if and only if (aRb and bRa) is an equivalence relation on A. What are the equivalence classes of this equivalence relation when R is the preordering specified in (a)?

2.4.5   Functions

Intuitively, a *function* from a given set A to a given set B is a device or rule which assigns a unique element of B to each element of A. In set theory this idea is given a precise formulation in terms of relations. Thus we define a function from A to B to be a relation f between A and B possessing the following property:

for any $a \in A$, there is a unique $b \in B$ for which afb.

In this situation we write $f : A \to B$. A is called the *domain*, and B the *codomain*, of f. For $a \in A$, we also write $f(a)$ or fa for the unique element b of B such that afb: $f(a)$ is called the *value* of f at a, or the *image* of a under f. A function $f : A \to A$ is called a (unary) *operation* on A.

EXAMPLE 2.2

· The fatherhood relation F on the set H of all human beings defined by aFb *if and only if b is the father of a* is an operation on H.

· The relation R between the set H of human beings and the set $\mathbb{N}$ of natural numbers defined by aRn *if and only if n is the number of children of a* is a function from H to $\mathbb{N}$.

· The relation R on $\mathbb{N}$ defined by $mRn \iff n = m^2$ is an operation on $\mathbb{N}$.

· For any set A, the identity relation on A is an operation on A. As such, it is called the *identity operation* on A and denoted by 1_A.

Functions or operations can have *more than one variable.* For example, the operation of addition on the set of natural numbers and the operation of conjunction on the set of all statements both involve two variables. Formally, an n–ary operation on a set A is defined to be a function $f : A^n \to A$. The value of f at an n–tuple $\langle a_1, \ldots, a_n \rangle$ is written $f(a_1, \ldots, a_n)$.

EXERCISES 2.4.6

* 1. Let $f : A \to B$, $g : B \to C$. Prove that $g \circ f$ is a function from A to C, and that, for any x in A, $(g \circ f)(x) = g(f(x))$. Prove also that $f = 1_B \circ f = f \circ 1_A$.

2. A function $f : A \to B$ is said to be *one-to-one* if, for any $x, y \in A$, $f(x) = f(y) \to x = y$.

   (a) Which of the functions in the examples above are one-to-one?

   (b) If $f : A \to B$ and $g : B \to C$ are both one-to-one, prove that $g \circ f$ is also.

3. Let $f : A \to B$ be a function, and X a subset of A. The *image* of X under f is the set $f[X]$ consisting of all elements of B of the form $f(x)$ with $x \in X$ (i.e., $f[X] = \{ y \mid \exists x \in X(y = f(x)) \}$). The function $f : A \to B$ is said to be *onto* B if $f[A] = B$.

   (a) Prove that if $X, Y \subseteq A$, then $X \subseteq Y \Rightarrow f[X] \subseteq f[Y]$.

 * (b) Prove that if $X, Y \subseteq A$, then $f[X \cup Y] = f[X] \cup f[Y]$. Does this remain true when "$\cup$" is replaced by "$\cap$"?

   (c) If $f : A \to B$ and $g : B \to C$ are both onto, prove that $g \circ f : A \to C$ is also.

4. Let $g : A \to B$ be a function, and $Y \subseteq B$. The *pre-image* of Y under g is the set $g^{-1}[Y] = \{ x \mid g(x) \in Y \}$.

   (a) Prove that if $Y, Z \subseteq B$, then $g^{-1}[Y \cup Z] = g^{-1}[Y] \cup g^{-1}[Z]$, $g^{-1}[Y \cap Z] = g^{-1}[Y] \cap g^{-1}[Z]$, and $g^{-1}[B \setminus Y] = A \setminus g^{-1}[Y]$.

    * (b) Prove that, for any $X \subseteq A$, $X \subseteq g^{-1}[g[X]]$, and that g is one-to-one if and only if $X = g^{-1}[g[X]]$ for all $X \subseteq A$.

        (c) Prove that, for any $Y \subseteq B$, $g[g^{-1}[Y]] \subseteq Y$, and that g is onto B if and only if $g[g^{-1}[Y]] = Y$ for all $Y \subseteq B$.

2.5   Interpretations of Languages for Predicate Logic

We now return to the idea of an interpretation of the language $\mathcal{L}$, using the concepts of set theory to make the idea precise.

    In section 2.3.1 we noted that to specify a language $\mathcal{L}$, it was enough to specify its non-logical vocabulary (and to specify whether $\mathcal{L}$ was with or without identity). That done, the recursive formation rules in definitions 2.4 and 2.3, which remain the same for all languages, generated the grammatical expressions of the language. We will make use of this fact when assigning meanings to the grammatical expressions of the language. That is, roughly speaking, we will set things up so that to assign "meanings" to all the grammatical expressions of the language it will be enough to assign meanings to the non-logical vocabulary of the language. This will be sufficient because we will specify rules, parallel to the formation rules, which will allow one to determine precisely the "meaning" of any grammatical expression from this information. We begin, then, with a statement of what will be required to assign "meanings" to the non-logical vocabulary.

DEFINITION 2.7 An *interpretation* $\mathcal{M}$ of a language $\mathcal{L}$ consists of:

    1. A *non-empty* set M called the *domain* or *universe* of $\mathcal{M}$.

    2. To each name a, an assignment of a specific *element* of M, denoted by $a^{\mathcal{M}}$, and called the *interpretation under $\mathcal{M}$* of a.

    3. To each n-place function f symbol, an n-place *operation* on M, denoted by $f^{\mathcal{M}}$ and called the *interpretation under $\mathcal{M}$* of f. (So $f^{\mathcal{M}} : M^n \rightarrow M$.)

    4. To each n-place predicate symbol P, an assignment of a definite subset of A^n, denoted by $P^{\mathcal{M}}$, and called the *interpretation under $\mathcal{M}$* of that predicate symbol. (So the interpretation of a 1-place predicate symbol will simply be a subset of M, while the interpretation of an n-place relation symbol will be an n-place relation on M.)

    We can now turn to the first part of assigning "meaning" to the *logical* vocabulary. We begin with the individual variables. As one would expect by their name, these do not have a *fixed* meaning. Rather, each variable, as we say, *ranges over* the domain of the interpretation, which is to say that it might take *any* value in that domain. We handle this by considering different ways the values of the variables might be fixed (temporarily, so to speak).

DEFINITION 2.8 A *valuation* v in $\mathcal{M}$ is an assignment of an element of M, the domain of $\mathcal{M}$, to each individual variable. That is, v is a function with domain the set $\{v_1, v_2, \ldots\}$ and codomain M. If v is a valuation and $d \in M$, we will use $v(x/d)$ to denote the valuation which assigns the same element as v to all variables, except perhaps for the variable x, which gets d assigned to it.

The reader will recall that the grammatical expressions of $\mathcal{L}$ come in two sorts, the terms and the formulas. The terms are used to refer to objects in the domain, while (at least some of) the formulas are used to express statements. We now have enough information to specify which object in M is denoted by each term of $\mathcal{L}$.

DEFINITION 2.9 (INTERPRETATION OF TERMS) We assign to each term t of $\mathcal{L}$ its *interpretation in $\mathcal{M}$ under the valuation v*, which we denote by $[t]_\mathcal{M}^v$, as follows.

1. For a variable x, $[x]_\mathcal{M}^v = v(x)$.

2. For a name a, $[a]_\mathcal{M}^v = a^\mathcal{M}$.

3. If f is an n–place function symbol and $t_1, \ldots, t_n$ is a list of n (not necessarily distinct) terms, then $[f(t_1, \ldots, t_n)]_\mathcal{M}^v = f^\mathcal{M}([t_1]_\mathcal{M}^v, \ldots, [t_n]_\mathcal{M}^v)$.

EXAMPLE 2.3
1. First, suppose that $\mathcal{L}$ contains a 2–place function symbol f, that M is the set of natural number $\mathbb{N}$, and that $f^\mathcal{M}$ is the operation of addition on the natural numbers. The expression $f(x, y)$ thus means $x + y$ in $\mathcal{M}$. This as yet doesn't refer to any particular natural number, for the familiar reason that x and y are variables. Under a particular valuation v, though, each of x and y will be assigned some natural number. So if $v(x) = 7$ and $v(y) = 5$, then $[f(x, y)]_\mathcal{M}^v$ will be $f^\mathcal{M}(v(x), v(y)) = f^\mathcal{M}(7, 5) = 7 + 5 = 12$. If $\mathcal{L}$ also includes the names a and b, and $a^\mathcal{M} = 4$ and $b^\mathcal{M} = 5$, then $[f(a, b)]_\mathcal{M}^v$ will be $4 + 5 = 9$. Notice that in this case the valuation v plays no role in the calculation. This is an instance of an important fact: if no variables occur in a term, then its interpretation in $\mathcal{M}$ does not depend on the valuation. We call terms in which no variable occurs *closed terms*. In the case of a closed term t we can write $[t]_\mathcal{M}$ in place of $[t]_\mathcal{M}^v$, and will do so on occasion.

2. Suppose $\mathcal{L}$ contains two 1–place function symbols f and g, that $\mathcal{M}$ has as its domain the set of human beings, and that $f^\mathcal{M}$ assigns each person his or her father while $g^\mathcal{M}$ assigns each person his or her mother. Then $g(f(x))$ will assign to each person x his or her paternal grandmother, $g(g(x))$ will assign each person x his or her maternal grandmother, and so on.

We now parallel the rules for formation of formulas (in definition 2.4) by *rules for determining the truth values of each formula under an interpretation, given a valuation.* We do so in three stages.

DEFINITION 2.10 Let $\mathcal{L}$ be a language for predicate logic, $\mathcal{M}$ an interpretation for $\mathcal{L}$, and v a valuation in $\mathcal{M}$. For each formula φ of $\mathcal{L}$, we define *the interpretation of φ in $\mathcal{M}$ under v*, which we denote by $[\![\varphi]\!]_{\mathcal{M}}^{v}$, as follows.

Atomic formulas If P is an n–place predicate symbol of $\mathcal{L}$ and $t_1,\ldots,t_n$ are terms of $\mathcal{L}$, then $[\![Pt_1 \ldots t_n]\!]_{\mathcal{M}}^{v}$ is *true* if $\langle [t_1]_{\mathcal{M}}^{v},\ldots,[t_n]_{\mathcal{M}}^{v}\rangle \in P^{\mathcal{M}}$. Otherwise it is false. If $\mathcal{L}$ is a language with identity, then $[\![t_1 = t_2]\!]_{\mathcal{M}}^{v}$ is true if $[t_1]_{\mathcal{M}}^{v}$ and $[t_2]_{\mathcal{M}}^{v}$ are the same element of M. Otherwise it is false.

Notice that if all of $t_1,\ldots,t_n$ are closed terms, then the values of $Pt_1 \ldots t_n$ and $t_1 = t_2$ will not depend on v. So if Q is an atomic *statement*, we can write $[\![Q]\!]_{\mathcal{M}}$ instead of $[\![Q]\!]_{\mathcal{M}}^{v}$.

Truth-functional formulas If φ and ψ are formulas of $\mathcal{L}$, then

1. $[\![\neg\varphi]\!]_{\mathcal{M}}^{v}$ is true if $[\![\varphi]\!]_{\mathcal{M}}^{v}$ is false, and it is false otherwise.

2. $[\![\varphi \wedge \psi]\!]_{\mathcal{M}}^{v}$ is true if $[\![\varphi]\!]_{\mathcal{M}}^{v}$ is true and $[\![\psi]\!]_{\mathcal{M}}^{v}$ is true. Otherwise it is false.

3. $[\![\varphi \vee \psi]\!]_{\mathcal{M}}^{v}$ is true if at least one of $[\![\varphi]\!]_{\mathcal{M}}^{v}$ and $[\![\psi]\!]_{\mathcal{M}}^{v}$ is true. Otherwise it is false.

4. $[\![\varphi \rightarrow \psi]\!]_{\mathcal{M}}^{v}$ is true if at least one of $[\![\neg\varphi]\!]_{\mathcal{M}}^{v}$ and $[\![\psi]\!]_{\mathcal{M}}^{v}$ is true. Otherwise it is false.

Notice that these definitions are essentially the same as the truth tables for classical propositional logic, which is to say that these connectives have the same meaning in classical propositional and predicate logic. So employing the usual definition of $\longleftrightarrow$, it is easy to show that $[\![\varphi \longleftrightarrow \psi]\!]_{\mathcal{M}}^{v}$ will be true if $[\![\varphi]\!]_{\mathcal{M}}^{v}$ and $[\![\psi]\!]_{\mathcal{M}}^{v}$ are both true or both false, and false otherwise. (Of course, in predicate logic more is involved in determining the truth values of the components of a truth functional formula (i.e., of φ and ψ in the above definition) than just a truth value assignment and the truth tables themselves.)

Quantified formulas

1. $[\![(\forall x)\varphi]\!]_{\mathcal{M}}^{v}$ is true if $[\![\varphi]\!]_{\mathcal{M}}^{v(x/d)}$ for *each $d \in M$*.

2. $[\![(\exists x)\varphi]\!]_{\mathcal{M}}^{v}$ is true if $[\![\varphi]\!]_{\mathcal{M}}^{v(x/d)}$ for *at least one $d \in M$*.

All this is best explained by examples.

EXAMPLE 2.4
1. Consider again the earlier example where $\mathcal{L}$ contains the two-place function symbol f which $\mathcal{M}$ interprets as addition, the names a and

b interpreted to be 4 and 5, respectively, and suppose now that $\mathcal{L}$ is a language with identity. Then $[\![(\exists x)f(a,x) = b]\!]^v_{\mathcal{M}}$ will be true if and only if there is at least one $n \in \mathbb{N}$ such that $[\![f(a,x) = b]\!]^{v(x/n)}_{\mathcal{M}}$. That is, x must be able to be assigned some natural number n as its value so that $f^{\mathcal{M}}(a^{\mathcal{M}}, n) = b^{\mathcal{M}}$, i.e. $4 + n = 5$. Since 1 is a natural number, this statement is *true*. (Note that there is no *name in* $\mathcal{L}$ which, under $\mathcal{M}$, names the number 1, but that this is irrelevant to the truth of the statement at hand.)

If we consider the formula $(\forall x)f(a,x) = b$, on the other hand, it will be *false*. For it to be true, it would have to be the case that *whatever* value in $\mathbb{N}$ was assigned to n, $4 + n = 5$ was true, which is obviously not the case.

2. Suppose $\mathcal{L}$ contains a 1-place predicate symbol P, one binary relation symbol R and one name n. Consider the interpretation $\mathcal{M}$ whose domain is $\mathbb{N}$, and under which $P^{\mathcal{M}}$ is the set of odd numbers, $R^{\mathcal{M}}$ is the "less than" relation $<$, and $n^{\mathcal{M}}$ is the number 1. Let us determine the truth values under $\mathcal{M}$ of the statements

   (a) $\exists x(Px \wedge Rxn)$

   (b) $\forall x \exists y(Py \wedge Rxy)$.

For the first, we can calculate as follows. For any valuation v in $\mathcal{M}$,

$$[\![\exists x(Px \wedge Rxn)]\!]^v_{\mathcal{M}} \text{ is true}$$
$$\Longleftrightarrow \text{ for some } a \in \mathbb{N}, [\![Px \wedge Rxn]\!]^{v(x/a)}_{\mathcal{M}} \text{ is true}$$
$$\Longleftrightarrow \text{ for some } a \in \mathbb{N}, [\![Px]\!]^{v(x/a)}_{\mathcal{M}}$$
$$\text{and } [\![Rxn]\!]^{v(x/a)}_{\mathcal{M}} \text{ are both true}$$
$$\Longleftrightarrow \text{ for some } a \in \mathbb{N}, a \in P^{\mathcal{M}} \text{ and } R^{\mathcal{M}}(a,1)$$
$$\Longleftrightarrow \text{ for some } a \in \mathbb{N}, a \text{ is odd and } a < 1.$$

But this last statement is clearly false, since 0 is the only natural number less than 1. It follows that the statement is false under $\mathcal{M}$.

For the second, we can calculate thus: for any valuation v in $\mathcal{M}$,

$[\![\forall x \exists y (Py \wedge Rxy)]\!]^{v}_{\mathcal{M}}$ is true

$\iff$ for any $a \in \mathbb{N}$, $[\![\exists y (Py \wedge Rxy)]\!]^{v(x/a)}_{\mathcal{M}}$ is true

$\iff$ for any $a \in \mathbb{N}$, there is at least one $b \in \mathbb{N}$

such that $[\![Py \wedge Rxy]\!]^{v(x/a,y/b)}_{\mathcal{M}}$ is true

$\iff$ for any $a \in \mathbb{N}$, there is at least one $b \in \mathbb{N}$

such that both $[\![Py]\!]^{v(x/a,y/b)}_{\mathcal{M}}$

and $[\![Rxy]\!]^{v(x/a,y/b)}_{\mathcal{M}}$ are true

$\iff$ for any $a \in \mathbb{N}$, there is at least one $b \in \mathbb{N}$

such that $b \in P^{\mathcal{M}}$ and $\langle a, b \rangle \in R^{\mathcal{M}}$

$\iff$ for any $a \in \mathbb{N}$, there exists at least one $b \in \mathbb{N}$

such that b is odd and $a < b$.

This last statement is obviously true, and accordingly the statement we were testing is true under $\mathcal{M}$.

Notice that the valuation v is only doing any work in these examples by allowing us to use its variants such as $v(x/a)$ to consider all the different values a quantified variable might take. This is because in these examples we are considering statements, rather than formulas which include free occurrences of variables. In fact, it is not hard to see that the following proposition is true.

PROPOSITION 2.1 *Let $\mathcal{M}$ be an interpretation of $\mathcal{L}$, P a statement of $\mathcal{L}$. Then P is true in $\mathcal{M}$ under* some *valuation if and only if P is true in $\mathcal{M}$ under* every *valuation.*

EXERCISES 2.5.1
  1. In each case, determine in the examples the truth value of each statement under the interpretation specified.

  *   (a) Consider $\mathcal{L}$ and $\mathcal{M}$ as in the previous example.

          i. $\exists x \forall y (Px \wedge Rxy)$.
         ii. $\forall x \exists y (\neg Py \wedge Rxy)$.
        iii. $\forall x \forall y [Rxy \rightarrow \exists z (Rxz \wedge Rzy)]$.

  *   (b) Let $\mathcal{L}$ be as above but lacking the name a. Let $\mathcal{M}$ have as its domain the set of human beings, let $P^{\mathcal{M}}$ be the set of males and let $R^{\mathcal{M}}(x, y)$ mean "x is a parent of y."

          i. $\forall x \exists y (Ryx \wedge Py)$.
         ii. $\forall x \forall y (Rxy \rightarrow x \neq y)$.
        iii. $\forall x \forall y \forall z (Rxz \wedge Ryz \wedge Px \wedge Py \rightarrow x = y)$.

2. Prove that the statement $\exists x[Px \land \forall y(Py \to y = x)]$ is true under an interpretation $\mathcal{M}$ if and only if the set $P^{\mathcal{M}}$ contains exactly one element. Formulate sentences which are true under an arbitrary interpretation $\mathcal{M}$ if and only if $P^{\mathcal{M}}$ contains:

   (a) At most one element
   * (b) At most two elements
   * (c) At least two elements
   * (d) Exactly two elements
   (e) At most three elements
   (f) At least three elements
   (g) Exactly three elements

2.6 Validity, Satisfiability, and Models

DEFINITION 2.11 An argument or inference with premises $P_1, \ldots, P_n$ and conclusion C formulated in a language $\mathcal{L}$ for predicate logic is said to be (classically, quantificationally) *valid* if, for any interpretation $\mathcal{M}$ of $\mathcal{L}$, whenever all of $P_1, \ldots, P_n$ are true under $\mathcal{M}$, so is C. In that case, we say that the conclusion is a (classical, quantificational) *logical consequence* of the premises. A statement of $\mathcal{L}$ is said to be a (classical, quantificational) *logical truth* or to be (classically, quantificationally) *valid* if it is true under any interpretation. A set S of statements is said to be (classically, quantificationally) *satisfiable* or *consistent* if there is an interpretation under which all the statements in S are true: such an interpretation is called a (classical) *model* of S. A statement P is said to be *independent* of a set of statements S if there is an interpretation under which each statement in S is true but P is not.

EXAMPLE 2.5
The sentence

$$\forall y \exists x Rxy \tag{2.1}$$

is a *logical consequence* of the sentence

$$\exists x \forall y Rxy. \tag{2.2}$$

For if $\mathcal{M}$ is an interpretation with domain M under which 2.2 is true, then

there exists an $a \in M$ such that, for all $b \in M, \langle a, b \rangle \in R^{\mathcal{M}}$.

In that case, choosing a fixed $a \in M$ so that $\langle a, b \rangle \in R^{\mathcal{M}}$ for all $b \in M$, it follows that

$$\text{for all } b \in M, \; [\![Rxy]\!]_{\mathcal{M}}^{v(x/a,y/b)} \text{ is true}$$
$$\Longleftrightarrow \; \text{for all } b \in M, \; [\![\exists x Rxy]\!]_{\mathcal{M}}^{v(y/b)} \text{ is true}$$
$$\Longleftrightarrow \; \text{statement 2.2 is true under } \mathcal{M}.$$

The sentence

$$\exists y \forall x Rxy \tag{2.3}$$

is *not* a logical consequence of the sentence

$$\forall x \exists y Rxy. \tag{2.4}$$

For consider the interpretation $\mathcal{M}$ with domain $\mathbb{N}$ in which $R^{\mathcal{M}}$ is $<$, the "less than" relation. Then 2.4 is true under $\mathcal{M}$ just when

for any $a \in \mathbb{N}$, there exists $b \in \mathbb{N}$ such that $a < b$,

which is evidently true. On the other hand statement 2.3 is true under $\mathcal{M}$ just when

there exists $b \in \mathbb{N}$ such that, for all $a \in \mathbb{N}$, $a < b$,

which is evidently false (since there is no greatest number). It follows also that the set of statements consisting of 2.4 together with the negation of 2.3 is *satisfiable*, and that 2.3 is independent of 2.4.

EXERCISES 2.6.1
1. Establish the validity of the following statements by giving arguments of the sort presented in this section.

  * (a) $\neg \forall x Px \longleftrightarrow \exists x \neg Px$.
    (b) $\neg \exists x Px \longleftrightarrow \forall x \neg Px$.

2. Which of the following sets of statements are satisfiable? In each of the satisfiable cases, supply an interpretation under which all of the statements are true. [You may find the attempt to use trees to answer this question instructive.]

    (a) $\forall x Px$, $\forall x (Px \rightarrow \exists y Rxy)$, $\exists x \exists y \neg Rxy$.
  * (b) $\forall x \exists y Rxy$, $\forall x \exists y \neg Rxy$.
    (c) $\forall x \neg Rxx$, $\forall x \forall y \forall z [(Rxy \wedge Ryz) \rightarrow Rxz]$, $\exists x \exists y \exists z (Rxy \wedge Ryz \wedge Rzx)$.

2.7   Correctness and Adequacy

We will prove the correctness and adequacy of the tree method for languages of predicate logic without identity and without function symbols. The modifications which must be made to these proofs to extend them to predicate logic with identity and function symbols will be dealt with in exercises at the end of this section.

2.7.1 Some Difficulties

In Chapter 1 we showed the correctness of trees for classical propositional logic by showing that if a tree starts with a satisfiable finite set of statements S, then the tree has a completed open path. Adequacy was demonstrated by showing how a valuation which satisfied a finite set S of statements could be "read off" from any completed open path in a tree that starts with S, which allowed us to infer that if there is a completed open path in a tree that starts with S, then S is satisfiable.

We will employ essentially the same strategies for showing correctness and adequacy for the tree method for classical predicate logic. However, there are some important complications in the present case.

In the case of classical propositional logic, all the rules were *rule-correct* and *rule-complete* (cf definition 1.21), and this made it possible to state our proofs of correctness and adequacy very simply. By exercise 1 of the previous section, the negated quantification rules are both correct and complete. Not so for the instantiation rules, however.

First we notice that each of the instantiation rules calls for the introduction of *new* names, i.e. names which do not occur anywhere on the branches on which the consequences of the application of the rule are to be entered (though in the case of universal instantiation it only calls for this in some situations). This is a problem for the rule-correctness of these rules. For suppose we are applying one of the instantiation rules to a statement which is a member of S, the set of statements with which a tree begins. Because there is no guarantee that the newly introduced name is in the basic vocabulary of $\mathcal{L}$, where $\mathcal{L}$ is the language for predicate logic in which S is formulated, there can be valuations for S which are not valuations for the consequence of the application of the rule, and so there might be valuations in which S is satisfied while the consequence statement is not. Let's ignore this problem momentarily for the sake of making clear a couple of other problems.

Ignoring the above problem for present purposes, the rule of universal instantiation is clearly correct. However, it is *not* rule-complete. That is, the truth of the conclusions of an application of the rule is not sufficient to ensure the truth of the premise. This, after all, is why we don't tick a universal formula after the application of this rule. If we consider only the premise and conclusions of a single application of this rule, it is always possible that there be *other* elements of the domain which fail to satisfy the universal formula, even though all the elements named in the conclusions satisfy it.

On the other hand, the existential instantiation rule is clearly complete. If Pn is true under a valuation, then $\exists x Px$ will be true under that valuation also. However, the truth of $\exists x Px$ is not in general sufficient to guarantee the truth of Pn for any particular n. The truth of the latter on a given valuation ensures that there is *at least one* element of UD which satisfies Px, but the element named by n needn't be such an element.

A second source of complications for proving correctness and adequacy in the predicate logic case is that in the classical propositional case we could prove that every tree that starts with a finite set S of statements of the language of propositional logic terminates eventually with either a closed tree or a tree which includes a completed open path. This fact also was helpful in our proofs. In the predicate logic case, though, this helpful property no longer obtains, for a couple of different reasons.

First, there are some sets of statements of predicate logic whose trees simply *will never terminate.* For instance, consider the tree:

$$\forall x \exists y F x y$$
$$\exists y F a y \quad \checkmark$$
$$F a b$$
$$\exists y F b y \quad \checkmark$$
$$F b c$$
$$\vdots$$

Clearly each application of universal instantiation to the first statement will produce an existential statement. But each application of existential instantiation will require the introduction of a new name, hence another application of universal instantiation. We are clearly in a loop that is not going to terminate.

Secondly, the rules for classical propositional logic required no particular ingenuity on the part of the person constructing the trees. Sometimes ingenuity might lead one to a short tree associated with a set, while applying the rules in a different order would have led to a more complex tree for the same set, but in the end both the ingenious and the foolish will be led to the same result (i.e., either to a closed tree or to a complete tree with an open path) as long as they apply the rules correctly. In this sense, the tree method for classical propositional logic is immune to stupidity. However, in the predicate logic case it is possible to apply rules correctly but, owing to a lack of ingenuity, to fail to obtain the appropriate result. For instance, consider the tree:

$$\exists x \forall y \neg F x y$$
$$\forall x \exists y F x y$$
$$\exists y F a y \quad \checkmark$$
$$F a b$$
$$\exists y F b y \quad \checkmark$$
$$F b c$$
$$\vdots$$

There is nothing illegal about this tree. But in this case, unlike the previous one, one would have to be very short sighted to continue in this way, since the following tree closes:

$$\exists x \forall y \neg Fxy \quad \checkmark$$
$$\forall x \exists y Fxy$$
$$\forall y \neg Fay$$
$$\exists y Fay \quad \checkmark$$
$$Fab$$
$$\neg Fab$$
$$\times$$

The point is simply that in cases like this, some insight (admittedly small in this case) is required to get the tree to close, and so the rules as so far presented are not "foolproof" in the same way as those for the propositional case.

2.7.2 Dealing with the Difficulties

We will first consider the problems raised by the possibility of trees which do not terminate. We begin by distinguishing a special class of trees.

DEFINITION 2.12 A tree that starts with a finite set of statements S is *systematic* if it is constructed in accordance with the following procedure.

1. Decompose all truth-functional and existential statements on the tree and all statements in the sets of consequences of the applications of these decompositions which are either truth-functional or existential. (Close branches as appropriate, of course.)

2. Apply universal instantiation to every universally quantified statement $\forall x \varphi$ on every path on which $\forall x \varphi$ occurs. (Close branches as appropriate, of course.) Return to stage 1.

The virtue of systematic trees is that they eliminate the need for ingenuity in the construction of trees for predicate logic. That is, if there is *any* tree associated with a finite set S of statements which closes, then any systematic tree associated with S will close (though we won't pause to prove this fact here). The availability of systematic trees for any finite set S of statements will prove useful when we come to prove adequacy of the tree method. However, it is not a good idea to adopt the construction of systematic trees as a general practice, because where there is a systematic tree which closes (or which has a completed open path) associated with S, there will typically be a much shorter non-systematic tree which does the same.

In the first example of a non-terminating tree, the problem was not a lack of ingenuity on the part of the person constructing the tree. There are some sets of statements for which there exists no associated tree which terminates in either a closed tree or a tree with a completed open path. Non-terminating trees are certainly not closed, of course. Rather than speaking of closed and open trees, then, we will speak of trees which are closed and those which *do not close*, where the latter sort include both trees which have a complete open path and those which do not terminate.

REMARK 2.2 The existence of non-terminating systematic trees is closely related to an important difference between classical predicate logic and classical propositional logic. Classical propositional logic is *decidable* in the sense that for any argument with a finite set of premises there is an algorithm for determining whether or not the argument is valid, i.e. a general procedure which can be followed and which will always, in a finite number of steps, determine whether or not the argument is valid. The tree method described in chapter 1 is one such method. On the other hand, though we will not prove the fact here, there is no such general procedure for classical predicate logic. That the tree method is not such a procedure manifests itself in the existence of infinite paths. As we shall see, the procedure is correct and adequate, and so every valid argument has an associated tree which closes—and all its *systematic* trees close eventually. So only invalid arguments have open systematic trees. However, this does not amount to a decision procedure because there is no general procedure for telling, at an arbitrary stage in the construction of a so-far open tree, whether the reason it has not yet closed is because it will never close, or whether it will close after a finite number of further steps. Since there are non-terminating trees, there is also no assurance that carrying on will eventually lead to an improvement in this condition.

We next introduce the tools which will allow us to prove the correctness and adequacy of the tree method in spite of the non-rule-correctness of existential instantiation and the non-rule-completeness of universal instantiation. The tools will be in the form of a series of definitions and lemmas.

DEFINITION 2.13 A language for predicate logic $\mathcal{L}$ is a *sublanguage* of another such language $\mathcal{L}^+$ if every item in the non-logical vocabulary of $\mathcal{L}$ is included in the non-logical vocabulary of $\mathcal{L}^+$. Note that it follows that every term and formula of $\mathcal{L}$ is a term or formula of $\mathcal{L}^+$. A mathematical structure $\mathcal{M}$ is a *reduct* of a structure $\mathcal{M}^+$ if every relation, operation or distinguished element of $\mathcal{M}$ is also a relation, operation, or distinguished element of $\mathcal{M}^+$.

Note that if $\mathcal{L}$ is a sublanguage of $\mathcal{L}^+$, then any interpretation $\mathcal{M}^+$ of $\mathcal{L}^+$ has a reduct which is an interpretation of $\mathcal{L}$.

LEMMA 2.2 *Let $\mathcal{L}$ be a sublanguage of $\mathcal{L}^+$, and let $\mathcal{M}^+$ be an interpretation of $\mathcal{L}^+$. Let $\mathcal{M}$ be the reduct of $\mathcal{M}^+$ which results by deleting from $\mathcal{M}^+$ those relations, operations and distinguished elements which interpret non-logical basic vocabulary of $\mathcal{L}^+$ which is not also non-logical basic vocabulary of $\mathcal{L}$.*

Then for any grammatical expression of $\mathcal{L}$, and for every valuation, the interpretation of that expression is the same in $\mathcal{M}$ and in $\mathcal{M}^+$.

To prove the lemma, first note that the valuations in $\mathcal{M}$ and in $\mathcal{M}^+$ are exactly the same, because each has M as its universe.

To show the result for a term t, we need to consider three cases.

1. If t is a variable x, $[x]_{\mathcal{M}}^{v} = v(x) = [x]_{\mathcal{M}^+}^{v}$.

2. If t is a name a, $[a]_{\mathcal{M}}^{v} = a^{\mathcal{M}} = a^{\mathcal{M}^+} = [a]_{\mathcal{M}^+}^{v}$.

3. If t is an n-place function symbol f, and supposing $[t_i]_{\mathcal{M}}^{v} = [t_i]_{\mathcal{M}^+}^{v}$ for each $i = 1, \ldots n$,

$$[f(t_1, \ldots, t_n)]_{\mathcal{M}}^{v} = f^{\mathcal{M}}([t_1]_{\mathcal{M}}^{v}, \ldots, [t_n]_{\mathcal{M}}^{v})$$
$$= f^{\mathcal{M}^+}([t_1]_{\mathcal{M}^+}^{v}, \ldots, [t_n]_{\mathcal{M}^+}^{v})$$
$$= [f(t_1, \ldots, t_n)]_{\mathcal{M}^+}^{v}$$

because $f^{\mathcal{M}} = f^{\mathcal{M}^+}$, since $\mathcal{M}$ is a reduct of $\mathcal{M}^+$.

For formulas, there are once again three cases to consider.

1. For atomic formulas:

$$[\![t_1 = t_2]\!]_{\mathcal{M}}^{v} = 1 \text{ iff } [t_1]_{\mathcal{M}}^{v} = [t_2]_{\mathcal{M}}^{v}$$
$$\text{iff } [t_1]_{\mathcal{M}^+}^{v} = [t_2]_{\mathcal{M}^+}^{v}$$
$$\text{iff } [\![t_1 = t_2]\!]_{\mathcal{M}^+}^{v} = 1$$

(by the proof above for terms). The case for n-place non-logical predicates is similar.

2. For truth-functional formulas: Suppose that $[\![\varphi]\!]_{\mathcal{M}}^{v} = [\![\varphi]\!]_{\mathcal{M}^+}^{v}$ and $[\![\psi]\!]_{\mathcal{M}}^{v} = [\![\psi]\!]_{\mathcal{M}^+}^{v}$. Then if the expression in question is $\varphi \wedge \psi$,

$$[\![\varphi \wedge \psi]\!]_{\mathcal{M}}^{v} = 1 \text{ iff } [\![\varphi]\!]_{\mathcal{M}}^{v} = 1 \text{ and } [\![\psi]\!]_{\mathcal{M}}^{v} = 1$$
$$\text{iff } [\![\varphi]\!]_{\mathcal{M}^+}^{v} = 1 \text{ and } [\![\psi]\!]_{\mathcal{M}^+}^{v} = 1 \quad \text{iff } [\![\varphi \wedge \psi]\!]_{\mathcal{M}^+}^{v} = 1.$$

The proofs for $\vee, \rightarrow$ and $\neg$ are similar.

3. For quantificational formulas: Suppose that $[\![\varphi]\!]_{\mathcal{M}}^{v(x/u)} = [\![\varphi]\!]_{\mathcal{M}^+}^{v(x/u)}$ for every $u \in$ UD. Then

$$[\![\forall x \varphi]\!]_{\mathcal{M}}^{v} = 1 \text{ iff } [\![\varphi]\!]_{\mathcal{M}}^{v(x/u)} = 1 \text{ for all } u \in \text{UD.}$$
$$\text{iff } [\![\varphi]\!]_{\mathcal{M}^+}^{v(x/u)} = 1 \text{ for all } u \in \text{UD.}$$
$$\text{iff } [\![\forall x \varphi]\!]_{\mathcal{M}}^{v} = 1$$

The $\exists$ case is similar.

COROLLARY 2.3 *With L, M and M^+ as in the above lemma, if a set of statements of L is satisfied in M^+, then it is satisfied in M.*

DEFINITION 2.14 (SOUNDNESS OF A RULE) We say that a tree rule r is *rule-sound* if whenever the premise of r is true on some interpretation, then there is an interpretation on which the premise and at least one of r's lists of premises are all true.

This definition differs from the definition for rule-correctness, because rule-correctness requires that if the premise is true on an interpretation, then one of its lists of premises must be true on *that very interpretation*. Rule-soundness requires only that they all be true under *some* interpretation.

The above corollary should make it obvious that universal instantiation is rule-sound. Recall that the reason it is not, strictly speaking, rule-correct is that it is possible that a newly introduced name n need not be in the language L in which a universally quantified premise is interpreted. However, that language is a sublanguage of the one we get by adding n to the basic vocabulary of L, and we may extend the interpretation M of L to an interpretation M^+ of the new language which assigns n to any element of UD. The original interpretation is a reduct of the new one, hence the premise remains true, and if the premise is true in M^+, then the conclusion in which n occurs will need to be true as well.

Existential instantiation is also rule-sound. Here there are two cases to consider. First, it might be that the premise $\exists x \varphi$ is true under an interpretation M under which n is not assigned to any distinguished element, and so the consequence $\varphi(n)$ is not interpreted in M. In this case we can construct an interpretation M^+ like M except that we choose an element $u \in M$ such that $[\![\varphi]\!]_M^{v(x/u)} = 1$ and set $n^{M^+} = u$. By the corollary, the premise remains true in M^+, and the conclusion is true by construction. The other case we must consider is that it is possible that the premise is true under an interpretation and the conclusion *false*. For instance, if we consider an interpretation M where UD $= \mathbb{N}$ in which the one place predicate Px is interpreted by "x is prime," $\exists x Px$ is obviously true. But if we consider the case where $n^M = 4$, Pn is false in M. However, we can obviously get a structure M' from M by leaving M the same except that $n^{M'} = 3$.

The remaining problem is that universal instantiation is not rule-complete. A look back at the proof of the adequacy of the tree method for the propositional case shows that the non-completeness of a rule will require significant modifications to the method used there. In the propositional case we could assign an interpretation to each atomic statement of a completed open branch, and then rely on the completeness of the rules to show that the non-atomic statements could not fail to be true if all the shorter statements on the branch (i.e., their premises, among other statements) were all true. We can't get this argument to work with an incomplete rule in the mix. But notice that what is shown in the propositional case is that *every* valuation which makes all the atoms which occur on a completed open path true satisfies every statement on the path. But to demonstrate satisfiability, it is sufficient to show that there is *at least one* valuation which does this. And the non-rule-completeness of universal instantiation will not prevent us from doing that. The following definitions and lemmas will help us do so.

LEMMA 2.4 *Suppose τ is a tree which fails to close. Then either τ has at least one path which is a completed open path or τ has a non-terminating branch.*

To see this, first notice that if an occurrence of a statement P in a tree has infinitely many occurrences of statements which occur below it, then the first statement in one of the paths which extend below that statement also has infinitely many occurrences of statements below it. For the paths below the occurrence of P result from the application of one of the rules, and each rule allows at most two branches below P. Supposing there are two, if the first statement in both branches was above only finitely many occurrences of statements, then the occurrence of P would likewise be above only finitely many statements, since the sum of two finite numbers is finite.

Now suppose that τ neither closes nor contains a completed open branch. Then if this tree were continued forever, there would be infinitely many occurrences of statements in the tree. Hence there will be infinitely many statements which occur below the first statement, say Q, in the tree. We get a non-terminating branch as follows: begin with Q, and call it stage 1; at each stage, choose one of the statements below it which has infinitely many statements which occur below it, and call that statement stage $n + 1$. This process will not terminate, so the path which proceeds from stage to stage is a non-terminating path.

This lemma might look too obvious to even require proof. However, it is at this point that our proof requires appeal to a *choice principle* of some sort.[4] Notice that the "instructions" describing the process in the preceding paragraph are not ones which a person could typically carry out when constructing a tree. For while we know that *at least one* of the paths below a given node has infinitely many occurrences of statements below it, we don't have any general method for telling *which one it is*. What the choice principle does for us in the proof is to guarantee that the series of selections exists, even though nobody is in a position actually to carry out these selections. Choice principles have generated much argument in the philosophy of mathematics and are the subject of a large and fascinating

---

[4]Our lemma follows directly from *König's Lemma*, which asserts that there is an infinite path in any tree with infinitely many nodes if there are at most finitely many paths extending below each node. König's Lemma is an equivalent principle to the famous set theoretic principle called the Axiom of Choice, which was perhaps the most controversial principle in 20th Century philosophy of mathematics. However, to prove the adequacy of the tree method for classical predicate logic, we could get by with a principle strictly weaker than the Axiom of Choice. An investigation of this would lead us too far afield from the main point of this section, so we simply leave which choice principle we are appealing to unspecified.

literature. Thus it is worth noting that it is at this seemingly innocuous point that these principles are relied on, and that it is also at this point that some mathematicians would not accept our proof.

To demonstrate the adequacy of the tree method, we need to show that every finite set of statements which is not associated with any closed tree is satisfiable. We will do this in two stages: first we show that each such set of statements has an associated tree which includes a path whose nodes form a special sort of set, known as a *Hintikka set*; secondly, we appeal to a lemma which says that each Hintikka set is satisfiable.

DEFINITION 2.15 A set of statements S of a language $\mathcal{L}$ is a *Hintikka set* if it meets the following conditions:

1. There is no atomic statement P such that $P \in S$ and $\neg P \in S$.

2. If $\neg\neg P \in S$, then $P \in S$.

3. If $P \wedge Q \in S$, then $P \in S$ and $Q \in S$.

4. If $\neg(P \wedge Q) \in S$, then $\neg P \in S$ or $\neg Q \in S$.

5. If $P \rightarrow Q \in S$, then $\neg P \in S$ or $Q \in S$.

6. If $\neg(P \rightarrow Q) \in S$, then $P \in S$ and $\neg Q \in S$.

7. If $P \vee Q \in S$, then $P \in S$ or $Q \in S$.

8. If $\neg(P \vee Q) \in S$, then $\neg P \in S$ and $\neg Q \in S$.

9. If $\neg \exists x \varphi \in S$, then $\forall x \neg \varphi \in S$.

10. If $\exists x \varphi \in S$, then $P(n) \in S$ for some n.

11. If $\neg \forall x \varphi \in S$, then $\exists x \neg \varphi \in S$.

12. If $\forall x \varphi \in S$, then there is at least one name a such that $\varphi(a) \in S$, and $\varphi(n) \in S$ for every n that occurs in S.

LEMMA 2.5 *If S is a Hintikka set, then S is satisfiable.*

To see this, let $\mathcal{M}$ be the following structure.

· The UD, M, is the set $\{ t \mid t$ is a term which occurs in $S \}$. If this set is empty, $M = \{1\}$.

· For a name a, $a^{\mathcal{M}} = a$.

· For an n-place function symbol f, and $t_1, \ldots, t_n \in M$, $f^{\mathcal{M}}(t_1, \ldots, t_n) = f(t_1, \ldots, t_n)$.

· For an m-place predicate P, and $t_1, \ldots, t_m \in M$, let $P^{\mathcal{M}} = \{ \langle t_1, \ldots, t_m \rangle \mid Pt_1 \ldots t_m \in S \}$. (That is, $Pt_1 \ldots t_m$ is true if and only if $Pt_1 \ldots t_m \in S$.)

EXERCISES 2.7.1
Show that S is satisfied in $\mathcal{M}$. [Argue by induction on the complexity of a statement P.]

2.7.3 The Proofs

THEOREM 2.6 (CORRECTNESS OF THE TREE METHOD)
If a finite set S of statements of a language for predicate logic is satisfiable, then through any tree which starts with S there will be a path which does not close.

To prove this, observe first that, if all the statements occupying nodes in a path ψ of a tree are true under some interpretation $\mathcal{M}$, then ψ is open, since if a statement and its negation both occupied nodes in ψ then one of these statements would have be false in $\mathcal{M}$.

Now suppose that there is some interpretation $\mathcal{M}$ under which all members of S are true. Consider the following property of a tree τ.

(∗) τ starts with S and contains a path ψ such that all statements occupying nodes of ψ are true under some interpretation.

By the observation above, any tree satisfying (∗) contains an open path.

We claim that, if τ has property (∗), so does any tree τ^* obtained from τ by applying a tree rule. For suppose that (a) all the statements occupying nodes in a certain path ψ through τ are true under $\mathcal{M}$ and (b) we extend τ to τ^* by applying a tree rule to one of its statements. Clearly we may assume that this statement is in ψ, for if not, then ψ is unaffected, and is a path of τ^* and so all of its statements are true under $\mathcal{M}$. Accordingly, in the transition from τ to τ^* the path ψ is extended to a new path, or split into two paths. If the rule applied is any rule other than the two instantiation rules, the rule is correct and so all the statements in the new path, or in at least one of the new paths, are true under $\mathcal{M}$. If the rule in question is an instantiation rule, then the rule is sound, and so there is an interpretation $\mathcal{M}'$ under which all the statements in the new path are true. Thus τ^* has the property (∗), as claimed.

It follows that *any* tree starting with S has the property (∗), and which hence fails to close.

As an immediate consequence, we obtain the

THEOREM 2.7 (ARGUMENT CORRECTNESS OF THE TREE METHOD)
If a tree associated with an argument is closed, the argument is valid.

Now we prove the converse of the correctness result, that is, the

THEOREM 2.8 (ADEQUACY OF THE TREE METHOD)
If there does not exist a tree that begins with a finite set S of statements which closes, then S is satisfiable.

To prove this, note that if no tree for S closes then there is a systematic tree τ for S which does not close. By lemma 2.4, τ contains either a completed open path or a non-terminating path, ψ. We claim that the nodes of ψ form a Hintikka set.

First, suppose ψ is a completed open branch. The first condition is met, since if it were not the path would be closed. For all the remaining conditions, if P is a node of ψ which satisfies the antecedent it must also satisfy the consequent, or else the path is not complete, since these conditions are essentially re-statements of the tree rules.

So suppose ψ is a non-terminating branch. Once again, the first condition is met, because ψ does not close. But this tree is systematic. Hence every existential or truth-functional statement which occurs on ψ will have been decomposed within a finite number of steps after its appearance (during one of the implementations of stage 1), so all the remaining conditions but the final one will be met. Finally, the recurring passages through stage 2 will guarantee that if $\forall x \varphi$ occurs in ψ, then $\varphi(a)$ will occur for every name which ever turns up in S. Hence the final condition is met as well.

By lemma 2.5, the set containing the nodes of ψ is satisfiable. Since S is a subset of that set, S, too, is satisfiable.

As an immediate consequence, we obtain the

THEOREM 2.9 (ARGUMENT ADEQUACY OF THE TREE METHOD)
If an argument is valid, then there is a closed tree associated with it.

The argument-correctness and argument-adequacy results we have demonstrated refer to cases where the argument has a *finite* set of premises. There are situations in logic where it is useful to be able to talk about, for instance, the entailment of a statement P by an *infinite* class S of statements. To this end, let us introduce the

DEFINITION 2.16 A set of statements S is *tree-consistent* if there is no tree beginning with a finite subset of S which closes.

We now prove the

LEMMA 2.10 *If S is a tree-consistent set of statements, whether finite or infinite, then S is contained in a Hintikka set.*

For if we prove this lemma, from Lemma 2.5 we immediately get the

THEOREM 2.11
If S is tree-consistent, then S is satisfiable.

Since S entails P if and only if $S \cup \{\neg P\}$ is unsatisfiable, this theorem in effect extends the argument-adequacy result to the infinite case: if $S \cup \neg P$ is inconsistent, then there must be a tree beginning with a finite subset of it which closes, and so there is a closed tree associated with an argument which takes as its premises a finite subset of S and as its conclusion P.

In effect, we prove the lemma by modifying the definition of a systematic tree to cover the case in which S is infinite. Suppose that we have enumerated the members of S as $P_1, P_2, \ldots$. We make the following definition:

1. $S_0 = S$

2. $S_{n+1} = S_n \cup V$, where V is one of the sets of conclusions which results by the application of the appropriate tree rule to P_n. In cases where P_n has more than one premise set, we include clauses analogous to this one: if P_n is $Q \vee R$, then $V = \{Q\}$ if $S_n \cup \{Q\}$ is tree-consistent. Otherwise $V = \{R\}$.

3. $S^* = \bigcup \{S_n \mid n \in \mathbb{N}\}$.

Notice that this definition makes implicit use of a choice principle. At any stage where there are distinct consequence sets, we can be sure that at least one of them can be consistently joined to the existing set, so we "choose" one. However, there is no general purpose procedure which would allow a person to actually make this choice at every stage.

Next, we make another definition building atop the previous one:

1. $T_0 = S$

2. $T_{n+1} = T_n^*$.

3. $T^* = \bigcup \{T_n \mid n \in \mathbb{N}\}$.

We leave as an exercise the proof that if S is tree-consistent, then T^* is a Hintikka set. The only difficulty is in showing that the requirement that if $\forall x P x$ is in the set, then, for all a which occur in the set, Pa is in the set is met. In the earlier case, this was guaranteed by the back and forth nature of systematic trees, the requirement that one decompose all truth functional and existential formulas before turning to the universal formulas. We can't use this method in the case where S might be infinite, since there might be infinitely many truth functional and existential statements in S and so decomposing all of them first would mean that the universal formulas would never be decomposed at all. In effect, what needs showing is that the above definitions of S^* and T^* nevertheless ensure the satisfaction of the condition.

From the theorem we can prove the following important result.

THEOREM 2.12 (COMPACTNESS THEOREM)
If every finite subset of S is satisfiable, then S is satisfiable.

For if every finite subset of S is satisfiable, then every finite subset is tree-consistent. But S is tree-inconsistent only if there is a finite subset of S which is tree-inconsistent, so S is tree-consistent. Hence S is satisfiable.

EXERCISES 2.7.2
We consider here the changes which must be made to the above proof to make it a proof for the tree rules for languages with identity.

1. Two modifications are necessary to show correctness for the case of predicate logic with identity.

    (a) We began the proof of correctness by arguing that if all statements on a path are true under $\mathcal{M}$, then the path is open. However, the reasons offered are no longer sufficient, since in predicate logic with identity we have *two* closure rules, rather than one. Provide a proof which shows that the result holds also for predicate logic with identity.

    * (b) We must show that if all statements occupying nodes of a path ψ in a tree τ are true under some interpretation, and if ψ^* is a path resulting by an application of the identity rule, then all the statements in ψ^* are true under some interpretation. For this it will suffice to show either that the identity rule is correct, or that it is sound in a suitable sense. So, either show that the identity rule is rule-correct, or if this is not possible formulate a suitable sense in which it is rule-sound.

2. There are several modifications needed to prove adequacy for the case of predicate logic with identity.

    (a) We must modify our definition of a *systematic* tree, by deleting the instruction to return to step 1 from the description of step 2, and adding a third stage to the process sketched in definition 2.12.

    3. Repeatedly apply the Rule for Identity until the tree has the property: if $a = b$ occurs at a node and P is a statement on a branch in which $a = b$ occurs, and Q is a statement which results by replacing b in P at one or more places by a, then Q occurs on that branch. Return to stage 1.

    (b) We modify the definition of a Hintikka set by adding two further clauses.

    13. No formula of the form $a \neq a$ occurs on the path.
    14. If $a = b \in S$, P is a statement which contains b, Q results from P by replacing b one or more times by a, and $P \in S$, then $Q \in S$.

    So, show that with the revised definitions the following claims are true:

    *   i. If a systematic tree for a set of statements does not close, then it has at least one path the nodes of which form a Hintikka set.

        ii. The set of statements in a Hintikka set is satisfiable.

3. We now consider the modifications necessary to handle the case in which the language $\mathcal{L}$ includes operation symbols.

(a) Notice that in the presence of operation symbols there is another sort of correct, unterminating tree which *could be made to terminate.* Consider the tree

$$\forall x P f(x)$$
$$\forall x \neg P x$$
$$P f(a)$$
$$P f f(a)$$
$$P f f f(a)$$
$$\vdots$$

This tree is correct, and non-terminating, but it is obvious that there is a tree for the first two statements which closes. Modify the definition of a systematic tree in a way which will take this problem into account.

(b) Suppose that a function term fx occurs in some statement with that occurrence of x bound by a universal quantifier. Show that any path of which that statement is a node is either closed or infinite.

4. Show that if S is tree-consistent, then T^* is a Hintikka set.

Chapter 3

Using and Extending Predicate Logic: Postulates, Sorts and Second-Order Logic

In Chapter 2, we presented classical predicate logic and discussed some of its important properties. We adverted in Chapter 1 to the fact that it is not uncommon to encounter the view, more or less explicitly defended, that classical predicate logic *is* logic, or at least that it's all the logic anyone needs to know. What is not clear from what we have said so far is *why* classical predicate logic should hold such a privileged position. The reasons for this are many and interesting. Some have to do with certain of its technical properties (it is the strongest logic which is complete, compact, and for which every (countable) satisfiable set of statements has a model whose domain is a set of natural numbers, for instance) which would take us too far afield to do justice to here. A less technical reason for this view is the fact that predicate logic is a system in which central concepts of mathematics can be elegantly presented. Mathematical reasoning is in some sense very general, and so one might argue that a logical system appropriate for handling mathematics will have the right degree of generality to be considered the one true logic, applicable across all domains. It turns out, though, that mathematics is also a source of examples which show that classical predicate logic has some important limitations. We will look at some of these examples and at two ways of extending predicate logic to avoid different sorts of limitations, by (1) using many sorted languages, and (2) using second-order quantification. These examples therefore indirectly motivate the discussion of the other non-standard logics which will occupy the rest of this book.

3.1 Postulate Systems

A mathematical *structure* is made up of four sorts of things: a set which is called the *domain* of the structure; a set of *distinguished elements* from the domain; for each positive integer n, a set of n-place *relations* on the domain; and for each positive integer n, a set of n-place *operations* on the domain. Note that it is structures that we use to interpret languages of predicate logic. More precisely, to interpret $\mathcal{L}$ we can use structures whose number of distinguished elements matches the number of names in $\mathcal{L}$, whose number of n-place relations, for each n, matches the number of n-place predicates of $\mathcal{L}$, and whose number of n-place operations, for each n, matches the number of n-place function symbols of $\mathcal{L}$.

A useful oversimplification for introducing novices to the various subdisciplines in mathematics (which usually are called "theories") is to say that all mathematics is concerned with the study of some or other structures. Some areas are concerned with the properties of a particular important structure. For example, number theory is the investigation of the set of natural numbers, with distinguished element 0, no predicates (other than identity), a one-place operation which assigns to each number its successor, and two binary operations of addition and multiplication. Other areas of mathematics, such as group theory, graph theory, model theory, category theory, and so on, investigate a whole class of structures, namely the classes of groups, graphs, models and categories, respectively.

Obviously, this practice only makes sense because the elements in each of these classes have some important property in common—that is, as we might say, they fall under some important mathematical concept. It is often possible and useful to make precise what the elements of these classes of structures have in common by presenting the relevant mathematical concepts by means of *postulates* (sometimes called *axioms*) formulated as sentences of predicate logic. In such cases we can state succinctly what it means to be, say, a *group*. It is precisely to be a *model* of the set of sentences which is used to present the concept of *group* in predicate logic—i.e., to be an interpretation on which all the sentences in the set are true.

Let us elaborate on this by considering some examples. We begin by noting that in writing and talking about systems of postulates it is customary to place binary operation symbols between arguments, rather than in front of them: thus, for example, one writes $x + y$ instead of $+xy$.

In the following example of a postulate system, we use a dot $\cdot$ written between arguments as a binary operation symbol. We also assume the presence of a name e.

DEFINITION 3.1 The following pair of sentences are the *postulates for a multiplicative system* or (as in mathematicians' succinct jargon) a *monoid*.

$$\forall x \forall y \forall z [x \cdot (y \cdot z) = (x \cdot y) \cdot z] \tag{M1}$$
$$\forall x [e \cdot x = x \cdot e = x] \tag{M2}$$

(Here we have written $e \cdot x = x \cdot e = x$ for $e \cdot x = x \cdot e \land x \cdot e = x$. Similar abbreviations will be employed below.) M1 is the *associativity postulate*, and M2 asserts that e is a *neutral element* under the "multiplication." A model of these postulates is called a *monoid*. The interpretation of $\cdot$ is called the operation of *multiplication* or *composition* on the monoid and that of e the *neutral element* of the monoid.

EXAMPLE 3.1 (MONOIDS)

1. *The additive monoid of natural numbers.* In this interpretation the domain is the set $\mathbb{N} = \{0, 1, 2, \ldots\}$ of natural numbers, $\cdot$ is interpreted as the addition operation on natural numbers, and e names 0.

2. *The multiplicative monoid of natural numbers.* This interpretation has the same domain $\mathbb{N}$ as 1, but $\cdot$ is interpreted as the multiplication operation on natural numbers, and e names 1.

3. *The additive monoid of integers.* In this interpretation the domain is the set $\mathbb{Z}$ of all integers (positive, negative, and zero), $\cdot$ is interpreted as the addition operation on integers, and e names 0.

4. *The multiplicative monoid of integers.* This interpretation has the same domain as 3, but $\cdot$ is interpreted as the multiplication operation on integers, and e names 1.

5. *The multiplicative monoid of positive rationals.* In this interpretation the domain is the set of all positive rational numbers (i.e., fractions), the interpretation of $\cdot$ is the operation of multiplication of fractions, and e names 1.

6. *The monoid of operations on a set A.* In this interpretation the domain is the set of all one-place operations on a set A, the interpretation of $\cdot$ is the operation $\circ$ of composition of operations, and e names the identity operation.

We now consider some examples of statements which are true in every monoid. It follows from the results in Chapter 2 that we can show this in each case by constructing an appropriate tree which closes. (As was shown in the concluding exercises of Chapter 2, in the presence of operation symbols one will rarely get *complete* open branches on a tree and so the method is of limited use for finding counterexamples. We shall be using it primarily to construct proofs in this chapter.)

In presenting some of these trees we shall omit some obvious steps. We mark places where we have done so with ellipses. We will explain what is replaced by some ellipses in the first few trees. We trust that with a bit of practice it will become obvious how to fill in the gaps.

Neutral elements are unique: $\forall y[\forall x(x \cdot y = x) \rightarrow y = e]$.
Proof:

$$\forall x \forall y \forall z[x \cdot (y \cdot z) = (x \cdot y) \cdot z]$$

$$\forall x(e \cdot x = x \cdot e = x)$$
$$\neg \forall y[\forall x(x \cdot y = x) \to y = e] \quad ✔$$

$$\exists x \neg [\forall x(x \cdot y = x) \to y = e] \quad ✔$$
$$\neg [\forall x(x \cdot a = x) \to a = e] \quad ✔$$
$$\forall x(x \cdot a = x)$$
$$a \neq e$$
$$e \cdot a = e$$
$$e \cdot a = a \cdot e = a$$

$$\vdots$$

$$e \cdot a = a$$
$$a = e$$
$$\times$$

Here the line $e \cdot a = a \cdot e = a$ is from line 2 by universal instantiation. The ellipsis replaces the nodes $e \cdot a = a \cdot e$ and $a \cdot e = e$ (and the node after the ellipsis is from these two lines by the rule for identity).

Inverses are unique: $\forall x \forall y \forall z[y \cdot x = e = x \cdot z \to y = z]$.
Proof:

$$\forall x \forall y \forall z[x \cdot (y \cdot z) = (x \cdot y) \cdot z]$$
$$\forall x[e \cdot x = x \cdot e = x]$$
$$\neg \forall x \forall y \forall z[y \cdot x = e = x \cdot z \to y = z] \quad ✔$$

$$\vdots$$

$$\neg [b \cdot a = e = a \cdot c \to b = c] \quad ✔$$
$$b \cdot a = e = a \cdot c \quad ✔$$
$$b \neq c$$
$$b \cdot a = e$$
$$e = a \cdot c$$
$$e \cdot b = b \cdot e = b \quad ✔$$
$$e \cdot b = b \cdot e$$
$$b \cdot e = b$$
$$b \cdot e = b \cdot e$$
$$b \cdot e = b \cdot (a \cdot c)$$
$$b = b \cdot (a \cdot c)$$

$$\vdots$$

$$b \cdot (a \cdot c) = (b \cdot a) \cdot c$$

$$b = (b \cdot a) \cdot c$$
$$b = e \cdot c$$

$$\vdots$$

$$e \cdot c = c \cdot e = c$$

$$\vdots$$

$$e \cdot c = c$$
$$b = c$$
$$\times$$

(The first ellipsis of this tree replaces a series of nodes which instantiate a pattern readers should familiarize themselves with. From line 3 one obtains $\exists x \neg \forall y \forall z[y \cdot x = e = x \cdot z \rightarrow y = z]$. By existential instantiation on that formula we obtain $\neg \forall y \forall z[y \cdot a = e = a \cdot z \rightarrow y = z]$. Another application of negated universal followed by an application of existential instantiation will yield $\neg \forall z[b \cdot a = e = a \cdot z \rightarrow b = z]$, and another repetition yields the statement at the node after the ellipsis. In general, a statement which is the negation of another statement beginning with a sequence of universal quantifiers will yield, eventually, a statement from which that sequence of universal quantifiers has been erased, and the variables bound by those quantifiers have each been replaced by a distinct, new variable. The statement $b \cdot e = b \cdot e$ is from the statement $b \cdot e = b$ *applied to itself.* That is, since $b \cdot e = b$ occurs on the lone path in this tree, we can replace b in any statement on the path by $b \cdot e$, and we had done so in $b \cdot e = b$ itself. The statement $b \cdot (a \cdot c) = (b \cdot a) \cdot c$ results from three applications of universal instantiation to line 1. $e \cdot c = c$ results from $e \cdot c = c \cdot e = c$, by a pattern we have already seen.)

We now enlarge the vocabulary for the monoid postulates by adding a new one-place operation symbol *, which we write following its argument, thus: x^*, a^*. The postulates for the mathematical systems known as *groups* consist of M1 and M2, together with the sentence

$$\forall x (x \cdot x^* = e). \tag{M3}$$

Any model of M1, M2 and M3 is called a *group*: the interpretation of * is called the *inverse operation* of the group. For example, the additive monoid of integers is a group in which the inverse operation is *subtraction*, and the multiplicative monoid of positive rationals is a group in which the inverse operation is *reciprocation*, that is, the inverse of a fraction m/n is the fraction n/m.

The following *cancellation law* is true in every group.

$$\forall x \forall y \forall z (x \cdot z = y \cdot z \rightarrow x = y). \tag{M4}$$

This is so because the tree below closes.

$$\forall x \forall y \forall z[x \cdot (y \cdot z) = (x \cdot y) \cdot z]$$

$$\forall x(e \cdot x = x \cdot e = x)$$
$$\forall x(x \cdot x^* = e)$$
$$\neg \forall x \forall y \forall z(x \cdot z = y \cdot z \rightarrow x = y) \quad \checkmark$$

$$\vdots$$

$$\neg(a \cdot c = b \cdot c \rightarrow a = b) \quad \checkmark$$
$$a \cdot c = b \cdot c$$
$$a \neq b$$

$$\vdots$$

$$a \cdot (c \cdot c^*) = (a \cdot c) \cdot c^*$$
$$b \cdot (c \cdot c^*) = (b \cdot c) \cdot c^*$$
$$c \cdot c^* = e$$
$$a \cdot e = (a \cdot c) \cdot c^*$$
$$a \cdot e = (b \cdot c) \cdot c^*$$
$$a \cdot e = b \cdot (c \cdot c^*)$$
$$a \cdot e = b \cdot e$$

$$\vdots$$

$$a \cdot e = a$$
$$b \cdot e = b$$
$$a = b \cdot e$$
$$a = b$$
$$\times$$

(Most of these patterns should be familiar. The second ellipsis replaces four nodes: two sets of two applications of universal instantiation to line 1; the third line after that ellipsis is by universal instantiation on line 3; the next several nodes are by the identity rule—note that $a \cdot e = (b \cdot c) \cdot c^*$ results from the previous statement by replacing $a \cdot c$ by $b \cdot c$; the first two statements after the final ellipsis result from line 2 in the familiar way.)

EXERCISES 3.1.1
Using trees as above, prove that each of M5 - M8 below follow from lower numbered Ms:

* M5 $\forall x(x \cdot x^* = x^* \cdot x = e)$

M6 $\forall x \forall y \forall z(z \cdot x = z \cdot y \rightarrow x = y)$

M7 $\forall x \forall y(x \cdot y = e \rightarrow y = x^*)$

* M8 $\forall x[(x^*)^* = x]$

3.1.1 Postulate Systems for Arithmetic

The non-logical vocabulary for arithmetic includes a one-place operation symbol s, two binary operation symbols $+$ and $\times$, and a name 0. The standard interpretation $\mathcal{N}$ of this vocabulary is the familiar natural number system, specified as follows:

Domain The set $\mathbb{N} = \{0, 1, 2, \ldots\}$ of natural numbers.

Interpretation of s The (immediate) successor operation $(\ ) + 1$.

Interpretation of $+$ **and** $\times$ The usual operations of addition and multiplication.

Interpretation of 0 The number zero.

Thus the domain and successor operation of the standard interpretation may be represented by the following diagram, which we shall refer to as *diagram $\mathcal{N}$*:

$$0 \longrightarrow 1 \longrightarrow 2 \longrightarrow 3 \longrightarrow \cdots$$

in which each arrow proceeds from an element to its successor.

The postulates for *basic arithmetic* are the following

B1 $\forall x \forall y (x \neq y \longrightarrow sx \neq sy)$.

B2 $\forall x (0 \neq sx)$.

B3 $\forall x [x \neq 0 \longrightarrow \exists y (x = sy)]$.

B4 $\forall x (x + 0 = x)$.

B5 $\forall x \forall y [x + sy = s(x + y)]$.

B6 $\forall x (x \times 0 = 0)$.

B7 $\forall x \forall y [x \times sy = (x \times y) + x]$.

These postulates are all true in the standard interpretation. The first three express familiar facts about the successor operation:

B1 Distinct natural numbers have distinct successors.

B2 Zero is the successor of no natural number.

B3 Every nonzero natural number is a successor.

The next two postulates tell us how to add in this notation:

B4 Adding 0 has no effect.

B5 $x + (y + 1) = (x + y) + 1$.

In this notation each numeral $1, 2, 3, 4, \ldots$ is represented by a string of ss of the appropriate length followed by 0, as in

$$1 = s0 \quad 2 = ss0 \quad 3 = sss0 \quad 4 = ssss0, \quad \ldots.$$

Here is a tree justifying the inference of $2 + 2 = 4$ from B4 and B5:

$$\forall x(x + 0 = x)$$
$$\forall x \forall y(x + sy = s(x + y))$$
$$ss0 + ss0 \neq ssss0$$

$$ss0 + 0 = ss0$$
$$\forall y(ss0 + sy = s(ss0 + y))$$
$$ss0 + s0 = s(ss0 + 0)$$
$$ss0 + ss0 = s(ss0 + s0)$$
$$ss0 + ss0 = ss(ss0 + 0)$$
$$ss0 + ss0 = ssss0$$
$$\times$$

(Lines 6 and 7 are both results of applying UI to line 5. At line 8, $ss0 + s0$ is replaced by $s(ss0 + 0)$, while in line 9 $ss0 + 0$ is replaced by $ss0$.)

Finally, the two remaining postulates reduce multiplication to repeated addition:

B6 Multiplying by 0 yields 0.

B7 $x \times (y + 1) = (x \times y) + x$.

EXERCISES 3.1.2
Using the tree test, show that arguments from one or more of the postulates of basic arithmetic to the following sentences are valid:

    1. $0 \neq s0$.

    2. $s0 \neq ss0$.

    3. $0 \neq ssss0$.

*   4. $ss0 \neq ssss0$.

    5. $0 + ss0 = ss0$.

*   6. $0 \times ss0 = 0$.

Basic arithmetic has a property known as *incompleteness*. By this is meant that there are certain statements true in the standard interpretation (the natural number system) which are *independent* of basic arithmetic. For instance, although each of the statements

$$0 \neq s0, \quad s0 \neq ss0, \quad ss0 \neq sss0, \quad \ldots$$

is provable in basic arithmetic (see the preceding exercises for the first two), the corresponding generalization

$$\forall x(x \neq sx) \tag{3.1}$$

is *not*. Similarly, *none* of the following generalizations are deducible in basic arithmetic, even though all their particular instances are:

$$\forall x(0 + x = x) \tag{3.2}$$
$$\forall x \forall y \forall z[x + (y + z) = (x + y) + z] \tag{3.3}$$
$$\forall x \forall y(x + y = y + x) \tag{3.4}$$
$$\forall x(0 \times x = 0) \tag{3.5}$$
$$\forall x \forall y[sx \times y = (x \times y) + y] \tag{3.6}$$
$$\forall x \forall y(x \times y = y \times x) \tag{3.7}$$

To establish the independence of 3.1–3.7 from the postulates of basic arithmetic, we must supply a model of basic arithmetic, that is, an interpretation in which B1–B7 are true, but in which 3.1–3.7 are false. It is easy to check that the following interpretation J does the job:

Domain The natural numbers together with two additional distinct objects $ and @.

Interpretation of s Indicated by the diagram below, which we shall refer to as *diagram J*, in which each arrow leads from a member of the domain to its successor:

$$0 \longrightarrow 1 \longrightarrow 2 \longrightarrow 3 \longrightarrow \cdots \circlearrowright \$ \circlearrowright @$$

Note that the only arrow leading to $ is the one beginning at $.

Interpretation of $+$ **and** $\times$ As usual when the arguments are both natural numbers. When one or both arguments are $ or @, the values are given by the tables below, in which n is any natural number, and $n^>$ is any nonzero natural number:

+	n	$	@
n		@	$
$	$	@	$
@	@	@	$

×	0	$n^>$	$	@
n			$	@
$	0	@	@	@
@	0	$	$	$

It is easy to see that B1 is true in J. Since any pair of distinct natural numbers have distinct successors, we only need to consider pairs where at least one of the pair is either $ or @. But this is clear, since each of these is its own successor, they are distinct, and neither is a natural number while the successor of any natural number is again a natural number. It is similarly easy to see that B2–B7 are true in $\mathcal{J}$, provided you read the tables properly. (The first argument is to be read off the leftmost vertical column, the second off the horizontal row at the top. Thus notice in the first table that $0 + \$ = \$$, while $\$ + 0 = @$. This establishes the falsity of 3.2 in $\mathcal{J}$.)

EXERCISES 3.1.3
Check that $\mathcal{J}$ establishes the remaining independence claims made above.

The incompleteness of basic arithmetic implies that it also fails to be *categorical*. A set of postulates is said to be *categorical* if all of its models are *isomorphic* (Greek *iso*: "same," *morphe*: "form") in the sense that the same diagram serves for all of them, apart from the re-labeling of nodes. The non-categoricity of basic arithmetic can be seen immediately from the fact that the standard interpretation $\mathcal{N}$ is not isomorphic to the interpretation $\mathcal{J}$ defined above. For no re-labeling of nodes can ever convert diagram $\mathcal{N}$ into diagram $\mathcal{J}$, since the latter contains loops and the former doesn't.

Incompleteness of basic arithmetic is a kind of deductive weakness: certain sentences that one would expect to be able to prove turn out not to be provable. This weakness can be to a great extent overcome by adding to it a new rule known as the *principle of mathematical induction*. Informally, this is the rule of arithmetic which states:

> for any property φ of natural numbers, if $\varphi(0)$, and if, for any number n, $\varphi(n + 1)$ follows from $\varphi(n)$, then every number has the property φ.

It follows from this that, if φ is a property of natural numbers such that $\varphi(0)$ is true but $\varphi(a)$ is false for some number a, then there must be some number n for which $\varphi(n + 1)$ does not follow from $\varphi(n)$, that is, for which $\varphi(n)$ is true but $\varphi(n + 1)$ is false. It is this consequence that we express in the form of the new tree rule:

RULE 3.1 (MATHEMATICAL INDUCTION (MI)) If statements of the form $P(0)$ and $\neg P(t)$ both occupy nodes of an open path of a tree, choose a name b new to the path and enter $P(b)$ and $\neg P(sb)$, the statements which result by replacing each occurrence of t in $P(t)$ and $\neg P(t)$ by b and sb, respectively, at the bottom of the path. Do not tick any of the nodes.

$$P(0)$$

$$\vdots$$

$$\neg P(t)$$

$$P(b)$$
$$\neg P(sb)$$

For reasons similar to those discussed for existential instantiation in the previous chapter, this rule is not correct, but it is clearly *sound* in the same sense in which existential instantiation is sound.

Let us show that sentence 3.1 above follows from B1 and B2 when we are allowed to use rule MI. Here is the appropriate closed tree:

$$\forall x \forall y (x \neq y \rightarrow sx \neq sy)$$
$$\forall x (0 \neq sx)$$
$$\neg \forall x (x \neq sx) \qquad\qquad ✔$$

$$0 \neq s0$$
$$\exists x \neg (x \neq sx) \qquad\qquad ✔$$
$$\neg a \neq sa$$
$$b \neq sb$$
$$\neg sb \neq ssb \qquad\qquad ✔$$
$$sb = ssb$$
$$b \neq sb \rightarrow sb \neq ssb \qquad\qquad ✔$$

$\neg b \neq sb$	$sb \neq ssb$
×	×

Here we applied MI to the two statements $0 \neq s0$ and $\neg a \neq sa$, taking $P(a)$ to be the sentence $a \neq sa$.

EXERCISES 3.1.4

1. Show that MI is unsound in the interpretation $\mathcal{J}$ of basic arithmetic given above. That is, find a statement P for which the premises of MI are true under $\mathcal{J}$, but the sentences forming the conclusion cannot be simultaneously true. (Hint: consider the sentence $a \neq sa$.)

* 2. Use MI to derive statements 3.2 and 3.5 above from (some of) the postulates of basic arithmetic.

3. Derive the following inference form from MI:

$$P(0)$$
$$\forall x[P(x) \rightarrow P(sx)]$$
$$\overline{}$$
$$\forall x P(x)$$

4. Consider the following "rule" ("the ω-rule"):

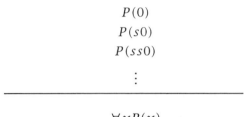

This rule stipulates that a universal generalization follows from the infinite set of premises consisting of its instances for all numeral values of the universally generalized variable. It is an *infinitary* rule allowing an infinite branch to close. The rule is clearly correct for the standard interpretation.

   (a) Show that the ω-rule is unsound for the interpretation $\mathcal{J}$ above.

* (b) Sketch the general appearance of trees, using the ω-rule but not MI, for the inference of statement 3.1 above from B1 and B2, and sentence 3.2 above from B4 and B5.

3.1.2 Noncategoricity of First-Order Peano Arithmetic

We have seen that basic arithmetic fails to be categorical. What is the situation in this regard when the first-order induction principle is added? Is the resulting theory, *first-order Peano arithmetic*, **B**, categorical? In fact, it is not. To establish this we require theorem 2.12, which we restate here.

THEOREM 3.1 (COMPACTNESS THEOREM)
If each finite subset of a set S of first-order statements has a model, then so does S.

We shall use the Compactness Theorem to prove a result stronger than the noncategoricity of **P**, namely:

THEOREM 3.2
The theory **T** *consisting of all the first-order statements true in the standard model* $\mathcal{N}$ *of arithmetic is not categorical.*

Since **T** clearly includes **P**, the noncategoricity of **P** follows immediately. Indeed, it follows that *there can be no first-order theory of arithmetic which is categorical.*

Here is one nifty way to obtain this result. First recall that a natural number $\geqslant 2$ is said to be *prime* if it is divisible only by itself and 1; in the opposite event it is said to be *composite*. Now, it is the case that in $\mathbb{N}$ there are *arbitrarily long strings of consecutive composite numbers*. For, given any n, the sequence $(n+1)!+2, (n+1)!+3, \ldots, (n+1)!+(n+1)$ is a sequence of n consecutive composite numbers. On the other hand, it is well known that in $\mathbb{N}$ there are *arbitrarily large prime numbers*. It follows that in $\mathbb{N}$ there can be *no infinite sequences of consecutive composite numbers*, because if such existed, it would have to consist of all the numbers greater than some fixed n, in violation of the fact that there is a prime number exceeding n.

Now, the property of being composite can be expressed by the formula

$$\mathrm{Comp}(x) \equiv \exists y \exists z (y \neq 1 \wedge z \neq 1 \wedge x = y \times z).$$

The fact that there are no infinite consecutive sequences of composite numbers in $\mathbb{N}$ may then be equivalently stated:

(∗) For no $n \in \mathbb{N}$ can all the following sentences be true in $\mathcal{N}$:

$$\mathrm{Comp}(n), \mathrm{Comp}(s(n)), \mathrm{Comp}(ss(n)), \ldots$$

We shall use the compactness theorem to produce a model $\mathcal{M}$ of **T** whose domain M contains an element a for which all the sentences

(∗∗) $\mathrm{Comp}(a), \mathrm{Comp}(s(a)), \mathrm{Comp}(ss(a)), \ldots$

are true in $\mathcal{M}$ (where a in these formulas is a name for the element $a \in M$). Thus a is the first element of an infinite sequence of consecutive composite "numbers." From this and (∗) it follows immediately that $\mathcal{M}$ and $\mathcal{N}$ are not isomorphic; since both are models of **T**, the latter is not categorical.

To obtain $\mathcal{M}$, we first add a new name a to the vocabulary of first-order arithmetic and consider the set **T**′ of statements consisting of **T** together with all the statements listed in (∗∗). Consider any finite subset F of **T**. Clearly, for some n, F is included in the set

$$\mathbf{T}_n = T \cup \{\mathrm{Comp}(a), \mathrm{Comp}(s(a)), \ldots \mathrm{Comp}\, s^n(a)\}.$$

Now, each $\mathbf{T}_n$ has a model. For consider the extension $\mathcal{N}^*$ of the standard interpretation $\mathcal{N}$ in which the name a is assigned the value $(n+1)!+2$. $\mathcal{N}^*$ is by definition a model of **T** and since the interpretation of a, together with its n successors, are composite, the statements $\mathrm{Comp}(a), \mathrm{Comp}(s(a)), \ldots, \mathrm{Comp}(s^n(a))$ are also true in $\mathcal{N}^*$. Accordingly, $\mathcal{N}^*$ is a model of $\mathbf{T}_n$. So each $\mathbf{T}_n$, and hence each finite subset of **T**′, has a model. The Compactness Theorem now implies that **T**′ itself has a model $\mathcal{M}$, which by construction is a model of **T** possessing the required property of not being isomorphic to $\mathcal{N}$.

EXERCISES 3.1.5

*   1. Show that for any n, $(n+1)!+2, \ldots, (n+1)!+(n+1)$ are all composite.

*   2. Show that for any prime number n, there is prime number k with $n < k \leqslant (n+1)$.

3. Consider the $\mathcal{L}$ which results by adding a new name c to the first-order language $\mathcal{L}$ of arithmetic. Consider the set of statements $C = \{0 \neq c, s0 \neq c, ss0 \neq c, \ldots\}$. Show that every finite subset of $\mathbf{T} \cup C$ is satisfiable. Use the Compactness Theorem to provide an alternative proof that $\mathbf{T}$ is not categorical.

3.2   Many Sorted Logic

3.2.1   Introductory Remarks

In English (and other natural languages) there are different quantifiers for different types of domain, for example, various universal quantifiers.

Domain	Places	Times	People	Things
Quantifier	Everywhere	Always	Everyone	Everything

It is convenient to introduce similar devices into our formal logical notation. The method is best illustrated by an example.

Consider the following vocabulary:

Px x is a person

Qx x is a politician

Tx x is a time

$Fxyz$ x can fool y at (time) z.

Then the statement "There is someone who can fool only himself and all politicians all of the time" may be symbolized in our customary notation as

$$\exists x[Px \land \forall y[Py \rightarrow [\forall z(Tz \land Fxyz) \rightarrow (x = y \lor Qy)]]].$$

This rather involved expression may be simplified by introducing different sorts of letter to indicate individuals satisfying P (i.e., persons) or T (times). Thus, if we agree to use letters x, y for persons, and letters t, u for times, the statement above assumes the simpler "many sorted" form:

$$\exists x \forall y[\forall t[Fxyt \rightarrow (x = y \lor Qy)]].$$

The advantage here is that we no longer need to employ explicit predicates to restrict the "range" of the variables. Notice that in order to transcribe this many-sorted statement back into its original "one-sorted" form we need to replace $\forall x$ by $\forall x(Px \rightarrow \ldots)$, $\exists y$ by $\exists y(Py \land \ldots)$ and $\forall t$ by $\forall z(Tz \rightarrow \ldots)$.

EXAMPLE 3.2

Many sorted languages are in some cases much more natural than unsorted languages for presenting postulate systems. For instance, if presenting David Hilbert's famous axioms for geometry, it is extremely useful to have available different sorts of variables. Let us use p, q, r as variables for *points*, l, m, n for *lines*, and let the predicate Opl mean that (point) p lies on (line) l. Hilbert's first group of postulates are the following *incidence axioms*:

1. $\forall p \forall q [p \neq q \rightarrow \exists l (Opl \wedge Oql) \wedge \forall m (Opm \wedge Oqm \rightarrow m = l)]$ (any two distinct points p and q lie on one and only one line).

2. $\forall l \exists p \exists q (p \neq q \wedge Olp \wedge Olq)$ (there are at least two points on every line).

3. $\exists p \exists q \exists r [p \neq q \wedge q \neq r \wedge p \neq r \wedge \neg \exists l (Olp \wedge Olq \wedge Olr)]$ (there are three points p, q, r not all on a line).

These three axioms enable us to define *triangle*, but not *right angle*.

A second set of postulates are called the *axioms of order*. We introduce a three place relation, $Bpqr$, to be understood as "p lies between q and r (and p, q, r lie on one line)."

4. $\forall p \forall q \forall r [Bpqr \rightarrow Bprq]$ (if p is between q and r, then p is between r and q.

5. $\forall p \forall q \forall l [p \neq q \wedge Olp \wedge Olq \rightarrow \exists r \exists r' (Olr \wedge Olr' \wedge Brpq \wedge Bqpr')]$ (if p and q are distinct points on a line l, then there exists on l a point r between p and q and a point r' such that q is between p and r').

6. $\forall p \forall q \forall r [p \neq q \wedge q \neq r \wedge p \neq r \wedge \exists l (Olp \wedge Olq \wedge Plr) \rightarrow Bpqr \vee Bqrp \vee Brpq \wedge \neg (Bpqr \wedge Bqrp) \wedge \neg (Bqrp \wedge Brpq) \wedge \neg (Bpqr \wedge Brpq)]$ (if p, q, and r are three distinct points on a line l, then exactly one of these three is between the other two.

With these axioms we can define the segment pq, where p and q are distinct points.

Hilbert introduces many further sets of axioms—*congruence axioms*, which would allow a definition of right angle, *parallel postulates*, *completeness axioms*, and so on. For our purposes, it is most important to note that these postulates are relatively straightforward in a sorted language, while an unsorted presentation of the same axioms would be quite cumbersome.

3.2.2 Many Sorted Languages and Their Interpretations

The basic definitions for languages and their interpretations need some adjustments if we are to work with many sorted predicate logics. First, what language is appropriate for a particular purpose will depend on the number of distinct sorts we want to be able to quantify over. Let us consider the case where we have a particular set of sorts, S, in mind. We describe the changes we need to make to the specification of a language $\mathcal{L}$ for predicate logic described in section 2.3.1. We will need to modify our specification of the logical vocabulary by requiring that our language $\mathcal{L}_{ms}$ includes

1. For each sort $s \in S$, a (countably) infinite set of variables $v_1^s, v_2^s, v_3^s, \ldots$.

As the examples of predicates in many sorted logic show, an important difference between many sorted languages and unsorted predicate languages is that they require that only terms referring to the right sort of object can occur in certain places if an expression is to be grammatical. (It is ungrammatical to speak of a point running through two other points, or to speak of fooling a time at a particular person rather than the other way round.) We must build such restrictions into our specification of the non-logical vocabulary. So, the *non-logical vocabulary of* $\mathcal{L}_{ms}$ consists of

1. A set of *non-logical predicates*, $P_1, P_2, P_3 \ldots$. Each predicate is assigned a number $\geqslant 1$ called its *arity*. If the arity of P is n, then P is also assigned a *signature* $\langle s_1, \ldots, s_n \rangle$, where $s_i \in S$, for each $i = 1, \ldots, n$.

2. A (possibly empty, finite but non-empty, or infinite) set of *names*, each of which is equipped with a signature s for some $s \in S$. We say that a name with signature s is a *name of sort s*.

3. A (possibly empty, finite but non-empty, or infinite) set of *function symbols*. Each function symbol is assigned a number $n \geqslant 1$ called its *arity*. If the arity of f is n, then f is assigned a signature $\langle s_1, \ldots, s_n \rangle \rightarrow s_{n+1}$, where $s_1, \ldots, s_{n+1} \in S$.

The idea here is that each term will refer to an object of a particular sort, and predicates can be turned into grammatical expressions of the language only by including in each slot a term of the appropriate sort, as determined by the signature of that predicate. Hence we need also to modify our recursive specifications of the terms and formulas of our language. We begin by specifying the terms:

1. An individual variable or name of sort s is a *term of sort s*.

2. If f is an n-place function symbol with signature $\langle s_1, \ldots, s_n \rangle \rightarrow s_{n+1}$, and $t_1, \ldots, t_n$ is a sequence of terms of sorts $s_1, \ldots, s_n$ respectively, then $f(t_1, \ldots, t_n)$ is a term of sort s_{n+1}.

3. Nothing else is a term.

If a term t is of sort s, we often indicate this by writing t_s.

We can get a suitable definition of a *formula of* $\mathcal{L}_{ms}$ by modifying the definition of a formula for a predicate language $\mathcal{L}$ in two of its clauses.

1. If P is an n-place predicate symbol with signature $\langle s_1, \ldots, s_n \rangle$ and $t_1, \ldots, t_n$ are terms of sorts $s_1, \ldots, s_n$ respectively, then $Pt_1 \ldots t_n$ is a *formula* of $\mathcal{L}_{ms}$.

2. If φ is a formula of $\mathcal{L}_{\text{ms}}$ and x_s is a variable of sort s which occurs in φ, and neither $(\forall x_s)$ nor $(\exists x_s)$ occurs in φ, then $(\forall x_s)\varphi$ and $(\exists x_s)\varphi$ are both *formulas of $\mathcal{L}_{\text{ms}}$*.

The remaining clauses from the definition of formulas of $\mathcal{L}$ remain unchanged. The definitions of *free* and *bound* occurrences of variables, of *statements*, and so on, need not change beyond adding subscripts indicating that variables now are of different sorts.

   With these modifications in the notion of a language, we need to make corresponding changes in the notion of an *interpretation*. If $\mathcal{L}_{\text{ms}}$ is a many sorted language for predicate logic, and S is our set of sorts, an interpretation $\mathcal{M}$ will consist of:

1. For each $s \in S$, a non-empty set M_s, called the *domain of s*.

2. An assignment, to each name of sort s, if there are any, of a definite element of M_s.

3. An assignment, to each function symbol of signature $\langle s_1, \ldots, s_n \rangle \to s_{n+1}$, of a function $M_1 \times \cdots \times M_n \to M_{n+1}$.

4. An assignment, to each predicate symbol of signature $\langle s_1, \ldots s_n \rangle$, of a subset of $M_1 \times \cdots \times M_n$ (i.e., to a relation among members of the appropriate domains).

Two related points should be noted about these definitions. First, there is no requirement that the domains of the various sorts be disjoint. We could have one sort interpreted by the set of *women*, for instance, and another by the set of *people*. Secondly, we have therefore not built in any grammatical requirement that atomic statements involving the *identity predicate* need have terms of the same sort occurring on both sides of the identity sign. On some interpretations there will be true identity statements where the terms involved are of different sorts.

   Two final, rather obvious adjustments—both essentially merely requiring the addition of appropriate subscripts—remain to be made. A *valuation* will now need to be an assignment of an element of M_s to each variable of sort s. And in the definition of truth of a formula φ under an interpretation $\mathcal{M}$ and valuation v, we need to adjust the clauses for quantified formulas. If x_s is the universally (existentially) quantified variable, then the clause will need to require truth for each (at least one) member of M_s, rather than of M.

3.2.3   Reducing Many Sorted to Unsorted Logic

In the introductory remarks to this section we indicated that for many purposes the adoption of many sorted logic can be a significant convenience.

Indeed, it is often preferred to unsorted first-order logic in computer science and linguistics, for instance, both because of the already noted naturalness of many sorted logic for dealing with the interpretations people have in mind in such applications, and because improved versions of certain metatheoretical results important in these disciplines are available for the many sorted case. We will not further pursue the investigation of these advantages here.

On the other hand, there is a sense in which many sorted predicate logic is no stronger than unsorted predicate logic. This sense is made explicit by the result we will now sketch, which is that many sorted logic is *reducible* to unsorted logic. We begin by first defining a *translation* of an arbitrary (but fixed for the duration of this discussion) many sorted language $\mathcal{L}_{ms}$ into an unsorted language $\mathcal{L}$. We then show how to convert any many sorted interpretation of $\mathcal{L}_{ms}$ into an interpretation of the unsorted language $\mathcal{L}$ so that the translation of any true sentence is a true sentence in the resulting unsorted interpretation. But to show a sort of equivalence between the original and its translation, we will also need to consider how to transform unsorted structures interpreting $\mathcal{L}$ into sorted interpretations as well. Finally, we prove the theorem which shows that this process is appropriately called a *reduction*.

DEFINITION 3.2 (TRANSLATION OF $\mathcal{L}_{ms}$ INTO $\mathcal{L}$) The non-logical vocabulary of $\mathcal{L}$ will include all the non-logical vocabulary of $\mathcal{L}_{ms}$. Furthermore, if S is the set of sorts of $\mathcal{L}_{ms}$, then $\mathcal{L}$ includes a one-place predicate S_s for each sort $s \in S$. We will take the variables of $\mathcal{L}_{ms}$ to all be variables of $\mathcal{L}$.[1] We now define a function tr, which takes the grammatical expressions of $\mathcal{L}_{ms}$ into the class of grammatical expressions of $\mathcal{L}$.

1. For a variable x_s, $\mathrm{tr}(x_s) = x_s$, and for a name c_s, $\mathrm{tr}(c_s) = c_s$.

2. For function terms, $\mathrm{tr}(f(t_1, \ldots, t_n)) = f(\mathrm{tr}(t_1), \ldots, \mathrm{tr}(t_n))$.

3. For atomic formulas, $\mathrm{tr}(P(t_1, \ldots, t_n)) = P(\mathrm{tr}(t_1), \ldots, \mathrm{tr}(t_n))$.

4. For truth functional formulas, $\mathrm{tr}(\varphi \wedge \psi) = \mathrm{tr}(\varphi) \wedge \mathrm{tr}(\psi)$, etc.

5. For quantified formulas, $\mathrm{tr}(\exists x_s \varphi) = \exists x_s (S_s(x_s) \wedge \mathrm{tr}(\varphi))$ and $\mathrm{tr}(\forall x_s \varphi) = \forall x_s (S_s(x_s) \rightarrow \mathrm{tr}(\varphi))$.

DEFINITION 3.3 (CONVERSION OF MANY SORTED TO UNSORTED STRUCTURES) Given a many sorted structure $\mathcal{M}$, we construct a corresponding unsorted structure $\mathcal{M}'$ from it as follows:

1. Let M' be the union of all the M_s for $s \in S$.

---

[1] We assume here, for simplicity, that there are at most countably many sorts in $\mathcal{L}_{ms}$, or else the set of variables of $\mathcal{L}$ will be uncountably large. The proof could be modified to avoid making this assumption, but this would introduce complications which obscure the basic structure of the proof.

2. The distinguished elements of each M_s remain distinguished elements of M'.

3. For each $f^{\mathcal{M}} : M_1 \times \cdots \times M_n \rightarrow M_{n+1}$, M' has an operation $f^{\mathcal{M}'} : M'^n \rightarrow M'$. If $f^{\mathcal{M}}(t_1, \ldots, t_n)$ is defined, then we put $f^{\mathcal{M}'}(t_1, \ldots, t_n) = f^{\mathcal{M}}(t_1, \ldots, t_n)$. If it was not defined, we let $f^{\mathcal{M}'}(t_1, \ldots, t_n)$ be an arbitrary but fixed element of M'.

4. For $P^{\mathcal{M}}$, which is a subset of $M_1 \times \cdots \times M_n$, we set $P^{\mathcal{M}'} = P^{\mathcal{M}}$. ($P^{\mathcal{M}}$ is after all a subset of M'^n. The effect is to make the corresponding predicate P true of exactly the same n-tuples in the unsorted structure as it was in the many sorted structure.)

5. For each S_s, we include in $\mathcal{M}'$ a property to interpret it. $S_s^{\mathcal{M}'} = M_s$.

It is now straightforward to prove

THEOREM 3.3
Let φ be a statement of $\mathcal{L}_{\mathrm{ms}}$. Then φ is true in a many sorted structure $\mathcal{M}$ if and only if $\mathrm{tr}(\varphi)$ is true in the corresponding unsorted structure $\mathcal{M}'$.

EXERCISES 3.2.1
Prove this theorem. (Hint: First note that any many sorted valuation in $\mathcal{M}$ is a valuation in $\mathcal{M}'$. Now prove the more general statement that for any grammatical expression (i.e., any term or formula) of $\mathcal{L}_{\mathrm{ms}}$, and any many sorted valuation v in $\mathcal{M}$, the interpretation of that expression is the same in $\mathcal{M}'$ as it is in $\mathcal{M}$. Argue by induction on the form of well formed expressions.)

As noted above, we need also to be able to consider how we might convert an unsorted structure appropriate for the interpretation of $\mathcal{L}$ into a many sorted structure for $\mathcal{L}_{\mathrm{ms}}$. If we begin with the structure $\mathcal{M}'$ defined above, it is obvious how to turn it back into a sorted structure, of course. But if we begin with an arbitrary structure for $\mathcal{L}$, the process needn't be so straightforward, for three reasons. First, the predicate S_s need not be satisfied by an element of the universe of discourse in an unsorted structure, but the domain for the sort S_s must be non-empty. Secondly, a constant c_s might be interpreted by some element of the universe which doesn't satisfy S_s. Finally, and similarly, $f(s_1, \ldots, s_n)$ needn't satisfy S_{n+1}, for an f with signature $\langle s_1, \ldots, s_n \rangle \rightarrow s_{n+1}$. To circumvent such problems, we make the following

DEFINITION 3.4 An unsorted structure $\mathcal{M}$ for $\mathcal{L}$ is *sortable* if and only if it is a model of the following sentences:

1. $\exists x S_s x$ for every $s \in S$.

2. $\forall x_1 \ldots x_n (S_1 x_1 \wedge \cdots \wedge S_n x_n) \rightarrow S_{n+1} f(x_1, \ldots, x_n)$, for every function symbol f with signature $\langle s_1, \ldots, s_n \rangle \rightarrow s_{n+1}$.

3. $S_s c_s$ for every constant c of signature s.

If $\mathcal{M}$ is a sortable structure for $\mathcal{L}$, then we can define a structure $\mathcal{M}^+$ for $\mathcal{L}_{ms}$, essentially by reversing the process for converting a many sorted structure to an unsorted one.

EXERCISES 3.2.2
Suppose $\mathcal{M}$ is a sortable unsorted structure for $\mathcal{L}$.

1. Formulate a description of $\mathcal{M}^+$, the appropriate many sorted structure for $\mathcal{L}_{ms}$. (You will need to (a) identify all the domains, one for each $s \in S$; (b) identify the interpretation for each constant, function symbol, and predicate symbol in $\mathcal{L}_{ms}$—note that the functions and relations in $\mathcal{M}$ will in general be defined for more n-tuples than the functions of $\mathcal{M}^+$ should be.)

2. Use the *sortability* of $\mathcal{M}$ to explain why your definitions work. That is, check that the result is a many sorted structure for $\mathcal{L}_{ms}$.

THEOREM 3.4
A sentence φ of $\mathcal{L}_{ms}$ is true in $\mathcal{M}^+$ if and only if tr(φ) *is true in $\mathcal{M}$.*

EXERCISES 3.2.3
1. Prove this theorem. (Hint: prove a more general result for all grammatical expressions.)

2. Verify that if $\mathcal{M}$ is a sorted model for $\mathcal{L}_{ms}$, then $\mathcal{M}'^+ = \mathcal{M}$. Show also that if $\mathcal{M}$ is a sortable structure for $\mathcal{L}$, then $\mathcal{M}^{+'} = \mathcal{M}$.

Finally, we can state explicitly the sense in which many sorted logic is reducible to unsorted logic.

THEOREM 3.5
If $\Gamma \cup \{\varphi\}$ is a set of sentences of $\mathcal{L}_{ms}$, then $\Gamma \vDash \varphi$ if and only if tr(φ) *is true in every* sortable *unsorted model in which* tr(ψ) *is true for every $\psi \in \Gamma$.*

To prove this, begin by supposing that $\Gamma \vDash \varphi$, and let $\mathcal{M}$ be an unsorted model in which tr(ψ) is true for every $\psi \in \Gamma$. By theorem 3.4, $\mathcal{M}^+$ is a model of Γ, so it is also a model of φ, and so $\mathcal{M}$ is a model of tr(φ) by the same theorem.

Next, suppose that the second condition holds, and suppose that $\mathcal{M}$ is a many sorted model of Γ. Then $\mathcal{M}'$ is a sortable unsorted model (by exercise 2) and by theorem 3.3 it's also a model of tr(ψ) for every $\psi \in \Gamma$. So tr(φ) is true in $\mathcal{M}'$, too, whence we conclude that φ is true in $\mathcal{M}$.

3.3   Second-Order Logic

Predicate logic is also known as *first-order logic*, because in forming its sentences quantification, even in many sorted logic, is restricted to individuals, that is, to *first-order* entities. Second-order logic is an extension of first-order logic which allows existential and universal quantification of *second-order* entities such as predicates, relations, and operations. There are many claims we might make in English which are only naturally represented as involving such quantification. As examples of second-order statements, consider:

1. $\forall x \forall y [x = y \longleftrightarrow \forall P(Px \rightarrow Py)]$

2. $(\forall x)(\forall y)(\exists R)Rxy$.

The first of these asserts that individuals are identical just when one possesses every property the other does, a claim often associated with Leibniz. The second asserts that any two individuals are related in some way or other. In these sentences the P is used as a one-place predicate variable, for properties of individuals, and the R is used as a binary relation variable, for relations between individuals.

Another example is the sentence

3. $\forall P[[P0 \wedge \forall x(Px \rightarrow Psx)] \rightarrow \forall xPx]$, which expresses the *principle of mathematical induction* discussed in section 3.1.1.

3.3.1   Languages and Interpretations

Languages

The formation and interpretation rules for statements of second-order logic are straightforward extensions of the corresponding first-order rules. We will consider the formation rules first, and will suppose as a basis for our discussion that we are given a first-order (unsorted) language $\mathcal{L}$, and modify it to describe the corresponding second-order language $\mathcal{L}_{so}$.

Note first that, in the second-order case, all the non-logical vocabulary, plus the identity sign if it is part of $\mathcal{L}$—that is, all the predicate symbols and function symbols of $\mathcal{L}$, in addition to the names of individuals—count as *names*. To our *logical vocabulary* we must add different sorts of *variables*.

DEFINITION 3.5 In addition to the *individual variables* of $\mathcal{L}$, we have for each natural number n, the following basic vocabulary in $\mathcal{L}_{so}$.

Predicate variables $P_1^n, P_2^n, P_3^n, \ldots$

Operation variables $f_1^n, f_2^n, f_3^n, \ldots$

We call the relevant n the *arity* of the variable in question. We will omit the subscript indicating the arity of these higher order variables, and will instead allow the context to make the arity clear. We will typically use P to denote a one-place predicate variable, and R to denote a two or more place predicate variable. Note that we also use P and R to denote predicates. Again, the context will make clear which is required in any particular case.

We must expand the classes of terms and atomic formulas. More precisely, we must have additional clauses in the definitions which specify the classes of terms and of formulas. If f is an n-place function variable and $t_1, \ldots, t_n$ a sequence of terms, then $f(t_1, \ldots, t_n)$ is a *term* of $\mathcal{L}_{so}$. If P is an n-place predicate variable, and $t_1, \ldots, t_n$ is a sequence of terms of $\mathcal{L}_{so}$, then $Pt_1 \ldots t_n$ is an *atomic formula* of $\mathcal{L}_{so}$.

Finally, we must also add a clause to our definition of a formula which allows quantification over higher-order variables. If φ is a formula of $\mathcal{L}_{so}$ in which the higher order variable P (or f) occurs, and in which neither $\forall P$ nor $\exists P$ ($\forall f$ nor $\exists f$) occurs, then $(\forall P)\varphi$ and $(\exists P)\varphi$ $((\forall f)\varphi$ and $(\exists f)\varphi)$ are both formulas of $\mathcal{L}_{so}$. The notion of a free occurrence of a second-order variable is a straightforward generalization of the definition for individual variables. A *statement* of $\mathcal{L}_{so}$, also called a *sentence* of $\mathcal{L}_{so}$, is a formula in which no variable of either order occurs freely.

Interpretations

A structure which interprets the first-order language $\mathcal{L}$ also interprets the second-order language $\mathcal{L}_{so}$. The interpretations of the names of $\mathcal{L}_{so}$ are then properties (i.e., subsets of UD), or relations of the appropriate number of argument places (i.e., sets of n-tuples of individuals from UD), n-ary operations on UD, or particular individuals selected from within UD, exactly as they were before.

The extra work involved in interpreting second-order languages therefore is all carried out by the extra machinery required to extend these interpretations to quantified formulas. First, we need a more general notion of a *valuation*.

DEFINITION 3.6 A *second-order valuation* in a structure $\mathcal{M}$ is a mapping of the following sort:

1. Each individual variable x is mapped to a member of M.

2. Each n-place predicate variable is mapped to an n-place relation on UD (where a one-place relation is taken to be a property).

3. Each n-place function variable is mapped to a member of the set of operations from UD^n to UD.

We extend the notation $v(x/d)$ from the case of individual variables to include the case where x is a higher order variable and d is a member of the appropriate class.

The clauses for interpreting formulas involving second-order quantifiers under a particular valuation are then directly analogous to those for first-order quantifiers.

Given all this machinery, the notions of *validity*, *consistency* and *model* are automatically extended to second-order sentences.

3.3.2   Second-Order Trees

The tree method can be applied to reasoning that involves second-order sentences—second-order reasoning—in essentially the same way as for first-order reasoning. For instance, let us apply the tree test for validity to the sentence (1) above. We get the tree below.

$$\neg\forall x\forall y[x = y \longleftrightarrow \forall P(Px \to Py)]$$

$$\vdots$$

$$\neg[a = b \longleftrightarrow \forall P(Pa \to Pb)] \qquad\qquad ✔$$

$a = b$	$a \neq b$
$\neg\forall P(Pa \to Pb)$ ✔	$\forall P(Pa \to Pb)$
$\exists P\neg(Pa \to Pb)$ ✔	$a = a \to a = b$
(∗∗) $\neg(Ka \to Kb)$ ✔	
Ka	$a \neq a$ $a = b$
$\neg Kb$	× ×
Kb	
×	

✔(∗) appears to the right of $a = a \to a = b$.

To obtain line (∗), we applied UI (extended in the obvious way to second-order sentences) to the sentence $\forall P(Pa \to Pb)$ immediately above by choosing the instance of the predicate variable P to be the expression $a = x$, that is, the property of *being a*. To obtain line (∗∗), we applied EI (extended in the obvious way to second-order sentences) to the sentence $\exists P\neg(Pa \to Pb)$ immediately above by introducing a new predicate name K and substituting it for P. The tree is then seen to close, so that the statement in question is a second-order logical truth. This means, in effect, that in second-order logic identity $x = y$ can be defined as $\forall P(Px \to Py)$.

Similarly, in the case of sentence (2), we get a tree which begins

$$\vdots$$

$$\neg \exists R R a b \qquad ✔$$
$$\forall R \neg R a b$$
$$\neg (a = b \vee a \neq b)$$

$$\vdots$$

where the last displayed line is obtained by second-order UI by choosing for R the relation $x = y \vee x \neq y$. This tree will obviously close. But this example also illustrates the need to be slightly more precise about the instantiation rules, since the relation $x = y \vee x \neq y$ does not explicitly occur on the tree in advance of its substitution for R.

We take the negated quantifier rules to be obvious enough that they do not require restatement.

For the instantiation rules, it will be helpful to have some terminology and notation.

DEFINITION 3.7 A formula ψ of second-order logic which is not a statement is called an *n-place relation expression*, where n is the number of *distinct free variables* in ψ. If $n = 1$, we often call ψ a *property expression*. Note that according to this description an n-place relation symbol is also an n-place relation expression.

If φ is a formula in which an n-place predicate variable R occurs, and ψ is an n-place relation expression, we shall write $\varphi[R/\psi]$ for the formula which results if all occurrences of R are replaced by ψ (and, if necessary, the variables in ψ are replaced by the variables and constants, in the same order, that are attached to R in φ). So, for example, if R is a binary relation variable and φ is $Rxy \vee Ryz \rightarrow Rxy$, and ψ is $f(x) = y$, then $\varphi[R/\psi]$ will be $f(x) = y \vee f(y) = z \rightarrow f(x) = z$. If f is an n-place function variable and g is an n-place function name, we will write $\varphi[f/g]$ for the analogously defined formula in which f is replaced by g.

The rule of universal instantiation has two parts, one for function variables and one for relation variables.

RULE 3.2 (UNIVERSAL INSTANTIATION) 1. Given a statement of the form $\forall f \varphi$ occupying a node of an open path of a tree,

(a) If no name of a function of appropriate arity appears on the path, choose a function name g of appropriate arity and write $\varphi[f/g]$ at the foot of each path on which the statement occurs.

(b) if a name g of a function of appropriate arity appears in the path, write the statement which results replacing f in φ by g at its foot, unless that statement already occupies a node of the path (in which case writing it once more in the path would be redundant);

2. Given a statement of the form $\forall R\varphi$ where R is an n-place predicate variable, and *if ψ is an n-place relation expression such that all the non-logical vocabulary which occurs in ψ already occurs on the path,* the statement $\varphi[R/\psi]$ may be entered at the foot of the path.

In either case, the universally quantified statement should not be ticked.

Note that since $=$ is part of the logical vocabulary of the languages we are considering, the formula ψ substituted for R may be any formula constructed out of that symbol and the other logical vocabulary. For instance, if R is a one-place predicate variable and a occurs elsewhere on the path, $a = x$ could replace Rx, as could $a \neq x$, $x = a$, $x = a \lor x \neq a$, $\forall y(y = a \rightarrow x = y)$, etc.

For existential instantiation, we can simply add a second clause to the first-order existential instantiation rule which parallels the original:

RULE 3.3 (SECOND-ORDER EXISTENTIAL INSTANTIATION (EI)) For an unticked statement of the form $\exists R\varphi$ (or $\exists f\varphi$) occupying a node of an open path, check to see whether the path contains a node occupied by a statement which is like $\varphi[R/\psi]$ for some relation expression ψ of appropriate arity ($\varphi[f/g]$ for a function symbol of appropriate arity). If not, choose a predicate name (a function symbol) of the appropriate arity *that has not been used anywhere in the path* and write the statement which results by replacing P (f) in φ by that new symbol at its foot. When this has been done for every open path in which the statement $\exists P\varphi$ ($\exists f\varphi$) occupies a node, tick the node occupied by the given statement.

EXERCISES 3.3.1

1. Let R be a binary predicate variable. Each of the following pairs includes a statement and a two-place relation expression. For each, take the statement to be $\forall R\varphi$ and the relation expression to be ψ, and determine what $\varphi[R/\psi]$ is.

*   (a) $\forall R\exists x Rax$, $x = y \lor y = x$.

     (b) $\forall R(Rab \rightarrow Rba)$, Kxy.

*   (c) $\forall R\forall x\forall y\exists z[(Rxy \land Ryz \rightarrow Kxz) \rightarrow \forall w(Kww \rightarrow Rww)]$, $x = y$.

2. Using the tree method as above, show that the following arguments are valid.

     (a) $\forall P(Pa \rightarrow Pb)$, $\forall P(Pb \rightarrow Pc) \therefore \forall P(Pa \rightarrow Pc)$.

*   (b) $\forall P(Pa \rightarrow Pb) \therefore \forall P(Pb \rightarrow Pa)$.

3. Using the tree method, show that the following statements are valid in second-order logic.

     (a) $\exists X\forall y Xy$.

(b) $\exists X \forall y \neg X y$.

* (c) $\forall R[\forall x \forall y (Rxy \rightarrow \neg Ryx) \rightarrow \forall x \neg Rxx]$

3.3.3 The Strength of Second-Order Logic

We have seen that basic arithmetic has models that differ in essential respects from the standard interpretation—the natural number system. Sentence (3) above—the principle of mathematical induction—is a second-order sentence which is true in the standard interpretation, and, in a certain sense, only in that interpretation. The first, and crucial, step in demonstrating this is to establish what we shall call the

Exhaustion principle Models of the principle of mathematical induction are exactly those interpretations in which (the interpretations of the terms on) the list $0, s0, ss0, sss0, \ldots$ exhausts the whole domain of the interpretation.

To see this, suppose that $\mathcal{M}$ is a model of the principle. Then if L is (a name for) the property of being the interpretation under $\mathcal{M}$ of a name on the list, clearly $L0$ and $\forall x(Lx \rightarrow Lsx)$ are both true under $\mathcal{M}$. Since the induction principle has been assumed to be true under $\mathcal{M}$, so then will the sentence $\forall x Lx$. But the truth of this means precisely that every individual in the domain is named on the list.

Conversely, suppose that the domain of an interpretation $\mathcal{M}$ consists exactly of (the interpretations of) $0, s0, ss0, sss0, \ldots$. Let P be (a name for) any predicate defined on the domain of $\mathcal{M}$, and assume that $P0$ and $\forall x(Px \rightarrow Psx)$ are both true under $\mathcal{M}$. We claim that $\forall x Px$ is also true under $\mathcal{M}$. If not, then some element of the domain fails to satisfy $P^{\mathcal{M}}$. This element cannot be (the interpretation of) 0, and must therefore be (the interpretation of) $s^n 0$ for some $n \geqslant 1$ (here $s^n 0$ is 0 preceded by n ss). Choosing n to the least n which fails to satisfy $P^{\mathcal{M}}$, we have $n \geqslant 1$ and $Ps^{n-1}0$ both true under $\mathcal{M}$. Since $\forall x(Px \rightarrow Psx)$ is true under $\mathcal{M}$, it follows that $Ps^{n-1}0 \rightarrow Ps^n 0$ is true under $\mathcal{M}$, and hence $Ps^n 0$ is also true under $\mathcal{M}$. This contradiction shows that $\forall x Px$ must have been true under $\mathcal{M}$ after all. Accordingly

$$P0 \wedge \forall x(Px \rightarrow Psx) \rightarrow \forall x Px$$

is true under $\mathcal{M}$; since P was arbitrary, we conclude that the induction principle is true under $\mathcal{M}$.

It follows immediately from the exhaustion principle that in any model of the induction principle the postulate

B3 $\forall x[x \neq 0 \rightarrow \exists y(x = sy)]$

of basic arithmetic must also be true. In fact this postulate is derivable from the induction principle, as the following closed tree demonstrates. Here we use $S(x)$ as an abbreviation for $x \neq 0 \rightarrow \exists y(x = sy)$.

$$\forall P[[P0 \wedge \forall x(Px \to Psx)] \to \forall xPx]$$
$$\neg\forall xS(x)$$
$$[S(0) \wedge \forall x[S(x) \to S(sx)]] \to \forall xS(x)$$

$\neg[S(0) \wedge \forall x[S(x) \to S(sx)]]$ ✔ $\forall xS(x)$
✗

$\neg S(0)$ $\neg\forall x[S(x) \to S(sx)]$ ✔
$0 \neq 0$ $\vdots$
$\neg\exists y(0 = sy)$ $\neg[S(a) \to S(sa)]$ ✔
✗ $S(a)$
$\neg S(sa)$ ✔
$sa \neq 0$

$\neg\exists y\, sa = sy$ ✔
$\forall y\, sa \neq sy$
$sa \neq sa$
✗

The second-order induction principle has several non-isomorphic models, which shows that, taken by itself, it is not categorical. These models are based on the four diagrams below, in which the interpretations of s and 0 are displayed: as usual, each arrow goes from an element to its "successor." (Note that (d) is the standard interpretation.)

(a)   (b)   (c)

(d)

Clearly no one of these diagrams can be converted into another by re-labeling nodes, since they all contain different numbers of nodes: 1, 2, 3, and infinitely many. The interpretations are therefore non-isomorphic.

EXERCISES 3.3.2
Show that the induction principle is true in each of the interpretations diagrammed by (a) (b) and (c) (and of course (d)).

In contrast, the system—known as *second-order arithmetic*—obtained by adding postulates

B1 $\forall x \forall y (x \neq y \rightarrow sx \neq sy)$

B2 $\forall x (0 \neq sx)$

to the second-order induction principle is categorical, as we shall shortly establish.

EXERCISES 3.3.3
Show that B1 is false in interpretation (c), and B2 is false in both (a) and (b).

PROPOSITION 3.6 (SECOND-ORDER ARITHMETIC IS CATEGORICAL) *Any interpretation $\mathcal{M}$ in which B1, B2 and the second-order induction principle are all true is isomorphic to the standard interpretation $\mathcal{N}$.*

To prove this, we first note that, by the exhaustion principle, the domain of $\mathcal{M}$ consists of the interpretations of the names on the list

$$0, s0, ss0, sss0, \ldots. \tag{$*$}$$

The truth of B2 under $\mathcal{M}$ means that the sentences $0 \neq s0, 0 \neq ss0, 0 \neq sss0$ are all true under $\mathcal{M}$. The truth of B1 under $\mathcal{M}$ now implies that distinct members of the list ($*$) receive distinct interpretations under $\mathcal{M}$. (For if not, then, for example, $sss0 = sssss0$ would be true under $\mathcal{M}$ and three applications of B1 would show $0 = ss0$ to be true under $\mathcal{M}$, contradicting what we have already established.) It follows that the diagram of $\mathcal{M}$ looks like:

$$0 \longrightarrow s0 \longrightarrow ss0 \longrightarrow sss0 \longrightarrow \cdots$$

Clearly this diagram can be re-labeled so as to convert it into the diagram of the standard interpretation $\mathcal{N}$, viz.,

$$0 \longrightarrow 1 \longrightarrow 2 \longrightarrow 3 \longrightarrow \cdots$$

Therefore $\mathcal{M}$ and $\mathcal{N}$ are isomorphic.

The categoricity of second-order arithmetic means that—unlike basic arithmetic—it furnishes a complete characterization of the natural numbers with the successor function in the following sense:

PROPOSITION 3.7 *For any statement P in the vocabulary of second-order arithmetic, P is a logical consequence of second-order arithmetic if and only if P is true in the standard interpretation $\mathcal{N}$.*

To prove this, we observe that if P is a logical consequence of second-order arithmetic, it must be true in every model of it, and so in particular it must be true in $\mathcal{N}$. Conversely, suppose P is true in $\mathcal{N}$, and let $\mathcal{M}$ be any model of second-order arithmetic. Since second-order arithmetic is categorical, $\mathcal{M}$ is isomorphic to $\mathcal{N}$, so since P is true in $\mathcal{N}$, it must also be true in $\mathcal{M}$. Therefore P is a logical consequence of second-order arithmetic.

3.3.4   Metatheory of Second-Order Logic

We have seen that first-order trees are *correct*, that is, any first-order tree with a satisfiable set of initial sentences contains an open path. As we recall, this followed from the fact that all the first-order tree rules are *sound* in the sense that, for any such rule r, if the premise of an application of r is true under a given interpretation, then there is an interpretation under which all the sentences in at least one of r's lists of conclusions are also true. It is easily seen that this remains the case when r is any of the second-order tree rules of universal or existential instantiation. Accordingly, second-order trees are *correct* in the same sense as first-order trees.

First-order trees were also shown to be *adequate*. That is, if every first-order tree starting with a given set G of initial sentences contains an open path, then G is satisfiable. But this is not the case for second-order trees, as is demonstrated by the example below.

If A is a set, it is clear that the following conditions are equivalent:

1. A is finite;

2. Any one-to-one operation $f : A \to A$ is onto A.

Condition 2 can be expressed as the second-order sentence

$$\forall f[\forall x \forall y(fx = fy \to x = y) \to \forall x \exists y(x = fy)] \tag{P}$$

in which f is a unary operation variable. Any model of P must then be finite.
Consider next the second-order sentence

$$\exists R[\forall x \neg Rxx \land \forall x \forall y \forall z(Rxy \land Ryz \to Rxz) \land \forall x \exists y Rxy], \tag{Q}$$

where R is a binary relation variable. This sentence expresses the assertion that there exists a strict ordering on the domain of discourse with no maximal element. Clearly any model of Q must be infinite.

Since any model of P is finite, and of Q infinite, the set $G = \{P, Q\}$ is unsatisfiable. But any (second-order) tree with G as its set of initial sentences contains an open path. For such a tree must develop essentially as follows.

$$P$$
$$Q$$
$$\vdots$$
$$\forall x \neg Sxx \land \forall x \forall y \forall z(Sxy \land Syz \to Sxz) \land \forall x \exists y Sxy \qquad (\dagger)$$
$$\forall x \forall y(gx = gy \to x = y) \to \forall x \exists y(x = gy)$$

$$\neg\forall x \forall y(gx = gy \to x = y) \qquad\qquad\qquad \forall x \exists y(x = gy)$$

$$\vdots \qquad\qquad\qquad\qquad\qquad\qquad \vdots$$
$$(A) \qquad\qquad\qquad\qquad\qquad\qquad (B)$$

As the tree grows, the sentence P will not be used again since no operation symbols were present initially apart from the operation variable f. And it is easy to see that the remaining active sentences (all first-order) in each of the two branches (A) and (B) are satisfiable. To obtain a model of those in branch (A), we need only take its domain to be the set $\mathbb{N}$ of natural numbers, the interpretation of S to be the strict less than relation $<$, and that of g to be the function sending every natural number to 0. For those in (B), the model is the same except that the interpretation of g is the identity function on $\mathbb{N}$. It follows from the correctness theorem that as the tree grows, each of the two branches will contain an open path, and so *a fortiori* the tree will never close.

Therefore any tree with initial set G will contain an open path even though G is unsatisfiable. So if we write S for the sentence $\neg(P \wedge Q)$, then S is valid, but our argument above shows that no tree starting with $\neg S$ will close. Accordingly, *the tree test for validity is inadequate in the second-order case*. Now it might be surmised that this inadequacy has arisen merely as the result of failing to include enough second-order tree rules, so that one might hope to discover others whose inclusion would render the resulting trees complete. But any such hope would be in vain, for it can be shown that, no matter what new rules we add, second-order trees will remain inadequate.

This can be proved by showing that the existence of an adequate set of rules for second-order trees would yield an effective procedure for enumerating the (first- and second-order) sentences true in the standard model of arithmetic $\mathcal{N}$. Since it follows from a famous result of Tarski—his "undefinability of arithmetical truth" theorem, the proof of which will be sketched in passing in our discussion of provability logic in the next chapter—that no such procedure can exist, there can likewise be no complete set of rules for second-order trees.

Let us sketch how such an enumeration of the true sentences of arithmetic can be obtained from a complete set of rules for second-order trees. Let A be the conjunction of the axioms of second-order arithmetic. We have seen that the logical consequences of A are precisely the sentences true in $\mathcal{N}$. That is, for any (first- or second-order) sentence B of the language of arithmetic,

$$B \text{ is true in } \mathcal{N} \iff A \to B \text{ is valid.}$$

Now suppose that there were a complete set of tree rules adequate for establishing validity of second-order sentences. Then the sentences true in N can be effectively enumerated in the following way. First, we assign a code number to each symbol in the language of second-order arithmetic. Next, we define the *complexity* of a sentence to be the larger of the number of symbols appearing in it and the maximum code number of any such symbol. This enables us to define the *degree* of a tree to be the larger of the number of sentences it contains and the maximum code number of a symbol occurring in it. Clearly there are only finitely many trees having a given degree. If B is a sentence true in $\mathcal{N}$, then $A \to B$ is valid and so there is a closed tree with initial sentence $\neg(A \to B)$. Of all such trees, there will be one of least degree n, say; we call n the *order* of B.

For any given number n, the *standard listing* of the finitely many sentences of order n is defined as follows: we place a sentence U before another, T, if either U contains fewer symbols than T or, if they contain the same number of symbols, the code number of the symbol occurring in U in the first place at which U and T differ is smaller than that of the corresponding symbol occupying the same place in T.

Finally we obtain an enumeration of all the sentences true in $\mathcal{N}$ by placing, for $m < n$, the standard listing of true sentences of order m before that of order n.

The fact that no adequate set of rules for second-order trees exists indicates that the meaning of the second-order quantifiers "for all functions," "for all relations," or "for all subsets" cannot be completely captured in a formal way. But it turns out that the second-order tree rules are complete for interpretations in which the second-order quantifiers are construed in a suitably weakened sense. This can be motivated by reconsidering the tree above with its initial sentences P,Q.

The sentence P, which expresses the finiteness of the domain of discourse, comes out false under any interpretation with an infinite domain— for definiteness one with domain $\mathbb{N}$—because the quantifier $\forall f$ in it is interpreted as "for any function $f : \mathbb{N} \to \mathbb{N}$." On the other hand, in specifying the interpretations under which the relevant first-order sentences in the tree are true, we needed to name just two operations on $\mathbb{N}$, namely, the identity function and a particular constant function (and others would have done just as well). Now, because each of these interpretations has domain $\mathbb{N}$, P is false under both; however, if we were to change the meaning of $\forall f$ from "for any function $f : \mathbb{N} \to \mathbb{N}$" to "for any function $f : \mathbb{N} \to \mathbb{N}$ which is constant or the identity," then the sentence P would come out true. Thus, by changing the meaning of the second-order quantifier, the connection between open paths and satisfying interpretations is re-established.

This suggests that adequacy can be achieved for the second-order tree rules by weakening the interpretation of the second-order quantifier $\forall f$ to mean "for all prescribed functions," where by prescribed is meant "being a member of a prescribed set of functions on the domain of discourse." (Here corresponding changes must be made in the interpretation of $\forall P$, $\forall R$ and the second-order existential quantifiers.) This indeed turns out to be true, and the fact is proved in much the same way as in the first-order case. But, as we have seen, no set of rules can be adequate when the second-order quantifiers are understood in their original sense of "for all ... without restriction." This is what is meant when we say that *second-order generality is not capturable by formal rules.*

Second-Order Logic is a Genuine Extension

In our discussion of many sorted logic, we saw a few of the obvious benefits of working with such a language rather than with a standard unsorted first-order language. However, we also saw that many sorted logic is *reducible* to first-order logic. This has led many authors to conclude that the advantages of many sorted languages are merely practical, and that as a matter of theory whatever can be done in a many sorted language could already be done—though perhaps at the cost of less clarity—in standard first-order logic. It is therefore said that many sorted logic is not a genuine *extension* of first-order logic.

The move from first-order to second-order logic *is* a genuine extension, in the sense that it allows us to do things which could not be done in unsorted first-order logic (hence, not in sorted first-order logic, either). One example is that in second-order logic, but not in first-order logic, we were able to give a *categorical* set of axioms for arithmetic. This is something which cannot be done in first-order logic, as we have seen. There is a precise sense, then, in which there are things which can be expressed in second-order logic which cannot be expressed in first-order logic.

One can see a sort of trade-off in the move from first-order to second-order logic. One gains extra expressive power by making this move. The price one pays for this extra expressive power is that one must work with notions which are not capturable by formal rules.

Chapter 4

Introducing Contextual Operators: Modal Logics

In the narrowest sense, *modal logic* is the study of (various kinds of) *necessity*, *possibility*, and related notions—the so-called *alethic* modalities. The term "alethic" comes from the Greek *alethea*, "truth", and the suggestion is that these notions express various *modes of truth*. They form an independent field of study because they play an important role in our reasoning and yet are not expressible, at least in any natural way, in the sorts of classical logic we have looked at so far. However, it turns out that many other features of our reasoning which likewise have no natural expression in propositional or predicate logic—reasoning about what can be *known* (called *epistemic* logic, from the Greek *episteme*, "knowledge"), reasoning about propositional attitudes like *belief* (called *doxastic* logic, from the Greek *doxa*, "opinion"), reasoning about *obligations* and *permissibility* (called *deontic* logic, from the Greek *deon*, "duty"), and even more specialized cases like reasoning about what is *provable* and what not (usually simply called *provability logic*, but sometimes called *apodeictic* logic, from the Greek *apodeiknunai*, "demonstrate")—all have useful representations which treat the respective central notions in a manner parallel to the treatment of necessity and possibility in modal logic. It has therefore become common practice to provide a unified treatment of all these notions and as a consequence also to refer to all these related systems as "modal logics." We think this usage is somewhat unfortunate, but will follow it nonetheless because it has become quite standard. We will also use the term "contextual logics" to refer to these systems, using a name derived from the following account of what these various systems have in common.

In classical propositional logic we think of a statement as being simply true or false, with no reference to context. However, there are many statements in natural languages whose truth is in some way context-dependent. For instance,

> *It is raining here*

is a context-dependent statement of the kind we have in mind: its truth depends on the exact location of "here," and this is something which depends on the context in which the statement was uttered.

Another example of a context-dependent statement is

> *It is raining over a 10 square mile circular region centred 50 miles north of here.*

There is a connection between these two types of statement. Let us write simply *A* for the partial statement "It is raining." Then "It is raining at (place) *x*" is the same as

> *A holds at x.*

We might deal with the other statement thus: Given a place *x*, call any place *y* within a 10 square mile circular region centred 50 miles north of *x* a *place of relevance to x*, and the set of such places the *region of relevance determined by x*: it will of course vary with *x*. We agree to write □*A* (read "box *A*") for the partial statement *It is raining over a region of relevance*, that is, *It is raining at every place of relevance*. In that case, the statement

> *It is raining over a 10 square mile circular region centred 50 miles north of x*

may be written

> □*A holds at x.*

Similarly, if we agree to write ◊*A* (read "diamond *A*") for the partial statement

> *It is raining at a place of relevance,*

then the statement

> *It is raining somewhere within a 10 square mile circular region centred 50 miles north of x*

may be written

> ◊*A holds at x.*

The symbols □ and ◊ are unary statement forming operators, which, like ¬, when applied to a statement (such as "It is raining") yield new statements: if *P* is a statement, so are □*P* and ◊*P*. They are called *contextual* or *modal* operators. As should be clear from the example above, these operators act as a sort of quantifier, with the □*P* asserting something about what happens at all relevant places, while ◊*P* asserts something about what happens at *some* relevant place.[1] With this in mind, it should be clear why, understanding $\neg$ and $\longleftrightarrow$ in the same bivalent way we adopted in earlier chapters, we have

$$\neg\Diamond P \longleftrightarrow \Box\neg P \quad \text{and} \quad \neg\Box P \longleftrightarrow \Diamond\neg P.$$

What makes it appropriate to call these operators "contextual" is the obvious dependence of the statement on the context of utterance for its truth value.[2] We might say that in the example the context *frames* the discussion by doing two things. (1) It determines what things can count as "here." (2) It determines which places are relevant to one another. In the other sorts of logic mentioned above the context can profitably be thought of as doing similar work, viz.: (1) It determines a set of things which will play a role analogous to the one played by places in our example. (2) It will determine a relation akin to "relevance of places to one another" in our example. We will call it, rather blandly, the *relatedness* relation.

4.1   The Propositional Modal Language and Models

4.1.1   The Language

We describe the syntax of a suitable language $\mathcal{L}_{ML}$ by indicating the changes that need to be made to the language $\mathcal{L}$ of propositional logic introduced in Chapter 1.

First, in addition to statement letters and the usual logical connectives, we need two new primitive symbols, $\Box$ and $\Diamond$.

Secondly, we must add a clause to the definition of statements of $\mathcal{L}$, to get the following:

DEFINITION 4.1 (DEFINITION OF STATEMENT OF $\mathcal{L}_{ML}$)
  1. Any statement letter is a statement.

---

[1] As one might expect, if one views $\Box$ and $\Diamond$ as quantifiers ranging over "places," and takes the places to be a *sort*, one finds many interesting relationships between modal logics and many sorted predicate logics. Many modal logics can be *reduced* to many sorted first-order logic (in the same sense in which many sorted logic can be reduced to unsorted logic). Some, e.g., so-called dynamic logics, cannot (though in this case a reduction to a many sorted higher-order logic is possible). An extended discussion of these matters can be found in Maria Manzano, *Extensions of First Order Logic*, (Cambridge Tracts in Theoretical Computer Science 19, Cambridge University Press 1996).

[2] Of course, this is not to deny that other sentences depend on context to fix their truth values. Whether or not "Keith plays the drums" is true depends on which of the many people named "Keith" is in question, and that is information usually provided by the context in which the sentence is uttered. To a first approximation, the difference between the cases is this: In this case we are relying on the context to fix the *sense* of the sentence—until we know which Keith is in question, we don't know what claim is being made. In a case like "It is raining here," we know perfectly well the meaning of the sentence, and yet are not in a position to know whether the claim made with it is true until the context fixes which "here" is in question. It is part of the very meaning of the word "here" that what it refers to depends on the context in which it is used.

2. If P and Q are statements, so too are $(P \wedge Q)$, $(P \vee Q)$, $(P \rightarrow Q)$, $\neg P$.

3. If P is a statement, then $\Box P$ and $\Diamond P$ are both statements.

4. Nothing else is a statement.

Notice that this doesn't merely mean that, for instance, $\Diamond(A \wedge B)$ is a statement of $\mathcal{L}_{ML}$, but that $(\Diamond A \wedge \Diamond B)$, $\Box(\Diamond A \wedge \Diamond B)$, and so on, are statements. The grammatical rules of $\mathcal{L}_{ML}$ do not merely permit the application of modal operators to statements of $\mathcal{L}$, they allow the result to be treated as a statement to which any of the other clauses of the definition apply.

Finally, we must modify the discussion of omitting parentheses from Chapter 1 by noting that, just as with negation (the other monadic operator in the language), the scope of $\Box$ and $\Diamond$ is to be read as being as short as possible. In particular, if the left member of a pair of parentheses or brackets is immediately preceded by a modal operator, then it cannot be omitted. So $\Diamond A \wedge B$ is the same statement as $(\Diamond A \wedge B)$, and must not be confused with $\Diamond(A \wedge B)$.

4.1.2 Interpretations

As one might expect from the introductory remarks for this chapter, the formal definition of an *interpretation* of a statement of $\mathcal{L}_{ML}$ involves both of the components provided by a context when it frames a discussion. Thus we make the

DEFINITION 4.2 A *frame* is a pair $\langle W, R \rangle$, where W is a non-empty set and R is a binary relation on W. We call the members of W its *points*, or the *localities* of the frame, and if xRy, we say that y is R-*related to* x.

The letter "W" is used because one often sees the points of a frame referred to as "worlds." This usage derives from the fact noted above that the other systems of logic currently under discussion are called "modal logics" because of their structural similarity to alethic modal logic, and it is thought by many that the appropriate sort of entity to play a role akin to a "place" in our contextual example above is a *possible world*. The relation R is often referred to as the "accessibility relation." We will avoid both these usages because they give rise to misleading pictures when discussing some of the other, non-alethic logics we are considering. We hope that the notion of *location* is in such common use in various metaphorical forms that it won't call to mind such misleading pictures; we have chosen the unfamiliar word "locality" as a reminder that being R-related is not always a spatial matter.

DEFINITION 4.3 A (propositional modal) *model* is a frame equipped with an *interpretation*. If $\mathcal{F} = \langle W, R \rangle$ is a frame, then an interpretation I in $\mathcal{F}$ is a function which assigns to each pair consisting of a point from W and a statement letter A an element of the set of truth values $\{\top, \bot\}$, i.e.,

$I : W \times SL \longrightarrow \{\top, \bot\}$, where SL is the set of statement letters. The triple $\mathcal{M} = \langle W, R, I \rangle$ is called a *model based on $\mathcal{F}$*.

Notice that what this amounts to is that I supplies a (propositional) valuation *for each point in W*: think of it as telling us *which atomic statements are true at each locality* in the frame.

   Suppose $\mathcal{M} = \langle W, R, I \rangle$ is a model. We can build a definition for the relation $\mathcal{M} \vDash_w P$, "P is true at w in the model $\mathcal{M}$," by adapting the definition of $[\![\cdot]\!]^V$ of classical propositional logic.

DEFINITION 4.4 (TRUTH AT A LOCALITY UNDER AN INTERPRETATION)
  1. If P is atomic, $\mathcal{M} \vDash_w P$ iff $I\langle w, P \rangle = \top$.

  2. The clauses for $\wedge, \vee, \rightarrow$, and $\neg$ are just the truth tables from Chapter 1, relativized to localities. So, $\mathcal{M} \vDash_w P \wedge Q$ iff $\mathcal{M} \vDash_w P$ and $\mathcal{M} \vDash_w Q$, and similarly for the others.

  3. $\mathcal{M} \vDash_w \Box P$ iff $\forall x \in W$, if wRx then $\mathcal{M} \vDash_x P$.

  4. $\mathcal{M} \vDash_w \Diamond P$ iff $\exists x \in W$ such that wRx and $\mathcal{M} \vDash_x P$.

   We will also say that a statement P is *true in a model* $\mathcal{M} = \langle W, R, I \rangle$ (and will write $\mathcal{M} \vDash P$) if $\mathcal{M} \vDash_w P$ for all $w \in W$. P is *valid in a frame* $\mathcal{F} = \langle W, R \rangle$ (written $\mathcal{F} \vDash P$) if $\mathcal{M} \vDash P$ for all $\mathcal{M}$ based on $\mathcal{F}$. A *schema* is true in a model (or valid in a frame) if all instances of the schema have that property. If Γ is a set of statements, we will write $\mathcal{M} \vDash \Gamma$ (or $\mathcal{F} \vDash \Gamma$) if each element of Γ is true in $\mathcal{M}$ (or valid in $\mathcal{F}$).

   A good way to familiarize oneself with the semantics is to show that certain schemes are valid while others are not. For instance,

PROPOSITION 4.1 $\Box(P \vee \neg P)$ *and* $\Box(P \rightarrow Q) \rightarrow (\Box P \rightarrow \Box Q)$ *are true in all models, hence valid in all frames.*

   This can be shown as follows. (1) It is clear from the definition of truth at a locality that, whatever statement of $\mathcal{L}_{\mathrm{ML}}$ P happens to be, it will get either the value $\top$ or $\bot$ at each locality. Since $P \vee \neg P$ is a classical tautology, and since at each locality the truth value of truth-functional formulas is calculated according to the usual classical truth tables, it is true at all points in all models. Therefore for any w in any $\mathcal{M}$, $\mathcal{M} \vDash_x P \vee \neg P$ for all x such that wRx. (2) Suppose $\mathcal{M} \vDash_w \Box(P \rightarrow Q)$ and $\mathcal{M} \vDash_w \Box P$. Let x be any locality such that wRx. Then $\mathcal{M} \vDash_x P$ and $\mathcal{M} \vDash_x P \rightarrow Q$, so $\mathcal{M} \vDash_x Q$, by the definition of the truth of an $\rightarrow$-statement at a locality. So $\mathcal{M} \vDash_w \Box Q$.

EXERCISES 4.1.1
Show that the following statements are valid in all frames.

  1. $\Diamond(P \rightarrow Q) \rightarrow (\Box P \rightarrow \Diamond Q)$.

  2. $\Box(P \rightarrow Q) \rightarrow (\Diamond P \rightarrow \Diamond Q)$.

*   3. $\Box(P \wedge Q) \longleftrightarrow (\Box P \wedge \Box Q)$.

     4. $\Diamond(P \vee Q) \longleftrightarrow (\Diamond P \vee \Diamond Q)$.

Conversely, to show that a schema is *not valid*, it suffices to supply an instance of the schema, and a point in a model in which the instance is false. Some caution needs to be exercised here, since invalid schemas can have valid instances. (For instance, $B \to B$ is an instance of $P \to Q$, but the former is obviously valid while the latter is obviously not. Indeed, every valid conditional statement is an instance of this invalid schema.) It is therefore a good idea to construct one's counterexamples to the validity of schemas by referring to sentence letters (by using A, B, C, etc.) rather than using variables ranging over formulas (i.e., P, Q, etc.).

PROPOSITION 4.2 $\Diamond(P \vee \neg P)$ *and* $\Box P \to P$ *are not valid schemas.*

We can prove these claims as follows. (1) Let $W = \{w\}$ and $R = \varnothing$. Then for *any* interpretation I, $\mathcal{M} \not\models_w \Diamond(A \vee \neg A)$, because there is no x such that wRx. (2) (We could use the same model as was used in (1), but this one might be clearer.) Put $W = \{x, y\}$, let wRx but *not* wRw, xRx, nor xRw. Finally, let $I(x, A) = \top$ but $I(w, A) = \bot$. Then $\mathcal{M} \models_w \Box A$, since $\mathcal{M} \models_x A$ and x is the *only* locality such that wRx. However, $\mathcal{M} \not\models_w A$, so $\mathcal{M} \not\models_w \Box A \to A$.

EXERCISES 4.1.2
    1. Show that the following formulas are not valid in all frames.

        (a) $\Box A \to \Box\Box A$.
        (b) $\Box(A \to B) \to (\Box A \to \Diamond B)$.
        (c) $\Diamond A \to \Box A$.
    *   (d) $\Box(A \vee B) \to (\Box A \vee \Box B)$.

*   2. Show that $\Diamond(A \vee \neg A)$ and $\Box A \to \Diamond A$ have exactly the same models.

     3. Describe a frame in which $\Box(A \wedge \neg A)$ is valid.

The following proposition gathers together some useful facts which we will need later. The (straightforward) proofs are left as exercises.

PROPOSITION 4.3 *For any model* $\mathcal{M}$,

     1. *If P is a truth-functional tautology, then* $\mathcal{M} \models P$.

     2. *If $\mathcal{M} \models P$ and $\mathcal{M} \models P \to Q$, then* $\mathcal{M} \models Q$.

     3. *If $\mathcal{M} \models P$, then* $\mathcal{M} \models \Box P$.

     4. *Parts (1)–(3) of this proposition still hold if $\mathcal{M}$ is replaced by $\mathcal{F}$.*

4.1.3   Classes of Frames and Different Logics

A significant fact, one which lies behind the potential of these formal semantics to serve as a device for interpreting the operators in several different ways, is that there is often an interesting relationship between *properties of the relation R* and *schemas of $\mathcal{L}_{ML}$*. For instance,

PROPOSITION 4.4 *Let $\mathcal{F} = \langle W, R \rangle$ be a frame. Then*

1. *R is reflexive (i.e., $\forall w\,(wRw)$) iff $\Box P \to P$ is valid in $\mathcal{F}$.*

2. *R is transitive (i.e., $\forall x, y, z (xRy \wedge yRz \to xRz)$) iff $\Box P \to \Box\Box P$ is valid in $\mathcal{F}$.*

To see (1), suppose R is reflexive and, for some interpretation I, $\mathcal{M} \vDash_w \Box P$. Since R is reflexive, wRw and so $\mathcal{M} \vDash_w P$. Conversely, suppose $\Box P \to P$ is valid in $\mathcal{P}$. Suppose not(wRw). Let I be an interpretation such that $I(w, A) = \top$ for all and only x such that wRx. Then $\mathcal{M} \vDash_w \Box A$, but $\mathcal{M} \nvDash_w A$. So $\mathcal{M} \nvDash_w \Box A \to A$, hence $\mathcal{M} \nvDash \Box A \to A$, a contradiction.

For (2), suppose R is transitive and, for some interpretation I, $\mathcal{M} \vDash_w \Box P$. We need to show $\mathcal{M} \vDash_w \Box\Box P$. That is, we need to show that if wRx, then $\mathcal{M} \vDash_x \Box P$. Which is to say, we need to show that if xRy, then (if wRx then $\mathcal{M} \vDash_y P$). But if wRx and xRy, then wRy by transitivity. So $\mathcal{M} \vDash_y P$, since $\mathcal{M} \vDash_w \Box P$. Conversely, suppose $\mathcal{F} = \langle W, R \rangle$ and $\Box P \to \Box\Box P$ is valid in $\mathcal{F}$. Suppose wRx and xRy, but not wRy. Let I be a valuation such that $I(x, A) = \top$ iff wRz. Then $\mathcal{M} \vDash_w \Box A$ and $\mathcal{M} \nvDash_y A$. But since xRy, $\mathcal{M} \nvDash_x \Box A$, so $\mathcal{M} \nvDash_w \Box\Box A$, a contradiction.

EXERCISES 4.1.3
Show that for $\mathcal{F} = \langle W, R \rangle$:

*   1. *R is serial (i.e., $\forall w \exists x (wRx)$) iff $\Box P \to \Diamond P$ is valid in $\mathcal{F}$.*

2. *R is symmetric (i.e., $\forall w, x (wRx \to xRw)$) iff $P \to \Box\Diamond P$ is valid in $\mathcal{F}$.*

3. *R is euclidean (i.e., $\forall w, x, y (wRx \wedge wRy \to xRy)$) iff $\Diamond P \to \Box\Diamond P$ is valid in $\mathcal{F}$.*

4. Find properties of R which are necessary and sufficient for R to validate each of the schemas: $P \to \Box P$; $\Box(P \wedge \neg P)$.

Results like these help to explain why this semantics is so useful and popular. Sometimes schemes are antecedently thought to be important, perhaps because they seem an obvious feature of a correct analysis of some interesting notion. For instance, if a statement is *necessarily true*, then whatever else can be said about it, it seems the least we will be able to say is that it is true. Hence, if $\Box P$ is interpreted to mean that P is necessarily true, then wherever $\Box P$ is true P must be true as well. Hence, $\Box P \to P$ should be valid. It follows from the proposition above that not every frame can be one appropriate for the analysis of necessary truth—we can safely restrict attention to those frames in which the R is reflexive. Conversely, if we are analyzing a notion where we can be confident that a semantics of this sort is appropriate and where the "localities" should be related in a way which is transitive, then we will know that the notion is one governed by the principle that $\Box P \rightarrow \Box\Box P$. In epistemic logic, for instance, one might take the points to be "states of information" and xRy to mean that y is a state we could get to from x by further investigation. That relation should clearly be transitive, so whatever notion $\Box$ formalizes on this interpretation—some might suggest that it captures the property of *being known*, though others would not agree—must obey that principle.

It is sometimes useful to be able to discuss a particular *class* of frames, for instance all the frames where R is reflexive. Let C be such a class. We write $C \vDash P$ if P is valid in every $\mathcal{F} \in C$.

It is also useful to have available an abstract notion of a "logic" as simply a set of statements which has certain useful properties.

DEFINITION 4.5 A *contextual logic* (which we shall simply call *a logic*) is a set Λ of statements of $\mathcal{L}_{\mathrm{ML}}$ such that:

1. Λ includes all classical propositional tautologies.

2. If P and $P \rightarrow Q$ are both in Λ, then so too is Q. (As we say, Λ is *closed under modus ponens*.)

Note that the set of classical propositional tautologies is itself a logic. So, too, is the set of all statements of $\mathcal{L}_{\mathrm{ML}}$. We call a logic Λ *smaller* than another logic Φ if $\Lambda \subseteq \Phi$.

EXERCISES 4.1.4
Show that the intersection of a non-empty set of logics is itself a logic. Show that for any set of statements of $\mathcal{L}_{\mathrm{ML}}$, there is a (unique) smallest logic which contains every member of that set of statements. [Hint: use the first fact to prove the second.]

The logic K is the smallest logic which contains every instance of the schema

$$\Box(P \rightarrow Q) \rightarrow (\Box P \rightarrow \Box Q) \tag{K}$$

which is *also* such that for any P, if P is in the logic, then so too is $\Box P$. (When a logic meets this latter condition, we say that it is *closed under the rule of necessitation*.) Any logic which includes all instances of the schema (K) and which is closed under necessitation is called a *normal modal logic*. So K is the intersection of all the normal modal logics.

It has become customary to use the notation

$$KS_1 \ldots S_n$$

to refer to the smallest normal modal logic containing the schemas $S_1, \ldots, S_n$. Set theoretically, this logic is:

$$\bigcap \{\Lambda | \Lambda \text{ is normal and all instances of } S_1, \ldots, S_n \text{ are in } \Lambda\}.$$

Many schemas have their own names. The names by now are little more than historical curiosities, but they are still widely used in the philosophical literature, so we will continue to use them here. Some examples:

$$\Box P \to \Diamond P \tag{D}$$

$$\Box P \to P \tag{T}$$

$$\Box P \to \Box\Box P \tag{4}$$

$$P \to \Box\Diamond P \tag{B}$$

$$\Diamond P \to \Box\Diamond P \tag{5}$$

$$\Box(P \wedge \Box P \to Q) \vee \Box(Q \wedge \Box Q \to P) \tag{L}$$

$$\Box(\Box P \to P) \to \Box P. \tag{W}$$

Some logics that are often discussed under a particular name include:

$$S4 = KT4$$

$$S5 = KT4B$$

$$G = KW$$

$$K4.3 = K4L$$

$$S4.3 = KT4L.$$

We say that a logic Λ is *sound* with respect to a class of frames C if

$$P \in \Lambda \quad \text{implies} \quad C \vDash P,$$

and that it is *complete* with respect to C if

$$C \vDash P \quad \text{implies} \quad P \in \Lambda.$$

The logic K, the smallest normal modal logic, is both *sound and complete* with respect to the *class of all frames.* Soundness follows directly from Exercise 4.1 and Proposition 4.3.

To establish completeness is a somewhat more complex undertaking. We will sketch one method of proving it, leaving some of the detail-checking as a series of exercises for intrepid readers. The technique we use will be useful below when considering logics other than K, so we will state things in ways slightly more general than necessary for our immediate purposes.

DEFINITION 4.6 (TERMINOLOGY) We will refer to the set containing precisely the statements of $\mathcal{L}_{\text{ML}}$ as **sent**. If $S \subseteq$ **sent**, we will write $S^{\Box}$ for $\{P \mid \Box P \in S\}$. A logic Λ is *consistent* if there is no P such that $P \in \Lambda$ and $\neg P \in \Lambda$. We will say that a set of statements $S \subseteq$ **sent** is a *maximal consistent set for the logic* Λ if:

1. $\Lambda \subseteq S$

2. There is no P in $\mathcal{L}_{\text{ML}}$ such that both $P \in S$ and $\neg P \in S$.

3. If T meets conditions (1) and (2) and $S \subseteq T$, then $S = T$.

A set S of statements is said to be a *maximal consistent* (simpliciter, i.e., not relative to any particular logic Λ) if it is consistent and for any consistent set T, if $S \subseteq T$, then $S = T$.

EXERCISES 4.1.5
Establish the following claims.

1. If $P \notin \Lambda$, there is a maximal consistent set T such that $\Lambda \subseteq T$ and $P \notin T$. [Hint: Consider the members of **sent** as an (obviously infinite) sequence $P_1, P_2, \ldots$. Recursively define the following sequence: $\Lambda^0 = \Lambda \cup \{\neg P\}$; $\Lambda^{n+1} = \Lambda^n \cup \{P_n\}$ if that set is consistent, and $\Lambda^{n+1} = \Lambda^n$ otherwise. Let $\Lambda^* = \bigcup\{\Lambda^n \mid n \in \mathbb{N}\}$. Show that each Λ^n is consistent, and deduce that Λ^* is consistent, too. Verify that Λ^* has the required properties.]

* 2. If S is a normal modal logic, then so is $S^\square$.

3. For any logic Λ and any statement P, $\square P \in \Lambda$ if and only if $P \in T$ for each maximal consistent set T such that $\Lambda^\square \subseteq T$. [Hint: One direction is obvious. For the other direction, use (1) and (2).]

The *Canonical Frame for* Λ, $\mathcal{F}_\Lambda$, is the frame which results by letting the set of points W be the set of maximal consistent sets for Λ, and letting two such sets s and t be R-related if and only if $s^\square \subseteq t$ (i.e., sRt if and only if $\square P \in s$ implies $P \in t$ for every statement P). The *Canonical Interpretation for* Λ is the interpretation I_Λ in $\mathcal{F}_\Lambda$ such that $I_\Lambda(s, A) = \top$ if and only if $A \in \Lambda$.

THEOREM 4.5 (FUNDAMENTAL LEMMA)
1. *For $s \in W$ and any statement P, $I_\Lambda(s, P) = \top$ if and only if $P \in s$.*

2. $\mathcal{F}_\Lambda \vDash P$ *if and only if $P \in \Lambda$.*

The first assertion is proved by induction on the formation of P. For atomic statements, it is true by definition, while for truth-functional P it follows from the fact that each member of W is a maximal consistent set. Suppose that the result holds for Q. Then

$$I_\Lambda(s, P) = \top \iff \forall t(uRt \implies I_\Lambda(t, Q) = \top)$$
$$\iff \forall t(u^\square \subseteq t \implies Q \in t) \quad (*)$$
$$\iff Q \in u^\square \text{ by exercise 3}$$
$$\iff \square Q \in u.$$

The step marked ($*$) is justified as follows: we are supposing that the result holds for Q. If $u^\square \subseteq t$, then uRt by the definition of R, hence $I_\Lambda(t, Q) = \top$, and so $Q \in t$ by the supposition.

The case for $\Diamond Q$ is left as an exercise.

For the second assertion, suppose $P \in \Lambda$. Then $P \in s$ for all s in W, so $\mathcal{F}_\Lambda \vDash P$ by (1). Conversely, if $P \notin \Lambda$ then, by exercise 1, there is a maximal consistent set s for Λ such that $P \notin s$. So $I_\Lambda(s, P) = \bot$, by (1), whence $\mathcal{F}_\Lambda \nvDash P$.

As a consequence, we obtain the

THEOREM 4.6 (COMPLETENESS THEOREM FOR K)
If P is valid in all frames, then $P \in K$.

For if P is valid in all frames, then P is valid in $\mathcal{F}_K$, so $P \in K$ by the fundamental lemma.

Having established the soundness and completeness of K for the class of all frames, we can use the results given at the end of the preceding section (and related results for other schemas) to get many soundness and completeness results with little additional effort. For instance, KT is sound and complete for the class of *reflexive* frames. The soundness result is immediate from the definitions of KT and of the relevant class of frames, together with proposition 4.4. To establish completeness, we need only to show that $\mathcal{F}_{KT}$ is reflexive. This is established as follows: KT includes the scheme $\square P \to P$. By the definition of R, sRs if and only if $\square P \in s$ implies $P \in s$ for every statement P. The points in W are maximal consistent sets, and every such set for KT will include $\square P \to P$, so this is clearly the case.

Similarly, we can show that $S4 = KT4$ is sound and complete with respect to the class of *reflexive and transitive* frames, $S5 = KT4B$ with respect to the class of *reflexive, transitive and symmetric* frames (i.e., those for which R is an *equivalence* relation), and so on.

EXERCISES 4.1.6
Show that

*   1. $\mathcal{F}_{K4}$ is transitive.

     2. $\mathcal{F}_{K5}$ is symmetric.

     3. $\mathcal{F}_{KD}$ is serial.

Once we have such soundness and completeness results, we have the great convenience of being able to choose whether to reason about conditions on logics or about the properties of R defining the relevant C when we try to show things like: $K45 = KB5$. In that case, it is much easier to reason about the properties of R. Suppose R is transitive and symmetric, and that sRt and sRu. By symmetry, tRs, so by transitivity tRu, and so R is euclidean. Next suppose that R is symmetric and euclidean and that

sRt and tRu. By symmetry, tRs, so sRu by euclideanness, and so R is also transitive.

EXERCISES 4.1.7
Show $S5 = KDB4 = KDB5 = KT5$.

REMARK 4.1

1. S5 is probably the best known contextual logic. This is because it is a good candidate for characterizing *logical necessity*, using Leibniz's suggestion that a sentence is necessarily true if it is true in *all possible worlds* and that it is possibly true if it is true in *at least one possible world*. As a first step to making this work, we need only consider the localities in a frame to be possible worlds. Note that S5 is sound and complete for the class of all frames in which R is an equivalence relation, which isn't the same as Leibniz's suggestion. However, S5 is also sound and complete with respect to the class of frames in which R is the *universal relation* (i.e., $\forall x, y (xRy)$). (This is not hard to show: first, a universal relation is an equivalence relation. To see the converse, suppose that $\nvDash_{S5} P$. Then there is an appropriate model in which P fails to hold in some world, w, say. We can turn this model into one in which R is universal by deleting all the worlds not accessible to w. Since the truth value of P in any world depends only on truth values in that world and in worlds R-related to w, P remains false in w. Accordingly, there is an $\mathcal{M}$ with R a universal relation such that $\mathcal{M} \nvDash P$.)

2. It is sometimes suggested that S4 is a good candidate for an epistemic logic, and that we can read $\Box P$ in S4 as the statement that "P is known."

3. The logic K4 is sometimes recommended as a doxastic logic, where $\Box P$ can be read as "it is believed that P." Note that this differs from S4 in that $\Box P \rightarrow P$, one of the schemes used to define S4, does not appear in K4—one wouldn't want the claim "if P is believed, then P" to be valid, whereas the claim "if P is known, then P" is much more plausible.

4. Finally, the schema (D) is a principle often argued to be valid in deontic reasoning, where $\Box P$ is interpreted as "P is obligatory" and $\Diamond P$ is interpreted as "P is permissible." KD is therefore recommended by some as a formalization of deontic logic.

EXERCISES 4.1.8
Each of the above logics corresponds to a particular class of frames. If it is sensible to regard the points of a frame for alethic modal logic as *possible worlds*, what would be a similarly sensible way to regard the points for each of epistemic, doxastic, and deontic logic?

   We mention in passing that while the correspondence between schemas involving $\Box$ and $\Diamond$ and easily described (first-order) properties of the relation

R in a class of frames is an important and useful feature of the semantics for contextual logics, some important schemes do not have a class of models characterized by any set of first-order sentences governing the relation R, simple or otherwise. Notable examples are

$$\Box(\Box P \rightarrow P) \rightarrow \Box P, \tag{W}$$

which is important in the *provability logic* we will discuss below, and *Mc-Kinsey's scheme*,

$$\Box\Diamond P \rightarrow \Diamond\Box P. \tag{M}$$

In cases such as this, the canonical model for the logic will indeed allow us to prove a completeness result, i.e. if $\mathcal{F}_\Lambda \vDash P$, then $P \in \Lambda$, but there will be $P \in \Lambda$ which are not valid in $\mathcal{F}_\Lambda$.

Conversely, there are also some natural first-order properties that do not correspond to any schema, for instance *irreflexivity* ($\forall x(\neg xRx)$), *anti-symmetry* ($\forall x, y(xRy \wedge yRx \rightarrow x = y)$), and *asymmetry* ($\forall x, y(xRy \rightarrow \neg yRx)$). The proofs of such results are quite difficult, and go beyond the scope of this book.[3]

4.2   Trees for Contextual Logics

As indicated by the examples with which this chapter began, we think of the truth values of contextual statements as being implicitly determined by contexts. This idea leads us to adopt the following tree rules for contextual statements. First, the

RULE 4.1 ($\Diamond$-RULE) If $\Diamond P$ occurs at some node in some locality in a tree, it can be ticked and a *new locality* can be introduced on every open path running through it, and P asserted at the new locality.

$$\frac{\Diamond P}{P}$$

Here we have incorporated a new device into our trees, namely that of *introducing a new point* or *moving from one locality to another*. We will in-dicate such a move by means of a solid horizontal line: thus two statements in a given path not separated by a horizontal line are said to be *at the same point* or *in the same locality*: it follows that a tree containing n horizontal lines contains $n + 1$ localities. It is important to understand that each appli-cation of the $\Diamond$ rule to statements appearing at the same point *requires the*

---

[3]For more information about the topics in this section, see chapters 1–4 of Robert Gold-blatt, *Logics of Time and Computation*, Second Edition (Stanford: CSLI Lecture Notes 7, 1992).

introduction of a separate and independent new locality. This is illustrated by the following example:

$$\Diamond P$$
$$\Diamond Q$$

$$P \qquad Q$$

Here it is important to note that *the fork through two (or more) horizontal lines does* not *indicate the splitting of the given path into two (or more) paths*; it signifies merely the introduction of two (or more) independent localities *within a single path.* Hence if *any one* of these localities closes, i.e., if all the paths at that point close, then the original path closes. In other words, *all* the localities on a path must be open for the path to be open. Thus, for example,

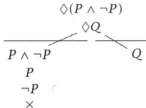

$$\Diamond(P \wedge \neg P)$$
$$\Diamond Q$$

$$P \wedge \neg P \qquad\qquad Q$$
$$P$$
$$\neg P$$
$$\times$$

is a closed tree, because it includes a single path which is closed.

Our second new rule is the

RULE 4.2 (□-RULE) If □P occurs at a node in some locality in a tree, and a *new locality* is introduced on some path running through it, then P may be asserted at the new locality (provided it doesn't already occur there).

$$\Box P$$
$$\cdots\cdots$$
$$P$$

Note that in presenting these rules a solid line will indicate that it is permissible to introduce a new locality, while a broken line means only that *if some other rule allows us to introduce a new locality*, then the rule in question allows us to assert something in it.

We also adopt the

RULE 4.3 (INTERCHANGE RULES) Tick an occurrence of $\neg\Diamond P$ occupying a node and enter $\Box\neg P$, in the same locality, at the foot of each open path containing the ticked node. Tick an occurrence of $\neg\Box P$ occupying a node and enter $\Diamond\neg P$, in the same locality, at the foot of each open path containing the ticked node.

$$\neg\Diamond P \quad ✔ \qquad \neg\Box P \quad ✔$$

$$\Box\neg P \qquad\qquad \Diamond\neg P$$

Finally, we declare a path to be closed only when it contains some state-ment and its negation *not separated by a horizontal line*, that is, *in the same locality.*

We write ■ for the system of tree rules consisting of the rules for the propositional operators, the □ and ◇ rules, the interchange rules, and the new rule for closing a path. This system is called *basic contextual logic.*

Let us use these new tree rules to establish some simple properties of the system. First, we show that the statement

$$\Box(P \to Q) \to (\Box P \to \Box Q)$$

is ■-valid.

$$\neg[\Box(P \to Q) \to (\Box P \to \Box Q)] \qquad ✔$$
$$\Box(P \to Q) \qquad (\#)$$
$$\neg(\Box P \to \Box Q) \qquad ✔$$
$$\Box P \qquad (*)$$
$$\neg\Box Q \qquad ✔$$
$$\Diamond\neg Q \qquad (†)$$
$$\rule{8cm}{0.4pt}$$
$$\neg Q \qquad (‡)$$
$$P \qquad (**)$$
$$P \to Q \qquad (\#\#)✔$$

$$\neg P \qquad\qquad\qquad\qquad Q$$
$$\times \qquad\qquad\qquad\qquad \times$$

Here (‡) is derived from (†) by the ◇-rule, and (**) from (*), as well as (##) from (#) by the □-rule.

Next, we show that, if P is ■-valid, then so is $\Box P$, and conversely. For the ■-validity of P means that there is a closed tree with initial statement $\neg P$:

$$\neg P$$
$$(*) \qquad \vdots$$
$$\times$$

This yields a closed tree

$$\neg\Box P \quad ✔$$
$$\Diamond\neg P$$
$$\rule{3cm}{0.4pt}$$
$$\neg P$$
$$(*) \qquad \vdots$$
$$\times$$

Here the nodes below the horizontal line reproduce the tree (*). So $\Box P$ is ■-valid.

Conversely, suppose that $\Box P$ is valid. Then there is a closed tree

$$\neg\Box P$$

$$(**) \qquad \vdots$$

$$\times$$

Now the only rule applicable to $\neg\Box P$ is the appropriate interchange rule, so that the tree $(**)$ must start with

$$\neg\Box P \ \checkmark$$
$$\Diamond\neg P$$

$$\vdots$$

$$\times$$

Similarly, the only rule applicable to $\Diamond\neg P$ is the $\Diamond$-rule, so $(**)$ must look like:

$$\neg\Box P \ \checkmark$$
$$\Diamond\neg P$$
$$\overline{\qquad\qquad}$$
$$\neg P$$

$$\vdots$$

$$\times$$

But then the portion of this tree below the horizontal line is a closed tree with initial statement $\neg P$. Accordingly P is ■-valid.

EXERCISES 4.2.1
1. By constructing closed trees, establish the validity of the statements

  * (a) $\Box(P \wedge Q) \longleftrightarrow \Box P \wedge \Box Q$.
    (b) $\Box P \rightarrow \Box(P \vee Q)$.
  * (c) $(\Box P \rightarrow \Diamond Q) \rightarrow \neg\Box\bot$ (Here $\bot$ is any contradiction, e.g. $A \wedge \neg A$).

2. Show that, if $\Box P \vee \Box Q$ is valid, then at least one of P and Q is valid. (Hint: consider a closed tree with initial statement $\neg(\Box P \vee \Box Q)$ and apply the same sort of analysis as was applied to the tree $(**)$ above.)

4.2.1 Proving Correctness for ■

The examples of the previous section are useful in proving the

THEOREM 4.7
The class of ■-valid sentences of $\mathcal{L}_{ML}$ is a normal modal logic. Hence K is included in ■.

For we have just shown that all instances of K are valid and that the set of ■–validities is closed under the rule of necessitation. That every truth functional validity is included follows from the fact that all the rules for classical propositional trees are included in basic contextual logic. To complete the proof, it suffices to show that the class of ■-validities is closed under modus ponens. But we have, in effect, already proved this in Chapter 1. What needs to be shown is that if there is a closed tree beginning with $\neg(P \rightarrow Q)$ and a closed tree beginning with $\neg P$, then there is a closed tree beginning with $\neg Q$. In the course of proving the Strengthened Soundness Theorem for PC, we employed "Extended Trees" for classical propositional logic, and in the proof of theorem 1.9 showed how to construct an extended tree beginning with $\neg Q$ which closes. But it follows from the adequacy of the tree method without LEM for trees that the same formulas are provable with trees and with extended trees in classical propositional logic, so the use of LEM for trees is dispensable, and so the system without LEM is also closed under modus ponens. Since all the classical propositional tree rules are also rules of ■, we can conclude that our current system is closed under MP, too.

Note that all ■–trees will terminate. There can be at most finitely many occurrences of $\Diamond$ or $\neg\Box$ in any finite set of sentences of $\mathcal{L}_{ML}$, and each tree begins with such a finite set. This implies that only finitely many new points may be introduced on any such tree. For such new points arise only through the application of the $\Diamond$-rule, each such application will be due to the presence of either $\Diamond$ or $\neg\Box$ somewhere in the original set, we will have ticked off the original sentence when the $\Diamond$-rule is applied, and there can be at most finitely many open paths running through the node on which any $\Diamond$ formula occurs. This means that the only rule which does not result in the original formula being ticked, the $\Box$ rule, will be applied at most finitely many times for each of the finitely many $\Box$ formulas occurring on the tree, because of the provision that it not be applied to put a statement at a locality where it already occurs. The only rules for which the statements in the set(s) of conclusions are not shorter than the premise are the interchange rules. But these result in statements which are no longer, and to which other rules which do reduce the length of statements are applicable. Finally, as we saw in Chapter 1, the process of making all possible applications of the truth-functional tree rules to a finite set of statements always terminates, and so there can be only finitely many applications of these rules at any given point on any ■–tree. Thus the process of constructing a tree will eventually reach the stage where the unticked statements occupying nodes of the tree are literals, or are $\Box$ sentences for which all allowable applications have already been made.

It is also not difficult to establish the

THEOREM 4.8 (CORRECTNESS OF BASIC CONTEXTUAL LOGIC)
Any ■-valid statement is true under every interpretation.

This can be established in much the same way as correctness was proved for propositional trees in section 1.2.

We begin by extending the definition of *correctness of a rule*. For the rules for the truth-functional connectives, or for the interchange rules, we say that it is *correct* if whenever its premise holds under a given interpretation, all the members in at least one of its sets of conclusions also hold under that interpretation. For the □- and ◊-rules, we say that either is correct if whenever its premise is true in a locality in some interpretation, its conclusion holds under the same interpretation *at every (respectively, some) locality R-related to the given one.* It is easily shown that all the rules are correct in this sense.

When discussing basic contextual logic, we will say the statements on a path are true *at appropriate localities in an interpretation I* if all the statements occupying nodes in a single locality on the tree (i.e. all those above the first horizontal line (if any), or all those between any pair of horizontal lines, or all those below a bottom horizontal line (if any)) are true at a single point on that interpretation; and these localities are *R*-related in *I* whenever two localities on the path are separated by a single horizontal line.

If a path is closed on a tree for basic contextual logic, a statement and its negation both must occur on nodes occurring on it in the same locality, so that there can be no interpretation on which all statements occurring on the path are true in the appropriate localities of the frame. So if all the statements on a path ψ are true in the appropriate localities under some interpretation, then ψ is open. Let I be an interpretation under which P is true. Then it follows from the correctness of the rules of basic contextual logic that if a tree τ has the property

($*$) τ starts with P and contains a path ψ such that all statements occupying nodes of ψ are true in the appropriate localities under I,

then so does any tree τ^* obtained from τ by applying a tree rule. So any tree starting with P will have an open path. So, if Q is ■-valid, i.e., if $\neg Q$ has a closed tree, $\neg Q$ is not satisfiable, and so Q is true under every interpretation.

4.2.2 Counterexamples

As in the case of classical propositional logic, the tree method for contextual logic can be used to generate *counterexamples* or *countermodels*, that is, interpretations in which invalid statements are false at some locality. We give a couple of examples which will serve to indicate the general procedure.

First, we will find a countermodel for $\Box A \to \Box\Box A$. Here we generate the following finished tree:

$$\neg(\Box A \to \Box\Box A) \; ✔$$
$$1 \qquad \Box A$$
$$\neg\Box\Box A \qquad ✔$$
$$\Diamond\neg\Box A$$

$$\neg\Box A \qquad ✔$$
$$2 \qquad A$$
$$\Diamond\neg A$$

$$3 \qquad \neg A$$

Since this tree contains *two* horizontal lines, it contains *three* localities which we label 1, 2, 3, and each locality is R-related to the one immediately below it. This may be represented by a diagram

$$1 \longrightarrow 2 \longrightarrow 3$$

in which the nodes represent localities and each arrow goes from a locality to the only one R-related to it. The diagram determines a frame $\mathcal{F} = \langle W, R \rangle$ in which $W = \{1, 2, 3\}$ and $R = \{\langle 1, 2 \rangle, \langle 2, 3 \rangle\}$. The countermodel will be an interpretation I in $\mathcal{F}$ making the initial statement of the tree false at the locality in which it appears. As with propositional trees we allow the truth values assigned to statement letters to be determined by whether they occur positively or negatively, only now this assignment will also depend on the *locality* in which they occur. We see that, in the tree above, A occurs positively at locality 2 and negatively at locality 3. So in our interpretation I we should define $I(2, A) = \top, I(3, A) = \bot$. (The value of $I(1, A)$ is irrelevant.) Our interpretation may then be displayed by the diagram

$$\top \qquad \bot$$
$$1 \longrightarrow 2 \longrightarrow 3$$

Let us verify that $\Box A \to \Box\Box A$ is false under I at locality 1. Since 2 is the only point R-related to 1, and $I(2, A) = \top$, it follows that $I(1, \Box A) = \top$. On the other hand, since 3 is a point R-related to 2, and $I(3, A) = \bot$, it follows that $I(2, \Box A) = \bot$. But this means that $I(1, \Box\Box A) = \bot$. Therefore $I(1, \Box A \to \Box\Box A) = \bot$, as claimed. So I is a countermodel for $\Box A \to \Box\Box A$.

Next, we find a countermodel for $\Box(A \lor B) \to \Box A \lor \Box B$. In this case we generate the following finished tree:

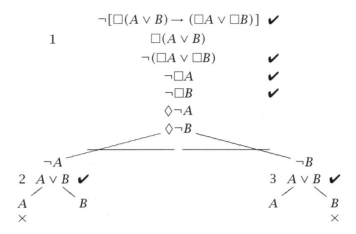

In this case the diagram of the interpretation I determined by the tree is, writing $\bot, \top$ and $\top, \bot$ for the truth values assigned to A, B respectively at points 2 and 3,

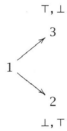

Let us verify that $\Box(A \lor B) \to \Box A \lor \Box B$ is false under I in locality 1. To begin with, since $I(2, A \lor B) = I(3, A \lor B) = \top$, and 2 and 3 are the only localities R-related to 1, it follows that $I(1, \Box(A \lor B)) = \top$. On the other hand, since $I(2, A) = I(3, B) = \bot$, it follows that $I(1, \Box A) = I(1, \Box B) = \bot$. Therefore $I(1, \Box A \lor \Box B) = \bot$, and so $I(1, \Box(A \lor B) \to (\Box A \lor \Box B)) = \bot$ as claimed.

EXERCISES 4.2.2

1. In a way similar to the two examples above, construct countermodels to the following statements:

    (a) $\Box A \to A$.

    (b) $A \to \Box A$.

*   (c) $\Box A \to \Diamond A$.

    (d) $\Diamond \Box A \to A$.

*   (e) $\Box(\Box A \to A) \to \Box A$.

2. Show that $\Box A \to \Box\Box A$ is true in the countermodel for $\Box A \to A$.

4.2.3   Proving Adequacy for ■

Just as we were able to show the correctness of ■-trees by suitably modifying the proof for classical propositional logic, so we show its adequacy by adapting the propositional proof. The proof will again essentially involve showing that a suitable interpretation can be "read off" from a complete open path on a tree.

However, we will need to adopt a notion from the metatheoretical proofs for predicate logic from Chapter 2. We will call a tree *systematic* if all truth-functional statements in any of its points are decomposed, and all possible applications of interchange rules are made, before any application of the ◇-rule to shift to another locality on the tree. We need this notion because in a non-systematic tree it is possible that, as a result of having prematurely shifted to a different locality by application of the ◇-rule, there will be an open path which includes undecomposed truth-functional formulas which we cannot decompose. Thus we could have a tree to which we can no longer apply rules, and which includes an open path, but which does not include a completed open path (i.e., a path on which all unchecked statements are literals, or are □-sentences to which we can no longer apply the □-rule).

We will say that a rule is *complete* if the truth of all the members of at least one of its sets of conclusions at appropriate points in some valuation is sufficient to guarantee the truth of its premise at the appropriate point in the same valuation. For the □-rule, we will say that, for each path on which □P occurs, its set of conclusions is composed of all occurrences of P at any point R-related to the locality of that occurrence of □P. It is clear that all the rules for ■-trees other than the □-rule are complete. For the truth-functional rules, this follows from the completeness of the rules noted in Chapter 1, together with the observation that the appropriate localities for the premises and conclusion will be the same in these cases. For the interchange rules and the diamond rule, this is obvious. Finally, in any *finished* tree, □ is complete, for in that case P will occur at every point R-related to the locality where □P occurs which is on an open path.

So suppose that there is an open path on a completed systematic tree starting with a set of statements S. Consider the interpretation under which the set of points consists of all the localities on that path, two localities on the path are R-related if and only if they are separated by exactly one horizontal line, and each statement letter is true at a locality if and only if it occupies a node in that locality in the tree. Then all the statements occupying nodes of that path are true at the points in which they occur in that interpretation.

For atomic statements, this is the case by definition. For a negated atom ¬A, this follows from the openness of the branch, which implies that A does not occur on it in the same locality as ¬A, and so the falsity of A at that point under the interpretation.

Now, suppose for reductio that P is a statement of shortest possible length which occurs at a node on the path but which is false at the appropriate point in the interpretation. It must be a non-literal, by the above. Since the tree is complete and systematic, some list of conclusions L must already be part of the path. P cannot be a truth-functional statement or a $\Diamond$ statement, since in that case the members of L are all shorter than P, hence are true under I, and by the correctness of the rules P would be true as well. If P is of the form $\neg\Diamond Q$ or $\neg\Box Q$, then L is either $\{\Box\neg Q\}$ or $\{\Diamond\neg Q\}$, which is to say that the set of premises includes a sentence equivalent to P. In the latter case, there must be another set of premises for the $\Diamond$ sentence occurring in L, and the correctness of the $\Diamond$-rule would imply the truth of all members of L; hence the correctness of the interchange rule would imply the truth of P. Finally, in the case where P has form $\Box Q$ (or $\neg\Diamond Q$), since the tree is complete, at every point which is R-related to the one where P occurs, the sentence Q (or $\neg Q$) will occur. Since that sentence is shorter than P, it will be true at all these points, and the correctness of the $\Box$-rule implies that P is true. Hence we have a contradiction, and so there can be no P which occurs at a node of the path which is false at the appropriate point in I.

This, coupled with our earlier proofs of the soundness and completeness of K for the class of all frames yields the

THEOREM 4.9
$K = \{P \mid P \text{ is } \blacksquare\text{-valid}\} = \{P \mid P \text{ is valid in all frames}\}.$

4.3 Other Systems of Contextual (Modal) Logic

The $\blacksquare$-system, as we have just proved, is suitable for contextual reasoning when the contexts in question impose *no conditions whatsoever* on which points are R-related to which. As we saw in section 4.1.3, many sorts of contextual reasoning, for instance systems advanced as formalizations of epistemic logic and alethic modal logic, (though not those of doxastic nor deontic logic) require that each point in a frame be R-related to itself, i.e., that aRa for any $a \in W$. A frame whose relation R satisfies this condition is called *reflexive*. Truth in reflexive frames is captured by adding the following $\Box$-elimination rule to our system $\blacksquare$ of tree rules:

RULE 4.4 ($\Box$-ELIMINATION) If $\Box P$ occupies a node, P may be entered *at the same locality* as that node (i.e., before any application of a rule which involves introduction of a horizontal line) on all paths not already containing an occurrence of P.

$$\Box P$$
$$P$$

We write $\blacksquare T$ for the resulting system of tree rules, because, clearly, $\Box P \rightarrow P$ becomes a valid schema in it (cf section 4.1.3).

On the other hand, the statement $\Box A \to \Box\Box A$ remains invalid. This can be seen by returning to the tree in section 4.2.2 which generates a countermodel for $\Box A \to \Box\Box A$. This tree can be finished in accordance with the rules of $\blacksquare T$ by adding a node with A on it at locality 1. Since we want the R-relation of our interpretation to be reflexive, the original relevance diagram must now have loops attached to each node, as in

However, when drawing these diagrams for reflexive systems, we shall take the loops as understood. In addition to assigning the value $\top$ to A at point 2, and $\bot$ at point 3, the interpretation must assign $\top$ to A at point 1. Then, as before, $\Box A \to \Box\Box A$ is false at point 1 under this interpretation.

EXERCISES 4.3.1
Construct countermodels to show that the following statements are invalid in $\blacksquare T$.

*   1. $\Diamond\Box A \to A$.

      2. $\Box(\Box A \to A) \to \Box A$.

   We also saw that in the formalization of several sorts of contextual reasoning, for instance doxastic, epistemic and alethic modal reasoning, it is natural to require that the R-relation be *transitive*: $(aRb \wedge bRc) \Rightarrow aRc$. A frame whose R-relation satisfies this condition is called *transitive*. Truth in transitive frames is captured by adding the following rule to the system:

RULE 4.5 ($\Box$-REPEAT) If $\Box P$ occurs at some node in a tree, and a *new locality* is introduced on some path running through it, then $\Box P$ may be asserted at the new locality (provided it doesn't already occur there).

$$\Box P$$
$$\cdots\cdots$$
$$\Box P$$

(Recall that the broken line indicates that if a new point is introduced, something may be asserted in it.) The resulting system is denoted by $\blacksquare 4$.

   The closed tree below shows that $\Box P \to \Box\Box P$ is valid in $\blacksquare 4$.

$$\neg(\Box P \to \Box\Box P) \; \checkmark$$
$$\Box P$$
$$\neg\Box\Box P \qquad \checkmark$$
$$\Diamond\neg\Box P \qquad \checkmark$$
$$\overline{}$$
$$\neg\Box P$$
$$\Box P$$
$$\times$$

Here the last line is derived from the second by the $\Box$-repeat rule.

EXERCISES 4.3.2
Show that the statement $\Diamond\Diamond P \to \Diamond P$ is valid in ■4.

Invalidity in ■4 is established, as before, by using trees to generate countermodels, only now the contextual structure in each countermodel must be
transitive. For instance, it will be found that this is the case for the countermodels for $\Box A \to A$ and $\Diamond\Box A \to A$ in exercise 4.3.1. So neither of these
two statements is valid in ■4.

The system ■T4 is obtained by combining ■T and ■4, in other words, by
adding both the □-elimination and □-repeat rules to ■. It captures truth
in *preordered* frames, those whose relevance relations are transitive and
reflexive, that is, *preorderings*.

EXERCISES 4.3.3
*   1. Show that the statements $\Diamond\Diamond P \longleftrightarrow \Diamond P$ and $\Box\Diamond\Box\Diamond P \longleftrightarrow \Box\Diamond P$ are valid
     in ■T4.

*   2. Show that the statements $\Box\Diamond A \to A$ and $\Diamond\Box A \to A$ are both invalid in
     ■T4.

We have had occasion to consider another possible condition on R-
relations, i.e., the condition that *all localities are R-related to one another*.
Call such frames *full*. (These are the the frames suitable for S5.) Let ■5 be
the system obtained from ■T4 by adding the two additional rules

RULE 4.6 ($\Diamond$-REPEAT) If $\Diamond P$ occurs at some locality in a tree, and a *new locality* is introduced on some path running through it, then $\Diamond P$ may be asserted
at the new locality (provided it doesn't already occur there).

$$\Diamond P$$
$$\cdots\cdots$$
$$\Diamond P$$

RULE 4.7 ($\Diamond$-ADJUNCTION) If P occurs at some locality in a tree, then $\Diamond P$
may be introduced, at the same locality, on every open path on which P
occurs.

$$P$$
$$\Diamond P$$

This system captures truth in full frames.

EXERCISES 4.3.4
*   1. Show that the following statements are valid in ■5.

    (a) $\Box P \longleftrightarrow \Diamond\Box P$.

    (b) $\Diamond P \longleftrightarrow \Box\Diamond P$.

    (c) $\Diamond\Box P \to P$.

Deduce that in ■5 any statement of the form $\$\$\ldots\$A$, where each $\$$ is either □ or ◇, is either equivalent to ◇A, or to □A.

*   2. By constructing a countermodel, show that the statement □◇$A \rightarrow A$ is invalid in ■5.

    3.   (a) Show that the tree rules

$$ P \qquad \Box P $$
$$ \Box P \qquad P $$

        are correct for interpretations in frames in which R is the *identity relation*, that is, in which *each locality is R-related only to itself*.

      (b) Show that the "premiseless" tree rule

$$ \Box P $$

        is correct for interpretations in frames in which the R-relation is *empty*, that is, in which *no localities are R-related to one another*.

We have yet to consider tree rules for the deontic interpretation of contextual logic. The only rule which would seem to be correct, beyond those of ■, is

RULE 4.8 (◇-INTRODUCTION) If □P occurs in some locality in a tree, then ◇P may be introduced, in the same locality, on every open path on which □P occurs.

$$ \Box P $$
$$ \Diamond P $$

This rule, given this interpretation, formalizes the principle that "whatever is obligatory is permissible." The system obtained by adding this rule to ■ is denoted by ■D.

EXERCISES 4.3.5

*   1. Show that the above rule for the deontic interpretation implies that the following "closure" rule is correct:

$$ \Box P $$

$$ \Box \neg P $$
$$ \times $$

    Find a counterexample which shows that ■D is not equivalent to the tree system which would result by adding this closure rule to ■. Show that nevertheless □$P \rightarrow$ ◇P is valid in that system.

    2. Why isn't ■T suitable for the doxastic interpretation? What about ■D?

4.3.1   Correctness and Adequacy for Trees

We proved above that K, the set of ■-valid statements, and the class of statements true in arbitrary frames are the same. We can use a similar approach for our other systems of tree rules. Because we have already showed that various other normal modal logics are sound and complete for particular classes of frames—say, that Λ is sound and complete for the class C—it suffices to show:

1. For every $P \in \Lambda$, P is provable in the tree system S.

2. If P is provable in tree system S, then P is true in every frame in C.

The proofs of 1 for various Λ are relatively straightforward. In the proof that K is included in the class of ■-valid statements, we showed that, for the case of ■, all instances of K are provable, that necessitation is valid, that all classical propositional tautologies are included, and that the set of provable formulas is closed under modus ponens. But these cases suffice to establish the same things for our other systems of tree rules, which include ■. So all that remains is to prove that all instances of the characteristic scheme(s) of the other normal modal logic are provable in a system of tree rules; it follows that the logic in question is included in the class of validities for that system of rules.

EXERCISES 4.3.6
Show each of the following to be true.

1. KT is included in the set of ■T-validities.

2. $K4$ is included in the set of ■4-validities.

3. $S4$ is included in the set of ■$T4$-validities.

4. $S5$ is included in the set of ■5-validities.

The basic idea involved in showing that every statement provable in a system of tree rules is valid in a class of frames is to show how to "read off" a counterexample to the validity of the statement from an open tree for the negation of the statement. There are some complications, however: (1) In both the cases of ■ and the trees for predicate logic, this could not be proved for open branches on *every* tree beginning this way, but instead required that we consider trees which were *systematic* in an appropriate sense. (2) In both these cases we also had to adjust the notion of the *completeness* of some of the rules from the simple one we were able to use in the case of classical propositional logic. It should thus be no surprise to discover that a large part of proving similar results in the present case is formulating appropriate definitions, for each set of tree rules, of "systematic tree" and "completeness of a rule" with respect to the relevant class of frames. (3) There is one further complication which we will have to consider in some cases. An earlier exercise showed that $\Box(\Box A \to A) \to \Box A$ is not provable in ■. But consider what happens when we attempt to show this in ■4.

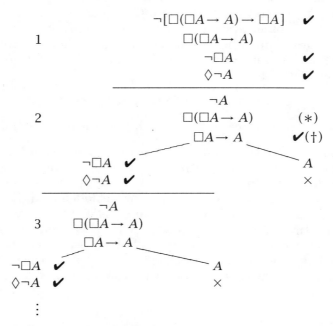

Here the node ($*$) is from the second node by $\Box$-repeat, and ($\dagger$) is from the same node by $\Box$-Rule. What is important to notice about this tree is that the locality 3 is exactly the same as locality 2, and it is easy to see that 3 will be followed by another point which is again just the same. The case is clearly analogous to the situation in predicate logic, where there were trees which never close, but which never become complete and open.

Let us take up (1)–(3) for the particular cases of the $\Box$-elimination and $\Box$-repeat rules. In each case, the requirements necessary for a tree to qualify as *systematic* are obvious. We need only ensure that all permissible applications of rules not introducing new points are performed before any rule is employed which introduces a new horizontal line. In the case of $\Box$-repeat, this means that all the $\Box$-statements at the preceding point must be carried forward into the present locality.

Turning to the sense in which these rules are complete, and recalling that for $\Box$-elimination it is the class of reflexive frames that we have in mind, it is not hard to see that the rule by itself is not complete (though it is obviously correct). In fact, it is the *combination* of the $\Box$-elimination *and* $\Box$-rules which is complete for this class of frames. For the $\Box$-rule alone does not guarantee that P will be true at all localities where $\Box P$ occurs, which is required if we restrict attention to reflexive frames. And the truth of P at localities where $\Box P$ occurs is not sufficient for the truth of $\Box P$ at those localities, since there might be other localities R-related to the one in question at which P must also be true. One way to deal with this problem is to define the set of conclusions *for an occurrence of* $\Box P$ in a ■T tree to be the occurrences of P at all the localities R-related to the one at which $\Box P$ occurs (i.e., those occurrences of P either introduced by an application of $\Box$-elimination or $\Box$-rule, or which made such application unnecessary at a particular point). Then, for systematic trees, this *combination* of $\Box$-rules is rule-complete. Similarly, in other systems where there is more than one rule for dealing with a single operator we will need to formulate notions of *set of conclusions* and *rule completeness* for these rules taken as a group.

EXERCISES 4.3.7

* 1. What is the appropriate notion of *set of conclusions* for $\Box$-statements in each of the the systems ■4 and ■$T4$ for which the combination of the various $\Box$-rules in each system turn out to be rule complete?

  2. What are the appropriate definitions of the *set of conclusions* for $\Box$- statements and $\Diamond$-statements in ■5?

With this modification, the proof that ■T is adequate for the class of reflexive frames is essentially complete, since it requires only minor changes in the wording of the proof of the adequacy of ■ for the class of all frames.

For ■4, we must deal with complication (3). The most straightforward proof of the adequacy of ■4 for transitive frames is to adopt the approach we have seen to work in the case of predicate logic. There we showed that an interpretation was provided not only by complete open paths, but also by any non-terminating path in a systematic tree. We can show that if no ■4 tree beginning with P closes, then there is an interpretation based on a transitive frame on which P is true at some (i.e., at the initial) locality, and so P is satisfiable, since there exist systematic trees which do not close, hence which include either complete open paths or non-terminating paths.

In the case of ■4, and several other systems, we can do better than this. Recall that our sample tree with a non-terminating path eventually began to repeat itself. In fact, any non-terminating path for a systematic ■4 tree will eventually begin to repeat itself. To see this, notice that all the rules for ■4 *do not increase* the length of the formulas to which they are applied, and most of them, in fact, decrease the length of these formulas. Clearly there can be only finitely many applications of rules *at any one point s*. Hence there can be at most finitely many formulas at s, and each of these is finite, and so has finitely many *subformulas*. Notice that there can be at most finitely many horizontal lines introduced beneath s, because there can be at most finitely many $\Diamond$-statements at s. At the locality beneath any of these horizontal lines, every statement will be a *subformula of some formula which occurs at s*, so the set of all statements occurring at this point is a subset of the set of subformulas of formulas which occur at s. Since there are finitely many such subformulas, there are only finitely many subsets of the set of such subformulas. So, since the "subset of" relation is transitive, if there is a non-terminating sequence of new points beginning from s, each point in this sequence will include a subset of the set of subformulas of s, and hence eventually the same subset must recur. Since the tree in question is assumed to be systematic, this implies that eventually the branch will give rise to a repeating sequence of similar localities.

This allows an alternative strategy for using trees for $\blacksquare 4$ to generate counterexamples. Say that on some path on a systematic tree locality s_i and the later locality s_{j+1} contain the same statements. Then in the interpretation we read off from the path, we need not put $s_j R s_{j+1}$. Instead, we may set $s_j R s_i$. It is not hard to verify that a statement will be true in s_j under the first interpretation if and only if it is true under the second, a task we leave as an exercise.

This is sufficient to establish that $\blacksquare 4$ (hence K4) has the *finite model property*: a statement is satisfiable in an interpretation based on a transitive frame if and only if it is satisfiable in an interpretation based on a transitive frame with a finite set of points.

EXERCISES 4.3.8

1. What modifications need to be made to the adequacy proof for $\blacksquare 4$ to turn it into an adequacy proof for $\blacksquare T4$ for the set of preordered frames? Does $\blacksquare T4$ have the finite model property?

*   2. Explain why the reasoning used here to establish that $\blacksquare 4$ has the finite model property does not apply to the system $\blacksquare 5$. Explain why it is possible nonetheless to use the first approach to show the adequacy of this system of rules (i.e., to show that an infinite, non-terminating path of a systematic tree gives rise to an interpretation on which the sentence tested is satisfied).

REMARK 4.2   S5 is in fact a decidable system, and so it would be possible to modify our system of tree rules to turn it into a decision procedure. $\blacksquare 5$, though, is not a decision procedure, which is the point of the previous exercise. To make it one would require employing rules of a very different sort from those used for the other systems we have considered. The difficulty is that trees, which are naturally constructed working down the page, are very good at considering all the possible interpretations of a formula when R is arbitrary, or is required to have only properties like *reflexivity* or *transitivity*, which are easily kept track of while moving down the page. In S5, though, R must also be *symmetric*. When moving down the page, the horizontal line does nicely for indicating R relations when these are required to go in one direction only. But once symmetry is required, a horizontal line means that the points on either side are R-related to one another, so the tree needs to work in two directions at once, so to speak. The result is that trees which yield a decision procedure for S5 must, in effect, allow one to add new statements to a point even after a new point has been opened below it (though this is often achieved by representing the various points in play as lists of numbers, rather than displaying them in a tree-like structure as we have done here).

4.4 Provability Logic

4.4.1 Arithmetic Provability and Contextual Logic

In Chapter 3 we showed that Basic Arithmetic is *incomplete*, i.e., there are sentences true in the standard interpretation of the natural numbers which are independent of Basic Arithmetic. This is not a special feature, though, of Basic Arithmetic, which is admittedly rather weak as formal theories of arithmetic go. Rather, one of Kurt Gödel's famous *incompleteness theorems* is that *any* formalized theory which contains a certain amount of arithmetic will be incomplete.[4]

We will avoid the details of Gödel's "arithmetization" procedure for effectively assigning code numbers to the symbols and expressions of the language of a given formal theory of arithmetic, though these are themselves interesting. We will simply note that he showed how to construct a formula of the language of the theory with two free variables, $\mathrm{prf}(x, y)$, which encodes the claim that y is (a number which is the code of) a sequence of formulas which are a proof in the formal system of (the formula which is encoded by) x. Thus, if we write $\ulcorner P \urcorner$ for the code of a formula P, the formula $\exists y \, \mathrm{prf}(\ulcorner P \urcorner, y)$ can be taken as the assertion that P is provable in the formal theory in question, because it will be provable precisely when P is provable (and so will be true in precisely those models of the theory in which P is true).

The connection with contextual logic arises when we agree to write $\Box(x)$ for $\exists y \, \mathrm{prf}(x, y)$ and $\Box P$ for $\Box(\ulcorner P \urcorner)$, where we are being systematically ambiguous about which formal theory's provability is in question. Whatever formalized theory we are considering, provided that within it a small amount of arithmetic can be proved, there will be a provability-formula for which we can employ this abbreviation. So, presuming for the rest of this discussion that we have a fixed formalized theory of arithmetic in mind when, for instance, we refer to provability, we have that

($*$) $\Box P$ is provable if and only if P is provable.

Indeed, this formula will satisfy all of the so-called *Hilbert-Bernays-Löb Provability Conditions*[5]:

---

[4]There are many important qualifications buried in this loose statement of Gödel's result. For instance, one needs to understand "formalized" in a quite restrictive sense. Among other things, one needs to disallow inference rules with infinitely many premises, such as the ω-rule discussed in Chapter 3. Similarly, we are being deliberately vague about "how much" arithmetic needs to be included in the theory before Gödel's results are provable. There are many useful discussions of Gödel's theorems which fill in many such details, for example George Boolos, *The Logic of Provability* (Cambridge, 1993), and Per Lindström, *Aspects of Incompleteness*, (Springer, 1997), but we pass them by as tangential to present concerns.

[5]These conditions have been isolated by logicians such as David Hilbert, Paul Bernays, Solomon Feferman and Martin Löb as conditions which will be met by "provability predicates" in formal systems of arithmetic and moreover as those conditions essential to proving Gödel's famous theorems. Each should be quite intuitive—for instance, the second says

1. If P is provable in the formal system, so is $\Box P$.

2. For every P, $\Box(P \to Q) \to (\Box P \to \Box Q)$ is provable in the system.

3. For every P, $(\Box P \to \Box\Box P)$ is provable in the system.

Note also that, in the relevant systems, all truth-functional tautologies will be provable, and the class of provable formulas will be closed under modus ponens. The result is that we can formalize the behaviour of $\Box$ so construed as a *normal contextual logic* in which, moreover, the principle (4) is valid. (Of course, if the formal system of arithmetic in question is *inconsistent*, then every statement P is provable—hence, so too is $\Box P$, both because of the condition above and because $\Box P$ is anyway one of the statements of the system).

Another result which we will state but not prove is the *arithmetical fixpoint theorem*: in any sufficiently rich formalized theory of arithmetic, for any formula of the language of that theory $\varphi(x)$ with one free variable, there is a sentence P of that language such that in the theory

$$\vdash P \longleftrightarrow \varphi(\ulcorner P \urcorner).$$

(We write "$\vdash P$" to abbreviate the statement of English that P is provable in the formal system. Unlike "$\Box P$," "$\vdash P$" is not itself a statement of the formal language.)

Of course, both $\Box(x)$ and $\neg\Box(x)$ are formulas of the language of the theory with one free variable. So each will have a fixpoint. Let us first consider the fixpoint for the latter. If $\vdash P \longleftrightarrow \neg\Box P$, P in effect is a formula which says "P is not provable." With this, we can easily establish

THEOREM 4.10 (GÖDEL'S FIRST INCOMPLETENESS THEOREM)
If the formal theory of arithmetic in question is consistent, there is a statement of the language of the theory which is neither provable nor refutable in the theory.

For suppose that P is provable in the theory, and that the theory is consistent. Then $\neg\Box P$ is also provable, because P is the fixpoint for $\neg\Box(x)$. But then P is not provable by ($*$), contradicting the supposition, which must therefore be false. So suppose that $\neg P$ is provable in the consistent theory. Then $\Box P$ is provable, and so, by ($*$), P is provable, too. Once again, a contradiction, and so $\neg P$ is not provable, either. Hence, if the theory is consistent, it is incomplete.

Looking again at the provability conditions enumerated above, it is perhaps not surprising that a notion of provability should conform to each of

---

that if a conditional is provable and so is its antecedent, then the consequent is provable. Condition 1 is obviously just half of the condition ($*$). It is stated in this form to make more obvious the analogy to the necessitation rule of normal contextual logics which is crucial to the use made of the provability predicate below.

them. But one might wonder whether it oughtn't also to validate the principle T, that $\Box P \to P$. After all, if a proof begins with true axioms, and the rules of inference preserve truth, then if P is provable, it should be true, and "P is true" is surely equivalent to P. Surprisingly, though, this reasoning doesn't work. The problem is that there is no formula available in arithmetic which can play the role "truth" plays in this reasoning. Indeed, it turns out that no consistent formal theory of arithmetic can have $\Box P \to P$ as a valid schema. To see this, consider again a fixpoint P for $\neg\Box(x)$, i.e. suppose that $\vdash P \longleftrightarrow \neg\Box P$. It follows that $\vdash \Box P \to \neg P$, so if T is a valid schema, then $\vdash \Box P \to (P \land \neg P)$. Since $(P \land \neg P)$ is refutable, $\vdash \neg\Box P$. So, $\vdash P$, and by necessitation, $\vdash \Box P$. But then $\vdash \neg P$ as well, and we have a contradiction.[6]

However, while T cannot be valid in general, the question of whether a sentence Q such that $\vdash Q \longleftrightarrow \Box Q$ is provable remains a natural one to ask—natural because such a Q is a fixpoint for $\Box(x)$, in contrast to the fixpoint P for $\neg\Box(x)$ used in proving the first incompleteness theorem, and so Q formalizes the claim that "Q is provable." It was investigation of this question which led Löb to his proof that one needn't even assume the provability of $Q \longleftrightarrow \Box Q$, but only the provability of the $\Box Q \to Q$ half of that claim, to ensure the provability of Q.

THEOREM 4.11 (LÖB'S THEOREM)
In a formalized theory of arithmetic strong enough to allow definition of $\Box$ *and the proof of the fixpoint theorem,* $\vdash \Box P \to P$ *implies* $\vdash P$.

Suppose $\vdash \Box P \to P$. By the fixpoint theorem, there is a sentence Q such that $\vdash Q \longleftrightarrow (\Box Q \to P)$. By necessitation, we have $\vdash \Box[Q \longleftrightarrow (\Box Q \to P)]$, and by the K scheme (twice) and propositional logic we have $\vdash \Box Q \to (\Box\Box Q \to \Box P)$. Since $\Box Q \to \Box\Box Q$ is valid, this reduces to $\vdash \Box Q \to \Box P$, which given the assumption in turn reduces to $\vdash \Box Q \to P$. But, looking back to what Q was a fixpoint for, we arrive at $\vdash Q$. By necessitation again, this yields $\vdash \Box Q$, whence $\vdash P$ by modus ponens.

We can reword Löb's theorem in the form of this further provability condition:

4. $\Box(\Box P \to P) \to \Box P$.

The modal logic of provability in (a consistent) formal arithmetic results by adding this scheme, which we earlier called W, to K4—though in normal modal logic, the presence of W makes 4 redundant, so the system is sometimes called KW rather than K4W. (Once again, we must add the qualifier about consistency because the modal logic for an inconsistent formal theory of arithmetic will be the inconsistent modal logic.)

---

[6]Note that this will double as a proof of a theorem cited but not proved in our discussion of second-order logic, namely *Tarski's famous theorem on the "undefinability of arithmetical truth."* For any formula of arithmetic with one free variable $\tau(x)$ which could reasonably be considered a predicate capturing the notion of arithmetical truth would need to satisfy the provability conditions noted above, and the condition T as well.

4.4.2 Frames for Provability Logic

It should be clear from the discussions in section 4.1.3 that the frames for
$K4W$ must be transitive, because schema 4 is valid, and that they will not
be reflexive, since T fails. We also noted in that section that there is no
first-order property which is satisfied by all and only frames satisfying W.
But this isn't to say that there is no class of frames for which $K4W$ is sound
and complete. In fact, there are two interesting classes for which this holds.

The first is the set of frames for which R is *transitive* and *converse well-
founded*. A relation on a set is *well-founded* if there is no *non-terminating
descending chain* of members of the set which have that relation to one
another. For instance (at least in standard set theories) the "member of"
relation is well-founded, because there can be no infinite descending chains
such that $\ldots z \in y \in x$. The converse of a relation R, recall, is the relation
R^{-1} defined by saying that $x R^{-1} y$ if and only if $y R x$. We say that a relation
on a set is *converse well founded* if and only if its converse is well-founded
on that set. So $\in$ is *not* converse well-founded, since $x \in \{x\} \in \{\{x\}\} \ldots$ for
whatever x you choose. Hence the sequence $x, \{x\}, \{\{x\}\}, \ldots$ is an infinite
sequence, each of which has $\in^{-1}$ to its predecessor in the sequence. So we
have an infinite descending chain

$$\ldots \{\{x\}\} \in^{-1} \{x\} \in^{-1} x.$$

It turns out that K4W shares the *finite model property* with many of the
other contextual systems we have considered: if there is a counterexample
to the validity in K4W of a formula, then there is a counterexample to its
validity in which the set W of points is finite. So, another class which will
have precisely the same valid formulas as the set of transitive and converse
well-founded frames is the class of frames in which W is finite and R is
transitive and converse well-founded. Which is to say, we can consider the
class of frames in which W is finite, and R is transitive and *irreflexive*, i.e.,
for every $s \in W$, it is not the case that sRs. (Neither finiteness nor converse
well-foundedness is a first-order property.)

EXERCISES 4.4.1
*   1. Show that for a transitive relation R on a finite set S, R is converse
       well-founded if and only if R is irreflexive.

While these classes of frames differ from those for the logics considered
earlier in that they are not first-order specifiable, the proofs of soundness
and completeness have the familiar form.

First, suppose there is a transitive frame $\mathcal{F} = \langle W, R \rangle$ in which (W) fails
for some P. Then there is an $s \in W$ where $\Box P$ is false and $\Box(\Box P \to P)$ is
true. By the first, there is a point t such that sRt and P is false at t, and by
the second $\Box P \to P$ is false at t. Hence $\Box P$ must be false at t, too. Hence
there is a point u such that tRu, and so for which wRu by transitivity, in
which P is false, and the same reasoning shows that $\Box P$ fails in u as well.

Hence we have an infinite chain of localities, $s, t, u, \ldots$ such that each bears R to the next member in the sequence, and in all of which except perhaps the first P fails. But this gives us an infinite descending chain

$$\ldots u R^{-1} v R^{-1} t,$$

which is to say that R is not converse well-founded. So if R is converse well-founded, the scheme W must be valid in the frame.

Now suppose that we have a transitive frame $\langle W, R \rangle$ in which R is not converse well-founded, i.e. that we have an infinite sequence of points $s_1, s_2, \ldots$, such that $s_i R s_{i+1}$ for every i. Consider the frame $\langle W', R' \rangle$, which results by setting $W' = \{s_1, s_2, \ldots\}$, and by making R' the restriction of R to W'. Let I be an interpretation in this frame on which $I(s_i, A) = \bot$ for every i. Then at $I(s_1, \Box A) = \bot$, since A is false in s_2. But at every point s_i in this sequence, $\Box A \rightarrow A$ is true, since A is false; and $\Box A$ is false because $s_i R s_{i+1}$. So $I(s_1, \Box(\Box P \rightarrow P)) = \top$, and so this instance of the (W) schema is false in s_1. So if the schema is true in a frame, the relation R in that frame is converse well-founded.

4.4.3 Trees for Provability Logic

We can get a system of tree rules for this system of modal logic by adding to ■4 the exotic looking rule:

RULE 4.9 (W–RULE) If $\Diamond P$ occurs at some node in some locality in a tree, a *new locality* may be introduced at the foot of each path on which that node occurs, and both P and $\Box \neg P$ may be asserted at the new point (provided it doesn't already occur there).

$$\frac{\Diamond P}{\Box \neg P}$$
$$P$$

(To get an idea of why this rule works, note that $\Diamond P$ is equivalent to $\neg \Box \neg P$, which says that $\neg P$ is not provable. Recall that by Löb's theorem the provability of $\neg P$ is equivalent to the provability of $\Box \neg P \rightarrow \neg P$, so the unprovability of $\neg P$ amounts to the unprovability of $\Box \neg P \rightarrow \neg P$. But in an adequate semantics this will mean that $\Box \neg P$ and P are both true at some locality.)

EXERCISES 4.4.2

1. Show that $\Box(\Box P \rightarrow P) \rightarrow \Box P$ is ■4W valid.

2. Show that $\Box A \rightarrow A$ is not valid in ■4W.

3. Show that $\Box A \rightarrow \Box(A \wedge \Box A)$ is valid in ■4W, and that $\Box(A \wedge \Box A) \rightarrow \Box \Box A$ is valid in ■.

Let $\perp$ be any refutable sentence of a formal theory of arithmetic, for instance $A \wedge \neg A$ for some A, or $0 = 1$. Then the statement $\neg \Box \perp$ is an assertion that the formal theory in question is *consistent*. For as we have seen in earlier chapters, a system which includes the rules of classical logic is *inconsistent* if and only if *every statement of the system is provable in the system*. Hence the *unprovability* of $\perp$ is equivalent to the system's consistency.

Consider the tree

$$
\begin{array}{ll}
\neg(\neg\Box\perp \rightarrow \neg\Box\neg\Box\perp) & \checkmark \\
\neg\Box\perp & \checkmark \\
\neg\neg\Box\neg\Box\perp & \checkmark \\
\Box\neg\Box\perp & (\dagger) \\
\Diamond\neg\perp & (*) \\
\hline
\neg\perp & \\
\Box\neg\neg\perp & (*) \\
\neg\Box\perp & \checkmark(\dagger) \\
\Diamond\neg\perp & \\
\hline
\neg\perp & \\
\neg\neg\perp & \\
\times &
\end{array}
$$

Here the second node marked $(*)$ follows from the first by the W-rule, and the second $(\dagger)$ from the first by the $\Box$-rule. What we have just proved is a *formalization* of the claim that: if the formal system of arithmetic in question is consistent, then the system cannot be proved (in that system) to be consistent.

That the statement $\neg\Box\perp$ is not provable in K4W can be shown more directly with the following open tree:

$$
\begin{array}{l}
\neg\neg\Box\perp \quad \checkmark \\
\Box\perp
\end{array}
$$

Note, again, that K4W is the modal logic appropriate for *consistent* theories of formal arithmetic, so the content of the first tree can be regarded as a formalized version of what is shown by the present tree.

So we have established

THEOREM 4.12 (GÖDEL'S SECOND INCOMPLETENESS THEOREM)
The "consistency sentence" $\neg\Box\perp$ of a consistent theory of formalized arithmetic cannot be proved within that theory. Furthermore, the formalized *Second Incompleteness Theorem, i.e., the statement $\neg\Box\perp \rightarrow \neg\Box\neg\Box\perp$, is provable in the theory.*

4.5 Multi-modal Logic

We pause here to briefly consider an obvious generalization which a deeper investigation of contextual logic would need to consider in detail. Many of the notions we have represented using contextual operators *interact* with one another when employed in our non-formal reasoning. For instance, in reasoning about what is *permitted* and *obligatory*, we may well need to take into account what is *possible* (if it is true that "ought implies can"), or what is *known*. The contextual systems we have considered so far involve just one pair of contextual operators at a time, and so have no way of representing the interdependence of these notions.

A language with more than one pair of contextual operators is called a *polymodal* or *multi-modal* language. Of course, in such a language one needs some means of distinguishing the various $\square$ and $\Diamond$ operators from one another. In languages with many sets of operators this is often accomplished by means of subscripts. We shall consider a *bi-modal* language, i.e., one with two pairs of operators, and so shall write one pair $\square$ and $\Diamond$ as usual, and write Δ and ∇ for the other. The syntax of the language is easily specified, by changing clause 3 of definition 4.1 to read:

3' If P is a statement, so are $\square P$, $\Diamond P$, ΔP and ∇P.

Of course, this means that expressions such as $\square \Diamond \Delta P \rightarrow \nabla P$ are statements.

The interest of such an addition to the language is in the principles which can be encoded in it which cannot be so encoded in a mono-modal system. The system ∎5 can usefully be regarded as a logic of alethic modality, i.e., we can read the statement $\square P$ as "P is necessarily true," and $\Diamond P$ is understood as "P is possibly true." If we couple ∎5 with ∎D by reading ΔP as "P is obligatory"and ∇P as "P is permissible," we can prove $\Delta P \rightarrow \Diamond \nabla P$:

$$\neg(\Delta P \rightarrow \Diamond \nabla P) \; ✔$$
$$\Delta P$$
$$\neg \Diamond \nabla P \qquad ✔$$
$$\square \neg \nabla P$$
$$\neg \nabla P$$
$$\nabla P$$
$$\times$$

Here the last line is obtained from the second by application of the $\Diamond$-Introduction rule, though of course now it would be better called ∇-Introduction. The proved statement is the rather obvious claim that "If P is obligatory, then possibly P is permissible."

However, not all trees in such a system will be so simple. To see why, consider what an interpretation for such a system must be like. First, a *bi-modal frame* will need to have *two* R–relations where a mono-modal frame has but one. In the present example, if W is our set of localities, then we shall need a relation $R_\square$ on W which is *reflexive, transitive,* and *symmetric,* i.e., which is an *equivalence,* since $R_\square$ will need to be a relation which makes the principles of ■5 valid. Similarly, R_Δ will need to be a *serial* relation on W. We must make the obvious modification to the definition of truth at a locality under an interpretation, by replacing clause 3 of definition 4.4 by the clause:

3' $\mathcal{M} \vDash_w \square P$ iff $\forall x \in W$, if $wR_\square x$ then $\mathcal{M} \vDash_x P$; $\mathcal{M} \vDash_w \Delta P$ iff $\forall x \in W$, if $wR_\Delta x$ then $\mathcal{M} \vDash_x P$.

The corresponding modifications must be made to the clause for ◊, as well.

This has obvious implications for the practice of constructing trees. The horizontal lines on trees for contextual logics represent changes from one locality to another which is R-related to it. When there is more than one R-relation under consideration, there is a need to keep track of *which R-relation the first locality has to the second.* One way to keep track is to annotate the horizontal lines. If a horizontal line is introduced by the application of, say, the ◊-rule to a ◊, we write $\square$ at the right end of the horizontal line; if the line is introduced by application of the ◊-rule to a ∇-statement, we instead write Δ at the right end of the line.

What we have said so far is enough to ensure that all statements of our expanded language which have the same form as theorems of ■5—that is, they can be obtained from such a theorem by uniformly replacing a formula P which occurs in it by some other formula, so that $\nabla P \rightarrow ◊\nabla P$ counts as having the same form as $P \rightarrow ◊P$ because it is obtained by replacing P with ∇P—are both provable in the revised system of tree rules and valid in the semantics, and likewise for the theorems of ■D. Moreover, there will be some statements which are valid but which do not share the form of any theorem of either of the original systems, such as $\Delta P \rightarrow ◊\nabla P$. But multi-modal systems are most interesting when one allows for rules which govern *interaction* between the operators. For instance, (perhaps for theological reasons?) one might want to introduce the following tree rule, which might be read as encoding the principle that "if P is necessarily the case, then P ought to be the case,"[7]

RULE 4.10 (□-Δ INTERACTION) If $\square P$ occurs in some locality in a tree, then ΔP may be introduced, in the same locality, on every open path on which $\square P$ occurs.

$$\square P$$
$$\Delta P$$

---

[7]The principle encoded in this rule, and the gloss on it, are borrowed from one of several multi-modal systems considered in Melvin Fitting, "Logics With Several Modal Operators," *Theoria* 3 (1969): 259–266. For a more general study of multi-modal logics see Sally Popkorn, *First Steps in Modal Logic* (Cambridge: Cambridge University Press, 1994).

With this rule available, we can prove $\Delta P \rightarrow \Diamond P$ as follows:

$$\neg(\Delta P \rightarrow \Diamond P) \; \checkmark$$
$$\Delta P$$
$$\neg \Diamond P \qquad \checkmark$$
$$\Box \neg P$$
$$\Delta \neg P$$
$$\nabla \neg P$$
$$\overline{} \; \Delta$$
$$\neg P$$
$$P$$
$$\times$$

The statement $\Delta \neg P$ is by $\Box$-Δ Interaction, of course, and the node above the horizontal line is by the ∇ introduction rule of ∎D. The Δ to the right of the horizontal line indicates that the line results from application of the ∇-rule (i.e., the relevant version of the $\Diamond$ rule for this set of operators), and tells us that we may apply the Δ rule to introduce P into the locality below the horizontal line. We have proved here a principle which encodes the principle that "ought implies can."

Clearly we shall need to introduce a further condition on the class of bi-modal frames to get a semantics appropriate for this system of rules. In particular, we need to consider the class of bi-modal frames $\langle W, R_\Box, R_\Delta \rangle$ where W is non-empty, $R_\Box$ is an equivalence relation on W, R_Δ is a serial relation on W, and, furthermore, *if $w R_\Delta w'$, then $w R_\Box w'$.*

EXERCISES 4.5.1

1. Explain why the condition on bi-modal frames is required if the $\Box$-Δ interaction rule is to be valid.

2. Use trees to determine which of the following are valid in the bi-modal system discussed in this section.

  * (a) $\Box P \rightarrow \nabla P$.

   (b) $\Box \Delta P \rightarrow \Delta \Diamond P$.

   (c) $\Box \Delta P \rightarrow \Diamond \Delta P$.

  * (d) $\Delta \Box P \rightarrow \Delta \Diamond P$.

4.6 Quantificational Contextual Logic

4.6.1 The Languages

We will spend very little time on the basic syntax here, and will entrust the details to the reader. We can get languages appropriate for quantificational contextual logic by making the same changes to the various languages for predicate logic as we made to the language for propositional logic to get $\mathcal{L}_{ML}$. That is, we add to our recursive definition of a formula of a language for predicate logic a further clause:

If P is a formula, then $\Box P$ and $\Diamond P$ are both formulas.

The free occurrences of variables of $\Box P$ and $\Diamond P$ are just the free occurrences of variables in P, so we need make no adjustment to our definition of *statements* (which we'll also sometimes call *sentences* in quantificational contextual logic). We will use $\mathcal{L}_{QM}$ to denote such a language, and where necessary will allow the context to fix which one is in question.

4.6.2 Introduction

A useful place to begin a consideration of logic which includes both quantifiers and the contextual operators $\Box$ and $\Diamond$ is to consider what happens if one simply adds the basic $\Box$-rule and $\Diamond$-rule to the rules for predicate logic. To this end, consider the tree

$$\neg[\Box(\forall x)Px \rightarrow (\forall x)\Box Px] \quad ✔$$
$$\Box(\forall x)Px$$
$$\neg(\forall x)\Box Px \qquad\qquad ✔$$
$$(\exists x)\neg\Box Px \qquad\qquad ✔$$
$$\neg\Box Pa \qquad\qquad ✔$$
$$\Diamond\neg Pa \qquad\qquad ✔$$
$$\overline{\qquad\qquad\qquad\qquad\qquad\qquad}$$
$$\neg Pa$$
$$(\forall x)Px$$
$$Pa$$
$$\times$$

This tree establishes that the formula $\Box(\forall x)Px \rightarrow (\forall x)\Box Px$ is provable merely by application of the rules of predicate logic and those of basic contextual logic. This suggests that this formula captures a basic principle in contextual logic. On the other hand, consider the tree

$$\neg[(\forall x)\Box Px \rightarrow \Box(\forall x)Px] \quad ✔$$
$$1 \qquad\qquad (\forall x)\Box Px$$
$$\neg\Box(\forall x)Px \qquad\qquad ✔$$
$$\Diamond\neg(\forall x)Px \qquad\qquad ✔$$
$$\Box Pa$$
$$\overline{\qquad\qquad\qquad\qquad\qquad\qquad}$$
$$\neg(\forall x)Px \qquad\qquad ✔$$
$$2 \qquad\qquad Pa$$
$$(\exists x)\neg Px$$
$$\neg Pb$$

This tree shows that simply adding the rules of basic contextual logic to those for predicate logic leaves the formula $(\forall x)\Box Px \rightarrow \Box(\forall x)Px$ unprovable. Moreover, adding the rules $\Box$-elimination and $\Box$-repeat would not make this tree close, either: rather, it would only add the statement Pa to locality 1 and the statement $\Box Pa$ to locality 2. This suggests that the formula in question should not be a valid principle in the quantification versions of the contextual systems corresponding to $\blacksquare$, $\blacksquare T$, $\blacksquare 4$ and $\blacksquare T4$, which is to say, it ought not to be valid in quantificational K, KT, K4 or S4. On the other hand, in quantified $\blacksquare 5$, we have the tree

$$\neg[(\forall x)\Box Px \rightarrow \Box(\forall x)Px] \qquad \checkmark$$
$$(\forall x)\Box Px$$
$$\neg\Box(\forall x)Px \qquad \checkmark$$
$$\Diamond(\forall x)\Box Px \qquad \Diamond\text{-intro}$$
$$\Diamond\neg(\forall x)Px \qquad \checkmark$$
$$\overline{}$$
$$\neg(\forall x)Px \qquad \checkmark$$
$$\Diamond(\forall x)\Box Px \qquad \checkmark(\Diamond\text{-repeat})$$
$$(\exists x)\neg Px \qquad \checkmark$$
$$\neg Pa$$
$$\Diamond\neg Pa \qquad \Diamond\text{-intro}$$
$$\overline{}$$
$$(\forall x)\Box Px$$
$$\Diamond\neg Pa \qquad \checkmark\Diamond\text{-repeat}$$
$$\overline{}$$
$$\neg Pa$$
$$Pa$$
$$\times$$

So, that formula is provable in the obvious version of quantified $\blacksquare 5$, and so, we might suspect, ought to turn out valid in quantified S5. This formula is an instance of the so-called *Barcan formula* (and the one considered previously is called, unoriginally, the *converse Barcan formula*). It is named for Ruth Barcan Marcus, a pioneer in the investigation of contextual logics, and we will consider it further below.

Finally, consider the tree

$$\neg(\forall x)(\forall y)[x = y \rightarrow \Box(x = y)] \quad ✔$$

$$\vdots$$

$$p = q \qquad\qquad ✔$$
$$\neg\Box p = q \qquad\qquad ✔$$
$$\neg\Box p = p$$
$$\Diamond p \neq p$$

$$p \neq p$$
$$\times$$

This tree uses only the rules for identity, for the quantifiers, and for ■. So we seem to have showed that $(\forall x)(\forall y)[x = y \rightarrow \Box(x = y)]$ should be valid in every quantified contextual logic with identity. And it is easily seen that a tree for $a = b \rightarrow \Box(a = b)$ will close in the same way. But then were $\Box$ to be interpreted as "necessity," we would seem to have a proof that for any x and y, if they are identical, then they are necessarily identical. This might be thought problematic, since philosophers have long thought that there are *contingent* identity statements: for instance, some have contended that mental states are brain states, though they *might* have been something else. Moreover, this seems clearly false for some everyday cases. Mackenzie King is Canada's longest serving Prime Minister, though someone else might have served longer, and indeed he might never have been elected at all. Some have taken this proof as showing that these views about contingent identity statements were misguided, and have used this proof as part of their case for some radical metaphysical conclusions. In response to the second sort of case, a common response has been to insist that one needs to distinguish *genuine names*, for which this principle holds, from descriptions, such as "Canada's longest serving Prime Minister," which designate individuals but which are not genuine names and for which this principle needn't hold. Thus, this simple proof also plays a role in debates about the nature of names.

We now have in front of us one formula, the Barcan formula, which is unprovable in the system one gets merely by adding the basic contextual rules to predicate logic. Some contend that this formula ought to be valid in a reasonable quantified contextual logic. The converse Barcan formula, on the other hand, seems to be an obvious consequence of the basic modal rules and the basic rules of predicate logic. As we shall see, some authors defend systems in which even the converse Barcan formula is invalid. The third formula shows that when we are considering contextual logics we ought to pay special attention to identity. We shall briefly consider three different semantics for contextual predicate logic, paying special attention to the status of these three formulas in each.

4.6.3   Semantics for Contextual Predicate Logic

A first idea of how the semantics for quantified contextual logic should go
can be had, as one might expect, by considering the modifications which
needed to be made to the semantics for classical propositional logic to get a
semantics for propositional contextual logic. In that case we added *frames*
and, in effect, provided an interpretation for the language of propositional
logic *for every locality in the frame.* Moreover, the logical operators in
propositional logic are interpreted in just their usual way—what goes on
in other localities is relevant to interpreting the $\Box$ and the $\Diamond$, but not the
other operators (except in that a $\Box$ or $\Diamond$ may be embedded in a subformula
of a truth-functional statement).

One might expect to be able to get a workable semantics for contextual
predicate logic in the same way, and this is more or less how each of the
three systems of semantics we shall consider proceeds. In propositional
logic an interpretation was just a valuation, i.e. an assignment of truth
values to all the statement letters. In predicate logic, it is *interpretations*,
that is, *structures appropriate to the language in question*, which play the
corresponding role, so in contextual predicate logic an interpretation will
need to supply a structure appropriate for the language for every locality
in the frame. Moreover, the clauses for interpreting the quantifiers will
remain as close as possible to their interpretations in the non-contextual
case. What is going on in other localities shall be relevant to interpreting
the $\Box$ and $\Diamond$, but not to interpreting the other logical operators, including
quantifiers (except that $\Box$ and $\Diamond$ may be embedded in a subformula of a
truth-functional or quantifier formula). In other words, $\exists x P x$ shall mean
"something exists *in this locality* which has P," and $\forall x P x$ shall mean "all
things *in this locality* have P."

However, this rough description of an approach to finding a semantics
leaves unanswered many questions about details. The various semantic
systems we shall consider arise from answering these questions in different
ways.

Fixed Domain Semantics

The first question of detail to be considered arises from the fact that each
structure for the language must have a *domain* or *universe of discourse*.
The question is simply how these domains are to be related to one another.
The first, and simplest, semantics results from requiring that *each such
structure must have the same domain.* Once we have decided to make this
requirement, a direct and simple way to ensure the validity of $a = b \rightarrow$
$\Box(a = b)$ for any names a and b is available. We require that any names
in the language be treated as *rigid designators*, i.e., that any name in the
language must receive the same interpretation (i.e., it must be assigned the
same object from the common domain) in every locality. However, we allow
that different predicates can be true of a given individual (or a sequence

of individuals if we're talking about a many-place predicate) at different points. So if Pa is true at one point, but false at another, it is the same individual, namely the one named by a, which is in question at both points, but a differs with respect to (at least) the property denoted by Px at the two points.

DEFINITION 4.7 A *type-1 contextual predicate model* for $\mathcal{L}_{QM}$ is an ordered quadruple $\mathcal{M} = \langle W, R, I, v \rangle$, where

1. $\langle W, R \rangle$ is a frame.

2. I is a function which assigns a structure for $\mathcal{L}_{QM}$ to each element of W. It is required that all such structures have some set D as their common domain, and that every name a receives the same interpretation in all such structures.

3. v is a mapping from the set of variables to D, the common domain of all these structures.

Next, we can define what it will mean for a formula φ to be true in a locality w in the model $\mathcal{M}$. We denoted this by $\mathcal{M} \vDash_w \varphi$, writing w in the subscript for $I(w)$, the structure assigned by I to the locality w.

DEFINITION 4.8 (TRUTH IN A LOCALITY)
1. If φ is atomic, $\mathcal{M} \vDash_w \varphi$ iff $[\![\varphi]\!]_w^V = \top$.

2. The clauses for $\wedge, \vee, \rightarrow, \neg, \forall$, and $\exists$ are as in classical logic, relativized to localities.

3. The clauses for $\square$ and $\lozenge$ are as in propositional contextual logic.

As we would hope given the introductory discussion above, the converse Barcan formula $\square\forall x\varphi \rightarrow \forall x\square\varphi$ is valid according to this semantics. For suppose the antecedent is true at some locality w. Then at every locality which is R-related to w, the set of things that have the property φ is the whole domain. But it clearly follows from this that every object has φ at every locality R-related to w, which is to say that $\square\varphi(x)$ is true for every x in any such locality.

However, this simplest semantics also has its drawbacks. For one thing, *the Barcan formula* $\forall x\square\varphi \rightarrow \square\forall x\varphi$ *is also valid in this semantics.* For suppose the antecedent is true in some locality w under some interpretation $\mathcal{M}$. Suppose that wRz. We know that $\square\varphi(x)$ is true in w, for every value of x. It follows that $\varphi(x)$ is true in z for every value of x. Which is to say that $\forall x\varphi$ is true in z. Since this holds for every z such that wRz, we have that $\square\forall x\varphi$ is true in w.

Should we be satisfied with a semantics which makes the Barcan formula valid? Perhaps the appropriate course is simply to add an extra rule governing the interaction of the quantifiers and the contextual operators which would *make* the formula provable. Not all philosophers would approve of this course of action. For suppose that □ is interpreted as "it is necessary that ...." Many have wondered why it should follow from the fact that *everything necessarily possesses a property* that it is *necessary that everything have that property*. Consider the claim that everything that actually exists is such that if it is a horse, then it doesn't fly: something we might symbolize by $\forall x \square (Hx \rightarrow \neg Fx)$. Does it follow that $\square \forall x (Hx \rightarrow \neg Fx)$? This seems to assert that it is a necessary truth that no horse flies. But, the thinking might go, it doesn't follow from the fact that Pegasus doesn't exist, and that nothing which actually exists could have been a flying horse (instead of what it actually is), that *Pegasus could not have existed.*

Note that this objection depends on supposing that a different "possible world" might have different individuals in it—in particular, it might have Pegasus in it—from those that exist in the actual world. One way to look at the type-1 semantics is as embodying the denial that this is possible, since we built into type-1 semantics the requirement that the same domain of individuals must be part of the structure for interpreting the language at each locality. The validity of the Barcan formula is in fact tightly connected to this constant domain assumption, as a close look at the argument above to show its validity makes clear. So we can expect a semantics which does not make it valid to be one in which the domain of quantification can vary from point to point.

Variable Domain Semantics: Growing Domains

Suppose, then, that validity of the Barcan formula is too high a price to pay for the simple answer to the question of how the various domains are to be related to one another. We must, then, allow some variation in these domains. The second sort of semantics we will consider allows for some variation, but it leaves in place a sort of "persistence" condition: if two localities w and x of a frame are such that wRx, then all the elements in the domain of a structure for w must *also* be elements in the domain of x—though if it is not the case that xRw, there might be elements in the second domain which are not in the first.

There are a few complications involved in making this work. In particular, we need to consider again our policy of assigning names to the same object in every locality. What do we do if the name b is assigned to an individual which is in the domain of x but *not* in the domain of w? If we insist that for each locality we have a structure appropriate for our language, then b, which is part of the language, must be assigned to some element of the domain of the interpretation for w, which doesn't include the element b designates in x, so we have incompatible requirements. We shall resolve this difficulty by allowing that the contextual interpretation must assign to each locality a structure appropriate for the language, *except* that it may fail to assign certain individual names to any individual. Furthermore, the requirement that names refer to the same individuals in every structure is replaced by the requirement that *names refer to the same individual in every structure where that individual is a member of the domain.*

These modifications resolve the immediate difficulty, but they raise another. What are we to say of the truth value of a statement such as Pb in a locality where the referent of b is not in the domain? We can no longer simply rely on the machinery set up for interpreting statements of predicate logic to answer this question, because that machinery assumes that the referent of b is in the domain. In the present instance we shall answer this question in the following way: if the referent of b is not in the domain of a locality w, then every statement in which b occurs *has no truth value.* It is sometimes said that in such a case there is a *truth-value gap* in which any statement in which b occurs falls.[8]

DEFINITION 4.9 A *type-2 contextual predicate model* is an ordered quadruple $\langle W, R, I, v \rangle$, where W and R are as in the type-1 semantics. As in a type-1 model, I assigns to each locality w a structure appropriate for $\mathcal{L}_{QM}$, or to *some language which is like $\mathcal{L}_{QM}$ but for the fact that some names from $\mathcal{L}_{QM}$ do not occur in it,* to each point. Instead of requiring a common domain, however, it is only required that if wRz, then the domain of $I(w)$ must be a subset of the domain of $I(z)$.

We use D to denote the *union* of all the domains assigned to the various points, and D_w to denote the domain of the structure assigned to w. (Note that this use of D is consistent with its usage in the common domain semantics.) We also modify our definition of a valuation in a structure: v is now a function which assigns *a member of D* to each individual variable.

We can now define $\mathcal{M} \vDash_w \varphi$. This definition is rather more complicated than the corresponding definition for type-1 semantics since we must allow for truth value gaps.

DEFINITION 4.10 (TRUTH AT A LOCALITY, TYPE-2)

1. If φ is atomic, $\{x_1, \ldots, x_n\}$ are all the free variables of φ, $\{c_1, \ldots, c_m\}$ are all the constants of φ, and $v(x_1), \ldots, v(x_n)$ and $[c_1]_M^v, \ldots, [c_m]_M^v$ are all in the domain of $I(w)$, then $\mathcal{M} \vDash_w \varphi = \top$ if $[\![\varphi]\!]_M^v = \top$, and $\mathcal{M} \vDash_w \varphi = \bot$ if $[\![\varphi]\!]_M^v = \bot$. If the antecedent condition is not met, then φ has no truth value.

2. For $\neg$, $\wedge$, $\vee$, and $\rightarrow$, the clauses are just as they are in classical logic, subject to the provision that if one of the component subformulas receives no truth value, then the complex formula doesn't get one either.

3. If φ is $\forall x \alpha$, then $\mathcal{M} \vDash_w \varphi = \top$ if for all d in *the domain of $I(w)$,* $\mathcal{M} \vDash_w \alpha$ in the model which results by replacing v with $v(x/d)$. φ is false at w if there is some d in the domain of w such that α is false

---

[8]The present approach in effect employs the same approach taken in the three valued Bochvar logic considered again in Chapter 5, and so involves many of the same problems considered there. We leave these matters aside for now.

at w in the model that results from replacing v by $v(x/d)$. φ has no truth value assigned otherwise.

4. If φ is $\exists x \alpha$, then $\mathcal{M} \vDash_w \varphi$ if for some d in the domain of w, $\mathcal{M} \vDash_w \alpha$ in the model resulting from replacing v by $v(x/d)$. φ is false at w if for all d in the domain of w, α is false at w in the model which results by replacing v by $v(x/d)$. Otherwise it is assigned no truth value.

5. If φ is $\Box \alpha$, then $\mathcal{M} \vDash_w \varphi$ iff for all y such that wRy, $\mathcal{M} \vDash_y \alpha$. φ is false in w iff for every y such that wRy, α has a truth value in y and that value is false in one such y. (Thus, φ gets no truth value in w iff there is a locality y such that wRy at which α gets no truth value.)

6. If φ is $\Diamond \alpha$, then $\mathcal{M} \vDash_w \varphi$ iff for every point such that wRy α gets a truth value at y and $\mathcal{M} \vDash_y \alpha$ in one of them. φ is false in w if α is false in all y such that wRy. (So φ gets no truth value in w iff there is a point y such that wRy and at which α gets no truth value.)

This is a complicated looking definition. The basic idea is simple, though. A formula will get the truth value one would expect, given the classical interpretation of the propositional connectives and the quantifiers and the usual interpretation of the modal operators, provided that there is enough information available to determine truth values for all the components that make up the formula. If this information doesn't exist, the formula is simply declared not to have a truth value in that locality.

Consider again the tree for the Barcan formula we drew on page 172. From it—more precisely, from it with the modifications described in the paragraph following the tree which make it a tree for ■$T4$—we can obtain a countermodel to the validity of the Barcan formula in the present semantics. The countermodel has two localities, 1 and 2. Since we are considering a tree for ■$T4$, $1R1$ and $2R2$ (i.e., R is reflexive) and $1R2$, but not $2R1$. The domain of 1 is $\{a\}$, while the domain of 2 is $\{a, b\}$. Since Pa occurs in both localities on the tree, Pa must be true in both in our interpretation. On the other hand, Pb is false in locality 2 and has no value in locality 1.

Note that D is identical to the domain of 2, and we clearly have met the constraint on domains. Pa is true in all localities R-related to 1, so $\Box Pa$ is true in 1. Since a is the only member of the domain of 1, $\forall x \Box Px$ is true at 1. However, since Pb is false at 2, $\forall x Px$ is false at 2. Since $1R2$, $\Box \forall x Px$ is false at 1. Hence this instance of the Barcan formula is false at 1.

Notice that this countermodel is an S4 model but *not* an S5 model. For in type-2 semantics, in any frame where R is an equivalence (or, indeed, any symmetric) relation, the Barcan formula is valid in the frame. For if wRz and R is symmetric, then zRw also holds. Since being R–related requires that the domain of the first point is a subset of the domain of the second, the fact that R is symmetric guarantees that the domains of R-related points are identical. So suppose that $\Box \forall x \varphi$ is false at w. Then there is a z with wRz and $\forall x \varphi$ false in z. Which is to say that there is an element of the domain of z which, plugged in for x, falsifies φ. Furthermore, φ will get a truth value in every locality accessible to w, since all such localities have the same domain. We can thus conclude from the falsity of φ in z and the fact that wRz that $\Box\varphi$ is false in w, from which we can conclude that $\forall x \Box\varphi$ is also false in w.

This is quite a satisfactory result. However, type-2 semantics has difficulties of its own. Notice that the formula $a = b \rightarrow \Box(a = b)$ is no longer valid in the strong sense of being true in all localities in all frames, since it is not true in localities where the referent of a or b is not part of the domain. One solution to this problem would be to give up the truth value gap approach in favour of what is sometimes called a *Russellian approach*.[9] On a Russellian approach, any atomic formula in which a non-referring term occurs is declared *false* rather than devoid of truth value. (The remaining clauses of the type 2 definition of truth at a locality do not need to be changed. The machinery for handling truth value gaps no longer does any work in a Russellian system, but it is harmless.) However, this raises other problems. In the truth value gap approach, a statement such as $a = a$ fails to have a truth value at localities where a fails to refer. This may be regarded as problematic, but it is probably less problematic than being forced to say, as one is on a Russellian approach, that $a = a$ is *false* in such localities, and so that $\Box(a = a)$ is *invalid*. Advocates of the truth value gaps approach may suggest that it is preferable to avoid that sort of problem at the expense of saying that statements such as $a = b \rightarrow \Box(a = b)$ (or $\Box(a = a)$), while not strictly speaking valid, have a sort of conditional validity: At any locality, if a and b exist and are identical, then they are necessarily identical.

Another objection to type-2 semantics is this: Once we allow for the possibility that which individuals exist can vary with locality, it is unclear what grounds the restriction that if wRz the domain of w needs to be contained in the domain of z. If the only justification is that this restriction is required to validate the converse Barcan formula, this restriction is unacceptably ad hoc.

Variable Domains: Kripke's Semantics

The final sort of semantics for quantified contextual logics we consider is one which it is useful to regard as motivated by the desire to circumvent the objections to type-2 semantics. There are two main adjustments to type-2 semantics. First, in answer to the question "What relation must there be between the domains at various localities?" it answers, "None," thus avoiding the ad hoc stipulation built into type-2 semantics. Secondly, in order to avoid the invalidity of certain statements which one would hope would be valid, rather than opting for truth value gaps, this semantics allows statements involving a name a to have a truth value at a locality even if a

---

[9]Some insight into why it is called "Russellian" can be found in the discussion of descriptions in Chapter 6.

does not refer to an individual which is in the domain at that locality. Unlike the Russellian approach, which also does this, the present approach allows for atomic statements involving a to be *true* at a locality, even if a is not in the domain at that locality. (Thus, "Pegasus is a horse" might be true in our world, even though Pegasus doesn't exist here.)

To make this work requires an adjustment to the notion of "structure for a language" which is more radical than the one required by type-2 semantics. The structures assigned by I to each locality are, in the present approach, a sort of hybrid. For each locality w, let us write D_w for the domain of the interpretation assigned by I to w. If we regard D_w as the domain of w, then the quantifiers range over the domain D_w as usual. But then the relations which interpret the atomic predicates of $\mathcal{L}_{QM}$ at w assign the values $\top$ or $\bot$ to *every n-tuple*, not just of members of that D_w, but of $D = \cup\{D_w \mid w \in W\}$, i.e., to all n-tuples involving members the domains at all localities. Alternatively, we can think of I as assigning a structure whose domain is D, so that the assignment of truth values to all n-tuples is to be expected. But then we must also regard I as picking out a subset of D for each w, which we might call the *inner domain* for w, over which the quantifiers range in locality w.[10] Finally, we require that a name a is assigned an interpretation in D. Thus the referent of a need not be in the inner domain of every locality, but it is in the inner domain of some locality. Furthermore, we require that $=$ be interpreted, at every locality, as the identity relation on D. The result is that $\forall x \forall y[x = y \rightarrow \Box(x = y)]$ and $a = b \rightarrow \Box(a = b)$, $a = a$, and $\Box(a = a)$ all are valid in type-3 semantics.

The definition of *truth at a locality* can be exactly as it was for type-2 semantics. However, in the present case this will have quite different results. Since the atomic formulas are now interpreted by relations which are defined on all of D, every atomic formula is assigned either $\top$ or $\bot$ at every point and every term refers, so all the qualifications about when φ receives no truth value simply never apply.

Some very interesting things happen in this semantics. First, since $\forall x$ is interpreted at w as meaning that *every x at w* has a certain property, we have the following possibility: it might well turn out that everything at w has P, but something *not at w* doesn't have that property. But notice that we are now assigning truth-values to all formulas at each point, even where the referent of a term does not exist at a point. So if b is assigned a value outside of the domain of w, it can happen that b does not have P, i.e., that Pb is false at w, but for every individual d in the domain of w, d is an element of $P^I(w)$. In such a case we have $\forall x Px \rightarrow Pb$ *failing to hold* at w. But this looks very much like a failure of a basic principle of predicate logic, viz. universal instantiation! A parallel problem can easily be described in which the formula $\forall x Px \rightarrow Py$ also turns out to be invalid.

Those who advocate this sort of semantics for contextual logics, most famously Saul Kripke, avoid the second problem by noting that the formula

---

[10] Inner and outer domains arise again in the discussion of free logic in Chapter 6.

in question is not a *statement*, since y occurs freely in it. One might opt for a system of predicate logic where *only statements* can count as logical truths. If one takes this view, the fact that $\forall x \varphi(x) \rightarrow \varphi(y)$ fails to be valid in type-3 semantics is nothing to worry about, since $\forall y[\forall x \varphi(x) \rightarrow \varphi(y)]$ *is* valid, and the second but not the first is a statement of classical predicate logic.

As for the first statement, one can argue that the falsity at w of $\forall x Px \rightarrow Pa$, where a does not exist at w, is something one ought not to find alarming, given the intended reading of the quantifiers. For such cases must mean something like: "Everything (that exists) has mass, therefore Pegasus has mass." As we shall see, examples of just this sort are used by some to motivate working in so-called free logic—hence to motivate giving up the standard semantics for non-contextual predicate logic—precisely to avoid making formulas of this form turn out valid.

Interestingly, and perhaps problematically, the Barcan formula now fails *even in quantificational S5.* For consider a type-3 model with two points, w and z, and let R be the universal relation on $D = \{a, b\}$. We are thus working with an S5 frame. Suppose $D_w = \{a\}$, while $D_z = \{a, b\}$. Let Pa be true in both localities, and Pb false in either. We can now calculate that $\forall x \Box Px \rightarrow \Box \forall x Px$ is false in w—it's exactly the same calculation used earlier to show that an instance of the Barcan formula failed in a type-2 S4 model, in fact.

More alarming is the fact illustrated by the following model: Modify the model from the previous example by putting $D_w = \{a, b\}, D_z = \{a\}$, letting Pa be true at both points, and letting Pb be true at w and false at z. In this model $\forall x Px$ is true at both points, so $\Box \forall x Px$ is true at w. However, $\Box Px$ is false at w, since Pb is false at z, which is R–related to w. So, since b is in D_w, $\forall x \Box Px$ also is false at w. This shows that *the converse Barcan formula also fails* to hold in type-3 modal S5 semantics.

The reason for alarm is this: we began our discussion with a tree which seemed to show that the converse Barcan formula is provable in the system which results by joining together, in the most obvious way, the rules of predicate logic and the basic $\Box$ and $\Diamond$ rules—and so we expected that this principle should be valid in *all* quantificational contextual logics. We also saw that while the Barcan formula fails to be provable in the simplest versions of quantified $\blacksquare$, $\blacksquare T$, $\blacksquare 4$, and $\blacksquare T4$, it is provable in $\blacksquare T5$, at least in its simplest form. Since the converse Barcan formula is not valid in type-3 modal semantics, and the Barcan formula is not valid in type-3 S5, we see that some modification, in particular some weakening of the tree rules for predicate logic, would need to be put in place for us to get a system of rules appropriate for type-3 semantics.

4.6.4 Concluding Remarks

We have briefly described three quite different approaches to the semantics of contextual predicate logic. Each of them presents significant difficulties, at least from certain points of view, some of which we have tried to illustrate. On the other hand, each of them is vigorously defended by some philosophers as the appropriate one, at least for certain purposes.

Indeed, the three types of semantics considered here are merely the beginning of the varieties of semantics available for quantified contextual logics. To mention just one more example, some philosophers object, at least for certain purposes, to the validity of $\forall x \forall y [x = y \rightarrow \Box(x = y)]$ and $a = b \rightarrow \Box(a = b)$, and so place restrictions on the application of the identity rules inside "modal contexts," i.e. inside the scope of a $\Box$ or $\Diamond$ operator.

In summary, it is probably wise to be aware that there is such a variety of systems of contextual predicate logic, and that the adoption of each has its *prima facie* costs and benefits. Such an awareness will presumably lead to careful scrutiny of claims that a particular system is the appropriate one for a particular purpose, and to a healthy scepticism about claims to be able to draw significant metaphysical conclusions on the basis of the validity of particular principles of quantified contextual logic.

EXERCISES 4.6.1

* 1. Explain why the countermodel which showed that the Barcan Formula is not valid in a type-3 S5 semantics does not suffice to show that it is not valid in type-2 S5 semantics. Is this the same reason that we cannot use the countermodel to the validity of the converse Barcan formula in type-3 semantics as a countermodel in type-2 semantics?

2. Which of the following are principles which ought to be valid in a reasonable system of contextual predicate logic. Explain.

    (a) $\forall x \Box(Ax \vee Bx) \rightarrow \forall x(\Box Ax \vee \Box Bx)$.

    (b) $\forall x \Diamond(Ax \vee Bx) \rightarrow \forall x(\Diamond Ax \vee \Diamond Bx)$.

  * (c) $\exists x \Diamond Ax \rightarrow \Diamond \exists x Ax$.

    (d) $\Diamond \exists x Ax \rightarrow \exists x \Diamond Ax$.

Chapter 5

Getting Away From Bivalence: Three-Valued and Intuitionistic Logic

In Chapter 1 we noted that in propositional logic one ends up with standard propositional logic if one accepts both *truth-functionality* and *bivalence*. In our discussion of contextual and modal logic in Chapter 4, we added operators to propositional logic which are *not truth functional*—for instance, P and Q might both be true at a locality w, and yet $\Box P$ is true while $\Box Q$ is false there. In the contextual logics we considered,[1] we continued to assume bivalence. However, many philosophers have argued that bivalence is not always an acceptable assumption. In this chapter we investigate two of the very many interesting sorts of logical systems which can result once one is willing to drop the assumption of bivalence.

In his influential analyses of the positions adopted by opponents of *realists* in various traditional philosophical disputes—for instance, *phenomenalists* in debates about material objects, *nominalists* in debates about the existence of universals, *behaviourists* in disputes about mental states, or *constructivists* in disputes about the existence of mathematical objects—Michael Dummett argues that a common thread among these positions is that they all deny that the entities discussed in these domains are *mind* (or *language*) *independent*. Dummett suggests that a consequence of such a view is that the *truth* of statements in such a domain should be *epistemically constrained*: roughly, there can be no truths in such a domain which are *unknowable in principle*. Again roughly, every truth must be *knowable* (at least in principle). Conversely, the falsehoods must be such that they can be known to be false, which we might abbreviate by saying that they must be *refutable*. But if this is what truth and falsehood amount to for

---

[1] Apart from type-2 contextual predicate logic, which introduced "truth value gaps."

184

statements in a particular domain, then, to begin with at least, there seems little reason to accept the principle of bivalence: it is unlikely that every statement is either knowable or refutable, and so we have little reason to think that all statements are either true or false. Note that, unlike a realist about a domain, an *anti-realist* is in no position to argue that in spite of the unknowability of the truth or falsity of a statement, a mind and language independent reality can be relied on to fix the truth values of claims which lie, even in principle, beyond our ken.

Dummett argues not just that it is natural for an anti-realist about a particular domain to reject bivalence, but also for the related but stronger claim that the acceptance of bivalence for the statements about a domain is in fact a *necessary condition* for being a realist about that domain—that the belief in a mind or language independent reality should commit one to the idea that this reality fixes the truth values of the statements of the domain, independently of our ability to determine what those truth values are. If this is right, then the rejection of bivalence is enough to qualify one as an anti-realist about the domain in question. But this leaves open the question of what the appropriate anti-realist logic would be for a domain where truth is epistemically constrained. Dummett argues that *intuitionistic logic*, to which the bulk of the present chapter is devoted, is the only well worked out logic for an epistemically constrained domain, though he by no means argues that it must be the logic for every domain for which an epistemically constrained notion of truth might be appropriate. In any event, since Dummett's arguments have been extremely influential in philosophy, there is much current debate in the literature in which the differences between intuitionistic and classical logic feature prominently. Students of philosophy need to be acquainted with intuitionistic logic if they want to be able to understand and participate in these debates.

Bivalence has been rejected not only on anti-realistic grounds. For instance, it has often been argued that statements involving vague predicates such as "x is red" can be used to make statements which are neither true nor false. This happens, it is suggested, when these predicates are applied to objects which are *borderline cases* for that predicate, such as a shade which is not evidently red, but not evidently pink, either. As another instance, it has often been suggested that claims which seem to generate paradoxes—such as "This sentence is false," which if true must be false, but which if false must be true—show that bivalence needs to be rejected, at least for such special cases. A natural first approach, if one has such an intuition, is to attempt to make do with three truth-values instead of two: true, false, and *indeterminate*, perhaps. While three-valued logics are regularly proposed in the literature as a solution to some philosophical problem or another, such approaches do not seem to us to be notable successes. However, we will begin this chapter by discussing some three-valued logics, both because they do come up fairly frequently in the literature and because doing so allows us to introduce some tools which will be useful when we come to the more important system of intuitionistic logic.

5.1   Three-Valued Logics

The virtue of adopting a logic with three truth values is presumably that it allows one to reject bivalence while departing as little as possible from familiar two-valued classical logic. In keeping with this motivation, we restrict attention to three-valued logics which meet the following conditions:

Truth functionality: The truth value of a complex statement is determined by the truth value(s) of its components. Thus we shall be able to present these logics by making a couple of modifications: we redefine a *valuation* to be a map from the set of sentence letters to the set $\{\top, I, \bot\}$, rather than to the set $\{\top, \bot\}$; and we give a new set of three-valued characteristic truth tables to replace the familiar two-valued tables of chapter 1.

Faithfulness: These three-valued truth tables should agree with the classical tables where the classical truth tables apply (i.e., if P and Q are both either $\top$ or $\bot$ on a valuation, then $\neg P$, $P \wedge Q$, etc., must receive the same truth value they would get by calculating according to the classical tables).

It is natural, for at least some applications, to regard those statements which get the value I as ones which might, at least in some cases, *come to be determined*, that is, which could acquire one of the classical truth values. For instance, if it is vagueness which makes a statement indeterminate, some new stipulation of how the vague vocabulary is to be used might make what was previously a borderline case one which is now determined one way or another. On such a view, it seems sensible to require also

Stability: If a complex statement has a determinate truth value, the change of one of its component statements from I to a determinate truth value cannot change the truth value of the complex statement.

If Stability is adopted as a further condition, there are only two three-valued logics we need to consider, namely the ones due to D.A. Bochvar and Stephen C. Kleene, discussed below.[2] However, we will also consider one non-stable three-valued logic, due to Jan Łukasiewicz, because it is often mentioned in the philosophical literature.

All three of these logics share the following characteristic truth table for negation:

P	$\neg P$
$\top$	$\bot$
$\bot$	$\top$
I	I

---

[2]What we call "Bochvar logic" is sometimes called "*strong* Kleene logic." In such cases, what we call "Kleene logic" is referred to as "*weak* Kleene logic."

It is for the other connectives that they differ:

		Bochvar			Kleene			Łukasiewicz		
P	Q	$P \wedge Q$	$P \vee Q$	$P \to Q$	$P \wedge Q$	$P \vee Q$	$P \to Q$	$P \wedge Q$	$P \vee Q$	$P \to Q$
⊤	⊤	⊤	⊤	⊤	⊤	⊤	⊤	⊤	⊤	⊤
⊤	⊥	⊥	⊤	⊥	⊥	⊤	⊥	⊥	⊤	⊥
⊤	I	I	I	I	I	⊤	I	I	⊤	I
⊥	⊤	⊥	⊤	⊤	⊥	⊤	⊤	⊥	⊤	⊤
⊥	⊥	⊥	⊥	⊤	⊥	⊥	⊤	⊥	⊥	⊤
⊥	I	I	I	I	⊥	I	⊤	⊥	I	⊤
I	⊤	I	I	I	I	⊤	⊤	I	⊤	⊤
I	⊥	I	I	I	⊥	I	I	⊥	I	I
I	I	I	I	I	I	I	I	I	I	⊤

The Bochvar truth tables can be summarized like this: if any component of a statement has the value I, then the statement has the value I, and the statement gets its classical value otherwise. The Kleene table encapsulates the idea that if the value of a component of a statement is sufficient, considering the classical truth tables, to determine the truth value of the statement (for instance, if the antecedent of a conditional is false), then the statement gets that value, even if another component of the statement is indeterminate. The Łukasiewicz table is the same as the Kleene table, except that $P \to Q$ gets the value ⊤ when both P and Q get the value I. Notice that stability is therefore not satisfied, for if we determine that the antecedent is true, the value of the conditional becomes I, and if we determine that the antecedent is ⊤ and the consequent ⊥, then the conditional becomes ⊥.

In Chapter 1 we defined an argument to be *valid* precisely if there is no case in which all its premises are true and its conclusion not true. We may continue to use the same definition even with three distinct truth values. The only difference in the present case is that what is ruled out is not merely the *falsity* of the conclusion in cases where the premises are all true, as is the case if we are assuming bivalence, but *the falsity or indeterminacy* of the conclusion. Similarly, a statement is *valid* if there is no truth value assignment on which it is either false or indeterminate.

In just the same way one can read off appropriate propositional tree rules from the classical truth tables, one can read off what the tree rules must be for any of these three-valued systems. We will presently do so for the Kleene and Łukasiewicz systems, but will first explain why trees for the Bochvar system are of little interest. First, we note that

PROPOSITION 5.1 *There are no valid statements in either Bochvar or Kleene logic.*

To see this, observe that, in both Bochvar and Kleene logic, if all the immediate components of a statement P receive the value I, then P itself has the value I. It follows that on a valuation where all the atoms which occur in P receive the value I, so, too, will P.

However, when one considers not the validity of *statements*, but the validity of *arguments*, the cases of Kleene and Bochvar logic are quite different. For in Bochvar logic, on any valuation under which *one* of the statement letters in P receives the value I, P will have the value I. While it doesn't quite follow that there are *no* valid arguments in Bochvar logic—"P, therefore P" remains valid, for instance, as does any argument with an unsatisfiable set of premises—it does follow that the class of such arguments is rather uninteresting, at least for present purposes. For if a single statement letter occurs in the conclusion but not in any premise, and the set of premises is satisfiable, the argument will be invalid.[3] As we shall see, Kleene logic has a somewhat more interesting class of valid arguments.

In constructing tree rules for three-valued Kleene logic, as one might expect from the fact that it meets the faithfulness and stability conditions, all the rules for classical propositional trees considered in Chapter 1 are correct. The same would be true for Bochvar logic. The systems differ because in the Kleene tables if the value of a component is sufficient to determine, classically, the value of the statement, then it will do so in the Kleene tables. So the rules from Chapter 1 are rule-complete as well as correct. However, as one might expect, the addition of a third truth value means our system of trees, even for Kleene logic, needs to be somewhat more complex.

5.1.1   Trees for Three-Valued Logic

Recall that each open path of a tree under construction in classical logic represents an attempt to construct a valuation demonstrating the satisfiability of the set of statements with which we began (and so a counterexample to the validity of an argument or statement if that is what we are testing). There are two main complications in the three-valued case.

REMARK 5.1 (NEW NOTATION) In classical trees the presence of the statement P on a path requires that P be true under any suitable valuation, while $\neg P$ requires its falsity. In a three-valued logic we need some way of indicating on trees that P has the value I. To this end, we introduce a new piece of notation—the letter I, used thus: $I(P)$—which allows us to express the indeterminacy of P in a purely formal way. Note that I is *not* to be regarded as a new logical operator, akin to $\wedge$ or $\neg$, nor do we regard $I(P)$ as a statement of our language for propositional logic. Rather, it is a *purely formal constituent of trees*. The I sign is only allowed to be placed *at the front* of any statement. Thus the brackets are used here merely for the sake of readability, since the I in $I\,P \wedge Q$ must refer to the whole statement $P \wedge Q$, and not merely to P.

---

[3]One way to circumvent this unfortunate absence of validities in Bochvar logic is to modify the definition of validity. For instance, one might stipulate that both $\top$ and I are *designated values*, and say that an argument is valid if there is no valuation on which all the premises have a designated value but the conclusion is false. We shall not pursue this approach here.

The second complication is that when testing for validity we now have available *two different sorts of counterexamples.* That is, an argument can be shown invalid by producing a valuation under which the premises are true and the conclusion false, but also might be shown invalid by producing a valuation under which the premises are true and the conclusion merely indeterminate. The simplest way to handle this complication is to adopt the following procedures:

REMARK 5.2 To show that an argument is *invalid*, it suffices to construct a tree which begins with (some subset of) the premises and *either* the *negation* of the conclusion *or* the conclusion *marked with I* which has a complete open path. On the other hand, to show that an argument is *valid* requires that one show neither sort of counterexample is possible, and so *two trees must be constructed and shown to close.* Note that if we are using the trees to test for *satisfiability* rather than for validity, *we need only to consider one tree*, since all sentences in the set must be *true* if the set is to be satisfiable.

Trees for Kleene Logic

The set of tree rules for three-valued Kleene logic, then, include all the rules listed for classical propositional logic (see page 1.3.1), and in addition the rules:

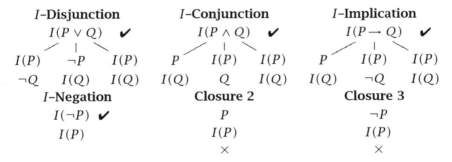

An important contrast between Kleene's and Bochvar's systems is that many classically valid arguments are valid in Kleene logic though not in Bochvar logic. For instance, the argument A, therefore $B \rightarrow A$ is invalid in Bochvar's system (consider a valuation under which A is true and B is indeterminate), but is valid in Kleene's system. To show the latter fact requires two trees. As will always be the case when constructing Kleene trees for a classically valid argument (or statement), the tree which begins with A and $\neg(B \rightarrow A)$ is routine. So consider the tree

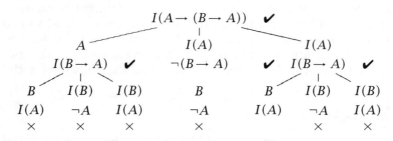

Since this tree closes as well, the argument in question is valid. On the other hand, to show that an argument or statement is not valid, a single tree suffices. For example, the tree

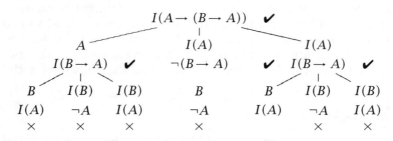

suffices to show that $A \rightarrow (B \rightarrow C)$ (hence the schema $P \rightarrow (Q \rightarrow P)$), which is classically valid, is not a valid statement in Kleene's system, because it shows that this statement will be indeterminate if A is indeterminate while B is true. Note that these two examples also show that what one might regard as the expected relationship between validity of arguments and validity of implication statements breaks down: in this system it is no longer the case that $P \rightarrow Q$ is a valid statement if and only if "P, therefore Q" is a valid argument.

EXERCISES 5.1.1

1. Construct trees which show the following arguments to be valid in Kleene's system.

   (a) $P \therefore Q \rightarrow P$.

   * (b) $\neg P \therefore P \rightarrow Q$.

   (c) $\neg(P \vee Q) \therefore \neg P \wedge \neg Q$.

2. Construct trees which show the following statements and arguments to be invalid in Kleene's system. (Hint: all are classically valid.)

   (a) $A \rightarrow A$.

   * (b) $A \wedge B \rightarrow A$.

   (c) $(A \rightarrow B) \vee (B \rightarrow A)$.

   (d) $\neg(A \wedge B) \rightarrow \neg A \vee \neg B$.

   (e) $A \vee \neg A$.

(f) $A \therefore B \to B$.

(g) $A \therefore B \vee \neg B$.

Trees for Łukasiewicz Logic

Since it is only with respect to the interpretation of $\to$ that Łukasiewicz's system differs from Kleene's, we can leave all Kleene tree rules in place apart from those for implication statements. In the Łukasiewicz system we use the rules:

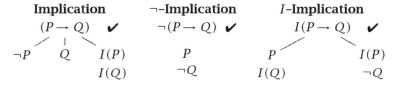

Implication	¬–Implication	*I*-Implication

As with trees for the Kleene system, strictly speaking we need two trees to show that any statement is valid, because there are two different ways in which it might fail to be valid. However, in the case of Kleene's system, if we were considering a formula we already knew to be a classical validity, we could avoid constructing the tree which begins with the negation of the statement to be tested, since that tree would simply be the classical tree. In the case of statements which contain no occurrences of $\to$, we can continue to reason this way in Łukasiewicz's system. If $\to$ occurs in the statement, however, we must be a bit more cautious, because the rule for $\to$ is not the familiar one from classical logic. If in the course of constructing the tree we encounter an unnegated $\to$ statement, we shall have I occurring on the tree.

Let's consider some examples. First, we show that $P \to (Q \to P)$ is valid. We leave it to the reader to check the tree for the negation of this statement. The other relevant tree is the following:

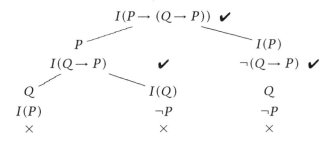

Thus, there are some statements which are not valid in the Kleene system which are valid in the Łukasiewicz system. On the other hand, there remain many classical validities which are not valid in this system. The following tree illustrates one such case.

$$I(A \lor \neg A) \; ✔$$

$$
\begin{array}{ccc}
I(A) & I(\neg A) \;✔ & I(A) \\
\neg\neg A \;✔ & \neg A & I(\neg A) \;✔ \\
A & I(A) & I(A) \\
\times & \times &
\end{array}
$$

EXERCISES 5.1.2

1. Construct trees which show the following statements to be valid in Łukasiewicz logic.

   (a) $P \rightarrow (Q \rightarrow Q)$.

   (b) $\neg\neg P \rightarrow P$.

   * (c) $(P \rightarrow Q) \lor (Q \rightarrow P)$.

2. Construct trees which show the following statements and arguments to be invalid in Łukasiewicz logic.

   (a) $A \rightarrow B \lor \neg B$.

   (b) $A \lor \neg A$.

   * (c) $\neg(A \land \neg A)$.

   (d) $A \rightarrow B \therefore \neg A \lor B$.

   (e) $A \rightarrow B \therefore \neg(A \land \neg B)$.

3. Let $\max(x, y)$ be an operation which chooses the *larger* of two numbers x and y (and which chooses x if they are equal), and let $\min(x, y)$ be the analogous operation which chooses the minimum. Take the truth values $\top$, $\bot$ and I to be the numbers 1, 0 and $\frac{1}{2}$. Show, using the definitions above, that:

   (a) $[\![A \land B]\!] = \min([\![A]\!], [\![B]\!])$.

   (b) $[\![A \lor B]\!] = \max([\![A]\!], [\![B]\!])$.

   * (c) $[\![A \rightarrow B]\!] = 1$ if $[\![A]\!] \leqslant [\![B]\!]$, and $1 - ([\![A]\!] - [\![B]\!])$ otherwise.

   (d) $[\![\neg A]\!] = 1 - [\![A]\!]$.

5.2   Intuitionistic Logic

The name "intuitionistic logic" derives from the origin of this system of logic in the work of a group of mathematicians and philosophers of mathematics in the first third of the 20th Century, centred around L.E.J. Brouwer, who were known as the *intuitionists*. By now, though, the name is more-or-less a historical curiosity. Most of those who nowadays regard it as the *correct* logic (perhaps as the correct logic for some specific purpose) are unlikely to buy much of Brouwer's philosophy, which tends towards solipsism. Moreover this system of logic has proved itself useful in many areas—in theoretical computer science, in proof theory, and in various newer approaches to the philosophy of mathematics which have quite different starting points from Brouwer's—so that it is a system which is taken seriously by many who don't think it is the correct logic, or who think that the notion of correctness is inapplicable in discussions of systems of logic.

5.2.1 Introduction—Constructivism

There are a great many interpretations of intuitionistic logic. We shall not be able to investigate all of them. However, it will be helpful to take a very brief look at the *constructivist* understanding of logic which motivates some advocates of intuitionistic logic. There are many versions of constructivism in mathematics and logic, and these differ in certain philosophically very significant respects. These philosophical differences can result in disagreements about which principles ought to be accepted, but there turns out to be quite general (though not unanimous) agreement on which propositional and first-order quantificational principles are genuinely constructive, even among views which differ sharply in areas such as set theory or higher-order quantification.

It is useful to begin by considering some unsolved problem in mathematics. Here is an example used by Brouwer. Consider the decimal expansion of $\pi = 3.14\ldots$. Almost nothing is known about regularities in this expansion. It is unknown, for instance, whether it contains a sequence of 9 nines. So, let $A(n)$ be the statement that "the nth decimal of π is a nine, and it is preceded by 8 nines." Now, in classical logic it is a logical truth that $\exists x A(x) \vee \neg \exists x A(x)$, and given bivalence it follows that there either *is* or there *is not* an n such that $A(n)$.

"But," a constructivist will ask, "why should we believe *that*?" Notice, first of all, that our failure to detect such a sequence of nines in the expansion of π as we have it so far is not much negative evidence, since even a few million decimal places is an infinitesimally small fragment of the whole expansion. On the other hand, it's certainly not *positive* evidence either. It is indeed tempting to believe that there must nevertheless be a fact of the matter—either there is such an n or there is not. But in this conviction the constructivist detects a commitment to a most unpalatable platonism— a platonism in which the complete decimal expansion of π is "out there" somewhere, outside of space and time, and the mere fact that we do not have and will never have access to it doesn't affect the fact that there either is or is not a sequence of 9 nines in it. This the constructivist finds to be a most unlikely story about what it is for a mathematical statement to be *true*. What it means for a mathematical statement to be true, the constructivists say, is that the statement is *provable* (and to say it is *false* is to say that it is *refutable*). The reasons offered by constructivists for saying this differ in detail, but they have to do with the fact that our only *grounds* for asserting the truth of mathematical claims involve proofs, with the fact that such an account is easier to square with the recognition that mathematics is a human activity—which is to say that it a construction of beings who fail to possess any evident method of grasping the mysterious seeming sort of mind-independent reality ("Plato's heaven") that would be required to fix truth values of statements if mathematical truth meant anything else—and with the difficulty of explaining why proofs should be regarded as evidence about the nature of some mind- and language-independent realm of mathematical objects.

If, as the constructivist contends, *mathematical truth* is *provability*, it is clear that we *cannot assert* the principle of bivalence. For we have *no reason* to think that $\exists x A(x)$ must be either provable or refutable. (Note that saying that one is unwilling to *assert* bivalence is *not* the same as *denying* it. Indeed, one might suspect the temptation to conflate these two things itself indicates an unspoken commitment to bivalence.) But if one is not committed to bivalence, it is not clear why one should be committed to the *law of excluded middle*, i.e., to the claim that $P \vee \neg P$ is a logical truth for every statement P: for a statement to be true it must be provable, and unless one can appeal to a general principle such as bivalence to license the proofs of statements of this form, the provability of a disjunction would seem to involve the provability of one of its disjuncts; the general faith in the provability or refutability of every statement is precisely what leads the constructivist to refuse to assert bivalence.

Considerations such as these lead constructivists to offer an alternative account of when one ought to be willing to assert statements involving logical operators. We give the merest sketch. First, given that truth means provability, what could the truth of $P \wedge Q$ be, except provability of both P and Q? The constructivist can agree with the classical logician that one may assert $P \wedge Q$ when and only when one is in a position to assert each of its conjuncts. More interestingly, the truth of $P \vee Q$, as in a bivalent system, means no more than the truth of P or the truth of Q, but to the constructivist this means the provability of P or the provability of Q. The result is that a constructivist will assert $P \vee Q$ *only if in a position to assert one of the disjuncts*. This is a very different account of assertability from the classical one, for classically we may assert $P \vee \neg P$ for cases where we haven't any idea which of P or $\neg P$ is assertable.

For the case of $P \rightarrow Q$, constructivists and classical logicians will disagree both about the meaning and about the conditions of assertion. If you think of what it means to prove a conditional claim, it is clear that (unlike the previous cases) such a proof need not—indeed is unlikely to—involve proofs of subformulas in the way the earlier cases did. Instead, such a sentence, according to a constructivist, says that *if* we can prove P, then we can also prove Q. How could *that* be established? Roughly speaking—for it is here that disagreements between different flavours of constructivism are likely to surface—the constructivist answer is that $P \rightarrow Q$ is proved if we have a *method* which we can use to convert any proof of P into a proof of Q. So a conditional sentence is proved by coming up with a method for manipulating proofs, and so it is a proof of a quite different sort from the earlier cases.

We can use this account of the truth of conditionals to capture the constructivist idea that the *falsity* of a statement is its *refutability*. For the fundamental method of refuting a statement is to show that it *could not be true*. In the hands of a constructivist, this amounts to the claim that it *could not be provable*. The canonical method for establishing such a claim is to show how any purported proof of the statement can be shown defective. On the basis of this reasoning, it is typical for formulations of intuitionistic logic to begin with a primitive sentence, $\bot$, which is the absurd sentence, and to take $\neg P$ to be *defined by* $P \rightarrow \bot$. (In order to use the same languages we used for classical logic, we shall take $\neg$ as to be primitive and define $\bot$ to be $P \wedge \neg P$ for an arbitrary but fixed statement P. The final result is equivalent.) Thus, given the above explanation of $\rightarrow$, $\neg P$ means that P has been *refuted* in the sense that it has been *reduced to absurdity*.

The constructivist interpretation of the propositional connectives yields a sort of *informal semantics*, in the sense that it tells us what a constructivist takes each connective to mean. But this leaves open the question of what a *formal* semantics appropriate for intuitionistic logic would be. Since such a semantics must allow for the possibility of statements which are neither provable nor refutable, hence which are neither true nor false, the classical truth tables clearly won't do. A natural first conjecture to test would be that the constructivist meaning of the connectives might be captured by some three-valued logic. But this cannot be right, nor will increasing the number of truth values to any finite number help, as is shown by the following result, due to Kurt Gödel.

PROPOSITION 5.2 *No truth-functional, faithful n-valued logic, for any fixed, finite n, can provide a semantics appropriate for intuitionistic propositional logic.*

To see this, first note that in intuitionistic logic $A \rightarrow A$ must come out a logical truth (any proof of A obviously can be "transformed" into a proof of A, by doing nothing to it). Thus any truth table for intuitionistic logic will need to share with Łukasiewicz logic the property that if two statements A and B receive the same intermediate value, $A \rightarrow B$ will receive the value $\top$.

Next, suppose that there are n truth values, and let $P_1, \ldots, P_{n+1}$ be distinct statement letters. Then under any valuation, for some $j, k \leqslant n + 1$, P_j and P_k must receive the same truth value. Under that valuation, $P_j \longleftrightarrow P_k$ (which is, we recall, an abbreviation for the statement $(P_j \rightarrow P_k) \wedge (P_k \rightarrow P_j)$) will receive the value $\top$. But it follows that the statement

$$(P_1 \longleftrightarrow P_2) \vee (P_1 \longleftrightarrow P_3) \vee \cdots \vee (P_1 \longleftrightarrow P_{n+1}) \vee (P_2 \longleftrightarrow P_3) \vee \cdots \vee (P_n \longleftrightarrow P_{n+1})$$

will get the value ⊤ under *any* valuation. That is, this statement will be valid in any such n-valued logic. But since each of the P_i is atomic, for any $i, j \leqslant n+1$ there will be valuations under which P_i is ⊤ and P_j is ⊥ and so on which $P_i \longleftrightarrow P_j$ is ⊥. Hence, this semantics is inappropriate for intuitionistic logic, since if it were appropriate the disjunction would be provable while no disjunct was provable, contrary to the constructivist meaning assigned above to disjunctions.

5.2.2   A More General Account

If we want a semantics for intuitionistic logic, clearly it must be of a different sort from truth tables. As we shall see, we can get one by noticing that what leads constructivists to the rejection of bivalence and so to revisions of logic is an unwillingness to make an assertion in the absence of a proof (or conclusive evidence of the provability of) the statement in question. Thus we have in play not merely the identification of truth with provability, but also the identification of legitimate assertibility and conclusive grounds. A constructivist will refuse to assent to $P \vee \neg P$ precisely when no conclusive grounds are available either for or against P. Looked at in this way, bearing in mind constructivists' insistence that proof is the only legitimate ground for claims to mathematical knowledge, the crucial feature of intuitionistic reasoning is that "not (known to be) true" is not the same as "(known to be) false."

   We see, then, that intuitionistic logic can be viewed as a kind of *epistemic* (or *apodeictic*) logic. The principal difference between them is that, in *epistemic* logic, as in any contextual logic, the statement operators □ and ◊ are introduced as explicit devices to represent knowledge (or conclusive evidence), thereby enlarging the class of statements, while the meaning of— and thus the logical principles governing—the statements on which they operate remains the same: simple truth or falsity. In intuitionistic logic, on the other hand, the criterion of evidence is, so to speak, injected into the meaning of the statements themselves. As we have seen above, this results in a change in the rules of reasoning.

Trees for Propositional Intuitionistic Logic

The tree rules we shall formulate for intuitionistic logic will involve a new piece of notation—the interrogative sign ?—which is akin to I as used in the trees for three-valued logics. It will allow us to express in a purely formal way the idea of a statement which is *not known to be true*. Thus, for any statement P, we will be able to write ?(P) and think of it as asserting that P is not known to be true, or that we do not possess conclusive evidence for P. Clearly ?(P) does not entail $\neg P$, that is, it does not entail that P is known to be false. As we have said, we do not regard ? as a new logical operator, nor do we regard ?(P) as a new statement of our logical system. Rather, expressions of the form ?(*P*) are to be viewed as *purely formal constituents of trees*. The ? sign is only allowed to be placed at the front of any statement. Thus, strictly speaking, no brackets are needed for writing interrogatives, and they are included only for the sake of readability: for example in ? *P* ∧ *Q* the ? sign must apply to the whole statement *P* ∧ *Q*, and not just to *P*.

As a kind of epistemic logic, intuitionistic logic is related to the system S4 of contextual logic considered in the previous chapter. Recall that this latter captures truth in *preordered* contextual structures, that is, those in which the *R*-relation is *reflexive* and *transitive*. These structures also furnish natural interpretations of statements of intuitionistic logic. When playing that role, *localities* in such structures should be thought of as *stages of knowledge*, and the *R*-relations as relations of *possible development of knowledge*. That is, if *a* and *b* are stages of knowledge, *aRb* is understood to mean that what is known at stage *b* is a possible development of what is known at stage *a*. When *R* is thought of in this way, it is quite natural to require it to be both reflexive and transitive.

We now state our tree rules for intuitionistic propositional logic. They are the following:

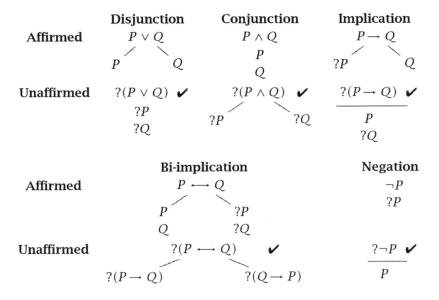

Transport rule. We are allowed to carry any statement not marked by "?" across any horizontal line introduced by the ?→ and ?¬ rules.

Closure rule. A path is closed when (and only when) both *P* and ?*P* occur on it not separated by a horizontal line. When this is the case, the path is marked, as before, by "×". (And, as usual, a tree is closed if all its paths are.)

Note that these rules—apart from those for $\neg$, $? \rightarrow$, $? \longleftrightarrow$ and $?\neg$ and the transport rule—are essentially the corresponding classical rules with "?" in place of "$\neg$." The $\neg$ rule is a device for converting $\neg P$ into an expression we can work with, since our rules are formulated in terms of "?" rather than "$\neg$." Clearly the negation rule allows us to close a path if both P and $\neg P$ occur on it not separated by a horizontal line. Note that the $\neg$ rule and the $\rightarrow$ rule are *correct*, but not *complete*—that $\neg P$ is true certainly implies that P is not (yet) known to be true, but the converse does not hold, and similarly for $\rightarrow$. Also note that we *do not* tick statements after application of a rule to an affirmed statement. This is because the transport rule means that such statements should not be "erased."

The $\rightarrow$ rule deserves a detailed explanation. The key point is that—in contrast with classical logic—implication in intuitionistic logic is not material implication: that is, $P \rightarrow Q$ is not equivalent to $\neg P \vee Q$. In classical logic, the justification for identifying $P \rightarrow Q$ with $\neg P \vee Q$ rests on the principle of bivalence, in particular on the claim that either P or $\neg P$ must be true. Then, if P is true, so is Q by the entailment of Q by P. Hence $\neg P \vee Q$. Since intuitionistic logic does not (as we have seen) satisfy the principle of bivalence, this justification breaks down. What rule should we then adopt for implication? Let us look at things from an epistemic standpoint. Asserting that "P implies Q" is known[4] amounts to asserting that, if P comes to be known, then so thereby will Q. Another way of putting this is to say that knowledge of $P \rightarrow Q$ means possessing a method for converting knowledge of P into knowledge of Q. In that case since in fact either P is known or P is not known, it follows that either P is not known or Q is known. This is the content of the $\rightarrow$ rule. Similar remarks apply to the $\longleftrightarrow$ rule.

Next, consider the $? \rightarrow$ rule. Recall that in contextual logic the horizontal line indicated passage to a new locality. Here the horizontal line may be taken to signalize advancement to a later stage of knowledge. Why is it needed? Because, to say that at some stage $P \rightarrow Q$ isn't known is to say that (for all that is known at that stage) it could turn out that, at some later stage, P comes to be known without thereby causing Q also to become known. This is the content of the $? \rightarrow$ rule.

To justify the $?\neg$ rule, we observe that to say that P isn't known to be false at a given stage is to say that it could turn out that P becomes known at some later stage. Or again, we can recall that intuitionistically $\neg P$ is equivalent to $P \rightarrow \bot$, so the $?\neg$ rule is simply the $? \rightarrow$ rule, together with the recognition that $?\bot$ is always true and so it is redundant to state it.

Two statements on the same path not separated by a horizontal line may be said to occur *at the same stage of knowledge*. The closure rule expresses the obvious fact that something can't be both known and not known at the same stage of knowledge.

The transport rule is designed to reflect a simple feature of our usual understanding of the claim that a statement is known to be true: if P is

---

[4]Henceforth the term "known," if used without qualification, will mean "known to be true."

known at some stage, then it is true, and so will continue to be true—and known—at all later stages. This property is called *persistence*.

It is important to note that in applying the ? → or ?¬ rules to statements on a single path *occurring at the same stage of knowledge*—that is, not separated by a horizontal line—it is necessary to introduce a separate and independent horizontal line for each such application. This is illustrated by

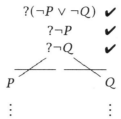

in which the fork is obtained by independent applications of the ?¬ rule to ?¬P and ?¬Q *within a single path*. If either side of this fork closes, then the whole path closes, just as was the case in contextual logic when two applications of the ◊ rule were made at a single point on a single path. So, for example, the tree

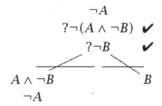

will *close*, because the left side of this path will close, even though the right side of the path is finished and open.

Note that the ? ⟷ rule is really just an application of ?∧ to ?(P → Q) ∧ (Q → P) which is obviously appropriate since P ⟷ Q is merely an abbreviation for that conjunction.

The tree test for validity is applied to intuitionistic statements in just the same way as for classical statements, except that ? replaces ¬. That is, to determine whether a statement P is intuitionistically valid, start a tree with ?P: if the tree closes in the new sense, P is valid. If it doesn't, then P is invalid and a countermodel can be read off from the tree, as we shall see later.

Here are some examples of intuitionistically valid statements. In each case, the tree closes through straightforward application of the above rules.

1. $P \rightarrow (Q \rightarrow P)$.

$$\frac{?[P \rightarrow (Q \rightarrow P)] \; \checkmark}{\begin{array}{c} P \\ ?[Q \rightarrow P] \quad \checkmark \end{array}}$$

$$\begin{array}{c} Q \\ ?P \\ P \\ \times \end{array}$$

2. $P \rightarrow [Q \rightarrow (P \wedge Q)]$.

$$\frac{?[P \rightarrow (Q \rightarrow (P \wedge Q))] \; \checkmark}{\begin{array}{c} P \\ ?[Q \rightarrow (P \wedge Q)] \quad \checkmark \end{array}}$$

$$\begin{array}{c} Q \\ ?(P \wedge Q) \end{array}$$

$$\begin{array}{ccc} ?P & & ?Q \\ P & & \times \\ \times & & \end{array}$$

3. $(\neg P \vee Q) \rightarrow (P \rightarrow Q)$.

$$\frac{?[(\neg P \vee Q) \rightarrow (P \rightarrow Q)] \; \checkmark}{\begin{array}{c} \neg P \vee Q \\ ?[P \rightarrow Q] \quad \checkmark \end{array}}$$

$$\begin{array}{c} P \\ ?Q \\ \neg P \vee Q \quad \checkmark \end{array}$$

$$\begin{array}{ccc} \neg P & & Q \\ ?P & & \times \\ \times & & \end{array}$$

EXERCISES 5.2.1
By constructing closed trees, show that each of the following statements is intuitionistically valid.

1. $[P \rightarrow (Q \rightarrow R)] \rightarrow [(P \rightarrow Q) \rightarrow (P \rightarrow R)]$.

2. $(P \wedge Q) \rightarrow P$.

3. $P \rightarrow (P \vee Q)$.

4. $(P \rightarrow R) \rightarrow [(Q \rightarrow R) \rightarrow [(P \vee Q) \rightarrow R]]$.

5. $(P \rightarrow Q) \rightarrow [(P \rightarrow \neg Q) \rightarrow \neg P]$.

6. $\neg P \rightarrow (P \rightarrow Q)$.

7. $[P \wedge (P \rightarrow Q)] \rightarrow Q$.

8. $[(P \vee \neg P) \rightarrow ((P \rightarrow Q) \rightarrow (\neg P \vee Q))]$.

9. $P \rightarrow \neg\neg P$.

* 10. $\neg\neg\neg P \longleftrightarrow \neg P$.

11. $(P \vee \neg P) \rightarrow (\neg\neg P \rightarrow P)$.

12. $P \wedge (Q \vee R) \longleftrightarrow (P \wedge Q) \vee (P \wedge R)$.

13. $P \vee (Q \wedge R) \longleftrightarrow (P \vee Q) \wedge (P \vee R)$.

14. $\neg (P \vee Q) \longleftrightarrow \neg P \wedge \neg Q$.

* 15. $(\neg P \vee \neg Q) \rightarrow \neg (P \wedge Q)$.

5.2.3 Semantics and Countermodels

We now give a precise definition of the idea of an *interpretation* of statements of intuitionistic logic, similar to that given for contextual statements.
For simplicity let us reserve the name "frame" for frames in which R is a
preordering. If $\mathcal{F} = \langle W, R \rangle$ is a frame, the localities in W will often be called
stages of knowledge. Instead of aRb, we will write $a \leqslant b$ (or $b \geqslant a$) and
read this "*b* is later than (or the same as) *a*." An (intuitionistic) valuation of
statements in a frame $\mathcal{F}$ is a function I which assigns, to each pair consisting of a member of W and a statement letter A, an element $I(a, A)$ of $\{\top, \bot\}$
in such a way that the condition

Persistence. For any statement letter A, if $I(a, A) = \top$ and $a \leqslant b$, then
  $I(b, A) = \top$.

is satisfied.
  We extend the interpretation to every statement of the language as follows.

DEFINITION 5.1 The interpretation of a statement P at a stage in the frame
$\mathcal{F}$ under the valuation I, denoted $I(a, P)$ is defined as follows:

1. If P is atomic, $I(a, P)$ is already defined.

2. $I(a, P \wedge Q) = \top \iff I(a, P) = I(a, Q) = \top$.

3. $I(a, P \vee Q) = \top \iff I(a, P) = \top$ or $I(a, Q) = \top$.

4. $I(a, \neg P) = \top \iff I(b, P) = \bot$ for all $b \geqslant a$.

5. $I(a, P \rightarrow Q) = \top \iff$ for all $b \geqslant a$, if $I(b, P) = \top$, then $I(b, Q) = \top$.

6. $I(a, P \longleftrightarrow Q)) = \top \iff I(b, P) = I(b, Q)$ for all $b \geqslant a$.

If $I(a, P) = \top$, we say that P is *true* (under I) *at stage a*. Thus the persistence condition stipulates that if a statement letter is true at some stage, it remains true at all later stages: its truth is, in a word, persistent. It is not difficult to show that then the truth of *any* statement is persistent in this sense. Notice also that, according to the second and third clauses, the truth of $P \wedge Q$ and $P \vee Q$ at a given stage is completely determined by the truth values of P and Q at that stage. However, this is not the case for $\neg P$, $P \rightarrow Q$, or $P \longleftrightarrow Q$. For example, according to the fourth clause, $\neg P$ is true at a given stage if and only if P has the value $\bot$ at all later stages (recall that "later" includes the given stage). And according to the fifth clause, $P \rightarrow Q$ is true at a given stage if and only if Q is true at *any later stage at which P is true*.

If P is true at every stage under I, we shall say simply that P is *valid under I*. If P is valid under I for every interpretation, we say that P is *valid in the frame*. If P is valid in every frame, we say that P is (*intuitionistically propositionally*) *valid*.

EXERCISES 5.2.2
1. Prove that if P is true at a stage under I, then it is true at every later stage. (Argue by induction on the formation of P.)

* 2. Prove that $I(a, \neg\neg P) = \top$ if and only if for all $b \geqslant a$ there is a $c \geqslant b$ such that $I(c, P) = \top$.

It can be shown without much difficulty that the rules we have given are correct (in the usual sense) for intuitionistic statements provided we take the truth of ?P at any stage as meaning that P has the value $\bot$ *at that stage*, with no reference to future stages. This means that, in using the tree method in the familiar way (that is, as for statements of contextual logic) to generate countermodels for intuitionistically invalid statements, statement letters will be assigned the value $\bot$ at stages where they occur preceded by ?. This will result in the truth values of statements changing from $\bot$ to $\top$ as knowledge "advances." While a trifle counterintuitive, it is the price that must be paid for employing just the two truth values $\top$ and $\bot$ in intuitionistic interpretations. It is, nevertheless, perfectly consistent, since, while truth is required to persist, the same is not demanded of the value $\bot$.[5] The most natural way to read the value $\bot$ at a stage might be as

---

[5] Alternatively, we might have employed three truth values at each stage. On this approach, each P would receive the value $\bot$ at a stage if and only if $\neg P$ received the value $\top$, and both truth and falsity would persist, though the third value would not. Of course, even working

"not yet known to be true," where this is taken to cover both cases where this is due to the fact that the statement in question is *known to be false* or to its being *as yet undecided.*

Just as for contextual logic, the tree method can be used to construct countermodels for statements of intuitionistic propositional logic. We conclude by constructing a countermodel for $(A \to B) \to (\neg A \lor B)$.

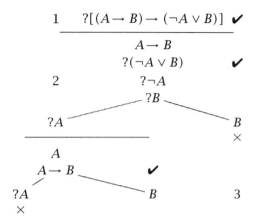

The tree is finished and has one open branch. That branch contains three stages of knowledge which we label 1, 2, 3. At stage 2, both $?A$ and $?B$ appear, so our interpretation will assign $\bot$ to A and B there. Similarly, at stage 3, it assigns $\top$ to both A and B. Thus the countermodel I will be an interpretation in the frame $\langle W, R \rangle$ where $W = \{1, 2, 3\}$, R is the usual "equal to or less than" relation on $\{1, 2, 3\}$, and $I(2, A) = I(2, B) = \bot$, $I(3, A) = I(3, B) = \top$. (To respect persistence we must also take $I(1, A) = I(1, B) = \bot$, but this fact will not figure in our calculations.) Clearly $I(2, A \to B) = \top$. On the other hand, since $I(3, A) = \top$, we have $I(2, \neg A) = \bot$, so that $I(2, \neg A \lor B) = \bot$. Therefore $I(2, (A \to B) \to (\neg A \lor B)) = \bot$, so I is a countermodel for $(A \to B) \to (\neg A \lor B)$.

EXERCISES 5.2.3
Using the tree method as above, construct intuitionistic countermodels for the following statements.

*   1. $\neg\neg A \to A$.

*   2. $A \lor \neg A$.

*   3. $(A \to B) \lor (B \to A)$.

    4. $\neg\neg A \lor \neg A$.

    5. $\neg(A \land B) \to (\neg A \lor \neg B)$.

with two truth values in the interpretations, "falsity persists," if falsity is taken to be truth of a negation, since $\neg P$, once true, remains true.

5.2.4 Metatheorems for Intuitionistic Propositional Logic

The proof of the correctness takes a by now familiar form. First, we shall modify our terminology slightly by saying that the expression ?P is *true at a stage of knowledge (or locality) s* under an interpretation I if and only if $I(s, P) = \perp$. This is an extension of the terminology because ?P isn't really a statement of the language, and so isn't, strictly speaking, interpreted by I at all. We speak in the sequel of the *expressions* which appear on a tree, since it is not only statements which occupy nodes of trees for intuitionistic logic. We correspondingly extend the notion of a set of expressions being *satisfied* by an interpretation, and hence being *satisfiable*, to include expressions which begin with ?.

We must establish the

LEMMA 5.3 *If a tree τ starts with some set S of expressions and includes a path ψ such that all expressions on the path are true at appropriate localities on some interpretation I, then any tree τ^* which results from the application of a tree rule to τ includes a path ψ^* such that all expressions on it are true at appropriate localities on some interpretation I^*.*

Here by "true at appropriate localities in an interpretation" we mean, as we did in our discussions of the metatheory for contextual logic, that all expressions which occur on a single path and which occur together before any horizontal line on a tree, or between a pair of horizontal lines on a tree, or after a final horizontal line on a tree, are true at a single locality under that interpretation.

To prove the lemma, first note that we may suppose that τ^* results from τ by application of a rule to some member of ψ, or else it suffices to note that ψ can serve as ψ^*, since all its members are true at appropriate localities under I. We then consider the various rules in turn. In effect, we show that all the rules are *rule-sound*. In fact, all these rules are not merely sound but *rule-correct*—that is, if the premise of the application of such a rule is true at some locality under I, then so too are all the members of some set of conclusions of that application of the rule. This is particularly obvious for the $\wedge$ and $\vee$ rules. A few of the cases are more interesting.

First, consider the $\rightarrow$ rule. By hypothesis, $P \rightarrow Q$ is true at some stage of knowledge w. But at $I(w, P)$ is either $\top$ or $\perp$. If it is $\top$, so too is $I(w, Q)$, or else $I(w, P \rightarrow Q) = \perp$. So either $I(w, P) = \perp$, in which case ?P is true at the appropriate locality in P, or Q is true at W.

For the ?¬ rule, suppose that $\neg P$ has the value $\perp$ at w. This is the case only if $\neg P$ does not have the value $\top$, which is to say that it is the case only if it is not the case that for every $x \geqslant w$, $I(x, P) = \perp$. But then there is some locality x such that $w \leqslant x$ and $I(x, P) = \top$.

The remaining cases are left as an exercise.

With this lemma we prove the

THEOREM 5.4 (CORRECTNESS OF THE TREE METHOD)
If a finite set S of expressions is satisfiable, then there is an open path through any tree starting with S.

If all the expressions on a path are true at appropriate localities under some valuation, then the path must be open. For P and $?P$ cannot both be true at a single locality, so the supposition that the path is closed is contrary to the requirement that all expressions are true at appropriate localities in an interpretation. Now, if S is satisfiable, then all members of S must be true at a single locality under some interpretation, which is to say that all statements in a tree beginning with S are true at appropriate points of some interpretation. But then any tree which begins with S will also have all its expressions true at appropriate points in some interpretation, and hence will have an open path.

From this, we get as an immediate consequence

THEOREM 5.5 (ARGUMENT CORRECTNESS)
If a tree associated with an argument closes, then the argument is valid.

The adequacy of the tree method may be shown in more than one way. We could use the method of constructing the *canonical frame* for a set of statements of intuitionistic propositional logic, in a manner similar to the one employed in our proof of completeness of K for the class of all frames in contextual logic. Instead, we use a method akin to that used in the proofs of the adequacy of tree methods for classical propositional and predicate logic. That is, we shall show that if every tree beginning with a set S of expressions is open, then some path of one such tree determines an interpretation in which the members of that set are all true at appropriate localities.

The outline of what such a proof will look like should be clear from discussion in earlier chapters. We need to take the following steps:

1. Give an appropriate specification of a *systematic tree* for intuitionistic propositional logic.

2. Define an appropriate modification of the notion of a Hintikka set—we shall call it a *Hintikka collection*—for intuitionistic propositional logic.

3. Show that every Hintikka collection is satisfiable.

4. Show that any non-terminating path of a systematic tree for intuitionistic logic provides a Hintikka collection.

The first step we leave as an exercise.

In coming up with an appropriate modification of the notion of a Hintikka set, we must consider two things. First, in the Hintikka sets considered in Chapter 2, there were no *localities* to consider. Obviously, the need to take localities into account will complicate our definition. Secondly, not all the expressions on an intuitionistic tree are statements, so we shall need somehow to take into account expressions beginning with $?$.

DEFINITION 5.2 A *Hintikka collection* will be a set H of sets, which we shall call the *Hintikka localities* in H. The Hintikka localities must meet the following conditions: Each must be a set of expressions S, all of which are either statements of $\mathcal{L}$ or are statements of $\mathcal{L}$ preceded by ?, and each must meet the following conditions:

1. There is no atomic statement P such that $P \in S$ and $?P \in S$.

2. If $P \wedge Q \in S$, then $P \in S$ and $Q \in S$.

3. If $?(P \wedge Q) \in S$, then $?P \in S$ or $?Q \in S$.

4. If $P \vee Q \in S$, then $P \in S$ or $Q \in S$.

5. If $?(P \vee Q) \in S$, then $?P \in S$ and $?Q \in S$.

6. If $\neg P \in S$, then $?P \in S$.

7. If $?\neg P \in S$, then for some Hintikka locality S' in H, $P \in S'$ *and*, if Q is a statement of $\mathcal{L}$ and $Q \in S$, then $Q \in H'$.

8. If $P \rightarrow Q \in S$, then $?P \in S$ or $Q \in S$.

9. If $?(P \rightarrow Q) \in S$, then for some Hintikka locality S' in H, $P \in S'$ and $?Q \in S'$, *and*, if Q is a statement of $\mathcal{L}$ and $Q \in S$, then $Q \in S'$.

From any Hinktikka collection H we can construct an interpretation I as follows. The frame will be $\langle H, \leqslant \rangle$, where for $S, S' \in H$, we put $S \leqslant S'$ if and only if every statement of $\mathcal{L}$ which is in S is also in S'. (Which is to say that all expressions in S which are not marked by ? are contained in S'.) For each atomic statement A, we set $I(S, A) = \top$ if and only if $A \in S$. To check that this is indeed an interpretation one needs only to verify that $\leqslant$ so defined is a preorder on H, but this is obvious from the transitivity of $\subseteq$.

LEMMA 5.6 *Let S be a Hintikka locality in a Hintikka collection H. If $P \in S$, then $I(S, P) = \top$, and if $?P \in S$, then $I(S, P) = \bot$, under the specified interpretation.*

The proof of this lemma is a straightforward argument by induction on the structure of P. If P is atomic, the lemma is true by definition. So suppose that the result holds for Q. If $\neg Q$ is in S, then for any S' such that $S \leqslant S'$, $\neg Q$ is in S'. But then, $?Q$ is also in S', and so $I(S', Q) = \bot$. If $?\neg Q \in S$, then there is an $S' \leqslant S$ with $Q \in S'$. Since the result is assumed to hold for Q, $I(S', Q) = \top$, and so $I(S, \neg Q) = \bot$.

The remaining cases are left as an exercise.

We also need the following

LEMMA 5.7 *The expressions on any non-closing path of a systematic tree determine a Hintikka collection.*

This follows straightforwardly from the systematicity of the tree and the close link between the tree rules and the definition of a Hintikka collection. Simply place all the expression occupying nodes of the path which occur in the same locality on the tree in the same Hintikka locality.

We are now in a position to establish the

THEOREM 5.8 (ADEQUACY THEOREM)
If there is a non-closing path through every tree starting with a given set S of expressions, then S is satisfiable.

For if there is a non-closing path through every tree beginning with S, there is a non-closing path through every systematic tree. But by lemma 5.7 each such non-closing path determines a Hintikka collection, whence by lemma 5.6, there is an interpretation under which every member of S will be true in the initial locality.

As an immediate consequence, we obtain

THEOREM 5.9 (ARGUMENT ADEQUACY)
If an argument is valid, then there is a closed tree associated with it.

EXERCISES 5.2.4
1. Complete the proof of lemma 5.3.

2. State an appropriate set of conditions for the construction of a *systematic* tree for intuitionistic propositional logic.

* 3. Complete the proof of lemma 5.6.

4. Prove lemma 5.7. (Hint: If the proof is difficult, the problem may be with your definition of a systematic tree.)

5. Show that every path of a systematic tree either closes, becomes a complete open path, or begins to repeat itself (i.e., produces a locality which includes precisely the same expressions, in the same arrangement, as a locality higher in the tree). Deduce that intuitionistic propositional logic is decidable.

5.2.5 Comparing Intuitionistic Logic to Other Logics

Many of the exercises in this chapter involve showing that certain statements which are valid in classical logic are no longer valid in intuitionistic logic. An obvious question in light of this is whether there are intuitionistically valid statements which are not classically valid. As we shall see, the answer to that question is "no." As we shall also see, there are many other interesting things which can be said about the relationship between these two systems.

We have noted above that the frames for intuitionistic logic are those in which the relation R is a *preordering* on W. These, of course, are precisely the same frames as are used in the interpretation of S4 (i.e., ■$T4$) in propositional modal logic. Of course, the *interpretations* differ in these two cases, because those for the intuitionistic case must satisfy the persistence condition, while those for S4 need not. Thus the class of interpretations of intuitionistic predicate logic is, in fact, a proper subset of the class of interpretations of S4. Since a statement is invalid if and only if there is a countermodel for it, and the previous statement amounts to the claim that there are fewer possible countermodels to intuitionistic statements than there are to S4 statements, we should expect the class of intuitionistic validities to be, in some sense, a subset of the S4 validities. Of course, things are not so simple, since the language of modal logic includes operators which do not appear in intuitionistic propositional logic, and some of the operators which are common to the two languages receive different interpretations in each. But it raises a natural question about whether there is some natural method of *translating* intuitionistic logic into S4.

Intuitionistic and Classical Propositional Logic

We begin by noting the following

PROPOSITION 5.10 *Every classical interpretation determines an intuitionistic interpretation.*

A classical interpretation is a valuation which becomes an intuitionistic interpretation by attaching it to the simple frame $\langle \{*\}, = \rangle$. From this we get the

THEOREM 5.11
Every intuitionistically valid statement is classically valid.

For if the statement is intuitionistically valid, it has no countermodels, and so in particular no countermodels in a one point frame.

Since we know that there are classically valid statements which are not intuitionistically valid, this theorem shows that one natural way to look at the relationship between classical and intuitionistic logic is to regard intuitionistic logic as a *subsystem* of classical logic, for the class of valid statements of intuitionistic logic is a proper subset of the class of classical validities.

However, there are other interesting ways to look at these relationships. Consider, for example, the following three ways of mapping the set of statements of propositional logic $\mathcal{L}$ into itself. Each is a *translation* of classical logic into intuitionistic logic in a sense we shall presently make precise. These translations are due, respectively, to Gerhard Gentzen, Andrei Kolmogorov, and Kurt Gödel.

t_1 (Gentzen)

1. $t_1(A) = \neg\neg A$ if A is atomic.
2. $t_1(\neg P) = \neg t_1(P)$.
3. $t_1(P \wedge Q) = t_1(P) \wedge t_1(Q)$.
4. $t_1(P \vee Q) = \neg[\neg t_1(P) \wedge \neg t_1(Q)]$.
5. $t_1(P \rightarrow Q) = t_1(P) \rightarrow t_1(Q)$.

t_2 (Kolmogorov)

1. $t_2(A) = \neg\neg A$ if A is atomic.
2. $t_2(\neg P) = \neg t_2(P)$.
3. $t_2(P \wedge Q) = \neg\neg[t_2(P) \wedge t_2(Q)]$.
4. $t_2(P \vee Q) = \neg\neg[t_2(P) \vee t_2(Q)]$.
5. $t_2(P \rightarrow Q) = \neg\neg[t_2(A) \rightarrow t_2(B)]$.

t_3 (Gödel)

1. $t_3(A) = \neg\neg A$ if A is atomic.
2. $t_3(\neg P) = \neg t_3(P)$.
3. $t_3(P \wedge Q) = t_3(P) \wedge t_3(Q)$.
4. $t_3(P \vee Q) = \neg[\neg t_3(P) \wedge \neg t_3(Q)]$.
5. $t_3(P \rightarrow Q) = \neg[t_3(P) \wedge \neg t_3(Q)]$.

Note that t_3 is the same as t_1, except for the clause for $(P \rightarrow Q)$. The Kolmogorov translation t_2 is often called the *double negation translation*, for obvious reasons.

These three mappings all share these interesting properties. For any statement P of $\mathcal{L}$, (1) P is classically equivalent to its translation $t_i(P)$; (2) $t_i(P)$ is *classically valid* if and only if it is *intuitionistically valid*. We shall not prove this for all three translations. We content ourselves with a series of exercises which give some idea of how these translations work, and which will supply enough hints to enable an energetic reader to construct proofs of his own.

EXERCISES 5.2.5

* 1. What, under each of t_1, t_2, and t_3, are the translations of the classical tautologies $A \vee \neg A$, $\neg\neg A \rightarrow A$, $\neg(\neg A \wedge \neg B) \rightarrow (A \vee B)$? (Assume that A and B are atomic.)

* 2. For each classical validity P in Question 1, show that P is classically equivalent to each of $t_1(P)$, $t_2(P)$ and $t_3(P)$, and that each of these is intuitionistically valid if and only if it is classically valid.

3. Observe that $(A \lor B) \lor C$ is classically equivalent to $A \lor (B \lor C)$, and that $A \lor B$ is classically equivalent to $\neg(\neg A \land \neg B)$. Hence $(A \lor B) \lor C$ is classically equivalent to this formula, which we call (∗): $\neg[\neg\neg(\neg A \land \neg B) \land \neg C]$. Similarly, $A \lor (B \lor C)$ is classically equivalent to (∗∗) $\neg[\neg A \land \neg\neg(\neg B \land \neg C)]$. Is $t_1(∗)$ intuitionistically equivalent to $t_1(∗∗)$? What about the translations of (∗) and (∗∗) under t_2 and t_3?

4. Show that $\neg P$ is classically valid if and only if $\neg P$ is intuitionistically valid. (Hint: Note that half of this proposition follows from an earlier theorem. Note that if $\neg P$ fails to be intuitionistically valid, then $I(x, \neg P) = \bot$ for some x and I, and so $I(y, P) = \top$ for some $y \geqslant x$. Consider the classical valuation v we get by setting $v(A) = I(y, A)$ for all atomic A.) Deduce that if P is classically valid, then $\neg\neg P$ is intuitionistically valid.

5. Show that t_2, the Kolmogorov "double negation translation," has the properties (1) and (2) described in the paragraph preceding these exercises. (Use the result of the preceding exercise.)

The solution to Question 3 shows that two classically equivalent formulas might be mapped respectively under a given translation function to two formulas that are *not* intuitionistically equivalent. More generally, we know that many theorems provable classically are not provable intuitionistically. But the mappings from classical logic into intuitionistic logic show that *relative to an appropriate translation* all theorems of classical logic are intuitionistically provable. Hence, it is often argued that classical logic and intuitionistic logic do not differ in *deductive strength* but in *expressive richness*. Intuitionistic logic allows, it is suggested, for more distinctions among formulas than does classical logic. For example, as we've seen, $P \lor Q$ and $\neg(\neg P \land \neg Q)$ are classically equivalent but are not intuitionistically equivalent. So, while we might expect that any distinction between formulas that holds classically can be recovered in intuitionistic logic, we ought not expect that all intuitionistic distinctions can be recovered classically ... at least not without extending classical logic by adding something to it.

One interesting feature of classical propositional logic was the *interdefinability* of the connectives. In Chapter 1 we established that the sets $\{\neg, \lor\}$, $\{\neg, \land\}$, as well as the sets including only the *Sheffer Stroke* $\{|\}$, and the *Peirce Arrow* $\{\downarrow\}$, are all expressively complete. So, too, is the set $\{\neg, \rightarrow\}$. It follows that, for each of these sets of connectives, all the other connectives can be defined in terms of its members. So in taking such a generous stock of primitive logical operations, we have built a good deal of redundancy into our logical system.

There is a good deal less redundancy in the case of intuitionistic logic. Let us say that a binary (unary) propositional connective $\star_1$ is *not definable in terms of* $\star_2, \star_3, \ldots, \star_n$ if there is no formula containing just the connectives $\star_2, \star_3, \ldots, \star_n$ and the atoms A and B (the atom A) which is equivalent to $A \star_1 B$ (to $\star_1 A$).

PROPOSITION 5.12 *In intuitionistic logic, $\vee$ is not definable in terms of $\rightarrow$, $\wedge$, $\neg$.*

To see this, let us write $\equiv$ for intuitionistic equivalence. Suppose that $\varphi = \varphi(A, B)$ is an $\vee$ free statement containing only the statement letters A and B, and that

$$\varphi \equiv A \vee B. \tag{5.1}$$

By the Gentzen translation, and noting that in intuitionistic logic $\neg\neg\neg P \equiv \neg P$,

$$t_1(\varphi) \equiv \neg(\neg A \wedge \neg B). \tag{5.2}$$

But examination of the translation rules for the connectives other than $\vee$ makes clear that $t_1(\varphi)$ is simply φ with A and B replaced uniformly by $\neg\neg A$ and $\neg\neg B$, respectively—i.e., $t_1(\varphi) = \varphi(\neg\neg A, \neg\neg B)$. So 5.2 gives

$$\varphi(\neg\neg A, \neg\neg B) \equiv \neg(\neg A \wedge \neg B). \tag{5.3}$$

But from 5.1 it follows that

$$\varphi(\neg\neg A, \neg\neg B) \equiv \neg\neg A \vee \neg\neg B.$$

This and 5.3 now give

$$\neg(\neg A \wedge \neg B) \equiv \neg\neg A \vee \neg\neg B,$$

which is easily shown to be false by construction of a tree which yields a countermodel.

EXERCISES 5.2.6
1. Show that $\wedge$ is not definable in terms of $\rightarrow$, $\vee$ and $\neg$. (Hint: Consider the frame with $W = \{x, y, z\}$, with $x < z$ and $y < z$. Let I be an interpretation such that $I(x, A) = \top, I(y, B) = \top$, and $I(z, A) = I(z, B) = \top$. Show that all $\wedge$ free formulas are equivalent to $\neg(A \rightarrow A)$ (i.e., they are intuitionistic contradictions), or are true at y or z.)

2. Show that $\rightarrow$ is not definable in terms of $\wedge$, $\vee$, and $\neg$. (Hint: Consider the same frame and interpretation as in 1. Show that for all $\rightarrow$ free statements φ, if $I(b, \varphi) = \top$, then $I(a, \varphi) = \top$.)

The reader will recall that a key part of Gödel's argument for Proposition 5.2 was that in an adequate account of intuitionistic propositional logic a disjunction will be valid only if one of its disjuncts is valid. We now show that this is the case in the system we have been calling intuitionistic propositional logic. This is an appropriate way to conclude this section, because this is perhaps the most fundamental difference between intuitionistic and classical logic.

THEOREM 5.13 (DISJUNCTION THEOREM)
If $P \vee Q$ is intuitionistically valid, then one of P and Q is intuitionistically valid.

For suppose that neither P nor Q is intuitionistically valid. Then there are systematic trees beginning with $?P$ and $?Q$ which do not close. Hence (given the nature of the above proof of the adequacy of the tree method) there are open paths in these systematic trees which determine a pair of interpretations $\langle W, \leqslant_W, I \rangle$ and $\langle X, \leqslant_x, J \rangle$ such that $I(w, P) = \bot$ and $J(x, Q) = \bot$, where w and x are the initial locality in their respective frames. We may assume that W and J are disjoint, since making them so is merely a matter of appropriate choice of labels for the localities on these trees.

We construct a new frame as follows. The set of localities shall be $L = W \cup X \cup \{a\}$, where a is a new individual which is in neither W nor X. We get a preordering on L as follows: for $y, z \in L$, $x \leqslant y$ if and only if $x \leqslant_W y$, $x \leqslant_x y$, or $x = a$. (In effect, we have welded the two distinct preorderings $\leqslant_W$ and $\leqslant_x$ by attaching a new bottom element, a, which is less than any element of either ordering, and the orderings above w and x are unchanged.)

We now define a new interpretation K. For each locality $z \in L$: for any atom A, if $z \in W$, $K(z, A) = I(z, A)$; if $z \in X$, then $K(z, A) = J(z, A)$; and $K(a, A) = \bot$.

Since P is not true at w under the interpretation I, it will also fail to be true at w under the interpretation K. (This can be established by a simple inductive argument on the structure of P, which shows that the interpretation of P at w is determined by the values assigned to atoms at localities $\geqslant w$.) Similarly, Q will not be true in x under K. Hence neither P nor Q is true in a under K, and so $P \vee Q$ is not true in K, either. But then $P \vee Q$ is not intuitionistically valid. The result follows by contraposition.

Intuitionistic Logic and S4

We now look at two translations of intuitionistic propositional logic into classical logic to which "something has been added," namely the contextual operators of ■$T4$ (i.e., S4). The first is due to Gödel, and the second to Alfred Tarski and J.C.C. McKinsey.

t_4 (Gödel)

    1. $t_4(A) = A$ if A is atomic.

    2. $t_4(\neg P) = \Diamond \neg t_4(P)$.

    3. $t_4(P \wedge Q) = t_4(P) \wedge t_4(Q)$.

4. $t_4(P \lor Q) = \Box t_4(P) \lor \Box t_4(Q)$.

5. $t_4(P \to Q) = \Box t_4(P) \to \Box t_4(Q)$.

t_5 (Tarski and McKinsey)

1. $t_5(A) = \Box A$ if A is atomic.

2. $t_5(\neg P) = \Box \neg t_5(P)$.

3. $t_5(P \land Q) = t_5(P) \land t_5(Q)$.

4. $t_5(P \lor Q) = t_5(P) \lor t_5(Q)$.

5. $t_5(P \to Q) = \Box[t_5(A) \to t_5(B)]$.

EXERCISES 5.2.7

* 1. What, under each of t_4 and t_5, are the translations into S4 of the intuitionistic validities $A \to \neg\neg A$, $(A \to B) \to (\neg B \to \neg A)$, $(A \lor B) \to \neg(\neg A \land \neg B)$.

* 2. Are the translations of $A \lor \neg A$ and $\neg\neg A \to A$ under t_4 and t_5 provable in ∎$T4$?

3. Show for each of t_4 and t_5 that, for any statement P of $\mathcal{L}$, P is intuitionistically valid if and only if $t_i P$ is valid in $S4$.

The final exercise shows the sense in which each of these is a *translation* of intuitionistic logic into a classical contextual logic. Some caution is in order when considering these translations, for it is possible to overestimate the extent of the linkage between intuitionistic logic and S4. So we conclude by pointing out some points to bear in mind.

First, while we may translate the theorems of intuitionistic propositional logic into S4, this by no means shows that the validities of S4 and the validities of intuitionistic logic are the same. Trivial examples which show this are those validities of classical propositional logic which are not intuitionistic validities. So these translations *embed* the intuitionistic validities *into* the set of validities of S4, but not *onto* that set.

Secondly, and not unrelatedly, with special reference to the Tarski and McKinsey translation, something should be said about the relationship between $P \to Q$ in intuitionistic logic and $\Box(P \to Q)$ in S4. In the past, presentations of modal logic often included an additional binary connective, often called a symbol of *strict implication*. However, in most systems the statement "P strictly implies Q" turns out to be equivalent to $\Box(P \to Q)$, so the extra connective is not often seen anymore. Tarski and McKinsey actually used a symbol for strict implication in clause 5 of their translation, but also showed how to convert it into the notation more commonly used nowadays.[6] That the relationship between these two notions is a close one

---

[6] J.C.C. McKinsey and Alfred Tarski, "Some Theorems About The Sentential Calculi Of Lewis And Heyting," *Journal of Symbolic Logic* **13** (1948): 1-15.

can be seen by comparing the relevant clauses of the respective definitions of "truth at a locality." For $P \rightarrow Q$ is true at w in an intuitionistic interpretation if and only if for all $x \geqslant w$, if $I(x, P) = \top$, then $I(x, Q) = \top$. In S4, $\Box(P \rightarrow Q)$ is true at w if and only if for all $x \geqslant w$, $I(x, P \rightarrow Q) = \top$, i.e., if and only if $I(x, Q) = \top$ in all cases where $I(x, P) = \top$. It follows easily from the fact that the Tarski and McKinsey translation *is* a translation that any intuitionistic statement which involves $\rightarrow$ as its only connective is valid only if its translation, which involves "strict implication" as its only connective, is valid in S4. But the converse is also true, for if $\Box(P \rightarrow Q)$ is valid, then there are no S4 models which are counterexamples to its validity. Since every intuitionistic model is an S4 model, this implies that there are no counterexamples to the validity of the intuitionistic statement of which $P \rightarrow Q$ is a translation, either. So, considered in isolation, it is natural to think of S4 strict implication and intuitionistic implication as essentially the same.

Of course, the qualification about being considered in isolation needs to be borne in mind. For there are many statements valid in S4 involving "strict implication" which are not translations of intuitionistically valid statements. For example, $\neg\neg A$ strictly implies A, but it does not intuitionistically imply it.

5.3   Intuitionistic Predicate Logic

We give here a brief introduction to some of the interesting features of intuitionistic predicate logic. We do not justify many of our claims by giving proofs of the metatheoretical results which underpin them.[7]

5.3.1   Interpretations

In the formal semantics for propositional intuitionistic logic, we employed a valuation which told us which atomic sentences are known to be true at each stage. Notice that this amounts to having a (classical) *truth-value assignment* for each stage (though we regard those sentences not assigned the value $\top$ as being "not (yet?) known to be true" instead of regarding them as false). In other words, we employed a *classical interpretation* of the language of propositional logic *for each stage*, subject to the persistence condition. We can do the same for the quantificational case: that is, we shall generate an intuitionistic interpretation in a particular frame for a language $\mathcal{L}$ for predicate logic by assigning a classical interpretation to the same language *for each stage*, subject to certain persistence conditions.

We shall need to have a *domain of individuals* at each stage. It is useful to think of these domains as containing only those objects which are *known*

---

[7]Readers interested in the details of these proofs will find most of them in Anil Nerode and Richard Shore, *Logic for Applications*, Second Edition (New York: Springer-Verlag, 1997).

at the given stage of knowledge to exist. For reasons similar to those which lie behind the persistence requirement, we will require that any object in the domain at stage a continues to be in the domain at any stage $b \geqslant a$. However, we must allow for the possibility that (thanks to new information, say) more objects come to be known to exist, and so that the domain of some later stage has an *increased* stock of individuals. (To this extent, then, semantics for intuitionistic predicate logic are akin to the "growing domain" semantics for contextual predicate logic.)

The fact that the domains of individuals can expand as knowledge increases means that we need to be careful about when we will be willing to say that $\forall x \varphi(x)$ is known to be true at stage a. In particular, it is not enough that all the individuals in the domain at a have the property φ. Instead, what shall be required is that all objects in the domain at a and *all objects in the domain of any stage later than a* must have that property.

More formally, then, let's describe a model for an arbitrary but fixed quantificational language $\mathcal{L}$ *without identity* (which, for simplicity, we will assume does not contain function symbols). We briefly consider languages with identity below.

DEFINITION 5.3 An *intuitionistic interpretation I for* $\mathcal{L}$ consists of:

1. An (intuitionistic) frame $\langle W, \leqslant \rangle$.

2. An assignment of a structure $\mathcal{M}^a$ for $\mathcal{L}$ (see definition 2.5) to each element a of W, subject to the following (persistence) conditions:

   (a) If $a \leqslant b$, the domain of $\mathcal{M}^a$ must be a subset of the domain of $\mathcal{M}^b$.

   (b) If $a \leqslant b$, P is an n-place predicate of $\mathcal{L}$, and $d_1, \ldots, d_n$ are elements of the domain of $\mathcal{M}^a$, and if $P^{\mathcal{M}^a}(d_1, \ldots, d_n) = \top$, then $P^{\mathcal{M}^b}(d_1, \ldots, d_n) = \top$.

3. A function V assigning each of the variables of $\mathcal{L}$ to some object which is in the domain of $\mathcal{M}^b$ for *at least one* $b \in W$.

Some comments on this definition are in order. The second condition on the allowable structures for different stages is just the persistence requirement familiar from the propositional case, revised for the present case. Notice that it only requires "once true, always true"; in particular, it does not prevent the "discovery" at some $b \geqslant a$ that objects satisfy some primitive predicate, even objects which already were known to exist at a—for instance, Pc might be true at b, but not true (yet) at a, even though the object denoted by c is in the domain of a. The final condition is a modification of the notion of a valuation used for classical quantificational logic. In particular, note that V might assign to a variable x a value not in the domain of interpretation of some stage (because that object only comes to be known to exist at a later stage, for instance). Our classical rules of interpretation provide us with no way of saying in such a case whether a formula such as Px is true or false under V. It is simplest to adopt an approach akin to the "Russellian" approach briefly considered in our discussion of contextual predicate logic, i.e., to count any formula containing a free variable which is assigned a value not in the domain of the interpretation at a as not known to be true (i.e., as $\perp$) at a.

DEFINITION 5.4 We define the truth value of a formula φ at a stage a under the interpretation I, denoted $I(a, \varphi)$ as follows:

1. If φ is atomic, $I(a, \varphi) = [\![\varphi]\!]^V$.

2. The cases for $\wedge, \vee, \rightarrow,$ and $\neg$ are the same, *mutatis mutandis*, as in the propositional case.

3. $I(a, \forall x\varphi) = \top$ if for all $b \geqslant a$ and all d in the domain of $\mathcal{M}^b$, $[\![\varphi]\!]_{\mathcal{M}^b}^{V(x/d)} = \top$.

4. $I(a, \exists x\varphi) = \top$ if there is a d in the domain of $\mathcal{M}^a$ such that $[\![\varphi]\!]_{\mathcal{M}^a}^{V(x/d)} = \top$.

5.3.2 Trees for Intuitionistic Predicate Logic

Now that we have described the semantics for intuitionistic quantificational logic, we turn to the tree rules for the quantifiers. Of course, we shall need instantiation rules.

RULE 5.1 ((INTUITIONISTIC) UNIVERSAL INSTANTIATION (IUI)) Given a statement of the form $\forall v\varphi(v)$ occupying a node of an open path of a tree,

1. if a name n appears in the path, write $\varphi(n)$ at its foot unless $\varphi(n)$ already occupies a node of the path in the same locality where the foot of the path occurs (in which case writing it once more in the path would be redundant);

2. if no name appears in the path, choose some name n and write $\varphi(n)$ at its foot.

Do not tick the line $\forall v\varphi(v)$.

RULE 5.2 (EXISTENTIAL INSTANTIATION (IEI)) Given an unticked statement of the form $\exists v\varphi(v)$ occupying a node of an open path, check to see whether the path contains a node occupied by a statement of the form $\varphi(n)$. If not, choose a name n *that has not been used anywhere in the path* and write the statement $\varphi(n)$ at its foot. When this has been done for every open path in which the statement $\exists v\varphi(v)$ occupies a node, tick the node occupied by the given statement.

$$\exists v\varphi(v) \qquad \checkmark$$
$$\varphi(n) \quad (n \text{ new})$$

In classical predicate logic, we needed only these two rules together with the very simple rules for negated quantifiers. We could make do with these simple rules because in classical logic the quantifiers are interdefinable. This is no longer the case in intuitionistic predicate logic. The result is that we need somewhat more complicated tree rules to handle quantified statements which are not known to be true at a given stage.

RULE 5.3 (? EXISTENTIAL INSTANTIATION (?EI)) Given an expression of the form $?\exists v\varphi(v)$ occupying a node of an open path of a tree,

1. if a name n appears in the path, write $?\varphi(n)$ at its foot in the same locality in which $?\exists v\varphi(v)$ occurs, unless $?\varphi(n)$ already occupies a node there (in which case writing it once more in the path would be redundant);

2. if no name appears in the path, choose some name n and write $?\varphi(n)$ at its foot in the same locality in which $?\exists v\varphi(v)$ occurs.

Do not tick the line $?\exists v\varphi(v)$.

RULE 5.4 (? UNIVERSAL INSTANTIATION (?UI)) Given an unticked statement of the form $?\forall v\varphi(v)$ occupying a node of an open path, draw a horizontal line at the foot of the path, choose a name n *that has not been used anywhere in the path*, and write the statement $?\varphi(n)$ at its foot. When this has been done for every open path in which the statement $?\forall v\varphi(v)$ occupies a node, tick the node occupied by the given statement.

$$?\forall v\varphi(v) \qquad \checkmark$$
$$\overline{\qquad\qquad}$$
$$?\varphi(n) \qquad (n \text{ new})$$

The $?UI$ rule requires a shift to a new stage. As in the propositional case, formulas not prefixed by ? may be transported over the shift line by the persistence condition. So, for example, instead of instantiating $\forall xFx$ by Fd, it is permissible (at least in non-systematic trees), and might be advisable, to transport $\forall xFx$ across a horizontal line before instantiating. Note also that once $\exists xPx$ or $?\forall xPx$ has been instantiated, it is ticked. Once ticked, we cannot transport $\exists xPx$ over a horizontal line, although its instantiation Pd can be transported. On the other hand $\forall xPx$ may be carried over a shift line even if it has already been instantiated.

Let us consider some examples which will show these rules in action. First, we can establish the intuitionistic validity of $\neg \exists x Px \rightarrow \forall x \neg Px$.

$$\frac{?\neg \exists x Px \rightarrow \forall x \neg Px}{\begin{array}{c} \neg \exists x Px \\ ?\forall x \neg Px \end{array}}$$

$$\frac{?\neg Pd}{\neg \exists x Px}$$

$$\begin{array}{c} Pd \\ \neg \exists x Px \\ ?\exists x Px \\ ?Pd \\ \times \end{array}$$

Here we used the persistence condition several times to move $\neg \exists x Px$ down the tree to where it was useful. Note that had we used the $\neg$ rule and the $?\exists$ rule to get $?Pd$ at an earlier stage, we would not have been able to move it down the tree to the stage where it could close the path. So, while it would have been correct to derive $?Pd$ at every stage, it is unnecessary.

For a second example, we prove $\forall x \neg Px \rightarrow \neg \exists x Px$.

$$\frac{?\forall x \neg Px \rightarrow \neg \exists x Px}{\begin{array}{c} \forall x \neg Px \\ ?\neg \exists x Px \end{array}}$$

$$\begin{array}{c} \exists x Px \\ \forall x \neg Px \\ Pd \\ \neg Pd \\ ?Pd \\ \times \end{array}$$

Countermodels

When an attempted proof results in a complete open path, we may use the path to "read off" a countermodel in the by now familiar way. However, in the present case we must keep in mind that it is possible for the domain of interpretation to *expand* as we move from one stage to another. So our procedure will be to take as the domain only those elements we are forced to include, either by the occurrence of names at that locality in the tree, or by the requirement that the domain at each stage must be a non-empty set. Let us consider some examples. First, consider the following tree for the formula $\neg \forall x Px \rightarrow \exists x \neg Px$.

$$?\neg \forall x Px \rightarrow \neg \forall x Px$$

$$\neg \forall x Px$$
$$?\exists x \neg Px$$
$$?\neg Pd$$

$$Pd$$
$$\neg \forall x Px$$
$$?\forall x Px$$

$$?Pe$$
$$Pd$$

As presented, this tree is not complete. For we may move the statement $\neg \forall x Px$ into the bottom stage, then by application of the $\neg$ and the $?\forall$ rules, open another stage which introduces another new individual. But it is clear that the path will not terminate. So there is a countermodel determined by this path. It would be an interpretation with an infinite number of localities arranged in a linear ordering. Moreover, beginning at the second stage, at each stage a new individual will appear which *is not yet known to have P*, but which, at the next stage, *comes to be known to have P*. However, with a bit of thinking and a willingness to double check one's work, a much simpler interpretation can be extracted.[8] For if we have an interpretation with two localities, 1 and 2, in their usual order, where the universe of 1 is the singleton set $\{d\}$ while the universe of 2 is $\{d, e\}$, and $I(1, Pd) = I(2, Pe) = \bot$, while $I(2, Pd) = \top$, we have our countermodel. For at every stage, $\forall x Px$ has the value $\bot$, since at every stage there is an individual for which Px is false. Hence $\neg \forall x Px$ is true at stage 1. But Pd is true at stage 2, so $\neg Pd$ is does not get the value $\top$ at stage 1. Since d is the only member of the domain at 1, it follows that $\exists x \neg Px$ is not true at stage 1. Hence the conditional in question is false at stage 1.

Now, it is perhaps not surprising that the following tree does not close. Many classical validities are not intuitionistically valid, after all.

$$?\forall x (Px \vee \neg Px)$$

$$?(Pd \vee \neg Pd)$$
$$?Pd$$
$$?\neg Pd$$

$$Pd$$

---

[8]Indeed, it would be possible to make this process much more rigorous, for instance by developing criteria which for cases of this sort tell us when we may stop constructing a non-terminating path and read off an interpretation, but we do not pursue this matter here so that we can keep our treatment of intuitionistic predicate logic brief. In any case, intuitionistic predicate logic, like classical predicate logic, is undecidable, and so there can be no reliable general procedure for doing this.

This tree yields an interpretation much like the propositional logic interpretations in which the law of excluded middle fails: an atomic statement has value $\perp$ at one stage, but the value $\top$ later.

More interesting is the following case. An exercise in our discussion of intuitionistic propositional logic implies that *every classical propositional tautology* becomes an *intuitionistically valid statement* if it is preceded by a double negation. In other words, while there are certain classical tautologies, such as $A \vee \neg A$, which may not be *asserted* in intuitionistic logic, they cannot be *consistently denied*, either, for to deny them is to assert something which implies an absurdity. Now consider the following tree:

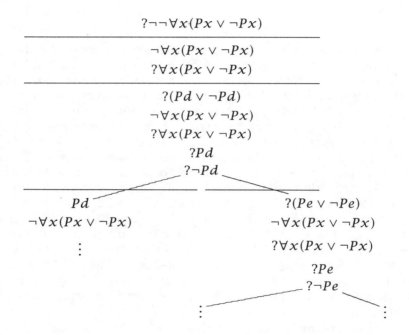

This tree is clearly not going to close, either. Thus the proposition in question is *not intuitionistically valid*. We see here a crucial difference between intuitionistic predicate and intuitionistic propositional logic. There are valid statements of classical predicate logic which may be consistently denied in intuitionistic logic.

In the present case, it is much easier to see that this tree will not close than it is to read a countermodel from the tree! Pursuing the tree for a few more stages suggests the following model. There is a recurring series of forks. On each of these, the leftmost fork is followed by a stage-shift, then another fork, while the right fork proceeds directly to another fork. So we could take the set $\{1, 2, 3, 3.1, 3.1a, 3.2, 3.1a1, 3.1a2, 3.21, 3.22, 3.1a1a, \dots\}$ for W. In general, each stage with a name ending in a 1 is followed by a stage whose name is the same but for an a appended to it, and any stage ending in either a or 2 is followed by a pair of stages designated by appending a 1 or a 2 to its name. We set $1 < 2 < 3$, and for all stages whose names begin with 3, we set one strictly earlier than the other if and only if the name of the first is a proper initial segment of the name of the second. We set the universe of 1, 2 and 3 to be an arbitrary individual. We choose domains so that an additional member is added to the domain of every stage whose name ends in 2 or in a. For convenience, let these new members have the name of the stage at which they first occur as members of a domain.

We interpret P as a property which all members of all domains eventually have; P is true of s at the first stage $a > s$ such that the name of a ends in a 1. (Recall that the individuals in the domains share names with the stages.) With this interpretation $\forall x (Px \lor \neg Px)$ has the value $\bot$ at every stage—for at every stage a there is an individual i such that i does not have P at a, and so $I(a, Pi) = \bot$, but such that Pi becomes true at some $b > a$, so $I(a, \neg Pi) = \bot$. But then by exercise 2 on page 202, $\neg\neg(Px \lor \neg Px)$ does not hold in locality 1 under this interpretation.

This countermodel includes infinitely many stages in W. This is *unavoidable* in this case. For consider the interpretation of $\neg\neg\forall x(Px \lor \neg Px)$ at some stage a in an interpretation which includes only finitely many stages. Then there will be a *final stage* in some path beginning with a, i.e. a stage $b \geqslant a$ such that there is no stage c such that $c > b$. But for every member n of the domain at that stage, either P (and so $Px \lor \neg Px$ holds of n), or P does not hold of n at b, in which case $\neg Px$ is true of n since b is a final stage, and again $Px \lor \neg Px$ is true of n. Since this is the case for all n in the domain of b, and since b is final, $\forall x(Px \lor \neg Px)$ is true at b, and so, by exercise 2 of page 202, $\neg\neg\forall x(Px \lor \neg Px)$ is true at a.

EXERCISES 5.3.1

1. For each of the following statements, use trees to determine whether or not it is intuitionistically valid. For those which are not, use the tree to recover a countermodel.

   * (a) $\exists y(\exists x Fx \to Fy)$.
   * (b) $\exists x(Fx \to \forall y Fy)$.
   * (c) $(\forall x Fx \lor \exists x \neg Fx) \to \exists x(Fx \to \forall y Fy)$.
   (d) $\exists x \neg Fx \to \neg\forall x Fx$.
   (e) $\forall x Fx \to \neg\exists x \neg Fx$.
   (f) $\neg\exists x \neg Fx \to \forall x Fx$.
   (g) $\neg\forall x \neg Fx \to \exists x Fx$.
   (h) $\exists x Fx \lor \forall x \neg Fx$.

2. Show that the statement $\forall x \neg\neg A(x) \to \neg\neg\forall x A(x)$ is *not* intuitionistically valid, though it *is* valid in every frame in which W is finite.

5.3.3 Intuitionistic Identity

Let us consider what happens when we add the usual rules for treating identity on trees to the rules for intuitionistic predicate logic. Consider, for example, this tree:

$$\frac{?\forall x \forall y (x = y \lor x \neq y)}{\frac{?\forall y (a = y \lor a \neq y)}{\frac{\begin{array}{c}?(a = b \lor a \neq b)\\ ?a = b\\ ?a \neq b\end{array}}{a = b}}}$$

It should not be surprising, perhaps, that this tree does not close. For the statement here shown to be invalid is a special case of the law of excluded middle, and it is not obvious why that should hold for identity statements when it does not in general hold for other sorts of statements.

There is a lesson here, though, which explains why we restricted attention to languages *without identity* when we described interpretations. For if we make the seemingly obvious move of interpreting =, at each stage, as identity, $\forall x \forall y (x = y \lor x \neq y)$ will turn out to be valid. Consider again the above tree. If we "read off" an interpretation in the obvious way, it is clear that we shall need to set $a = b$ *false* at the domain of the third stage, but *true* at the fourth stage. So, using the language of "stages of knowledge," we shall have to allow for the "discovery" that what were thought to be two things turns out upon further investigation to be one.

EXERCISES 5.3.2
Draw trees which establish the intuitionistic validity of the following: $\forall x (x = x)$, $\forall x \forall y (x = y \rightarrow y = x)$, $\forall x \forall y \forall z (x = y \land y = z \rightarrow x = z)$, and $\forall x \forall y (x = y \land Px \rightarrow Py)$. So all the *axioms* governing identity are provable in intuitionistic logic.

If = is interpreted by identity in the interpretations at each stage, we get a semantics appropriate for intuitionistic logic with *decidable identity* (i.e., with $\forall x \forall y (x = y \lor x \neq y)$ as an extra axiom). To get a more general semantics we need to modify our interpretation of = by treating it somewhat more like a non-logical basic predicate (that is, it can get a different interpretation in different structures), though not entirely since it must be interpreted by an equivalence relation related in the right way to the other primitive relations.

DEFINITION 5.5 To define an intuitionistic interpretation for a language *with identity*, we add the following conditions. The classical structure used to interpret the non-logical vocabulary of L at stage a must have appended to it a binary relation E such that:

1. E is an equivalence relation on the domain of the interpretation.

2. If P is an n-place predicate symbol of L and $x_1 E y_1, \ldots, x_n E y_n$, then $P x_1 \ldots x_n$ must receive the same intepretation as $P y_1 \ldots y_n$.

We specify that $a = b$ gets the value $\top$ at this stage if and only if the interpretation of a has the relation E to the interpretation of b. Note that identity statements, like all other statements in the language, are subject to the persistence requirement. So the relation used to interpret identity at an earlier stage will always be a subset of the relation used to do so at a later stage.

REMARK 5.3 The fact that intuitionistic logic does not in general have a decidable identity is important for the presentation of postulate systems in an intuitionistic setting. In many cases we need a stronger notion of inequality than $\neq$ provides in intuitionistic logic. For example, in the intuitionistic theory of real numbers we cannot show that $x \neq 0$ implies "x has an inverse," something which is trivially provable in the classical theory of real numbers. It is therefore usual to present the intuitionistic version of the postulates for the real numbers using a primitive *apartness* relation, $a \# b$, which, unlike identity, satisfies the condition that $\neg x \# y$ iff $x = y$ and $\forall z(x \# y \to x \# z \lor y \# z)$. The intuitionistic real numbers also do not satisfy *trichotomy*: $\forall x \forall y (x < y \lor x = y \lor y < x)$. However, there is still an important difference between a mere partial ordering in the intuitionistic setting and the sort of ordering of which the reals are an example (these are often called "pseudo-orderings"). The lesson is that trichotomy, with identity interpreted intuitionistically, becomes too strong a condition to express what the difference is between a partial ordering and the sort of ordering one finds on the reals. Thus even the theory of orderings, which is rather straightforward in a classical setting, in an intuitionistic setting turns out to be a subtle and interesting business.

Chapter 6

A Sampling of Other Logics

In this concluding chapter we shall briefly consider several topics not covered elsewhere in the book. Our treatment of each will be brief—each of the topics we shall consider could get a book-length treatment on its own, and most of them have had more than one—but will include enough material to provide the reader with an introduction. Of course, we can cover only a few of the many topics which might be included in a chapter of this sort. We have chosen topics which fit naturally with the material earlier in the book and which are encountered in the philosophical literature.

6.1 Fuzzy Logic

There are, in fact, many systems which go by the name "fuzzy logic," and they have been argued to be useful for many purposes. We shall consider only one such claim which is often advanced in the philosophical literature, namely that fuzzy logic can be used to explain away certain paradoxes which occur when one reasons with *vague* predicates. Consider the following argument:

1. A man with 10,000 hairs on his head is not bald.

2. Removing a single hair from the head of a person who is not bald will not make her or him bald.

   Therefore,

3. A man with no hairs on his head is not bald.

   This certainly seems to be a valid inference: for from the two premises it certainly follows that a man with 9,999 hairs on his head is not bald. But from this claim and the second premise it follows that a man with 9,998 hairs on his head is likewise not bald. And so on. But since the first premise is true (if this doesn't strike you as obvious, simply replace the number

10,000 with one where it does strike you as obvious) and the conclusion is obviously false, the validity of this argument would suggest that the second premise must be false. But if that premise is equivalent to "for any natural number n, if a person with n hairs on his or her head is not bald, then a person with $n - 1$ hairs on his or her head is not bald," and if we also accept classical logic, the falsity of this claim is equivalent to the truth of the claim that "for some n, a person with n hairs on his or her head is not bald, but a person with $n - 1$ hairs on his or her head is bald." And this strikes most—though, interestingly, not all—participants in the discussion as an extremely unlikely claim.

The key to dissolving this paradox, according to advocates of fuzzy logic as a logic of vagueness, is that one needs to recognize truth-values intermediate between truth and falsity. So, while the second premise is not true, it doesn't follow thereby that it is *false*. Instead, it receives some intermediate value. The reason the second premise of the paradox-generating argument seems plausible is that it is *much closer to true than to false*. We can thus explain away the paradox as follows: A valid inference involving two premises, one of which is true and the other of which is almost true, is not guaranteed to have a true conclusion, but is instead guaranteed to have one which is *close to true*. And if neither premise is true, but instead both have intermediate values, the truth value of the conclusion can decline even more. So, at some point in the chain of 9,998 inferences represented by the "and so on" in the argument purportedly showing the validity of the original inference, the truth value of the conclusion begins to bleed away. Eventually, some time before we reach 0 hairs, we arrive at a conclusion which is false.

It is usual in *fuzzy logic* to represent the range of truth values a proposition might take by the set of real numbers between 0 and 1 inclusive, which is denoted $[0, 1]$. In propositional fuzzy logic, then, a valuation becomes a map V which assigns each statement letter A a number $0 \leqslant V(A) \leqslant 1$. As usual, we shall often denote $V(A)$ by $[\![A]\!]_V$ (or simply by $[\![A]\!]$, when which V is in question is understood).

It remains to specify the conditions which fix the truth values of complex propositions.

DEFINITION 6.1

If P is $\neg Q$ for some statement Q, then $[\![P]\!]_V = 1 - [\![Q]\!]_V$.

If P is $Q \vee R$ for some statements Q and R, then $[\![P]\!]_V = \max([\![Q]\!]_V, [\![R]\!]_V)$.

If P is $Q \wedge R$ for some statements Q and R, then $[\![P]\!]_V = \min([\![Q]\!]_V, [\![R]\!]_V)$.

If P is $Q \rightarrow R$ for some statements Q and R, then $[\![P]\!]_V = 1$ if $[\![Q]\!]_V \leqslant [\![R]\!]_V$, and $[\![P]\!]_V = 1 - ([\![Q]\!]_V - [\![R]\!]_V)$ otherwise.

Two points are worthy of comment about this definition. First, as will be clear from a comparison of this definition with exercises 1.2.5 on page 21 and 3 on page 192, this semantics is a generalization of the representation of classical logic in binary arithmetic and of the three-valued Łukasiewicz logic discussed in Chapter 5, in the natural sense that if one restricts attention to the case where every statement letter is assigned values in the set $\{0, 1\}$ or $\{0, \frac{1}{2}, 1\}$, respectively, one gets these other systems. Secondly, while the first three clauses are fairly standard in propositional fuzzy logic, the fourth is less so. Indeed, the main source of variation in propositional fuzzy logic is in just what clause is adopted for the interpretation of conditional statements.

We will interpret the value 1 to be *true*, the value 0 *false*, and every other real number between 0 and 1 to be some truth value, as well. An argument is *valid* if under every valuation for which every premise has the value 1, the conclusion has the value 1 as well.

EXERCISES 6.1.1

1. Show that the following inferences are valid.

    (a) $P \rightarrow Q$, P, therefore Q.

    (b) $\neg P \rightarrow \neg Q$, therefore $P \rightarrow Q$.

*   2. Show that the inference from $P \rightarrow Q$ and P to Q has the further property that, on any valuation V, $1 - [\![Q]\!]_V$ is less than or equal to $(1 - [\![P]\!]_V) + (1 - [\![P \rightarrow Q]\!]_V)$. (If we think of $1 - [\![A]\!]$ as a measure of how "untrue" the statement A is, we can look at this result as showing that when one applies modus ponens, the conclusion is *no further from truth than the sum of the distance from truth of the two premises.*)

3. Show that the following statements are valid in fuzzy logic.

    (a) $P \rightarrow (Q \rightarrow P)$.

    (b) $P \rightarrow (Q \rightarrow Q)$.

*   (c) $\neg\neg P \rightarrow P$.

    (d) $(P \rightarrow Q) \vee (Q \rightarrow P)$.

How does this help us with the paradox-generating reasoning described earlier? For each $i = 1, \ldots 10,000$, let the statement letter P_i represent the statement that "A person with i hairs on his or her head is not bald." Let V be a valuation such that $[\![P_{10\,000}]\!] = 1$, $[\![P_0]\!] = 0$, and the other P_i get values distributed in the obvious way in between. Then for each i, $[\![P_i \rightarrow P_{i-1}]\!]_V = 1 - ([\![P_i]\!]_V - [\![P_{i-1}]\!]_V)$, which is 0.9999 in each case. But then the first step in the seemingly disastrous reasoning begins with the statements $P_{10\,000}$ and $P_{10\,000} \rightarrow P_{9999}$, which have the truth values 1 and 0.9999, respectively. While modus ponens is valid, it does no more than guarantee that the conclusion, P_{9999} has a truth value of at least 0.9999— which, indeed, it has on this valuation. But the next application of modus ponens gives a conclusion slightly further from being true—no further from truth than the sum of the distances of the premises from truth, in accordance with exercise 2, but further nonetheless. Indeed, each succeeding application of modus ponens, in this case, decreases the truth value of the conclusion by .0001, so after 10,000 steps we arrive at a truth value of 0, or false. This account is satisfying because it not only offers an explanation of why the premises seem plausible (i.e., because they are very nearly true), but it also meshes nicely with a natural reaction to the paradox-generating argument (i.e., that the problem is caused by *repeated application* of an argument which is harmless enough if only applied a few times).

However, there are other features of fuzzy logic which make it seem less appealing as a representation of reasoning about vague subject matters. One feature of vague predicates is that they have *borderline cases*: cases for which it is not clear whether the predicate applies to them or not. It's not hard to imagine someone with an amount of hair for which it is not clear whether or not it is the case that the person is bald, for instance. Or again, a one can easily call to mind a particular shade which falls between shades which are clearly red and those which are clearly orange, but which itself is not clearly one or the other. One objection to fuzzy logic as a representation of reasoning about vagueness runs as follows: Suppose that P represents the statement that "This shade is red," where the relevant shade is such a borderline case. If we suppose that $[\![P]\!] = \frac{1}{2}$, then also $[\![\neg P]\!] = 1 - \frac{1}{2} = \frac{1}{2}$, and $[\![P \wedge \neg P]\!] = \min(\frac{1}{2}, \frac{1}{2}) = \frac{1}{2}$. But, surely, the truth value of "This shade is red and this shade is not red" ought to be 0, not $\frac{1}{2}$, for whatever the color of an object it can't be *both* red and not red at the same time.

It is not impossible that somebody might fail to share this intuition, and would argue that what makes something a borderline case between two contrary properties is its having both of them to some degree. But there are other problems looming as well. Let's consider an example making use of atomic sentences in predicate logic.[1] Let a, b and c refer to three balls, and let Rx mean "x is red" while Sx means "x is small." Let

$$[\![Ra]\!] = 1 \qquad [\![Sa]\!] = \frac{1}{2}$$

$$[\![Rb]\!] = \frac{1}{2} \qquad [\![Sb]\!] = \frac{1}{2}$$

$$[\![Rc]\!] = \frac{1}{2} \qquad [\![Sc]\!] = 0$$

$$[\![Re]\!] = 0.4$$

Then $[\![Ra \wedge Sa]\!] = [\![Rb \wedge Sb]\!] = \frac{1}{2}$. But if someone were to request that you bring them a *small red ball*, isn't a, which is definitely red and borderline small, a better choice that b, which is borderline red and borderline small? Similarly, if you were asked to bring a ball which is either red or small, or as close as possible to meeting this condition at any rate, one might suppose that b is a better choice than c, which is borderline for colour, but is certainly

---

[1] This example is due to Dorothy Edgington, "Vagueness by Degrees," in Rosanna Keefe and Peter Smith, eds., *Vagueness: A Reader* (Cambridge, Mass.: MIT Press/Bradford Books, 1997). There is nothing essential about the use of a predicate language here. We use it only for the sake of readability.

not small (and might be huge). Finally, while $[\![Rb \wedge Re]\!] = 0.4$, which seems right since b is slightly redder than e, note that $[\![\neg Rb \wedge Re]\!] = 0.4$ as well. This seems very unlikely: if b is slightly redder than e, it seems that it should be *false* (i.e., it should have the truth value 0) that e is red and b is not.

   Whether or not fuzzy logic is an appropriate tool for analyzing reasoning about vague subject matters, it is argued to be useful in many other connections. It is therefore worthwhile to have some idea of what sorts of statements and argument are valid in this logic.

EXERCISES 6.1.2
Show the following statements and arguments to be invalid in fuzzy logic.

   1. $A \rightarrow (B \vee \neg B)$.

   2. $A \vee \neg A$.

* 3. $\neg(A \wedge \neg A)$.

* 4. $A \rightarrow B \therefore \neg A \vee B$.

   5. $A \rightarrow B \therefore \neg(A \wedge \neg B)$.

6.2   Algebraic Logic

Algebraic logic is a very large subject. We can motivate the small part of it to be presented here by considering a diagnosis of what has gone wrong in the final counterexample above. Considering the paradoxical results one gets when using classical logic to reason with vague concepts, it is natural to consider truth values intermediate between 0 and 1. Fuzzy logic uses the real numbers for these values, and this provides us with a convenient way of talking about how far away from being true or false a particular proposition is—the real numbers seem a particularly apt choice as a tool for talking about distances, whether real or metaphorical. But in this case, appearances are deceiving. For if b is *redder than* e, then *Re implies Rb*; that is, if e is *red enough* to count as red, then b must be red, as well. So Rb is naturally regarded as *closer to being true* than Re. And in general, it is quite natural to think of P's implying Q as Q's being *closer than P to being true* (more precisely, as its being *at least as close as P to being true—P does imply P, after all). The problem is due to the fact that the truth values of fuzzy logic are *totally ordered*, coupled with the way the truth values of negations are calculated.

   In a case where we assign a lower truth value to P than to Q because P implies Q, the conjunction of Q and $\neg P$ should be a contradiction, for $\neg P$ then implies $\neg Q$. But if Q has a non-zero truth value $< \frac{1}{2}$, then it could well turn out that the truth value of $Q \wedge \neg P$ is that same non-zero value. There's no natural way, compatible with the motivations for accepting fuzzy logic in the first place, for ruling out such problems. (Note that this shows that the problem here is closely related to the original complaint against fuzzy logic, which was that contradictory statements can get non-zero truth values as large as $\frac{1}{2}$.)

One way out of such problems is to retain intermediate truth values, only no longer to insist that they be totally ordered, requiring instead just that they be partially ordered. Of course, this means that there will in general be no natural way to assign numbers to the values. Moreover, without numbers, we will need other ways to calculate truth values for complex formulas. Obviously, we can't calculate the truth values of negations by subtraction, since we have no notion of subtraction to work with. But the reader will also recall that for a pair of elements a and b of a partially ordered set it will not always be the case that $a \leqslant b$ or $b \leqslant a$, so the notions of maximum and minimum don't apply in general to such pairs.

When dealing with small ordered sets (or large ones whose structure is very simple, such as the natural numbers), it is convenient to employ diagrams similar to those used in Chapter 3 to illustrate different models of Basic Arithmetic and so on. However, since we shall now be concerned to illustrate relations which are reflexive, we shall assume this without comment in the present diagrams. When we construct a diagram of a partially ordered set, we shall assign each element of a set to a node. If and only if $a < b$, we shall both place a lower on the page than b and draw a line—or a sequence of upward lines—connecting those nodes. We shall not draw horizontal lines, but we might place b lower than a on the page without connecting them on the page. When this happens, this means that b and a are non-comparable. Here are some examples of diagrams of partially ordered sets:

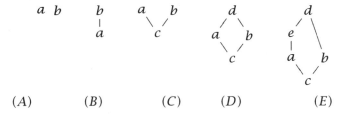

$\quad\quad\quad(A)\quad\quad\quad\quad(B)\quad\quad\quad\quad(C)\quad\quad\quad(D)\quad\quad\quad\quad\quad(E)$

Here (A) is a two element ordered set where $a \leqslant a$ and $b \leqslant b$, but a and b are non-comparable. (B) is the other sort of two element ordered set, where in addition $a < b$. Every two element ordered set is isomorphic to one or the other of these two ordered sets. In (C), $c < a$ and $c < b$, but a and b are non-comparable. Each of a and b is a *maximal element* of this set, in the sense that there is no element of the set greater than it. (D) and (E) are interesting ordered sets which it will be worth considering when doing some of the exercises.

We can get an idea of how conjunction and disjunction can be interpreted in a partially ordered set by holding to the idea that if P implies Q, then the truth value of P ought to be less than or equal to the truth value of Q. For

$P \wedge Q$ implies both P and Q; and for any other proposition C which implies both P and Q, C implies $P \wedge Q$. Dually, for any C to be implied by $P \vee Q$, it must be implied by *both* P and Q; and $P \vee Q$ is implied by each of P and Q. We thus specify the class of partially ordered sets we are interested in by means of the following definitions.

DEFINITION 6.2

1. Let $\langle L, \leqslant \rangle$ be a poset, and $X \subseteq L$. An *upper bound* for X is an element $y \in L$ such that for any $x \in X$, $x \leqslant y$. A *join*, or *supremum* for X is a *least* upper bound for X; i.e., if z is a join for X, then z is an upper bound for X and for any upper bound y for X, $z \leqslant y$. The definition of *lower bound* and of *meet*, or *infimum*, i.e., of *greatest lower bound*, are the same, except that $\leqslant$ is replaced by $\geqslant$.

2. A *lattice* is a non-empty partially ordered set $L = \langle L, \leqslant \rangle$ in which each pair of elements $\{x, y\} \subseteq L$ has a *join* in L, which we denote $x \vee y$, and a *meet* in L, denoted $x \wedge y$. We will often identify a lattice with its underlying set when confusion is unlikely.

3. A lattice L is *distributive* if for all $x, y, z \in L$,

$$x \wedge (y \vee z) = (x \wedge y) \vee (x \wedge z).$$

The notation should make obvious that the intention is that if a and b are the truth values of some statements, then $a \wedge b$ will be the truth value of the conjunction of those two statements, and $a \vee b$ of their disjunction. Comparing the facts about the logical behaviour of conjunctions and disjunctions mentioned above with the definitions of meet and join should make clear why it is natural to think of lattices as appropriate classes of truth values for modeling conjunction and disjunction. Of the ordered sets diagrammed above, (B), (D) and (E) are lattices. (A) and (C) are not because, in each case, a and b have no upper bound, and so no join. (B) and (D) are both distributive, but (E) is not: $e \wedge a = a$ and $e \wedge b = c$, so $(e \wedge a) \vee (e \wedge b) = a$, but $e \vee (a \wedge b) = e \vee c = e$.

We shall restrict attention to logics where the truth values form a *distributive* lattice. If one reads the $=$ as "if and only if," this will seem a natural constraint, so it is worth pointing out that not all interesting logics share this feature. In particular, *quantum logics* are logics in which the distributive law fails.

EXERCISES 6.2.1

1. Show that if L is a lattice then the following equations hold for any $x, y, z \in L$.

    (a) $x \wedge x = x = x \vee x$.

    (b) $(x \wedge y) \wedge z = x \wedge (y \wedge z)$ and $(x \vee y) \vee z = x \vee (y \vee z)$.

    (c) $x \wedge y = y \wedge x$ and $x \vee y = y \vee x$.

(d) $x \wedge (y \vee x) = x = (x \wedge y) \vee x$.

2. Explain why the poset $\langle \{a, b, c\}, \leqslant \rangle$, with $\leqslant$ defined so that $a \leqslant a$, $b \leqslant b$, $c \leqslant c$, $a \leqslant b$ and $a \leqslant c$, but $b \not\leqslant c$ and $c \not\leqslant b$ is a partially ordered set, but is not linearly ordered. Is it a lattice? Explain.

* 3. Show that in a distributive lattice, for any $x, y, z \in L$, $x \vee (y \wedge z) = (x \vee y) \wedge (x \vee z)$.

Of course, in most logical investigations we will want to have available some means of interpretation for $\neg$ and of $\rightarrow$, as well as $\wedge$ and $\vee$. To this end we shall introduce some further definitions.

DEFINITION 6.3 We will write 0 and 1 for the *least* and *greatest* elements of L, if they exist. Suppose L has 0 and 1. An element $y \in L$ is a *complement* for $x \in L$ if both $x \vee y = 1$ and $x \wedge y = 0$. If every element of L has a complement, we say that L is *complemented*.

EXERCISES 6.2.2

1. Suppose L is a lattice with 0 and 1. Show that, for any $x \in L$, $x \wedge 1 = x$ and $x \vee 0 = x$.

2. Show that if $x \leqslant y$ then, for any z, $x \wedge z \leqslant y \wedge z$ and $x \vee z \leqslant y \vee z$.

PROPOSITION 6.1 *An element of a distributive lattice has at most one complement.*

We can prove this proposition as follows. Suppose that both b and a are complements for x. Then

$$b = b \wedge 1 = b \wedge (x \vee a) = (b \wedge x) \vee (b \wedge a)$$
$$= 0 \vee (b \wedge a)$$
$$= (x \wedge a) \vee (b \wedge a)$$
$$= (x \vee b) \wedge a$$
$$= 1 \wedge a = a.$$

Obviously, then, in a complemented distributive lattice we can define a map $x \mapsto x^*$ taking each element x to its unique complement x^*.

DEFINITION 6.4 A *Boolean algebra* is a complemented distributive lattice.

We will assume that in each Boolean algebra $0 \neq 1$. We will prove some useful facts about Boolean algebras.

· First, note that in any lattice $a \leqslant b \iff a \wedge b = a \iff a \vee b = b$.

· Obviously for any element a of a Boolean algebra $a^{**} = a$, since both a^{**} and a are complements for a^*.

· Suppose $a \leqslant b$ in a Boolean algebra. Then $a \wedge b^* \leqslant b \wedge b^* = 0$. Suppose $a \wedge b^* = 0$. Then

$$a^* = (a \wedge b^*) \vee a^* = (a^* \vee a) \wedge (b^* \vee a^*)$$
$$= 1 \wedge (b^* \vee a^*)$$
$$= b^* \vee a^*$$

i.e., $b^* \leqslant a^*$. Now if $b^* \leqslant a^*$, then $b^* \vee b \leqslant a^* \vee b$, i.e., $1 \leqslant a^* \vee b$, hence $1 = a^* \vee b$. Finally, suppose $a^* \vee b = 1$. Then $a \wedge (a^* \vee b) = a$, so $a = (a \wedge a^*) \vee (a \wedge b) = 0 \wedge (a \wedge b) = a \wedge b$, i.e., $a \wedge b = a$, i.e., $a \leqslant b$. So we can conclude that in a Boolean algebra

$$a \leqslant b \iff b^* \leqslant a^* \iff a \wedge b^* = 0 \iff a^* \vee b = 1.$$

EXERCISES 6.2.3
Show that in a Boolean algebra

$$(a \wedge b)^* = a^* \vee b^* \qquad (x \vee y)^* = x^* \wedge y^*.$$

We have arrived at an interesting class of structures by attempting to add a reasonable notion of *negation* to (distributive) lattices, which we arrived at in turn from an analysis of conjunction and disjunction. We can, if we wish, get a notion of implication by defining it in terms of negation and disjunction, which is to say that we can simply take $P \rightarrow Q$ to be equivalent to $\neg P \vee Q$. Indeed, as we shall see, we are forced to do this in a complemented distributive lattice. But let's take a step back and consider whether anything interesting results if we add a notion of implication to distributive lattices, rather than beginning with negation.

First, of course, if $P \rightarrow Q$ is to represent that P implies Q, then $P \rightarrow Q$ together with P must imply Q. So, given our present understanding of $\leqslant$, we shall require that the truth value of $P \wedge (P \rightarrow Q)$ must be less than or equal to the truth value of Q. But now suppose that Z is a statement which, coupled with P, implies that Q. Then Z must imply $P \rightarrow Q$. For suppose Z. Then, if we suppose that P, we have available as assumptions both P and Z, which together imply Q, and so we have established, on the assumption that Z is so, that "if P, then Q" must hold—in other words, if $Z \wedge P$ implies, and so is less than or equal to Q, then Z implies, and so is less than or equal to, $P \rightarrow Q$. We thus arrive at the idea behind the following definition.

DEFINITION 6.5
  1. Let L be a lattice. For $a, b \in L$, the *arrow element from a to b* or the *relative pseudo-complement of a to b*, denoted $a \Rightarrow b$, if it exists, is the largest element $x \in L$ such that $x \wedge a \leqslant b$. A lattice L in which $a \Rightarrow b$ exists for all $a, b \in L$ is said to *have arrow elements* or to be *relatively pseudo-complemented*.

  2. A *Heyting algebra* is a relatively pseudo-complemented lattice with 0.

EXERCISES 6.2.4

1. Show that in any Heyting algebra $c \leqslant a \Rightarrow b$ if and only if $a \wedge c \leqslant b$. Deduce that $a \Rightarrow b = 1$ if and only if $a \leqslant b$, and that $a \wedge (a \Rightarrow b) = a \wedge b$.

* 2. Show that if L is a Boolean algebra, $a \Rightarrow b = a^* \vee b$, and so always exists. Hence all Boolean algebras are Heyting algebras.

3. Show that every Heyting algebra has a 1.

4. Show that Heyting algebras are distributive. [Hint: It suffices to show that for any element z in the lattice, $(a \wedge b) \vee (a \wedge c) \leqslant z$ if and only if $a \wedge (b \vee c) \leqslant z$.]

5. Every linearly ordered set with a top element and a bottom element is a Heyting algebra. Let L be such a linearly ordered set, and $a, b \in L$, with $a < b$. What are $a \wedge b$, $a \vee b$, and $a \Rightarrow b$? What is $a \Rightarrow 0$, if $a \neq 0$?

* 6. Suppose $\langle L, \leqslant \rangle$ is a distributive lattice, and that L is finite. Show that this lattice has a 0. Show that there is an arrow object $a \Rightarrow b$ for every pair of elements $a, b \in L$, and so this lattice is a Heyting algebra.

In a Heyting algebra $a \Rightarrow 0$ always exists, and is called the *pseudo-complement* of a. Each Boolean algebra is a Heyting algebra, and $a \Rightarrow 0 = a^*$. We therefore extend the a^* notation to denote the pseudo-complement of a in any Heyting algebra. On the other hand, not every Heyting algebra is a Boolean algebra. For instance, by exercise 5, a three element linearly ordered set is a Heyting algebra, but if one considers the middle member of this set, call it m, then $m^{**} \neq m$.

EXERCISES 6.2.5

* 1. Draw truth tables for a three-valued logic whose truth values form a three element linearly ordered set. What are some key differences between these truth tables and those for the three-valued logics considered in Chapter 5?

2. There is a set of exactly ten lattices such that all lattices with five or fewer elements are isomorphic to one of them. Identify these ten lattices. How many of these are Heyting algebras? How many are Boolean algebras? (Recall that we assume that a Boolean algebra has at least two members.)

Now that we have available two interesting classes of lattices, we may define two sorts of logic in much the same manner as we did in the case of fuzzy logic. First, we define a *Boolean valuation* to be a map which assigns to each statement letter a particular element of an arbitrary Boolean algebra, and a *Heyting valuation* to be such a map to elements of an arbitrary Heyting algebra. We then specify the following rules, which determine the truth values in the relevant algebra under a given valuation V.

DEFINITION 6.6

1. $[\![\neg P]\!]_V = [\![P]\!]_V{}^*$

2. $[\![P \wedge Q]\!]_V = [\![P]\!]_V \wedge [\![Q]\!]_V$

3. $[\![P \vee Q]\!]_V = [\![P]\!]_V \vee [\![Q]\!]_V$

4. $[\![P \to Q]\!]_V = [\![P]\!]_V \Rightarrow [\![Q]\!]_V$

Since a Boolean algebra is a Heyting algebra, and the operations * and $\Rightarrow$, which are in fact defined differently for the two cases, coincide in the Boolean case, we can use a single means for determining the truth values of complex statements for both cases.[2]

The definitions of validity, consistency, and so on, are the usual ones: a statement is *valid* if and only if it is true (i.e., has the value 1) under every valuation, for example. It turns out that Boolean valued logic is classical logic, and Heyting valued logic is intuitionistic logic. That is, an argument is valid in classical propositional logic if and only if it is valid in Boolean valued logic, and the same holds, *mutatis mutandis*, for intuitionistic logic. We will presently briefly indicate one way this can be shown, but will pause first to make a few philosophical observations about this.

First, note that this shows that one must keep straight the distinction between the *principle of bivalence* and the *law of excluded middle*, (i.e., in the propositional case, the requirement that $P \vee \neg P$ be valid for every P). For, as we have seen, in propositional logic the principle of bivalence coupled with the wish for a truth-functional logic forces classical logic on us (and so forces excluded middle on us, too, because it is valid in classical logic). On the other hand, classical logic, hence excluded middle, is quite compatible with there being more than two truth values, as is shown by the existence of Boolean valued logic.

Secondly, either of these logics seems to keep many of the advantages of fuzzy logic for dealing with, for instance, vagueness without being open to similar counterarguments. For in either of these logics, $[\![P \to Q]\!]_V = 1$ if and only if $[\![P]\!]_V \leqslant [\![Q]\!]_V$, for any V. The result is that if $P \to Q$ is true, then $P \wedge \neg Q$ must be *false*, i.e., have the truth value 0, because $Q \wedge \neg Q$ has that value and the value of P is less than or equal to the value of Q. On the other hand, the tools are still in place to defuse the paradoxical reasoning in much the same way as was done using fuzzy logic. In general, $[\![P \wedge (P \to Q)]\!] \leqslant [\![Q]\!]$, of course. Indeed, $[\![P \wedge (P \to Q)]\!] = [\![P]\!] \wedge [\![Q]\!]$. The result is that if we begin with a true statement ("a person with 10,000 hairs on his or her head is not bald") and a conditional which is not quite true, then the conjunction of these premises will yield a conclusion whose truth value is the truth value of the consequent of the conditional. And in the paradox-generating reasoning, this eventually becomes something

---

[2] Other interesting logics result when one considers other classes of lattices. These typically agree on the interpretation of $\wedge$ and $\vee$, but the interpretation of $\neg$ and $\to$ often differ, and in some cases are even absent altogether.

which has a truth value less than 1. At the next stage, then, the conclusion we can draw will have as a truth value the meet of that truth value, which is less than 1, and the truth value, itself less than 1, of a conditional. Hence it may be lower than either of them. And so on.

The proofs that Boolean valued logic is classical logic and that Heyting valued logic is intuitionistic logic can run in parallel. They are most easily proved using the respective propositional calculi.[3] We shall sketch the proof for the Boolean valued case, remarking on those places where something different needs to be done to get the proof to go through for the intuitionistic case.

First, we can show, where S is a set of statements and P is a statement, that if $S \vdash P$, then "S, therefore P" is a valid argument in Boolean valued logic. To show this, it suffices to show the following:

1. Every axiom of classical propositional calculus is valid in Boolean valued logic.

2. Modus ponens is a valid rule of inference in Boolean valued logic.

Each of these is easily proved. The second was in effect shown in exercise 1 on page 233, though it was shown there to be valid for all Heyting algebras and not merely for Boolean algebras. The first is established by checking each of the axiom schemes in turn. For instance, $P \rightarrow (Q \rightarrow P)$ is shown to be valid by showing that for any a, b in any Boolean algebra, $a \Rightarrow (b \Rightarrow a) = 1$. But as was seen in the exercises, in any Heyting algebra $a \Rightarrow (b \Rightarrow a) = 1$ if and only if $a \leqslant (b \Rightarrow a)$, and $a \leqslant b \Rightarrow a$ by the definition of an arrow element. (The proof for the intuitionistic case is just the same, except that we check a different set of axioms, and need to show them valid in all Heyting algebras instead of only in the Boolean algebras. As this example shows, often the same proof will work for both cases.) That the result follows can then be shown by considering what it means to prove a formula in a propositional calculus.

To show the converse is slightly trickier. Essentially, we shall use the set of premises of the argument, S, to construct an appropriate Boolean algebra, known as the *Lindenbaum algebra for S*. It will have the useful property that we can specify a natural ("canonical") valuation such that any statement P will receive the value 1 in the Lindenbaum algebra for S under the canonical valuation if and only if $S \vdash P$. It follows that $S \nvdash P$ if and only if P does not get value 1 under this interpretation. Hence if $S \nvdash P$, P does not have truth value 1 under all Boolean interpretations in which every member of S gets value 1. So, by contraposing, we get the result that if "S therefore P" is valid in Boolean logic, then $S \vdash P$.

Very briefly, the Lindenbaum algebra is constructed as follows. First, we divide the class of all statements into equivalence classes, by defining the

---

[3]The exercises on page 200, together with the preceding examples, are an adequate, if somewhat redundant, set of axiom schemes for intuitionistic propositional calculus.

equivalence relation $\sim_S$ as follows:

$$P \sim_S Q \iff S \vdash P \longleftrightarrow Q.$$

For each statement P, we denote the equivalence class $\{Q \mid Q \sim_S P\}$ by $[\![P]\!]_S$. All such equivalence classes are members of the set $B = \{[\![P]\!]_S \mid P \text{ is a statement}\}$. We can order B as follows:

$$[\![P]\!]_S \leqslant [\![Q]\!]_S \iff S \vdash P \to Q.$$

EXERCISES 6.2.6

1. Show that $\sim_S$ as defined above is indeed an equivalence relation.

2. Show that the definition of $\leqslant$ just introduced is a sound one in the sense that if $R \in [\![P]\!]_S$, then, for any z in B, $[\![P]\!]_S \leqslant z$ if and only if $[\![R]\!]_S \leqslant z$, and $z \leqslant [\![P]\!]_S$ if and only if $z \leqslant [\![R]\!]_S$.

3. Show that if S is consistent, then $\langle B, \leqslant \rangle$ is a Boolean algebra. That is:

   (a) Show that $\leqslant$ is a partial ordering. (For instance, $\leqslant$ will be reflexive because $P \to P$ is a propositional tautology for every P.)

   (b) Show that it is a lattice by showing that $[\![P \wedge Q]\!]_S$ will satisfy the definition of a meet for $[\![P]\!]_S$ and $[\![Q]\!]_S$, and similarly for $[\![P \vee Q]\!]_S$ and joins.

   (c) Similarly, show that it is distributive.

   (d) Show that in $\langle B, \leqslant \rangle$, $[\![P]\!]_S = 1$ if and only if $S \vdash P$ and $[\![P]\!]_S = 0$ if and only if $S \vdash \neg P$. (Since $S \vdash P \vee \neg P$ and $S \vdash \neg(P \wedge \neg P)$, $[\![\neg P]\!]_S$ is a (necessarily unique) complement for P.) Finally, if S is consistent, then $0 \neq 1$, because $\neg\neg(P \wedge \neg P)$ will not be provable, so we will have a Boolean algebra.

(The proof for the intuitionistic case will be similar, but will show only that the Lindenbaum algebra is a Heyting algebra, not that it is Boolean. For, in general, $P \vee \neg P$ is not provable from S, and so $[\![\neg P]\!]_S$ will not in general be a complement. Instead we must show that there is a 0 element ($[\![P \wedge \neg P]\!]_S$ serves nicely), and that $[\![P \to Q]\!]_V$ serves as an appropriate arrow element for $[\![P]\!]_S$ and $[\![Q]\!]_S$.)

The canonical valuation is simply the valuation which sends each sentence letter A to $[\![A]\!]_S$. Evidently under this valuation every P will have its own equivalence class as its truth value, and the argument sketched above goes through.

It is perhaps worth noting why we needed to construct the Lindenbaum algebra. We want to make use of the ordering naturally provided by the relationship of provability (which, recall, was what motivated us to make use of lattices as collections of truth values in the first place). However, provability only imposes a *preordering* on the class of statements. Since lattices are a particular sort of partial ordering, we perform the standard trick for converting a preordering into a partial ordering of the naturally occurring equivalence classes determined by that preordering (i.e., the classes of things each of which is $\leqslant$ the other according to that preordering) which was indicated in our discussion of orderings in Chapter 2.

6.3 Term Forming Operators and Free Logics

We conclude this book by considering two ways of modifying first-order predicate logic. Each eliminates some limitations imposed for the sake of simplicity in standard presentations of predicate logic.

When we characterized the languages of first-order logic, we made a fundamentally important distinction between the *terms* of the language (which, once interpreted, refer to elements of the domain of discourse) and the *formulas* of the language (which, once interpreted, say things about these individuals). We discussed three sorts of terms: *variables*, *names*, and *function expressions*. But natural languages and technical languages of various sorts include terms which are not naturally thought of as of any of these sorts. For instance, in English we can form *(definite, singular) descriptions*, such as "the present Dean of Arts" or "the author of Waverley." Such descriptions were symbolized earlier in the book by assigning *names* to them. But, unlike proper names, these names do more than refer to an object. They provide information *about* that object, for instance that it has the property denoted by the predicate which was used in forming the description. So, from the knowledge that the present Dean of Arts is amusing, one can infer that there is someone who is both amusing and who holds a position of responsibility in the university, but from the knowledge that Dean is amusing, no such knowledge is immediately available—that is, it is not available unless we know something else about Dean (perhaps that Dean is the present Dean of Arts). But, as we shall see, such terms are not like function terms, either, and they're obviously not variables.

An assumption we have built into our formal semantics is that the interpretation of any term in the language *must be a member of the domain of the interpretation*. However, this is not an assumption we generally make about the terms of ordinary languages. For instance, we can perfectly well produce arguments which include the term "the present King of France," or "Pegasus," even though those terms don't refer to any existing object. Relatedly, we assumed that the domain of any interpretation *must be a non-empty set*. (The terms of the language cannot be guaranteed to refer without this assumption.) But this has the unfortunate consequence that $(\exists x)x = x$ is *valid* in our semantics. It is often thought, though, that an existential claim such as this cannot be a *logical* truth. Such considerations have led some logicians to investigate *free logics* in which such assumptions are avoided.

6.3.1   Term Forming Operators

Introductory Remarks

An undergraduate pursuing a degree in philosophy won't likely go too long before running up against a discussion of the definite description operator ι and its seemingly inseparable traveling companions "the present King of France" and "the author of Waverley." If this student takes a course in the Philosophy of Mathematics, she or he is bound to be told that a crisis in the foundations of mathematics came about when the paradoxes, Russell's paradox in particular, showed that the *naive conception of set*, on which "any predicate has an extension," is inconsistent. Luckily, though, the world did not have long to wait before Zermelo (among others) invented the (apparently) consistent set theory sketched in Chapter 2, a crucial feature of which is that we cannot allow unrestricted application of the operation of forming extensions. That is, instead of an unrestricted rule which says that $\{\, x \mid Px \,\}$ is a set for all formulas Px, we only say that *if we already know that y is a set* then $\{\, x \in y \mid Px \,\}$ is a set. In this course a student may also run up against Hilbert's ε operator. The single axiom for ε is supposed to allow us to derive all the axioms that govern reasoning about the transfinite, and so, according to Hilbert's program in the foundations of mathematics, ε is the most important tool we have for ensuring that "no one shall be able to drive us from the paradise that Cantor has created for us."[4]

What the description operator ι, the set-abstraction operator $\{:\}$, and ε have in common is that they are all, from the point of view of formal logic, what we shall call *term forming operators*. We shall mean by this that in a formal language $\mathcal{L}$, for each variable x and each formula Px of $\mathcal{L}$ (in which x occurs, but in which there are no occurrences of $\forall x$, $\exists x$ nor results of previous applications of the term forming operator to x), application of the operator gives us a *term* of the language. In these cases the relevant terms are denoted by "$\iota x Px$," "$\{\, x \mid Px \,\}$," and "$\varepsilon x Px$" respectively; furthermore, while x was free in Px, it is no longer free in the term resulting from the application of the operator.

Let us expand on this last remark by considering why descriptions, for example, are not naturally thought of as function terms of the sort considered earlier in this book. Consider a functional expression like "father of ... ." In it, the dots must be filled in by a *term*. On the other hand, when we convert a predicate like " ... is a present King of France" to "the present King of France," we are, approximately, filling in the dots of "The ..." with a *formula*—slightly more formally, we apply "The x such that ..." to "x is a present King of France." If we apply a function to a term with a free variable (e.g., applying "father of ..." to x to get "father of x," or to "mother of x" to get "father of the mother of x") the result is an expression whose

---

[4]David Hilbert, "On the Infinite," translated by S. Bauer-Mengelberg, in Jan van Heijenoort, ed., *From Frege to Gödel: A Source Book for Mathematical Logic, 1879–1931*, (Cambridge, Mass.: Harvard University Press, 1967), pp. 367–392.

interpretation *depends on the interpretation of that same free variable.* But applying "The x such that ..." to "x is a present King of France" gives us an expression whose *interpretation does not depend on the value of x.* In other words, the procedure of forming descriptions *binds variables.*

This makes term forming operators, from the point of view of ordinary first-order logic, a somewhat strange hybrid. For in the usual presentations of first-order logic, the closest thing to something we might call a term forming operator is a function symbol. But these do not bind variables. Moreover, they operate on *terms*, and not on formulas. On the other hand, the only variable binding operators in such languages are quantifiers. But, from a grammatical point of view, the output of the process of appending a quantifier is a *formula*, not a term.

Syntax

We begin by describing the modifications which need to be made to the description of the syntax of an arbitrary language $\mathcal{L}$ (with identity but, for simplicity, without function symbols) for predicate logic to make it a description of a language which includes one term forming operator σ. We shall call the resulting language $\mathcal{L}_\sigma$.

First, the *basic vocabulary* of $\mathcal{L}_\sigma$ is the same as $\mathcal{L}$, but for one modification. The non-logical vocabulary remains the same, but the logical vocabulary includes one more item, namely the term forming operator σ.

More interestingly, when specifying which expressions of $\mathcal{L}_\sigma$ are grammatical, we can no longer proceed as we did in chapter 2, where we first defined the terms of the language, then, so to speak, built the formulas on top of the terms. For now which terms there are will depend on what formulas there are, and not merely the other way around. It is therefore convenient to give a single definition which determines both classes at once.

DEFINITION 6.7 The class of *terms* of $\mathcal{L}_\sigma$ and the class of *formulas* of $\mathcal{L}_\sigma$ are defined recursively as follows.

1. The individual variables and names of $\mathcal{L}_\sigma$ are *terms of $\mathcal{L}_\sigma$*.

2. If P is an n–place predicate symbol of $\mathcal{L}_\sigma$, and $t_1, \ldots, t_n$ is a sequence of (not necessarily distinct) terms of $\mathcal{L}_\sigma$, then $Pt_1 \ldots t_n$ is a *formula of $\mathcal{L}_\sigma$*.

3. If φ and ψ are formulas of $\mathcal{L}_\sigma$, then $(\varphi \wedge \psi)$, $(\varphi \vee \psi)$, $(\varphi \rightarrow \psi)$ and $\neg\psi$ are all *formulas of $\mathcal{L}$*.

4. If φ is a formula of $\mathcal{L}_\sigma$ and x is an individual variable which occurs in φ, and neither $(\forall x)$ nor $(\exists x)$ nor (σx) occurs in φ, then $(\forall x)\varphi$ and $(\exists x)\varphi$ are both *formulas of $\mathcal{L}$*.

5. If φ is a formula of $\mathcal{L}_\sigma$ and x is an individual variable which occurs in φ, and neither $(\forall x)$ nor $(\exists x)$ nor (σx) occurs in φ, then $(\sigma x)\varphi$ is a *term of $\mathcal{L}_\sigma$*.

6. Nothing else is either a *term of $\mathcal{L}_\sigma$* or a *formula of $\mathcal{L}_\sigma$*.

We shall often write $\sigma x P x$ (omitting the parentheses around σx), or even σ_P if it is clear which variable is being bound, when this seems to improve readability.

Examples: The ε- and τ-operators

We use the variable σ to refer to an arbitrary term forming operator in the above definitions. All term forming operators are alike at the level of elementary grammar. What distinguishes one operator from another are differences in the inferences which are licensed by the presence of each in a statement. Consider the behaviour of a pair of natural language analogs of term forming operators, the definite and indefinite articles. From "*the* black helicopter was spotted by the Montana militia," one may infer there was a single helicopter. On the other hand, "*a* black helicopter was spotted by the Montana militia" leaves open the possibility that there were other black helicopters which were not spotted.

We will briefly investigate two term forming operators introduced by David Hilbert and his collaborators in the 1920s. These turn out to have interesting properties, especially when they are added to intuitionistic predicate logic.

We have been using trees as our preferred method of proof in this book. However, as was indicated in Chapter 1, for some purposes other methods are preferable. Term forming operators turn out to be such a case. The problem is that for interesting term forming operators it is rather difficult to specify straightforward rules which capture their intended behaviour. (It is much easier to do so if we treat the logical system as a calculus.) For instance, an important pair of operators in the history of logic, both introduced by David Hilbert in the 1920s, are the *epsilon operator* and the *tau operator*. The intended behaviour of the epsilon operator can be characterized as follows: for any property $\varphi(x)$, there is an object (in the domain of discourse) which is the thing *most likely to have* φ, which we call $(\varepsilon x)\varphi(x)$. On the other hand, $(\tau x)\varphi(x)$ is the thing *least* likely to have $\varphi(x)$. It is fairly straightforward to specify this behaviour by adding a *new axiom* to a system of logic, in addition to the usual rules for predicate logic, whether intuitionistic or classical, considered as a calculus:

$$\exists x \varphi(x) \rightarrow \varphi((\varepsilon x)\varphi(x)) \qquad\qquad (\varepsilon)$$
$$\varphi((\tau x)\varphi(x)) \rightarrow \forall x \varphi \qquad\qquad (\tau)$$

To illustrate the difficulty of capturing such reasoning on trees, it helps to have available as an illustration a proof which shows that term forming operators can have interesting consequences in some contexts. Recall from the discussion of intuitionistic propositional logic in Chapter 5 that there are many classical tautologies which are not valid in intuitionistic logic. However, consider the following result:

THEOREM 6.2
In intuitionistic logic together with the τ axiom, $\{\forall x(x = c \lor x \neq c), b \neq c\} \vdash (P \rightarrow Q) \lor (Q \rightarrow P)$, for any statements P and Q.

To prove this, one begins by considering a formula which can be constructed by choosing a variable x which occurs in neither P nor Q,

$$(x = c \land P) \lor (x \neq c \land Q).$$

Call this formula $\alpha(x)$. Notice that we can prove, given our premises, that $(\forall x)\alpha(x) \longleftrightarrow P \land Q$, and so, given the τ axiom, that $\alpha(\tau_\alpha) \rightarrow P \land Q$. We also have, from our first premise, that $\tau_\alpha = c \lor \tau_\alpha \neq c$, so we can prove

$$[\alpha(\tau_\alpha) \rightarrow P \land Q] \land [\tau_\alpha = c \lor \tau_\alpha \neq c].$$

But if this is provable, then since the distributive laws are intuitionistically valid, so too must be

$$[(\alpha(\tau_\alpha) \rightarrow P \land Q) \land \tau_\alpha = c] \lor [(\alpha(\tau_\alpha) \rightarrow P \land Q) \land \tau_\alpha \neq c].$$

But in general if $(R \rightarrow S) \land T$, then $R \land T \rightarrow S$, so

$$[\alpha(\tau_\alpha) \land \tau_\alpha = c \rightarrow P \land Q] \lor [\alpha(\tau_\alpha) \land \tau_\alpha \neq c \rightarrow P \land Q]$$

is provable, too. But $\tau_\alpha = c$ and $\alpha(\tau_\alpha)$ together obviously imply P, while the latter together with $\tau_\alpha \neq c$ implies Q. So $[P \rightarrow (P \land Q)] \lor [Q \rightarrow (P \land Q)]$ is provable, whence $(P \rightarrow Q) \lor (Q \rightarrow P)$ is provable, too.

From a philosophical point of view, this is significant because it shows that the presence of the term forming operator τ, coupled with the assumption that there are two provably distinct objects, one of which is *decidable* in the sense that we can prove $\forall x(x = c \lor x \neq c)$, makes valid certain principles of *propositional logic*, for instance $(P \rightarrow Q) \lor (Q \rightarrow P)$, which are not valid in the absence of τ. (To show this, it suffices to construct a tree for intuitionistic predicate logic which yields a countermodel for the argument with the assumptions $\{\forall x(x = c \lor x \neq c), b \neq c\}$ and conclusion $(A \rightarrow B) \lor (B \rightarrow A)$. We leave this as an exercise.)

However, for present purposes we need to emphasize a lesson from the proof, rather than from the theorem itself. The proof required that we apply the τ axiom for a statement which is not a subformula of any of the statements of the premise set, nor of the conclusion. But there is no relatively straightforward and suitably efficient method which will lead one to consider $(\tau x)[(x = c \land P) \lor (x \neq c \land Q)]$, rather than any of indefinitely many other τ-terms. Hence there are no tree rules which at the same time are equivalent to the tau axiom and are easy to state and use. Similar examples could be generated for the epsilon operator.

We shall therefore work with tree rules which are *correct*, in the sense that anything which is provable using these rules in addition to those for (classical or intuitionistic) predicate logic will also be provable in the (classical or intuitionistic) predicate calculus to which the relevant operator has been added. However, the rules we formulate will not be adequate to prove *all* the validities of the systems of predicate logic. Moreover, when a tree rule (such as universal instantiation) states that *any* term may be substituted for a variable and the resulting formula placed at a node in a path, *this should no longer be understood as referring only to terms which occur already on the path.* Instead, *any term of the language* may be so substituted. This modification means that while the current trees are not very useful for showing that formulas are *unprovable* (because we no longer have a recipe which tells us when we have tried enough different terms), a closed tree still suffices to demonstrate validity—and the systems of rules, not being sufficient, were not of much use for showing invalidity, in any case.

RULE 6.1 (τ-RULE) Given a statement of the form $\varphi(\tau x\varphi)$ occupying a node of an open path of a tree,

  1. if a name n appears in the path, write $\varphi(n)$ at its foot unless $\varphi(n)$ already occupies a node of the path (in which case writing it once more in the path would be redundant);

  2. if no name appears in the path, choose some name n and write $\varphi(n)$ at its foot.

Do not tick the line $\varphi(\tau x\varphi)$.

RULE 6.2 (ε-RULE) Given an unticked statement of the form $\varphi(a)$ occupying a node of an open path, enter $\varphi(\varepsilon x\varphi)$ at its foot.

$$\varphi(a)$$
$$\varphi(\varepsilon x\varphi)$$

Consider first the formula $\exists x(\exists y Py \to Px)$. Exercise 3b on page 65 showed that this formula is valid in classical predicate logic, while exercise 1a on page 221 showed that it is not valid in intuitionistic predicate logic. However, the following tree shows that it *is* valid in intuitionistic predicate logic with the ε-operator.

$$?\exists x(\exists y P y \rightarrow P x)$$
$$?\exists y P y \rightarrow P(\varepsilon y P y) \ \checkmark$$
$$\overline{}$$
$$\exists y P y$$
$$?P(\varepsilon y P y)$$
$$P(\varepsilon y P y)$$
$$\times$$

(Strictly speaking, we should first infer Pa from $\exists y P y$ before applying the ε-rule in this tree. We shall often compress these two steps into one.) Notice that this tree is quite short thanks to a careful choice of which term to substitute for x in line 2. Had we substituted any other term, the tree could not have been so short, since there is only one term the ε-rule allows to be substituted for y when applied to $\exists y P y$.

Similarly, if τ is added to intuitionistic predicate logic, some classically valid but intuitionistically invalid principles become provable. For example,

$$?\exists y(P y \rightarrow \forall x P x)$$
$$?P(\tau x P x) \rightarrow \forall x P x \ \checkmark$$
$$\overline{}$$
$$P(\tau x P x)$$
$$?\forall x P x$$
$$\overline{}$$
$$?P(c)$$
$$P(\tau x P x)$$
$$P(c)$$
$$\times$$

Perhaps more interesting is that the following claim, the invalidity of which is one of the motivations behind the constructivists' rejection of classical logic, becomes valid in the presence of τ.

$$?\neg \forall x Px \rightarrow \exists x \neg Px$$
$$\neg \forall x Px$$
$$?\exists x \neg Px$$
_____
$$?\neg P(\tau x Px)$$
$$\neg \forall x Px$$
_____
$$P(\tau x Px)$$
$$\neg \forall x Px$$
$$?\forall x Px$$
_____
$$?P(b)$$
$$P(\tau x Px)$$
$$P(b)$$
$$\times$$

While we shall not prove it here, it can be shown that neither of these latter two formulas is provable in intuitionistic logic with ε, while the first is not provable in intuitionistic logic with τ. In the classical case, τ and ϵ turn out to be more closely related—indeed, each is definable in terms of the other.

EXERCISES 6.3.1
Draw trees for classical predicate logic, together with the rule for the mentioned operator in each case, which establish that the following two statements are provable.

*   1. $P(\varepsilon x \neg Px) \longleftrightarrow \forall x Px$.

    2. $P(\tau x \neg Px) \longleftrightarrow \exists x Px$

The reader will have noticed that we have been considering term forming operators as additions to intuitionistic rather than to classical logic. There is a good reason for this: in a sense that can be made precise, term forming operators are inert in classical logic.

To see this, it is useful to begin with a description of a very simple style of semantics for operators like ε and τ in classical logic. Let $P(x)$ be a formula with one free variable, x. Then (if $\mathcal{M}$ is a structure for the language and V is a valuation) we call the set $\{d \in M \mid [\![P(x)]\!]_{\mathcal{M}}^{v(x/d)} = 1\}$ the *truth-set* for $P(x)$ (in $\mathcal{M}$ under v. Henceforth we shall suppress this qualification). In classical logic any member of the truth-set for $P(x)$ will serve as an interpretation of $\varepsilon x Px$, and any member of the truth-set for $\neg P(x)$ will serve as an interpretation for $\tau x Px$. We can use this fact to produce a very simple semantics for these operators in classical logic.

A *choice function* f on a non-empty set S is a function $f : \mathcal{P}(S) \setminus \{\varnothing\} \rightarrow S$ such that, for every $T \subseteq S$ such that $T \neq \varnothing$, $f(T) \in T$. That is, for every non-empty subset of S, f "chooses" one of the members of that subset. It is an axiom of the usual versions of set theory that for every non-empty set S, there exists a choice function on S. Since a function is simply a special sort of set of ordered pairs, we may extend a choice function on S to a *special choice function on S* by adding to it the pair $\langle \varnothing, s \rangle$, where s is some arbitrary but fixed member of S (we could, for definiteness, set $s = f(S)$). A special choice function is defined on the whole of $\mathcal{P}(S)$, and not just on the non-empty subsets of S.

If $\mathcal{M}$ is a structure for a language $\mathcal{L}$, M is the universe of $\mathcal{M}$, and f is a special choice function on M, the pair $\langle \mathcal{M}, f \rangle$ will serve as a suitable structure for the language $\mathcal{L}_\sigma$. Just as it was convenient to give a single definition which simultaneously defined both the terms and the formulas of $\mathcal{L}_\sigma$, it is convenient to give a single definition which determines the interpretation of each grammatically correct expression of the language.

DEFINITION 6.8 We assign to each term t of $\mathcal{L}_\sigma$ its *interpretation in $\mathcal{M}$ under the valuation v*, which we denote by $[t]^v_\mathcal{M}$, and for each formula φ of $\mathcal{L}_\sigma$, we define *the interpretation of φ in $\mathcal{M}$ under v*, which we denote by $[\![\varphi]\!]^v_\mathcal{M}$, as follows.

1. For a variable x, $[x]^v_\mathcal{M} = v(x)$.

2. For a name a, $[a]^v_\mathcal{M} = a^\mathcal{M}$.

3. If f is an n–place function symbol and $t_1, \ldots, t_n$ is a list of n (not necessarily distinct) terms, then $[f(t_1, \ldots, t_n)]^v_\mathcal{M} = f^\mathcal{M}([t_1]^v_\mathcal{M}, \ldots, [t_n]^v_\mathcal{M})$.

4. If P is an n–place predicate symbol and $t_1, \ldots, t_n$ are terms, then $[\![Pt_1 \ldots t_n]\!]^v_\mathcal{M}$ is *true* if $\langle [t_1]^v_\mathcal{M}, \ldots, [t_n]^v_\mathcal{M} \rangle \in P^\mathcal{M}$. Otherwise it is false. If $\mathcal{L}$ is a language with identity, then $[\![t_1 = t_2]\!]^v_\mathcal{M}$ is true if $[t_1]^v_\mathcal{M}$ and $[t_2]^v_\mathcal{M}$ are the same element of M. Otherwise it is false.

5. If φ and ψ are formulas of $\mathcal{L}$, then

   (a) $[\![\neg\varphi]\!]^v_\mathcal{M}$ is true if $[\![\varphi]\!]^v_\mathcal{M}$ is false, and it is false otherwise.

   (b) $[\![\varphi \wedge \psi]\!]^v_\mathcal{M}$ is true if $[\![\varphi]\!]^v_\mathcal{M}$ is true and $[\![\psi]\!]^v_\mathcal{M}$ is true. Otherwise it is false.

   (c) $[\![\varphi \vee \psi]\!]^v_\mathcal{M}$ is true if at least one of $[\![\varphi]\!]^v_\mathcal{M}$ and $[\![\psi]\!]^v_\mathcal{M}$ is true. Otherwise it is false.

   (d) $[\![\varphi \rightarrow \psi]\!]^v_\mathcal{M}$ is true if at least one of $[\![\neg\varphi]\!]^v_\mathcal{M}$ and $[\![\psi]\!]^v_\mathcal{M}$ is true. Otherwise it is false.

6. If φ is a formula in which x occurs free, then

   (a) $[\![(\forall x)\varphi]\!]^v_\mathcal{M}$ is true if $[\![\varphi]\!]^{v(x/d)}_\mathcal{M}$ for *each $d \in M$*.

   (b) $[\![(\exists x)\varphi]\!]^v_\mathcal{M}$ is true if $[\![\varphi]\!]^{v(x/d)}_\mathcal{M}$ for *at least one $d \in M$*.

This much of the definition is merely a restatement of the definition of interpretation from chapter 2. We must add another clause which will interpret
the terms formed using σ. If σ is ε or τ, we can add the appropriate one
of the following clauses:

Interpretation of ε-terms If φ is a formula in which x occurs freely, and S
is the *truth-set* for φ (in $\mathcal{M}$ under v), $[\varepsilon x\varphi]_{\mathcal{M}}^{v} = f(S)$.

Interpretation of τ-terms If φ is a formula in which x occurs freely, and
S is the *truth-set* for $\neg\varphi$ (in $\mathcal{M}$ under v), $[\tau x\varphi]_{\mathcal{M}}^{v} = f(S)$.

It is not hard to see that the tree rules introduced for ε and τ are correct for this semantics. (To see this in the case of the τ-rule, notice that
$P(\tau xPx)$ will be *true* only in case $(\tau x)Px$ is *not* in the truth set of $\neg Px$.
But f is a special choice function on M, so this will only happen in the case
where the truth set of $\neg Px$ is empty, hence the case in which *every* member
of M is in the truth set of Px. The correctness of the ε rule is obvious.) Indeed, it is clear that every instance of the characteristic axioms for ε and τ
is correct under these interpretations. So we are now in a position to state
and sketch a proof of the following theorem.

THEOREM 6.3 (CONSERVATIVENESS OF ε AND τ IN CLASSICAL LOGIC)
*Let $S \cup \{P\}$ be a set of formulas in which the operators ε and τ do not occur.
Then P is provable from S in the system one gets by adding either ε or τ to
classical logic if and only if P is provable from S in classical predicate logic.*

One half of this claim is trivial, since every proof in classical predicate
logic is a proof in that logic to which further rules have been added.
So suppose that P is provable from S in the system one gets by adding
ε. (The case for τ is the same, *mutatis mutandis*.) As we have just observed,
this system is *correct* for the simple semantics just described, and so in
every structure for $\mathcal{L}_{\varepsilon}$, $\langle M, f \rangle$, if every member of S is true under a valuation
v, then P is true under that valuation as well. But *every structure for $\mathcal{L}$ gives
rise to structures for $\mathcal{L}_{\varepsilon}$, and the interpretations of expressions of $\mathcal{L}_{\varepsilon}$ in which
ε does not occur do not depend in any way on f.* So every member of S will
be true in $\langle \mathcal{M}, f \rangle$ under v if and only if every member of S is true in $\mathcal{M}$
under v, and similarly for P. It follows that in every classical structure $\mathcal{M}$,
if every member of S is true under v, then P is also true under v. But then
it follows from the *adequacy* of the proof methods for classical predicate
logic that P was provable from S in classical logic. In other words, ε *played
no essential role in the proof of P.*
The lesson of this theorem is that the addition of term forming operators
to classical logic results in no new deductive power for the logical system, in
the sense that *when we are talking about things we could talk about using the
unextended language,* the new rules don't yield any new valid arguments.
However, one shouldn't read this as telling us that these operators are use-
less in classical logic. The addition of term forming operators can be useful

because it might increase the *expressive* power of the formal language—for instance, the { : } notation we used to introduce *classes* in our discussions of set theory in chapter 2 was, essentially, a term forming operator. Moreover, the fact that we cannot prove new statements in which the operator does not occur obviously doesn't mean that we cannot prove new statements in which the operator *does* occur. Again, the example of the class terms of chapter 2 is instructive—one would expect some interesting statements of set theory to refer explicitly to particular sets (e.g., to $\{x : x \neq x\}$). The lesson of the theorem, though, is that these are not *logical* facts. Moreover, the theorem obviously generalizes to *any term forming operator* for which we can provide a semantics which is a straightforward extension of the usual semantics for classical predicate logic, i.e., which is such that: (1) we can prove the correctness of the system which results by adding the operator to classical logic for that semantics; (2) the interpretations of expressions in which the operator *does not occur* do not depend on the interpretations of the expressions in which it does.

As we have seen, the situation is different when we add term forming operators to intuitionistic logic. In the intuitionistic case, the addition of a term forming operator like ε or τ *makes valid* some inferences and statements which *are not valid in the absence of these operators*. Moreover, in the intuitionistic case we cannot be satisfied with a semantics which is quite so simple as the one sketched above, even for the simple illustrative purposes of this chapter. For notice that the semantics above means that if φ and ψ are a pair of formulas (in which x occurs free) which have the same truth set (in some $\mathcal{M}$ under some v), then $(\varepsilon x)\varphi$ and $(\varepsilon x)\psi$ will be the same. It follows that the semantics will make the following a valid scheme:

$$\forall x(\varphi \longleftrightarrow \psi) \rightarrow \varepsilon x \varphi = \varepsilon x \psi.$$

This was harmless enough in the classical case, at least in the sense that no new validities in which there is an occurrence of ε will result (though we might want to modify our semantics to make this scheme no longer valid for some purposes). But in the intuitionistic case, this scheme is far from harmless.

THEOREM 6.4
If in the intuitionistic predicate calculus with the ε-axiom, we add

$$\forall x(\varphi \longleftrightarrow \psi) \rightarrow \varepsilon x \varphi = \varepsilon x \psi$$

as an axiom scheme, then from $a \neq b$ we can prove $P \vee \neg P$ for any P.

To prove this, choose an x which is not free in P. Let us denote the expression $x = a \vee P$ by $Q(x)$, and the expression $x = b \vee P$ by $R(x)$.

Notice the following facts. First, $P \vdash \forall x(Q(x) \longleftrightarrow R(x))$, and so by appealing to the appropriate instance of the axiom scheme we have that $P \vdash \varepsilon x Q x = \varepsilon x R x$. It follows that $\varepsilon x Q x \neq \varepsilon x R x \vdash \neg P$. Notice also that

$\exists x Q x$ and $\exists x R x$ are each provable, and so by appeal to the ε-axiom we have $\vdash \varepsilon x Q x = a \vee P$ and $\vdash \varepsilon x R x = b \vee P$.

We now reason as follows. Since we can prove each conjunct, we can prove the conjunction

$$(\varepsilon x Q x = a \vee P) \wedge (\varepsilon x R x = b \vee P).$$

By the distributive law, then,

$$(\varepsilon x Q x = a \wedge \varepsilon x R x = b) \vee P.$$

Since we have as a premise that $a \neq b$, we can prove

$$\varepsilon x Q x \neq \varepsilon x R x \vee P.$$

But as we have seen, the left disjunct of this formula implies $\neg P$, so we can prove $\neg P \vee P$.

This is a striking result because, as we saw in our discussion of Heyting algebras and Boolean algebras, the addition of the law of excluded middle to intuitionistic logic makes valid *all* the principles of classical logic.

We have not presented a semantics for intuitionistic logic with term forming operators.[5] However, it can be shown that while ε added to intuitionistic logic makes valid some classically valid but intuitionistically invalid principles, it doesn't yield *all* of them. Thus, the extra assumption that *coextensive predicates* result in ε-terms which have the same referent carries a significant logical wallop. This is part of the reason that any semantics for these operators in the intuitionistic case needs to be more complicated.

6.3.2 Free Logics

There are two primary sources of motivation for the adoption of *free logics*. The first is that standard presentations of predicate logic all adopt, as a simplifying assumption, the requirement that the universe in every interpretation must be a *non-empty set*. However, this results in the validity of statements such as $\exists x (x = x)$. This statement might be read as asserting that "something exists." While this is obviously *true*, it's often felt that it is not a *logical truth*. More generally, it is sometimes contended that *logic* ought to be concerned with truths and principles of inference which are *subject neutral*, in the sense of holding in *every domain*—this, it would be argued, is what distinguishes, e.g., a *logical* rule of inference like *modus ponens* from a *non-logical* rule like the the principle of mathematical induction. But then predicate logic, properly speaking, ought to be concerned with what holds in *every* domain, including *empty* domains.

---

[5] Interested readers can find *algebraic* semantics for such operators in David DeVidi, "Intuitionistic ε- and τ-Calculi," *Mathematical Logic Quarterly*, **41** (1995): 523–546, and John L. Bell, "Hilbert's ε-Operator and Classical Logic," *Journal of Philosophical Logic*, **22** (1993): 1–18.

The other motivation is a reaction to another simplifying assumption in standard presentations of classical and intuitionistic predicate logic. The semantics for these logics are arranged such that *every term* in the language refers *to an element of the universe over which the quantifiers range.* Since one of these quantifiers has the meaning "there exists a ... ," this amounts to assuming that every term *refers to an individual which exists—* exists according to the interpretation, that is. But this seems to limit the usefulness of standard logic for understanding the reasoning we carry out in ordinary language, where we often find ourselves reasoning about things which *do not exist—*mythical or fictional characters (Pegasus or Sherlock Holmes, perhaps) or things we are mistaken in thinking to exist (containers of phlogiston, perhaps).

One response to the second sort of consideration is to try to avoid supplementing the tools already in hand by explaining away the problem. To use a standard example, on this approach one holds that the statement "The King of France is bald" is not correctly symbolized in predicate logic by Bk, because "The King of France" is *not a genuine name.* Instead, sentences containing descriptions of this sort are appropriately given a more elaborate symbolization. One well known analysis, due to Bertrand Russell, would symbolize the English sentence as

$$\exists x[Kx \wedge \forall y(Kx \rightarrow x = y) \wedge Bx].$$

That is, the English sentence says there is at least one individual who is the King of France, there is at most one individual who is the King of France, and that individual is bald.

For our purposes, there are two main difficulties for such an approach to reasoning about non-existent objects. First, it may be very well to say that *descriptions* like "the King of France" are not names, but often our reasoning about non-existent objects involves not descriptions, but names. For instance, we might well construct an argument involving the claim "Pegasus flies," or "Holmes played the violin." Russell's approach to this was to contend that *Pegasus* and *Holmes* are not *logically proper names.* Rather, they are disguised descriptions, and so sentences involving these expressions are subject to the same sort of analysis as are statements involving "the King of France." But we can be mistaken about whether the referent of an expression exists or not. Consider the statement "Moses wandered in the desert." It doesn't seem appropriate to say "the correct symbolization of this statement is Wm, but were we somehow to uncover conclusive evidence that Moses never existed we would thereby be discovering that some other symbolization is appropriate." That is, it doesn't seem right that empirical discoveries of that sort should at the same time count as evidence about what the statement *means.* Russell therefore accepted that *all* of what are usually classified as names in English are not *logically proper names.* (Indeed, at the time Russell was of the view that the only logically proper names are expressions which refer to items of direct experience, such as "this" and "that.") This position is one many have regarded as too much to swallow.[6]

The second worry about an approach such as Russell's is that his analysis does not allow for *truths* about non-existent individuals, and that it misidentifies what goes wrong in certain incorrect reasoning about such individuals. For notice that if we analyze "Holmes played the violin" on the model of Russell's analysis of "The King of France is bald," we must say that it is false. (It will be an existentially quantified statement, and whatever else we might say about Holmes, we can't say that he existed.) But many logicians and philosophers are of the opinion that it is *true* that Holmes played the violin, that the golden mountain is golden, and so on for properties of other non-existent individuals. Moreover, on Russell's account the inference from "Holmes played the violin" to "Somebody played the violin" is valid, but unsound. Those who think the premise true of course have another analysis of what is wrong with this reasoning: they contend that the inference is invalid, and more generally that one may only reason from the truth of a claim of the form Fa to one of the form $\exists x Fx$ if one knows that the individual referred to by a exists.

Many different free logics have been developed. Here we shall consider only one approach to free logic. It begins by adopting a (one-place) *existence predicate*, Ex, as a new item in our logical vocabulary. It has a status akin to the identity predicate which, though a predicate, counts as *logical* because, just like $\land$ or $\forall$, it *means the same thing under every interpretation*. Ex shall always mean *the individual referred to by x is a member of the universe of quantification*. The logic we consider shall allow for *empty universes of quantification*, and *names which do not refer to members of the universe of quantification*.

Trees for Classical Free Logic

We get a system of tree rules for a *classical free logic* by modifying the rules for classical predicate logic in two ways. First, we replace universal instantiation by the following rule:

RULE 6.3 (FREE UNIVERSAL INSTANTIATION) Given a statement of the form $\forall v \varphi(v)$ occupying a node of an open path of a tree, if a name n appears in the path, write $En \to \varphi(n)$ at its foot (unless $\varphi(n)$ or $En \to \varphi(n)$ already occupies a node of the path, in which case the addition of the new formula would be redundant).

---

[6]A possible view one might take is that the usual use of the word "name" is more or less right—that proper names in natural languages are genuine names which ought to be symbolized using small letters as we have been doing, but that descriptions are *not* genuine names, and so must be symbolized in some other way—perhaps Russell's. One way to make an account of this sort seem attractive is to consider the validity in quantified contextual logics of formulas of the form $a = b \to \Box(a = b)$. Most of the seeming counterexamples to this claim, like "If Bob is the tallest professor, then necessarily Bob is the tallest professor," seem to involve at least one description being symbolized by a or b.

Do not tick the node $\forall v\varphi(v)$.

$$(\forall x)\varphi(x)$$
$$\psi(n)$$
$$\vdots$$
$$En \rightarrow \varphi(n)$$

Notice that this rule dispenses with the second clause of the original rule for universal instantiation. That clause required that if no name occurred on a path on which a universal statement occurred, some new name had to be introduced and instantiated into the universal formula. The reader might recall that the original justification for that second clause was to ensure that the universe of any interpretation we read off an open path in a tree would be non-empty. Thus, it should be no surprise that this clause may be deleted if we want to allow for empty domains.

The other change is that instead of concluding $\varphi(n)$ from $\forall x\varphi(x)$, we may conclude only $En \rightarrow \varphi(n)$. This is required because the universal quantifier, $\forall x$, means "for all elements in the universe," while names like n might not refer to elements in the universe. So, for instance, in free logic we don't want to be able to infer from "all people have mass" to "Holmes has mass." The first is true, the second is not. The explanation, according to free logic, is that the quantifier in the premise ranges over existing people and is true of them, while Holmes is not a member of that set and so can consistently fail to have mass.

We replace the rule existential instantiation by the following rule:

RULE 6.4 (FREE EXISTENTIAL INSTANTIATION) Given an unticked statement of the form $\exists v\varphi(v)$ occupying a node of an open path, check to see whether the path contains a node occupied by a statement of the form $En \wedge \varphi(n)$, or one of the form $\varphi(n) \wedge En$, or two statements, one of the form $\varphi(n)$ and the other of the form En for identical n. If not, choose a name n *that has not been used anywhere in the path* and write the statement $En \wedge \varphi(n)$ at its foot. When this has been done for every open path in which the statement $\exists v\varphi(v)$ occupies a node, tick the node occupied by the given statement.

$$\exists v\varphi(v) \qquad \checkmark$$
$$En \wedge \varphi(n) \quad (n \text{ new})$$

While we have made use of the existence predicate Ex in our presentation of these rules, and have taken advantage of the convenience of taking it to be a new primitive predicate, there was in fact no need to take it as primitive, at least if we assume that we are working with languages *with identity*. For in such cases $(\exists x)x = a \longleftrightarrow Ea$ is valid, as is demonstrated by the following closed tree.

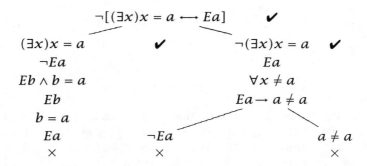

$$\neg[(\exists x)x = a \longleftrightarrow Ea] \qquad \checkmark$$

$$(\exists x)x = a \qquad\qquad \checkmark \qquad\qquad \neg(\exists x)x = a \quad \checkmark$$
$$\neg Ea \qquad\qquad\qquad\qquad\qquad Ea$$
$$Eb \wedge b = a \qquad\qquad\qquad\qquad \forall x \neq a$$
$$Eb \qquad\qquad\qquad\qquad\qquad Ea \to a \neq a$$
$$b = a$$
$$Ea \qquad\qquad \neg Ea \qquad\qquad\qquad a \neq a$$
$$\times \qquad\qquad\quad \times \qquad\qquad\qquad\qquad \times$$

EXERCISES 6.3.2
Construct trees which show each of the following statements to be valid in free classical logic.

*   1. $\forall x Px \wedge Et \to Pt$

    2. $Pt \wedge Et \to \exists x Px$

Interpretations and Countermodels

As with trees for (non-free) predicate logic, one may use trees to generate counterexamples which demonstrate the invalidity of arguments of free logic. Considering how this should work can provide some insight into an appropriate notion of an interpretation for languages of free logic. Consider the following simple tree:

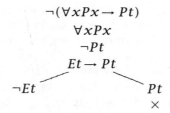

$$\neg(\forall x Px \to Pt)$$
$$\forall x Px$$
$$\neg Pt$$
$$Et \to Pt$$
$$\neg Et \qquad\qquad Pt$$
$$\times$$

This tree is finished. And of course $\forall x Px \to Pt$ *should* be invalid in free logic, in light of the above discussion of reasoning which allows for non-existent objects. The counterexample we read off from this tree will clearly need to be one in which t is interpreted to be an individual which *is not* a member of the universe of the interpretation—that is, it will need to be a *non-existent* individual. Also, t will need to be an object which *does not have* the property by which P is interpreted. On the other hand, the following tree will not close either:

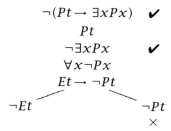

$$\neg(Pt \rightarrow \exists xPx) \quad ✔$$
$$Pt$$
$$\neg \exists xPx \quad ✔$$
$$\forall x \neg Px$$
$$Et \rightarrow \neg Pt$$

$$\neg Et \qquad\qquad \neg Pt$$
$$\times$$

The countermodel we read off this tree will again need to have t interpreted by an individual which is not a member of the universe, but in this case t must *have* the property we use to interpret P. So we must allow "nonexistent" objects to possess the properties (and to enter into the relations) which interpret the predicates of the language. And, of course, in free logic we no longer require that the universe of the interpretation be non-empty. We therefore make the following

DEFINITION 6.9 An *interpretation* $\mathcal{M}$ of a language $\mathcal{L}$ for free logic consists of:

1. A *non-empty* set M' called the *outer domain* of $\mathcal{M}$.

2. A (possibly empty) set M called the *domain* or *universe* of $\mathcal{M}$. It is required that $M \subseteq M'$.

3. To each name a, an assignment of a specific *element* of M', denoted by $a^{\mathcal{M}}$, and called the *interpretation under* $\mathcal{M}$ of a.

4. To each n–place predicate symbol P, an assignment of a definite subset of M'^n, denoted by $P^{\mathcal{M}}$, and called the *interpretation under* $\mathcal{M}$ of that predicate symbol. (So the interpretation of a 1–place predicate symbol will simply be a subset of M', while the interpretation of an n–place relation symbol will be an n–place relation on M'.)

And we extend the interpretation to all the grammatical expressions of the language in a manner very similar to that employed in classical predicate logic. However, we must first modify our definition of a *valuation*: it is now a map from the set of variables to the *outer domain* of the interpretation, not merely to the domain. It remains to give a definition which determines the interpretation of the rest of the language. Here we shall merely list those clauses of the definition which need comment. The other clauses are the same as in the classical predicate logic case.

DEFINITION 6.10 We assign to each term t of $\mathcal{L}$ its *interpretation in* $\mathcal{M}$ *under the valuation* v, which we denote by $[t]^v_{\mathcal{M}}$, as follows.

1. For a variable x, $[x]^v_{\mathcal{M}} = v(x)$.

2. For a name a, $[a]_{\mathcal{M}}^{v} = a^{\mathcal{M}}$.

For each formula φ of $\mathcal{L}$, we define *the interpretation of φ in $\mathcal{M}$ under v*, which we denote by $[\![\varphi]\!]_{\mathcal{M}}^{v}$, as follows.

Atomic formulas

1. If P is an n–place predicate symbol of $\mathcal{L}$ and $t_1, \ldots, t_n$ are terms of $\mathcal{L}$, then $[\![Pt_1 \ldots t_n]\!]_{\mathcal{M}}^{v}$ is *true* if $\langle [t_1]_{\mathcal{M}}^{v}, \ldots, [t_n]_{\mathcal{M}}^{v} \rangle \in P^{\mathcal{M}}$. Otherwise it is false.

2. If $\mathcal{L}$ is a language with identity, then $[\![t_1 = t_2]\!]_{\mathcal{M}}^{v}$ is true if $[t_1]_{\mathcal{M}}^{v}$ and $[t_2]_{\mathcal{M}}^{v}$ are the same element of M'. Otherwise it is false.

3. If t is a term, Et is true if $[t]_{\mathcal{M}}^{v} \in M$, and false otherwise.

The clauses for truth-functional formulas are obvious.

Quantified formulas

1. $[\![(\forall x)\varphi]\!]_{\mathcal{M}}^{v}$ is true if $[\![\varphi]\!]_{\mathcal{M}}^{v(x/d)}$ for *each* $d \in M$.

2. $[\![(\exists x)\varphi]\!]_{\mathcal{M}}^{v}$ is true if $[\![\varphi]\!]_{\mathcal{M}}^{v(x/d)}$ for *at least one* $d \in M$.

Notice that the clause which determines the interpretation of the predicate E, in effect, stipulates that its interpretation will always be the domain M of the interpretation. This formalizes the intuitive idea that an individual will satisfy the predicate E if and only if it exists, and that the domain is the collection of individuals which exist under the interpretation in question. Note carefully also the wording of the clauses for quantified formulas, which refer to the members d *of M*, i.e., of the domain, rather than of the outer domain. So a universally quantified formula might be true under an interpretation, even though there are members of the outer domain which do not have the property the formula asserts everything to have (and, dually, an existential formula can be false even if a member of the outer domain has the property the formula asserts something to have), provided that the individual in question is not also a member of the domain.

When reading a countermodel from a complete open path of a tree, one proceeds in much the same manner as in classical predicate logic: one must assign an interpretation to each name which appears on the path, and one assigns interpretations to the predicates so that the individuals assigned to the names satisfy or fail to satisfy the predicates, depending on whether the predicate or its negation appears on the path. The only additional complications in the present case are: (1) The set comprehending the interpretations of all names on the path is the *outer domain*, rather than the domain, of the interpretation. We assign the individual which interprets a name n to the *domain* if and only if En appears on the path. (2) If no names appear on the path, we must nevertheless include some individual in the outer domain since it is required to be non-empty even though the domain need not be. (This condition saves a lot of unnecessary work. For instance, it allows us to make a quite simple modification of the definition of a valuation rather than needing to consider what to do when there are no individuals available at all (rather than simply no existing individuals) to interpret the variables.)

Using this procedure, one interpretation which can be read off the completed open path in our tree for $Pt \rightarrow \exists x Px$ would have as its *outer domain* the set $\{1\}$, and for its domain $\varnothing$. It could interpret Px by "x is a natural number," and the name t by 1. Then since 1 is a natural number the antecedent of this formula is true, but since no member of the domain is a natural number (what with there being no members of the domain), the consequent is false.

Using these rules and definitions, it is possible to prove correctness and adequacy results by using methods similar to those used in chapter 2 to prove the corresponding results for classical predicate logic, though we shall not do so here.

EXERCISES 6.3.3
For each of the following formulas, construct a tree which either shows that it is valid in free classical logic, or which shows that it is invalid. If it is invalid, use the tree to construct a countermodel.

1. $(\forall x)x = x$

2. $(\exists x)x = x$

   *   3. $Et \longleftrightarrow t = t$

4. $Pt \wedge s = t \rightarrow Ps$

Free Intuitionistic Logic

In classical free logic we want it to follow from $\neg \forall x \varphi(x)$ that there is an *existent* n such that $\neg \varphi(n)$, and from $\neg \exists x \varphi(x)$ only that if a named individual exists then it fails to have φ. However, we do not need to introduce further rules to ensure this: the negated quantifier rules, followed by the free instantiation rules introduced above, give us these results automatically.

To get a system of tree rules for free intuitionistic logic is slightly more involved. The reason is that the existential and universal quantifiers are not interdefinable in intuitionistic logic as they are in the classical case. We therefore do not have the negated quantifier rules available in the intuitionistic case, and so we must take the existence predicate into account for quantified statements marked with ? as well. Moreover, because ? (unlike ¬) is not a part of the formal language and so cannot have as its scope one component of a complex statement, these rules need to have a slightly more elaborate structure than those above.

So, to get a system of tree rules for free intuitionistic logic: In addition to replacing the existential instantiation and universal instantiation by the free versions introduced in the preceding section, we replace the rule introduced in chapter 5 for ?∃ statements by the following:

RULE 6.5 (FREE ?-EXISTENTIAL RULE) Given an unticked, ?-marked statement of the form $?\exists v\,\varphi(v)$ occupying a node of an open path, if the name n occurs on the path, introduce a fork at the bottom of the path and place $?En$ at the foot of one path and $?\varphi(n)$ at the foot of the other.

$$?\exists v\,\varphi(v)$$
$$\psi(n)$$

$?En \qquad\qquad\qquad ?\varphi(n)$

We also replace the rule for ?∀ by the following:

RULE 6.6 (FREE ?-UNIVERSAL RULE) Given an unticked, ?-marked statement of the form $?\forall v\,\varphi(v)$ occupying a node of an open path, choose some name n which does not occur on the path, introduce a horizontal line at the foot of the path on which the statement occurs, and place the statements En and $?Pn$ below the horizontal lines.

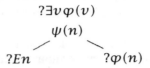

$$\frac{?\forall v\,\varphi(v)}{}\qquad \checkmark$$
$$E(n)$$
$$?\varphi(n) \quad (n\ \text{new})$$

The effects of moving from the usual formulation of intuitionistic predicate logic to free intuitionistic predicate logic, not surprisingly, parallel those of making the move in the classical case. For instance, the tree we used to show the invalidity of $\forall xPx \rightarrow Pt$ in classical free logic suffices, with a couple of simple modifications, to show its invalidity in intuitionistic logic as well.

$$\frac{?(\forall xPx \rightarrow Pt)}{}$$
$$\forall xPx$$
$$?Pt$$
$$Et \rightarrow Pt$$

$?Et \qquad\qquad\qquad Pt$
$$\times$$

Moreover, the modifications of the notion of an interpretation and the modifications we must make to the procedure for reading off countermodels from open paths of trees parallel the modifications in the classical case.

To arrive at an appropriate notion of interpretation, we add to the notion of a definition for intuitionistic predicate logic an *outer domain*, of which the domain for each stage of knowledge must be a subset. Once again, we allow that members of this outer domain which are not members of any domain can have properties and can enter into relations. And, once again, the interpretation of the existential and universal quantifiers must be understood as referring to members of the domains, and not to those members of the outer domain which are not members of any domain. In particular, $\exists x Px$ will be true at stage a if and only if there is a member of the domain of a which has the property P at a, while $\forall x Px$ shall mean that all those objects which are in the domain of a *or of any later stage* have the property P at every stage at which they exist. Finally, we now drop the requirement that the domain at each stage must be nonempty, though the outer domain must have at least one individual in it.

To get a method for reading interpretations from complete open paths, we must simply add to the method for non-free intuitionistic predicate logic the requirement that one include the interpretation of a name which occurs at a stage on a path in the domain of that stage if and only if Ea occurs on the path at that stage. If a occurs at a stage while Ea does not, then the interpretation of a must be a member of the outer domain, but it will not be part of the domain for the stage.

So the countermodel we get from the open path in the diagram above will have two stages of knowledge. Call them 1 and 2, and put $1 < 2$. The outer domain will have one element in it, say the number 0. However, since Et does not occur at either stage on this path, the domain at each stage is $\varnothing$. Finally, Px must be a property that 0 fails to have at stage 2, hence which it fails to have at stage 1. Then, vacuously, $\forall x Px$ is true at stage 1, because every object in the domain of 1 and of each later stage has the property P, since there are no such objects. However, since t is interpreted by 0, and 0 does not have the property P, Pt is not true at stage 1. So this does indeed serve as a countermodel.

EXERCISES 6.3.4
For each of the following claims, construct a tree which shows that it is true in free intuitionistic logic, or one which shows that it is false, and read off a countermodel which shows this falsity.

*   1. $\vdash \forall x Px \rightarrow \exists x Px$

     2. $\vdash \forall x Px \wedge Ea \rightarrow \exists x Px$

*   3. $\forall x (Px \wedge Ex) \rightarrow Q \vdash \exists x Px \rightarrow Q$

One way in which the move to free logic is more interesting in the intuitionistic than in the classical case is in the effect this move has on identity. In intuitionistic free logic, one can introduce a second equivalence relation which behaves slightly differently from the one which is captured by the tree rules, but which some might regard as a more appropriate formalization of the notion of identity. The two different notions might be characterized as follows: (1) if either a or b exists, then so does the other, and they are equal; (2) a and b both exist, and they are equal. It is the first of these which is captured by the tree rules for identity. However, one might take the other notion to be closer to what "identity" means if one doubts that non-existent individuals are the sorts of things which have identity conditions. In any case, in intuitionistic logic it turns out to be useful to have both notions available.

We shall introduce the notation $a \approx b$ to indicate the second notion of identity, and shall understand it to abbreviate the formula $Ea \wedge a = b$. From $a \approx b$ we can infer that both a and b exist, since $Ea \wedge a = b \rightarrow Eb$, as the following tree demonstrates:

$$?(Ea \wedge a = b \rightarrow Eb) \; ✔$$
$$\overline{}$$
$$Ea \wedge a = b \qquad ✔$$
$$?Eb$$
$$Ea$$
$$a = b$$
$$Eb$$
$$\times$$

EXERCISES 6.3.5

1. Use trees to establish that the following facts hold for any names a, b and c.

   (a) Symmetry, i.e., $a \approx b \rightarrow b \approx a$.

   (b) Transitivity, i.e., $[(a \approx b \wedge b \approx c) \rightarrow a \approx c]$.

   (c) Reflexivity, i.e., $a \approx a$.

   (d) Moreover, $c \approx c \longleftrightarrow Ec$.

2. The first three of these obviously hold if we replace $\approx$ by $=$. Establish that the fourth does not hold for $=$, i.e., that $Ec \longleftrightarrow c = c$ is not valid.

3. Explain why, in free logic, it is important to establish these facts for arbitrary names instead of simply proving the corresponding quantified statements (e.g., for reflexivity, $\forall x (x = x)$).

Since Ec is equivalent to $c \approx c$, from a purely formal point of view we could have begun our investigation of free intuitionistic logic by taking the relation $\approx$ as a primitive, and used it to introduce the existence predicate Ex, rather than the other way around. However, it would not have been possible to give an informal account of the intended meaning of $\approx$ without making use of the notion of existence, so it is more natural to introduce the existence predicate first. As in the classical free logic case, if we are considering only languages with identity we could define the existence predicate in terms of the existential quantifier and =. The proof is a tree which is not dissimilar to the one proving the corresponding fact for classical free logic.[7]

Having the two different notions of equivalence and the existence predicate available can be a considerable convenience. This is often the case when one is presenting postulates in an intuitionistic setting. For instance, the following postulates axiomatize a useful notion of a *hemilattice*:

S1 $E0$

S2 $\forall x \forall y [E(x \cup y) \rightarrow Ex \wedge Ey]$

S3 $\forall x (x \cup 0 = x)$

S4 $\forall x (x \cup x = x)$

S5 $\forall x \forall y (x \cup y = y \cup x)$

S6 $\forall x \forall y \forall z [x \cup (y \cup z)] = [(x \cup y) \cup z]$

A *semilattice* is a structure which has a join operation which obeys the laws which characterize a join in a lattice. (So if a semilattice also has a meet operation, it is a lattice.) However, in some circumstances it makes sense to speak of the operation of forming joins, but not to assume that this operation is *always* well defined. For instance, one might be working with the class of *consistent theories*, and the join of two consistent theories need not be consistent. A *hemilattice* is like a semilattice, except the operation of forming joins might be *partial*; i.e., there may be pairs x, y such that $x \cup y$ does not exist in the hemilattice.

Note that several of these laws are stated in terms of =. However, an algebraist may want to discuss the appropriate *structure preserving maps* for hemilattices. In classical mathematics, one would expect to see the requirement that for any a and b in a hemilattice, such a map f must satisfy the condition that

$$f(a \cup b) = f(a) \cup f(b).$$

However, we ought to leave open room for the possibility that $f(a) \cup f(b)$ turns out to exist, even though $a \cup b$ (and so $f(a \cup b)$) does not. As we have seen, this cannot be the case if an equation of this sort holds. On the other hand, if we require instead that for any a and b

$$E(a \cup b) \rightarrow f(a \cup b) \approx f(a) \cup f(b),$$

---

[7]If one is willing to build into one's theory the idea that for any pair a and b of non-existent individuals, $a \approx b$, then one may define = in terms of E and $\approx$ by setting $a = b$ to mean $Ea \vee Eb \rightarrow a \approx b$. This is the approach taken by Dana Scott, for instance, in "Identity and Existence in Intuitionistic Logic," in M.P. Fourman, et al. eds, *Applications of Sheaves*, Springer Lecture Notes in Mathematics, no. 753 (Berlin: Springer-Verlag, 1979), pp. 661-696. This approach runs contrary to the intuitive considerations we have used to motivate the discussion of free logic—in particular, it is most naturally built into the formal semantics by requiring that the outer domain contain a *single* non-existent object—so we do not pursue this approach here. In other respects we follow Scott quite closely.

we are closer to the mark.

There are many other cases in intuitionistic mathematics where the presence of the existence predicate, and the availability of two notions of equality, make for a more straightforward presentation of a notion. We conclude by noting one more case where this is so, one which combines term forming operators with free logic. Suppose we are considering a language $\mathcal{L}_\sigma$. Let us further suppose that σ in this case is a description operator ι, and that the crucial fact about descriptions is captured by the axiom scheme

$$\forall y[y = \iota x Px \longleftrightarrow \forall y(Px \longleftrightarrow x = y)], \qquad (\iota)$$

where y does not occur in Px. The machinery of free logic is useful here. For instance, certain facts about ι are naturally expressed using the E predicate, including

$$E(\iota x Px) \longleftrightarrow \exists y \forall x(Px \longleftrightarrow x = y)$$

and

$$E(\iota x Px) \rightarrow P(\iota x Px).$$

Moreover, the following two theorems illustrate a nice distinction, which can be perspicuously presented if we have available both $=$ and $\approx$.

$$\iota x Px = \iota x Qx \longleftrightarrow \exists y[\forall x(Px \longleftrightarrow x = y) \wedge \forall x(Qx \longleftrightarrow x = y)]$$
$$\iota x Px \approx \iota x Qx \longleftrightarrow \forall y[\forall x(Px \longleftrightarrow x = y) \wedge \forall x(Qx \longleftrightarrow x = y)].$$

Chapter 7

Solutions to ∗-ed exercises

7.1 Solutions for Chapter 1

Solutions to exercises 1.1.1

2. False. If the set of premises is inconsistent an argument is valid, regardless of the status of the conclusion.

Solutions to exercises 1.2.1

1(c) Not a statement, because there are more left than right parentheses (and the formation rules introduce parentheses in matched pairs).

2(a) $((\neg P \wedge \neg Q) \rightarrow \neg\neg P)$.

2(c) $(P \rightarrow ((Q \vee (R \wedge R)) \rightarrow P))$.

Solutions to exercises 1.2.2

2. This has the form

$$A \rightarrow B$$
$$\therefore \quad \neg B \rightarrow \neg A$$

The conclusion is false on only one line of the truth table:

A	B	$A \rightarrow B$	$\neg B \rightarrow \neg A$
$\top$	$\perp$	$\perp$	$\perp$

Since the premise is also false on this valuation, the argument is *valid*.

3. This has the form

$$A \to B$$
$$A \lor C$$
$$\neg B$$
$$\therefore \quad C$$

There are four lines in the truth table for which the conclusion is false:

A	B	C	$A \to B$	$A \lor C$	$\neg B$	C
⊤	⊤	⊥	⊤	⊤	⊥	⊥
⊤	⊥	⊥	⊥	⊤	⊤	⊥
⊥	⊤	⊥	⊤	⊥	⊥	⊥
⊥	⊥	⊥	⊤	⊥	⊤	⊥

On each row at least one premise is false. Hence the argument is *valid*.

Solutions to exercises 1.2.3

1. Suppose $A \equiv B$, and that A is true under the valuation V. Then $V(B) = \top$, since B is equivalent to A. Hence $A \vDash B$. A similar argument shows that $B \vDash A$.

   Now suppose that $A \vDash B$ and $B \vDash A$. If A is true under V, then so is B, since $A \vDash B$. If $V(A) = \bot$, then also $V(B) = \bot$, since $B \vDash A$. On every valuation either $V(A) = \top$ or $V(A) = \bot$, since our logic is bivalent. Hence $A \equiv B$.

3(b) The column in the following truth table for the statement in question is the same as the truth table for $\lor$.

A	B	$A \to B$	$(A \to B) \longleftrightarrow B$
⊤	⊤	⊤	⊤
⊤	⊥	⊥	⊤
⊥	⊤	⊤	⊤
⊥	⊥	⊤	⊥

Solutions to exercises 1.2.4

1. We know that $P \to Q \equiv \neg P \lor Q$. We can transform any statement R of $\mathcal{L}$ into an $\to$-free statement by applying the following procedure. First, determine which occurrence of $\to$ is of lowest rank. If there is no such occurrence, we are done. If there is such an occurrence, it is the main operator of a subformula $(P \to Q)$ of R. Replace that occurrence of $(P \to Q)$ by $(\neg P \lor Q)$. Call the result R'. Note that R' has one fewer occurrence of $\to$ than does R. Repeat the process on R' to obtain R''.

Eventually this process must terminate, since R can have only finitely many occurrences of $\rightarrow$.

It remains to show that when this process terminates the resulting formula is equivalent to R. It suffices to show that $S \equiv S'$ for any S. But this is clear from the nature of the truth table procedure for determining truth values: the truth value of S under a valuation V depends on the truth value of the subformula $P \rightarrow Q$. S' is the same formula as S, except at that occurrence of that subformula, and so depends for its truth value under V on the truth value of $\neg P \vee Q$ in exactly the same way. Since $V(P \rightarrow Q) = V(\neg P \vee Q)$, $V(S) = V(S')$.

5(c) $(A \wedge B \wedge C) \vee (A \wedge \neg B \wedge C) \vee (A \wedge \neg B \wedge \neg C) \vee (\neg A \wedge B \wedge C) \vee (\neg A \wedge B \wedge \neg C) \vee (\neg A \wedge \neg B \wedge \neg C)$.

Solutions to exercises 1.2.5

3. If $[\![A]\!] \leqslant [\![B]\!]$, then either $[\![A]\!] = 0$ or $[\![B]\!] = 1$. If $[\![A]\!] = 0$, $[\![A \rightarrow B]\!] = 1+0+0 = 1$. If $[\![A]\!] = [\![B]\!] = 1$, $[\![A \rightarrow B]\!] = 1+1+1 = 0+1 = 1$. Finally, if $[\![B]\!] = 0$ and $[\![A]\!] = 1$, $[\![A \rightarrow B]\!] = 1+1+(1 \cdot 0) = 0+0 = 0 = 1-(1-0)$.

Solutions to exercises 1.3.1

1(b)

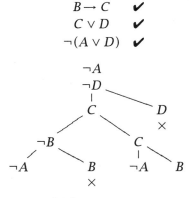

$$\neg A \vee B \quad ✔$$
$$B \rightarrow C \quad ✔$$
$$C \vee D \quad ✔$$
$$\neg(A \vee D) \quad ✔$$

There are two valuations which are counterexamples: $[\![A]\!] = [\![D]\!] = [\![B]\!] = 0$ but $[\![C]\!] = 1$, and $[\![A]\!] = [\![D]\!] = 0$ but $[\![C]\!] = [\![B]\!] = 1$.

2(b) The set is inconsistent, since the following tree closes:

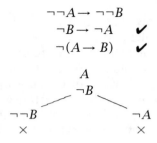

$$\neg\neg A \rightarrow \neg\neg B$$
$$\neg B \rightarrow \neg A \quad ✔$$
$$\neg(A \rightarrow B) \quad ✔$$

$$A$$
$$\neg B$$

$$\neg\neg B \qquad\qquad \neg A$$
$$\times \qquad\qquad\qquad \times$$

3(b) We need two trees to show that this formula is contingent. Each of the following trees has a finished open path.

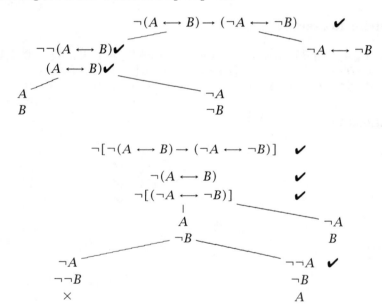

$$\neg(A \longleftrightarrow B) \rightarrow (\neg A \longleftrightarrow \neg B) \qquad ✔$$

$$\neg\neg(A \longleftrightarrow B)✔ \qquad\qquad\qquad \neg A \longleftrightarrow \neg B$$
$$(A \longleftrightarrow B)✔$$

$$A \qquad\qquad\qquad \neg A$$
$$B \qquad\qquad\qquad \neg B$$

$$\neg[\neg(A \longleftrightarrow B) \rightarrow (\neg A \longleftrightarrow \neg B)] \quad ✔$$

$$\neg(A \longleftrightarrow B) \qquad\qquad ✔$$
$$\neg[(\neg A \longleftrightarrow \neg B)] \qquad ✔$$
$$|$$
$$A \qquad\qquad\qquad\qquad \neg A$$
$$\neg B \qquad\qquad\qquad\qquad B$$

$$\neg A \qquad\qquad\qquad \neg\neg A \ ✔$$
$$\neg\neg B \qquad\qquad\qquad \neg B$$
$$\times \qquad\qquad\qquad\qquad A$$

4(b) Testing an argument with premises $P_1, \ldots P_n$ and conclusion C for validity is the same procedure as testing the set $\{P_1, \ldots P_n, \neg C\}$ for consistency. The argument is valid if and only if the set is inconsistent.

Solutions to exercises 1.4.1

1. Suppose a tree associated with an argument with premises $P_1, \ldots P_n$ and conclusions C closes. Then there is a tree starting with the set $\{P_1, \ldots, P_n, \neg C\}$ with no open path. Hence that set is unsatisfiable. Thus, for any valuation V satisfying $\{P_1, \ldots, P_n\}$, $V(\neg C) = \bot$, and so $V(C) = \top$—that is, under any valuation which makes all the premises true, the conclusion must be true. Hence the argument is valid.

Solutions to exercises 1.5.2

1. Easy: Use truth tables or trees.

Solutions to exercises 1.5.3

1(b) Suppose P is provable in propositional calculus. Then there is a sequence of formulas $P_1,\ldots,P_n$ which is a proof of $P_n = P$. We show that there is a natural deduction proof of each P_i for $i = 1,\ldots,n$. If P_i is an axiom, this follows from 1(a). So suppose P_k and $P_k \to P_i$ precede P_i in the sequence, and that each is has a natural deduction proof. We get a natural deduction proof of P_i by writing the proof of P_k, then appending the proof of $P_k \to P_i$, then appending P_i. This is a proper proof, since the two proofs employed here have no premises, and the addition of P_i is legitimate because $\to E$ is a rule of natural deduction.

Solutions to exercises 1.5.4

1.

1.	$A \vdash A$	Axiom
2.	$B \vdash B$	Axiom
3.	$\vdash A, \neg A$	From 1, by Right $\neg$
4.	$\neg B, B \vdash$	From 2, by Left $\neg$
5.	$\neg A \to \neg B, B \vdash A$	From 3,4, by Left $\to$
6.	$B, \neg A \to \neg B \vdash A$	From 5, Left-int
7.	$\neg A \to \neg B \vdash B \to A$	From 6, by Right $\to$
8.	$\vdash (\neg A \to \neg B) \to (B \to A)$	From 7, by Right $\to$

Notice that line 3 has a multiple conclusion.

2. We can use a proof similar to the one for the previous exercise:

1.	$A \vdash A$	Axiom
2.	$B \vdash B$	Axiom
3.	$\vdash A, \neg A$	From 1, by Right $\neg$
4.	$\neg B, B \vdash$	From 2, by Left $\neg$
5.	$\vdash \neg A, A$	From 3, by Right-int
6.	$B, \neg B \vdash$	From 4, by Left-int
7.	$A \to B, \neg B \vdash \neg A$	From 5,6, by Left $\to$
8.	$\neg B, A \to B \vdash \neg A$	From 7, Left-int
9.	$A \to B \vdash \neg B \to \neg A$	From 8, by Right $\to$
10.	$\vdash (A \to B) \to (\neg B \to \neg A)$	From 9, by Right $\to$

The following proof avoids multiple conclusions, and so is intuition-istically acceptable.

1.	$A \vdash A$	Axiom
2.	$B \vdash B$	Axiom
3.	$\neg B, B \vdash$	From 2, by Left $\neg$
4.	$B, \neg B \vdash$	From 3, by Left-int
5.	$A \rightarrow B, A, \neg B \vdash$	From 1,4 by Left $\rightarrow$
6.	$A, A \rightarrow B, \neg A \vdash$	From 5, by Left-int
7.	$A \rightarrow B, \neg B \vdash \neg A$	From 6, by Right $\neg$
8.	$\neg B, A \rightarrow B \vdash \neg A$	From 7, Left-int
9.	$A \rightarrow B \vdash \neg B \rightarrow \neg A$	From 8, by Right $\rightarrow$
10.	$\vdash (A \rightarrow B) \rightarrow (\neg B \rightarrow \neg A)$	From 9, by Right $\rightarrow$

7.2   Solutions for Chapter 2

Solutions to exercises 2.2.1

1(a)

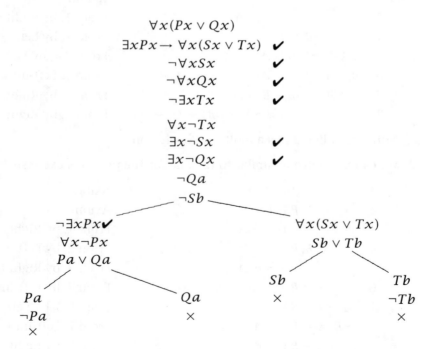

2(c)

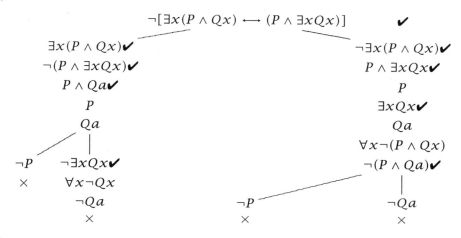

2(f)

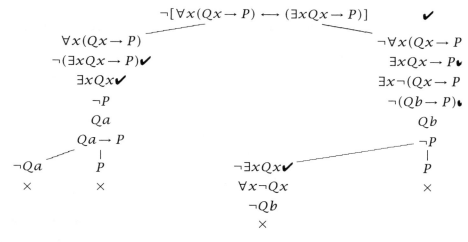

3(b)

$$\neg\exists x(\exists y Py \rightarrow Px)✔$$
$$\forall x\neg(\exists y Py \rightarrow Px)$$
$$\neg(\exists y Py \rightarrow Pa)✔$$
$$\exists y Py✔$$
$$\neg Pa$$
$$Pb$$
$$\neg(\exists y Py \rightarrow Pb)✔$$
$$\exists y Py$$
$$\neg Pb$$
$$\times$$

3(d)

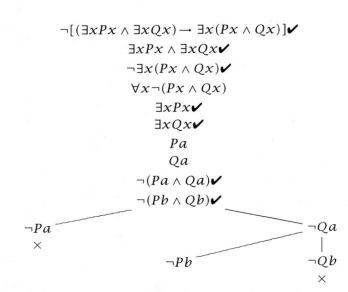

From the complete open path of this tree we get a countermodel with domain $\{a, b\}$, and interpretations of P and Q such that Pa and Qb are true, but Pb and Qa are false.

4(b)

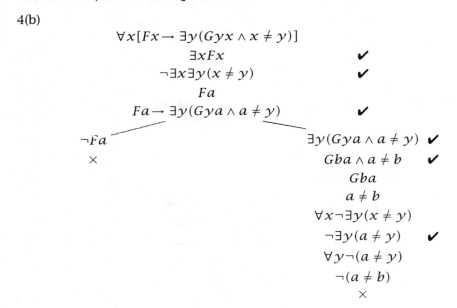

Solutions to exercises 2.3.1

1(c) Not a statement. To form this expression would have required pre-fixing $\forall x$ to a formula in which $\exists x$ already occurs—that is, in this expression $(\exists x)$ occurs in the scope of $(\forall x)$.

1(e) Not a statement. Only variables are bound by quantifiers, not names like a.

2(b) $\{x\}$. (x is free in its second occurrence.)

Solutions to exercises 2.4.1

1. Let A be any set. Then for any x, $x \in \emptyset$ is a false statement, so $x \in \emptyset \Rightarrow x \in A$ is a true one, hence $\emptyset \subseteq A$.

2(c) For any x, $x \in UD \iff x \in A \vee x \in CA$.

2(f) $x \in A \cup (B \cap C) \iff x \in A \vee (x \in B \wedge x \in C) \iff (x \in A \vee x \in B) \wedge (x \in A \vee x \in C) \iff x \in A \cup B \wedge x \in A \cup C \iff x \in (A \cup B) \cap (A \cup C)$.

2(i) $x \in C(A \cap B) \iff \neg(x \in A \cap B) \iff \neg(x \in A \wedge x \in B) \iff x \notin A \vee x \notin B \iff x \in CA \vee x \in CB \iff x \in CA \cup CB$.

3. We provide a partial solution. First, we show that (a) $\iff$ (b): $A \subseteq B \iff \forall x(x \in A \Rightarrow x \in B) \iff \forall x(x \notin B \Rightarrow x \notin A) \iff CB \subseteq CA$.

   (a) $\iff$ (c): $A \subseteq B \iff \forall x(x \in A \Rightarrow x \in B) \iff \forall x[(x \in A \vee x \in B) \iff x \in B] \iff A \cup B = B$.

   (a) $\iff$ (e): $A \cap CB = \emptyset \iff \forall x \neg(x \in A \wedge x \in CB) \iff \forall x(x \in A \Rightarrow x \notin CB) \iff \forall x(x \in A \Rightarrow x \in B) \iff A \subseteq B$.

4(b) Note that $B \subseteq (A \backslash B) \cup B$, so if $B \nsubseteq A$, then $(A \backslash B) \cup B \neq A$. If $A \cap B \neq \emptyset$, then $(A \backslash B) \backslash B \neq A$.

Solutions to exercises 2.4.2

2. Suppose $A \subseteq B$; then $\langle x, y \rangle \in A \times C \Rightarrow x \in A \wedge y \in C \Rightarrow x \in B \wedge y \in C \Rightarrow \langle x, y \rangle \in B \times C$. Conversely suppose $C \neq \emptyset$, and fix an element $c \in C$. If $A \times C \subseteq B \times C$, then $x \in A \Rightarrow \langle x, c \rangle \in A \times C \Rightarrow \langle x, c \rangle \in B \times C \Rightarrow x \in B$.

Solutions to exercises 2.4.3

2(b) We do the first part. $\langle x, y \rangle \in (S \circ R)^{-1} \iff \langle y, x \rangle \in S \circ R \iff \exists z(yRz \wedge zSx) \iff \exists z(zR^{-1}y \wedge xS^{-1}z) \iff \langle x, y \rangle \in R^{-1} \circ S^{-1}$.

Solutions to exercises 2.4.4

1. Let $U = [a]_R$, $V = [b]_R$ be two equivalence classes. If $U \cap V \neq \varnothing$, then there is c such that $c \in [a]_R$, $c \in [b]_R$, i.e., cRa and cRb, whence by symmetry aRc and cRb, so that aRb by transitivity. So if $x \in U$, then xRa, and, since aRb, xRb follows by transitivity. Therefore $U \subseteq V$; similarly $V \subseteq U$, so that $U = V$.

Solutions to exercises 2.4.5

1. We do the divisibility example. Since any natural number is divisible by itself, | is reflexive. Suppose n is divisible by m, and m by k. Then there are natural numbers a and b such that $ma = n$ and $kb = m$. But then $kba = n$ and ba is a natural number, so n is divisible by k, and | is transitive. However, each of 3 and 2 is less than 6 on this ordering, but neither is divisible by the other, so they are non-comparable.

3(b) We have for all a that aRa, so aSa. Suppose aSb and bSc. Then $aRb \wedge bRa \wedge bRc \wedge cRb$, hence by the transitivity of R (twice), $aRc \wedge cRa$. Finally, if aSb, then $aRb \wedge bRa$, hence $bRa \wedge aRb$, so bSa. The equivalence classes in (a) are the classes of logically equivalent statements.

Solutions to exercises 2.4.6

1. To show that $g \circ f$ is a function, we need to show that, for any $x \in A$, there is at most one $u \in C$ such that $\langle x, u \rangle \in g \circ f$. If $\langle x, u \rangle \in g \circ f$ and $\langle x, u' \rangle \in g \circ f$, then for some $b, b' \in B$ we have $\langle x, b \rangle \in f \wedge \langle b, u \rangle \in g$ and $\langle x, b' \rangle \in f \wedge \langle b', u' \rangle \in g$. Then $b = b'$ because f is a function and hence $u = u'$ because g is a function.

3(b) $z \in f[X \cup Y] \iff \exists x \in X \cup Y[z = f(x)] \iff \exists x \in X(z = f(x)) \vee \exists x \in Y(z = f(x)) \iff z \in f[X] \vee z \in f[Y] \iff z \in f[X] \cup f[Y]$. Hence $f[X \cup Y] = f[X] \cup f[Y]$. In general $f[X \cap Y] \subseteq f[X] \cap f[Y]$. But they are not always equal, for consider the function $f : \{0, 1\} \to \{0\}$ defined by $f(0) = f(1) = 0$, and let $X = \{0\}$, $Y = \{1\}$. Then $X \cap Y = \varnothing$, so $f[X \cap Y] = \varnothing$. But $f[X] = f[Y] = \{0\}$, so $f[X \cap Y] \neq f[X]$.

4(b) $x \in X \Rightarrow g(x) \in g[X] \Rightarrow x \in g^{-1}[g[X]]$. Hence $X \subseteq g^{-1}[g[X]]$. Now suppose that g is one-to-one. We already know that $X \subseteq g^{-1}[g[X]]$. If $y \in g^{-1}[g[X]]$, then $g(y) \in g[X]$, so $g(y) = g(x)$ for some $x \in X$, whence $y = x \in X$ since g is one-to-one. Therefore $g^{-1}[g[X]] \subseteq X$, so $X = g^{-1}[g[X]]$.

Solutions to exercises 2.5.1

1. (a) False, true, false; (b) all parts true.

2(b) $\forall x \forall y \forall z (Px \wedge Py \wedge Pz \rightarrow x = y \vee x = z \vee y = z)$.

2(c) $\exists x \exists y (Px \wedge Py \wedge x \neq y)$.

2(d) It suffices to form the conjunction of the answers to the previous two exercises, but this is more elegant: $\exists x \exists y [Px \wedge Py \wedge x \neq y \wedge \forall z (Pz \rightarrow z = x \vee z = y)]$.

Solutions to exercises 2.6.1

1(a) Suppose that $\neg \forall x Px$ is true under v in $\mathcal{M}$. Then $\forall x Px$ is false under v in $\mathcal{M}$, so it is not the case that Px is true under $v(x/d)$ for all $d \in M$. So, by bivalence, there is a $d \in M$ such that Px is false under $v(x/d)$, whence $\exists x \neg Px$ is true. Conversely, if $\exists x \neg Px$ is true under v, then Px is false under $v(x/d)$ for some $d \in M$. But then Px is not true under all $v(x/d)$, and $\forall x Px$ is false.

2(b) Satisfiable. Let the domain be the set of integers, and let Rxy be interpreted by $\leqslant$.

Solutions to exercises 2.7.2

1(b) The identity rule is obviously correct. If $\varphi(a)$ and $a = b$ are both true under an interpretation, then $\varphi(b)$ is true under the same interpretation.

2(b)(i) We only need to note that the path cannot include a formula of form $a \neq a$, or else the branch will close under the revised closure rule.

7.3   Solutions for Chapter 3

Solutions to exercises 3.1.1

M5

$$\forall x \forall y \forall z[x \cdot (y \cdot z) = (x \cdot y) \cdot z]$$
$$\forall x(e \cdot x = x \cdot e = x)$$
$$\forall x(x \cdot x^* = e)$$
$$\forall x \forall y \forall z(x \cdot z = y \cdot z \rightarrow x = y)$$
$$\neg \forall x(x \cdot x^* = x^* \cdot x = e)$$

$$\vdots$$

$$\neg(a \cdot a^* = a^* \cdot a = e)$$

$$\vdots$$

$$(a^* \cdot a) \cdot a^* = e \cdot a^* \rightarrow a^* \cdot a = e \qquad (M4)$$

$$\vdots$$

$$a^* \cdot (a \cdot a^*) = (a^* \cdot a) \cdot a^* \qquad (M1)$$
$$a^* \cdot e = e \cdot a^* \qquad (M2)$$
$$a \cdot a^* = e \qquad (M3)$$
$$a^* \cdot (a \cdot a^*) = e \cdot a^*$$
$$(a^* \cdot a) \cdot a^* = e \cdot a^*$$

$$(a^* \cdot a) \cdot a^* \neq e \cdot a^* \qquad\qquad a^* \cdot a = e$$
$$\times$$

$$a \cdot a^* \neq a^* \cdot a \qquad\qquad a^* \cdot a \neq e$$
$$a \cdot a^* \neq e \qquad\qquad\qquad \times$$
$$\times$$

M8

$$M1$$
$$\vdots$$
$$M7$$
$$\neg \forall x (x^{**} = x)$$

$$\vdots$$

$$a^{**} \neq a$$

$$\vdots$$

$$a^* \cdot a^{**} = e \qquad (M3)$$
$$a \cdot a^* = e \qquad (M3)$$

$$\vdots$$

$$a \cdot e = a \qquad (M2)$$
$$e \cdot a^{**} = a^{**} \qquad (M2)$$
$$a \cdot (a^* \cdot a^{**}) = (a \cdot a^*) \cdot a^{**} \quad (M1)$$

$$\vdots$$

$$(a \cdot a^*) \cdot a^{**} = a \cdot (a^* \cdot a^{**})$$
$$(a \cdot a^*) \cdot a^{**} = a \cdot e$$
$$(a \cdot a^*) \cdot a^{**} = a$$
$$e \cdot a^{**} = a$$
$$a^{**} = a$$
$$\times$$

Solutions to exercises 3.1.2

4.
$$\forall x \forall y (x \neq y \rightarrow sx \neq sy)$$
$$\forall x (0 \neq sx)$$
$$\neg ss0 \neq ssss0 \checkmark$$

$$ss0 = ssss0$$
$$0 \neq ss0$$

$$\vdots$$

$$0 \neq ss0 \rightarrow s0 \neq sss0 \checkmark$$

$\neg 0 \neq ss0$ $s0 \neq sss0$

$\times$ $\vdots$

$$s0 \neq sss0 \rightarrow ss0 \neq ssss0 \checkmark$$

$\neg s0 \neq sss0$ $ss0 \neq ssss0$

$\times$ $\times$

6.
$$\forall x (x + 0 = x)$$
$$\forall x \forall y [x \times sy = (x \times y) + x]$$
$$\forall x (x \times 0 = 0)$$
$$0 \times ss0 \neq 0$$

$$\vdots$$

$0 \times ss0 = (0 \times s0) + 0$	from 2
$(0 \times s0) + 0 = 0 \times s0$	from 1
$0 \times ss0 = 0 \times s0$	

$$\vdots$$

$0 \times s0 = (0 \times 0) + 0$	from 2
$(0 \times 0) + 0 = 0 \times 0$	from 1
$0 \times s0 = 0 \times 0$	
$0 \times 0 = 0$	
$0 \times s0 = 0$	
$0 \times ss0 = 0$	

$$\times$$

Solutions to exercises 3.1.4

2. We do the exercise for statement 3.2.

$$\forall x(x + 0 = x)$$
$$\forall x \forall [x + sy = s(x + y)]$$
$$\neg \forall x(0 + x = x) \checkmark$$

$$\vdots$$

$$0 + a \neq a$$
$$0 + 0 = 0$$
$$0 + b = b \qquad \text{by MI}$$
$$0 + sb \neq sb \qquad \text{by MI}$$

$$\vdots$$

$$0 + sb = s(0 + b)$$
$$0 + sb = sb$$
$$\times$$

4(b) Again, we do the exercise for statement 3.2.

$$\forall x(x + 0 = x)$$
$$\forall x \forall [x + sy = s(x + y)]$$
$$\neg \forall x(0 + x = x)$$

$$\vdots$$

$$0 + 0 = 0$$
$$0 + s0 = s(0 + 0)$$
$$0 + s0 = s0$$

$$\vdots$$

$$0 + sn = sn$$
$$0 + ssn = s(0 + sn)$$
$$0 + ssn = ssn$$

$$\vdots$$

$$\forall x(0 + x = x)$$
$$\times$$

Solutions to exercises 3.1.5

1. $(n + 1)! = 1 \times 2 \times 3 \times \cdots \times n + 1$ is divisible by each of $1, 2, \ldots, n + 1$, i.e., for any $m \leqslant n + 1$ there is a j such that $jm = (n + 1)!$. But then $(n + 1)! + m = (j + 1)m$, and $j + 1$ is neither 1 nor $(n + 1)! + m$.

2. Suppose n is prime, and let $p_1, \ldots, p_m$ be the primes $\leqslant n$. Then $p_1 \cdot \cdots \cdot p_m + 1$ is not divisible by any of $p_1, \ldots p_m$, so either it is prime or it is divisible by some prime $p > n$. In either case there is a prime greater than n. So there is no largest prime.

Solutions to exercises 3.3.1

1(a) $\exists x (a = x \lor x = a)$.

1(c) $\forall x \forall y \exists z [x = y \land y = z \to Kxz) \to \forall w (Kww \to w = w)]$.

2(b)

$$\forall P(Pa \to Pb)$$
$$\neg \forall P(Pb \to Pa) \checkmark$$
$$\exists P \neg (Pb \to Pa) \checkmark$$
$$Qb \to Qa \checkmark$$
$$Qb$$
$$\neg Qa$$
$$\neg Qa \to \neg Qb \checkmark$$

$$\neg\neg Qa \qquad\qquad\qquad Qb$$
$$\times \qquad\qquad\qquad\qquad \times$$

3(c)

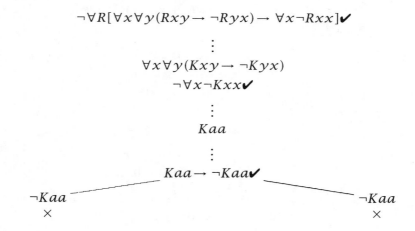

$$\neg \forall R[\forall x \forall y (Rxy \to \neg Ryx) \to \forall x \neg Rxx] \checkmark$$

$$\vdots$$

$$\forall x \forall y (Kxy \to \neg Kyx)$$
$$\neg \forall x \neg Kxx \checkmark$$

$$\vdots$$

$$Kaa$$

$$\vdots$$

$$Kaa \to \neg Kaa \checkmark$$

$$\neg Kaa \qquad\qquad\qquad\qquad \neg Kaa$$
$$\times \qquad\qquad\qquad\qquad\qquad\qquad \times$$

7.4   Solutions for Chapter 4

Solutions to exercises 4.1.1

3. $\mathcal{M} \vDash_w \Box(A \land B) \iff \forall x \in W, wRx \implies \mathcal{M} \vDash_x A \land B \iff \forall x \in W(wRx \implies \mathcal{M} \vDash_x A \text{ and } \mathcal{M} \vDash_x B) \iff \mathcal{M} \vDash_w \Box A \text{ and} \mathcal{M} \vDash_w \Box B \iff$

$\mathcal{M} \vDash_w \square A \wedge \square B.$

Solutions to exercises 4.1.2

1(d) Let $W = \{x, y, z\}$, with xRy and xRz. Suppose A is true while B is false at locality y, and B is true while A is false at locality z. Under this interpretation the formula is false at x.

2. Note that $\lozenge(A \vee \neg A)$ is true at x if and only if $\exists y \in W(xRy)$, since $A \vee \neg A$ is true at every locality. We show that this condition is also necessary and sufficient for the truth of $\square A \rightarrow \lozenge A$ at x. First, if there is no y such that xRy, $\square A$ is vacuously true and $\lozenge A$ is false. Secondly, suppose xRy. If A is false at y, then $\square A$ is false at x. If A is true at y, $\lozenge A$ is true at x. In either case, then, $\square A \rightarrow \lozenge A$ is true at x.

Solutions to exercises 4.1.3

1. Suppose $\mathcal{F}$ is serial and that $\mathcal{M} \vDash_w \square A$. Then $\exists x(wRx)$. So $\mathcal{M} \vDash_x A$, and so $\mathcal{M} \vDash_w \lozenge A$. Conversely, suppose $\square A \rightarrow \lozenge A$ is valid in $\mathcal{F}$ and w is a locality in $\mathcal{F}$ for which there is no x such that wRx. Then $\mathcal{M} \vDash_w \square A$, vacuously, but $\lozenge A$ is false at w.

Solutions to exercises 4.1.5

2. If P is a tautology, then $\square P$ is in S, since S is normal, hence closed under necessitation. So $P \in S^{\square}$. If P, $P \rightarrow Q$ are in $S^{\square}$, then $\square P$, $\square(P \rightarrow Q)$ are in S. But by the K scheme and modus ponens, $\square P \rightarrow \square Q$ is in S, whence by modus ponens again $\square Q$ is in S, and $Q \in S^{\square}$. The proofs that $S^{\square}$ includes all instances of K and that it is closed under necessitation are similar.

Solutions to exercises 4.1.6

1. $K4$ includes the scheme $\square P \rightarrow \square\square P$. Suppose xRy and yRz. By definition of R, this yields that $\square P \in x$ implies $P \in y$ and that $\square P \in y$ implies $P \in z$. So suppose $\square P \in x$. Then $\square\square P \in x$ since $K4$ (and so x, which is a maximal consistent set for $K4$) includes the scheme $\square P \rightarrow \square\square P$, whence $P \in z$. So $\square P \in x$ implies $P \in z$, i.e., xRz.

Solutions to exercises 4.2.1

1(a)

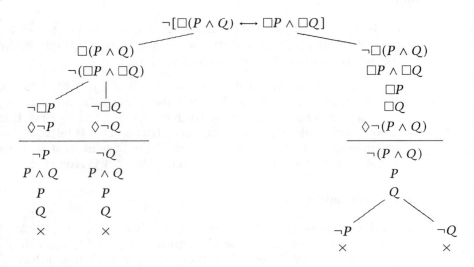

1(c)

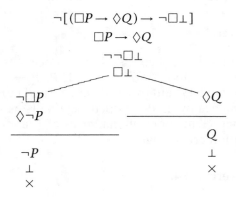

Solutions to exercises 4.2.2

1(c)

$$\neg(\Box A \rightarrow \Diamond A)$$
$$\Box A$$
$$\neg \Diamond A$$
$$\Box \neg A$$

⊤ or ⊥

1

1(e)

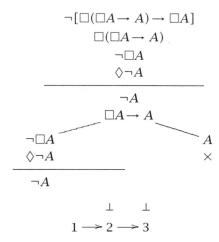

$$\neg[\Box(\Box A \to A) \to \Box A]$$
$$\Box(\Box A \to A)$$
$$\neg\Box A$$
$$\Diamond\neg A$$

$$\neg A$$
$$\Box A \to A$$

$$\neg\Box A \qquad\qquad A$$
$$\Diamond\neg A \qquad\qquad \times$$

$$\neg A$$

$$\bot \qquad \bot$$
$$1 \longrightarrow 2 \longrightarrow 3$$

Solutions to exercises 4.3.1

1.

$$\neg(\Diamond\Box A \to A)$$
$$\Diamond\Box A$$
$$\neg A$$

$$\Box A$$
$$A$$

$$\bot \qquad \top$$
$$1 \longrightarrow 2$$

Solutions to exercises 4.3.3

1. We do one of the two statements.

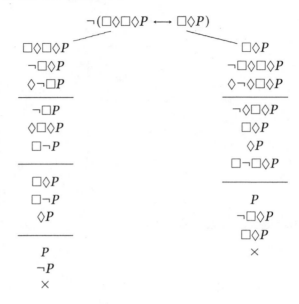

$$\neg(\Box\Diamond\Box\Diamond P \longleftrightarrow \Box\Diamond P)$$

$\Box\Diamond\Box\Diamond P$	$\Box\Diamond P$
$\neg\Box\Diamond P$	$\neg\Box\Diamond\Box\Diamond P$
$\Diamond\neg\Box P$	$\Diamond\neg\Diamond\Box\Diamond P$
$\overline{}$	$\overline{}$
$\neg\Box P$	$\neg\Diamond\Box\Diamond P$
$\Diamond\Box\Diamond P$	$\Box\Diamond P$
$\Box\neg P$	$\Diamond P$
$\overline{}$	$\Box\neg\Box\Diamond P$
$\Box\Diamond P$	$\overline{}$
$\Box\neg P$	P
$\Diamond P$	$\neg\Box\Diamond P$
$\overline{}$	$\Box\Diamond P$
P	$\times$
$\neg P$	
$\times$	

2. We do one of the two statements.

$$\neg(\Box\Diamond A \rightarrow A)$$
$$\Box\Diamond A$$
$$\neg A$$
$$\Diamond A$$
$$\overline{}$$
$$A$$

$$\bot \qquad \top$$
$$1 \longrightarrow 2$$

This tree *could* be continued by applying $\Box$-repeat, $\Box$-elimination, then the $\Diamond$-rule. Notice that locality 3 would be just the same as locality 2, and so could give us another similar locality 4. In such cases it is clear that there is no need to carry on. We shall justify the practice of stopping in such cases below.

Solutions to exercises 4.3.4

1 We give here trees for (a) and (c).

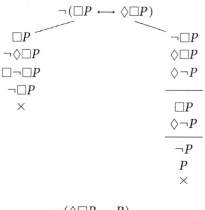

For any statement of the stipulated form $\$\$ \ldots \$A$, if there are more than two operators the leftmost pair will be $\Box\Box$, $\Diamond\Diamond$, $\Box\Diamond$, or $\Diamond\Box$. We know that the following "reduction laws" hold for the ∎5 operators: $\Box\Box P \longleftrightarrow \Box P$, $\Diamond\Diamond P \longleftrightarrow \Diamond P$, $\Box\Diamond P \longleftrightarrow \Diamond P$, and $\Diamond\Box P \longleftrightarrow \Box P$. So we may replace the leftmost two consecutive symbols of the statement by $\Box$ or $\Diamond$ as appropriate, and then continue the reduction procedure until there is only one operator to the left of A.

2. We can use a slight modification of the countermodel in exercise 4.3.3.

$$\perp \qquad \top$$
$$1 \longleftrightarrow 2$$

Solutions to exercises 4.3.5

1. Suppose our system has the $\Diamond$-introduction rule, and $\Box P$ and $\Box\neg P$ occur in the same locality. Then that path closes as follows:

$$
\begin{array}{c}
\vdots \\
\Box P \\
\Box\neg P \\
\Diamond P \\
\hline
P \\
\neg P \\
\times
\end{array}
$$

On the other hand, the set $\{\Box(P \wedge Q), \Box\neg P\}$ closes in $\blacksquare D$, but not in the system which results by adding the closure rule to $\blacksquare$. That a tree beginning with $\neg(\Box P \rightarrow \Diamond P)$ closes in that system is obvious.

Solutions to exercises 4.3.7

1. It suffices to use the same definition as in the $\blacksquare T$ case: the set of conclusions for an occurrence of $\Box P$ at a node in locality w of a tree are all occurrences of P in localities v on the tree such that wRv. (What differs from case to case is which v will satisfy the condition.)

Solutions to exercises 4.3.8

2. The reasoning does not apply because the $\Diamond$-adjunction rule for $\blacksquare 5$ *increases the length* of the statements to which it is applied. It is thus possible to have indefinitely many applications of tree rules in a locality before moving on to the next locality. What will make the general strategy work is a sensible definition of a systematic tree for $\blacksquare 5$. In particular, we cannot require that "all permissible applications of rules not introducing new points are carried out before any rule is applied which introduces a new horizontal line," as in the case of $\blacksquare$ and other systems considered above, for to do so would amount to requiring that no horizontal line ever be introduced on a $\blacksquare 5$ tree. One workable requirement is to insist that in a systematic tree $\Diamond$-adjunction may be applied to any P on a node of a tree provided that P does not occur at that particular node due to a previous application of $\Diamond$-adjunction—where we do not mean to include cases where, e.g., P results from $\Diamond$-adjunction at an earlier locality and occurs at its present node due to $\Diamond$-repeat. It will then be possible to show that any non-terminating path of a systematic tree yields a model in which the tested statement is true at the first locality.

Solutions to exercises 4.4.1

1. Suppose sRs. Then $sR^{-1}s$, and so $\ldots, s, s, s$ is a non-terminating descending chain for R^{-1}. Now suppose S is finite, and R is transitive. If there is an infinite chain $s_1 R s_2 R s_3 R \ldots$, then since S is finite there must be an $i < j$ such that $s_i = s_j$. But then $s_j R s_i$, since R is transitive, and so $s_j R s_j$, hence R is not irreflexive.

Solutions to exercises 4.5.1

2(a)

$$\neg(\Box P \to \nabla P)$$
$$\Box P$$
$$\neg \nabla P$$
$$\Delta \neg P$$
$$\Delta P \qquad \text{by } \Box \nabla$$
$$\nabla P \qquad \text{by } \nabla\text{-intro}$$
$$\overline{\hspace{4cm}} \, \Delta$$
$$P$$
$$\neg P$$
$$\times$$

2(d)

$$\neg(\Delta \Box P \to \Delta \Diamond P)$$
$$\Delta \Box P$$
$$\neg \Delta \Diamond P$$
$$\nabla \neg \Diamond P$$
$$\overline{\hspace{4cm}} \, \Delta$$
$$\neg \Diamond P$$
$$\Box P$$
$$\Box \neg P$$
$$\Delta \neg P \qquad \text{by } \Box \nabla$$
$$\Delta P \qquad \text{by } \Box \nabla$$
$$\nabla P \qquad \text{by } \nabla\text{-intro}$$
$$\overline{\hspace{4cm}} \, \Delta$$
$$P$$
$$\neg P$$
$$\times$$

Solutions to exercises 4.6.1

1. It is not a type-2 model because zRw but $D_z \not\subseteq D_w$. In type-2 S5 semantics, we get a fixed domain (at least among equivalence classes

of localities), hence the Barcan formula must be true in type-2 S5. The other countermodel fails to be a type-2 model for a similar reason.

2(c) This formula is equivalent to the converse Barcan formula, so one's opinion on its validity should be the same as one's opinion of converse Barcan.

7.5   Solutions for Chapter 5

Solutions to exercises 5.1.1

1(b) The tree for $\neg P$ and $\neg(P \to Q)$ is easy, and is left for the reader. The second tree is the following.

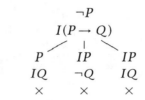

2(b)

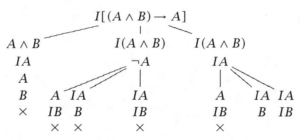

The statement is indeterminate under valuations in which A is indeterminate and B is either false or indeterminate.

Solutions to exercises 5.1.2

1(c) The tree which begins with the negation of the statement is routine, and is left for the reader.

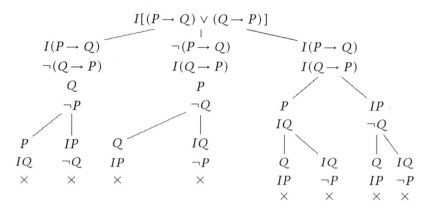

2(c)

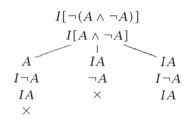

3(c) If either $[\![A]\!] = 0$ or $[\![B]\!] = 1$, then $[\![A \to B]\!] = 1$, and if $[\![A]\!] = [\![B]\!] = \frac{1}{2}$, then $[\![A \to B]\!] = 1$. These are all the cases where $[\![A]\!] \leqslant [\![B]\!]$. If $[\![A]\!] = 1$ and $[\![B]\!] = \frac{1}{2}$, then $[\![A \to B]\!] = \frac{1}{2} = 1 - (1 - \frac{1}{2})$. If $[\![B]\!] = 0$, then $[\![A \to B]\!]$ is $\frac{1}{2}$ if $[\![A]\!] = \frac{1}{2}$, and is 0 if $[\![A]\!] = 1$. In either case this is $1 - ([\![A]\!] - [\![B]\!])$.

Solutions to exercises 5.2.1

10.

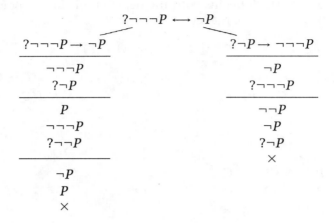

15.

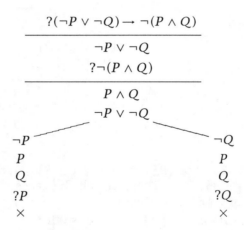

Solutions to exercises 5.2.2

2. $I(a, \neg\neg P) = \top \iff (\forall b \geqslant a)[I(b, \neg P) = \bot] \iff (\forall b \geqslant a)(\exists c \geqslant b)[I(c, P) = \top]$.

Solutions to exercises 5.2.3

1.

$$?\neg\neg A \rightarrow A$$

$$\neg\neg A$$
$$?A$$
$$?\neg A$$

$$A$$

$$\bot \qquad \bot \qquad \top$$
$$1 \longrightarrow 2 \longrightarrow 3$$

2.

$$?A \vee \neg A$$
$$?A$$
$$?\neg A$$

$$A$$

$$\bot \qquad \top$$
$$1 \longrightarrow 2$$

3.

$$?[(A \rightarrow B) \vee (B \rightarrow A)]$$
$$?(A \rightarrow B)$$
$$?(B \rightarrow A)$$

$$A \qquad\qquad\qquad\qquad B$$
$$?B \qquad\qquad\qquad\qquad ?A$$

$$\top\bot \qquad \bot\bot \qquad \bot\top$$
$$2 \longleftarrow 1 \longrightarrow 3$$

Solutions to exercises 5.2.4

3. Let P be $Q \vee R$ and suppose $P \in S$. Then either $Q \in S$ or $R \in S$, since S is a Hintikka locality. Suppose $Q \in S$. Then, since Q is of lower complexity than $Q \vee R$, by inductive hypothesis we have $I(S,Q) = \top$, whence $I(S,P) = \top$. Similarly, if $R \in S$. So suppose $?Q \vee R \in S$. Then $?Q \in S$ and $?R \in S$. So by inductive hypothesis we have $I(S,Q) = \bot$ and $I(S,R) = \bot$, whence $I(S,P) = \bot$.

Let P be $Q \rightarrow R$, and suppose $P \in S$. Then $?Q \in S$ or $R \in S$. By inductive hypothesis, then, we have that either $I(S,R) = \top$ or $I(S,Q) = \bot$, and either of these ensures that $I(S,P) = \top$. So suppose $?Q \rightarrow R \in S$. Then there is an S' such that $Q \in S'$ and $?R \in S'$ and $S \leqslant S'$. By inductive hypothesis, $I(S', Q) = \top$ and $I(S', R) = \bot$, hence we have $I(S, P) = \bot$.

The argument for $\wedge$ is very similar to the argument for $\vee$.

Solutions to exercises 5.2.5

1. We give some examples. $t_1(A \vee \neg A)$ is $\neg(\neg\neg\neg A \wedge \neg\neg\neg\neg A)$, while $t_2(\neg\neg A \to A)$ is $\neg\neg(\neg\neg\neg\neg A \to \neg\neg A)$, and $t_3(\neg(\neg A \wedge \neg B) \to (A \vee B))$ is $\neg[\neg(\neg\neg\neg A \wedge \neg\neg\neg B) \wedge \neg\neg(\neg\neg\neg A \wedge \neg\neg\neg B)]$.

2. We'll consider $A \vee \neg A$ which under t_1 and under t_3 is $\neg(\neg\neg\neg A \wedge \neg\neg\neg\neg A)$, and under t_2 is $\neg\neg(\neg\neg A \vee \neg\neg\neg A)$. It is easy to check by truth tables or classical trees that each of these is classically valid, hence classically equivalent to $A \vee \neg A$. It remains to show that these two statements are intuitionistically valid, which is easily done by drawing trees. (The validity of the t_1 translation should be obvious anyway, since it is the negation of a contradiction.)

Solutions to exercises 5.2.7

1. For example, $t_4(A \to \neg\neg A)$ is $\Box A \to \Box\Diamond\Box A$; $t_5[(A \to B) \to (\neg B \to \neg A)]$ is $\Box[\Box(\Box A \to \Box B) \to \Box(\Box\neg B \to \Box\neg A)]$.

2. For example, $t_4(A \vee \neg A)$ is $\Box A \vee \Box\Diamond\neg A$, which is easily shown to not be ∎$T4$ valid by drawing a tree. $t_5(\neg\neg A \to A)$ is $\Box(\Box\Diamond\Box A \to \Box A)$ which is also not ∎$T4$ valid.

Solutions to exercises 5.3.1

1(a)

$$?\exists y(\exists x Fx \to Fy)$$
$$?\exists x Fx \to Fd$$
$$\overline{}$$
$$\exists x Fx$$
$$?Fd$$
$$Fe$$

The countermodel will have $W = \{1, 2\}$, $D_1 = \{d\}$, $D_2 = \{d, e\}$, and Fd is false in both 1 and 2, while Fe is true in 2.

1(b)

$$?\exists x (Fx \rightarrow \forall y Fy)$$
$$?Fd \rightarrow \forall y Fy$$
$$\overline{}$$
$$Fd$$
$$?\forall y Fy$$
$$\overline{}$$
$$?Fe$$
$$Fd$$

The countermodel has $W = \{1,2,3\}$ in their usual ordering. $D_1 = D_2 = \{d\}$, while $D_3 = \{d,e\}$. The relevant interpretation must set Fd true in 2 and 3, and e false in 3. For then Fd is true in 2 but $\forall x Fy$ is false there (because of the falsity of Fe at a stage later than 2). Hence $Fd \rightarrow \forall y Fy$ is false in 1. Since d is the only member of the domain at 1, the existential statement must be false there.

1(c) The statement is valid.

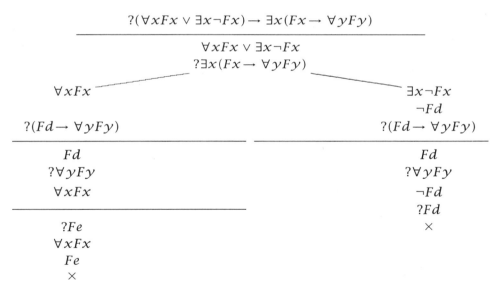

7.6   Solutions for Chapter 6

Solutions to exercises 6.1.1

2. There are 2 cases to consider. If $[\![P]\!] \leqslant [\![Q]\!]$, then $[\![P \rightarrow Q]\!] = 1$, so $(1 - [\![P]\!]) + (1 - [\![P \rightarrow Q]\!]) = 1 - [\![P]\!]$, and $1 - [\![Q]\!] \leqslant 1 - [\![P]\!]$. If $[\![P]\!] > [\![Q]\!]$, then $[\![P]\!] - [\![Q]\!] = r$, where $0 < r \leqslant 1$. Now $(1 - [\![P]\!]) + [1 - (1 - r)] = (1 - [\![P]\!]) + r = [\![Q]\!]$.

3(c) $[\![P]\!] = r$ for some r such that $0 \leqslant r \leqslant 1$, and $1 - (1 - r) = r$. So $[\![\neg\neg P]\!] = [\![P]\!]$, hence $[\![\neg\neg P \to P]\!] = 1$.

Solutions to exercises 6.1.2

3. If $[\![A]\!] = \frac{1}{2}$, $[\![\neg A]\!] = 1 - \frac{1}{2} = \frac{1}{2} = \max(\frac{1}{2}, \frac{1}{2}) = 1 - \max(\frac{1}{2}, \frac{1}{2}) = [\![\neg(A \wedge \neg A)]\!]$.

4. If $[\![A]\!] = [\![B]\!] = \frac{1}{2}$, then $[\![A \to B]\!] = 1$. However, $[\![\neg A]\!] = \frac{1}{2}$, so $[\![\neg A \vee B]\!] = \max(\frac{1}{2}, \frac{1}{2}) = \frac{1}{2}$.

Solutions to exercises 6.2.1

3.

$$
\begin{aligned}
x \vee (y \wedge z) &= [x \vee (x \wedge z)] \vee (y \wedge z) &&\text{by 1(d)} \\
&= x \vee [(x \wedge z) \vee (y \wedge z)] &&\text{by 1(b)} \\
&= x \vee [(z \wedge x) \vee (z \wedge y)] &&\text{by 1(c)} \\
&= x \vee [z \wedge (x \vee y)] &&\text{by distributivity} \\
&= [x \wedge (x \vee y)] \vee [z \wedge (x \vee y)] &&\text{1(d)} \\
&= [(x \vee y) \wedge x] \vee [(x \vee y) \wedge z] \\
&= (x \vee y) \wedge (x \vee z) &&\text{by distributivity}
\end{aligned}
$$

Henceforth we often perform several obvious steps involving laws like 1(a)-(d) at the same time and without comment.

Solutions to exercises 6.2.4

2. First, $(a^* \vee b) \wedge a = (a^* \wedge a) \vee (b \wedge a) = 0 \vee (b \wedge a) = b \wedge a \leqslant b$. It remains to show that if $c \wedge a \leqslant b$, then $c \leqslant a^* \vee b$. Note that $(c \wedge a) \vee a^* = (c \vee a^*) \wedge (a \vee a^*) = (c \vee a^*) \wedge 1 = c \vee a^*$. If $a \wedge c \leqslant b$, then $(a \wedge c) \vee a^* \leqslant b \vee a^*$, i.e., $c \vee a^* \leqslant b \vee a^*$, hence $c \leqslant b \vee a^*$.

6. Let $a_1, \ldots, a_n$ be all the elements of L. Then $a_1 \wedge \cdots \wedge a_n \leqslant a_i$ for all $i = 1, \ldots, n$, so $a_1 \wedge \cdots \wedge a_n$ is a minimal element of L. Suppose a_k is also minimal. Then we have both $a_1 \wedge \cdots \wedge a_n \leqslant a_k$ and $a_k \leqslant a_1 \wedge \cdots \wedge a_n$, hence these two elements are equal by anti-symmetry. So $a_1 \wedge \cdots \wedge a_n$ is the unique minimal element of L, i.e., it is 0.

Now let $a, b \in L$. Let $S = \{a_i \mid a_i \wedge a \leqslant b\}$. Let $s_1, \ldots, s_m$ be the (finitely many) elements of S. This set is non-empty, because b is in it. Write $\bigvee S$ for $s_1 \vee \cdots \vee s_m$. (Take this to be s_1 if there is only one element is S.) We claim $\bigvee S = a \Rightarrow b$. For if $c \wedge a \leqslant b$, then $c \in S$, hence $c \leqslant \bigvee S$. It remains to show that $\bigvee S \wedge a \leqslant b$. But by the distributive law, $\bigvee S \wedge a = (s_1 \wedge a) \vee \cdots \vee (s_m \wedge a)$. (The finiteness of S is relied on here.) But each $s_i \wedge a \leqslant b$, by the definition of S; hence the join of all of them must be $\leqslant b$.

Solutions to exercises 6.2.5

1. The table for negation is this:

P	$\neg P$
$\top$	$\bot$
$\bot$	$\top$
I	$\bot$

For the other connectives we have:

P	Q	$P \wedge Q$	$P \vee Q$	$P \to Q$
$\top$	$\top$	$\top$	$\top$	$\top$
$\top$	$\bot$	$\bot$	$\top$	$\bot$
$\top$	I	I	$\top$	I
$\bot$	$\top$	$\bot$	$\top$	$\top$
$\bot$	$\bot$	$\bot$	$\bot$	$\top$
$\bot$	I	0	I	$\top$
I	$\top$	I	$\top$	$\top$
I	$\bot$	0	I	0
I	I	I	I	$\top$

The negation table is different: if $[\![A]\!] \neq 0$, then $\neg A$ is false. This is characteristic of linearly ordered lattices. One important result of this is that $A \wedge \neg A$ always takes the value 0. Notice also that as with fuzzy logic and Łukasiewicz logic, $A \to B$ is true if and only if $[\![A]\!] \leqslant [\![B]\!]$. However, this table differs with those systems when $[\![A]\!] > [\![B]\!]$ by setting $[\![A \to B]\!] = [\![B]\!]$ in that case. Like Łukasiewicz logic, it is non-faithful because it assigns $A \to B$ the value 1 when each of A, B has the value I.

Solutions to exercises 6.3.1

1.

$$\neg[P(\varepsilon x \neg Px) \longleftrightarrow \forall x Px]$$

Solutions to exercises 6.3.2

   1.

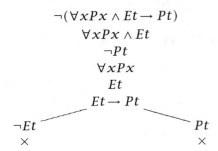

Solutions to exercises 6.3.3

   3.

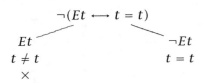

The countermodel has outer domain $\{t\}$, and inner domain $\varnothing$.

Solutions to exercises 6.3.4

  1. The tree for this statement is trivial: after application of the ?$\rightarrow$ rule, no further rules can be applied. The reason is that any interpretation with an empty domain for some stage (and, of course, a non-empty outer domain) will be one which falsifies this formula at that stage.

3.

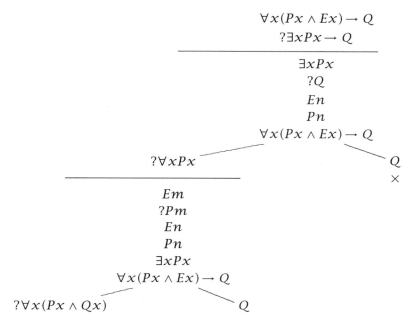

The countermodel has $W = \{1, 2, 3\}$ in their usual order. $D_1 = \varnothing$, $D_2 = \{n\}$, $D_3 = \{n, m\}$. Pn is true at each of 2 and 3, and Pm is false at 3. Q is false at 2 and true at 3. Since m exists at 3 and Pm is false there, $\forall x (Px \wedge Ex)$ is false at all three stages, hence the first conditional is true. However, at stage 2 $\exists x Px$ is true while Q is false, so the second conditional is false at stage 1.

Index